Is Anybody Listening?

KHALAF AHMAD AL HABTOOR

IS ANYBODY LISTENING?

How world leaders ignored prescient warnings on the Middle East

AKKADIA
PRESS

First published in 2016
Copyright © 2016 by Khalaf Ahmad Al Habtoor

The moral right of the author has been asserted

Every reasonable effort has been made to trace copyright holders of material
reproduced in this book, but if any have been inadvertently overlooked the publishers would be
glad to hear from them.

The opinions expressed in this work are those of the author and do not necessarily
reflect the views of Akkadia Press Ltd.

Akkadia Press
61/6 Elm Row
Edinburgh EH7 4AQ
United Kingdom
www.akkadiapress.uk.com
ISBN 978-0-9935845-2-7

Illustrated by Yasser Gaessa
Designed by Peter Burgess
Typeset in Eames Century and Amplitude
Printed in Dubai by Oriental Press
Photo credits
page vi: © Mercer University
page viii: © National Council on US–Arab Relations

Other books by Khalaf Ahmad Al Habtoor
Khalaf Ahmad Al Habtoor – The Autobiography
(Motivate Publishing, 2013)

Contents

Foreword

JIMMY CARTER

FOR ALMOST TWENTY years my friend Khalaf Al Habtoor has been
sharing his ideas through his writings and publishing *Al Shindagah*
magazine. Mr Al Habtoor enjoys a reputation as a successful
businessman, a generous philanthropist, as well as an outspoken
commentator on world affairs. I have enjoyed reading his frequent
articles regarding international events and the Arab perspective on key
issues in the Middle East. I look forward to reviewing these writings in
his anthology *Is Anybody Listening?*

Rosalynn and I have enjoyed spending time with Khalaf at his
beautiful ranch in Khawaneej, Dubai, and visiting with his children and
grandchildren. As a farmer, I enjoyed seeing the estate's free roaming
animals alongside world-class facilities and polo fields. We have shared
special time together at The Carter Center in Atlanta and at other locations
around the globe.

Over the past few years, Khalaf Al Habtoor and I have become
personal friends. We have exchanged thoughts on the state of the world
and the role of the United States and the United Arab Emirates in facing
these issues. We agree that our planet is facing enormous challenges, and
these threats often are being ignored. While we may not always agree on
the way forward, it is good to know that he is willing to call attention to the
issues of the day and to urge action.

No one knows what the next few years will bring, but I am confident
that Khalaf Al Habtoor will continue to offer his opinions to leaders in an
effort to make the world a better place.

JIMMY CARTER
President of the United States of America (1977–1981)

Introduction

DR JOHN DUKE ANTHONY

DR KHALAF AHMAD AL HABTOOR – author of the edited and
very worthwhile compilation of *Is Anybody Listening?*, a series of articles
and essays on Iran, Iraq, Syria, Yemen, Lebanon, Palestine and Egypt
– is no ordinary observer of Arabia and the Gulf's modernization and
development. He is practically synonymous with both, having long
had a hand in each. His is a household name from one end of Arabia
and the Gulf to the other and especially within and among the six Gulf
Cooperation Council (GCC) countries: Bahrain, Kuwait, Oman, Qatar,
Saudi Arabia and the United Arab Emirates (UAE). As such, he has long
been referred to as an "unofficial ambassador" of the UAE – from which
he hails.

From humble beginnings nearly half a century ago, the outspoken
businessman, educator, author and philanthropist turned his small
business into one of the region's largest conglomerates, with commercial
interests spanning the Middle East, Europe and the United States. Along
the way, he has published numerous articles and essays (many of them
appearing in the magazine *Al Shindagah*) in addition to a well-received
book: his autobiography, published in 2012. His major concerns and the
objects of his ongoing keen analyses have been a wide range of important
issues impacting the GCC region and beyond. For more than a decade he
has been producing these incisive, exceptionally well-written treatises,
and has been offering equally insightful assessments of what most needs to
be done to enhance regional security, defence, stability and peace – the four
keys to the prospects for prosperity.

Against this backdrop has been a mainly Western, and especially and
increasingly an American, false narrative interspersed with a growing
number of damaging and dehumanizing images of Arabs and Muslims
and of Arab and Islamic culture overall. One would hope there would be
reason to anticipate or expect that this often ugly, inaccurate and unfair
caricature of the Arab countries, the Middle East and the Islamic world
as a whole – particularly their people's cultures and values – would show
signs of winding down. Sadly, it is in the so-called democratic bastions of
mainly Western countries that one reads and hears the most outlandish

predictions and prognostications about the present and future prospects even of the more economically well-endowed, stable and robust GCC countries. One hardly need look far to find such evidence in abundance – in the media, in the film industry, in the candidacies of politicians eager to be elected or appointed to public office and among pundits of every stripe. For this reason alone, Dr Al Habtoor's *Is Anybody Listening* could hardly be more timely, relevant and appropriate. The volume is also a handy reference to some of the most cutting-edge issues and dynamics of the day, and for the musings of one of the region's most prolific and astute analysts, one could take it along to read on any visit to the region.

Dr Al Habtoor's extraordinary rags-to-riches life is just that: extraordinary. It dates from before oil was discovered in the emirate of Dubai. It is a story of one who was born and raised in a family unlike most in the country, for his had, and has maintained, simultaneous roots in the neighbouring emirate of Abu Dhabi. These two leading men in the Emirates – Dubai's Sheikh Rashid Bin Saeed Al Maktoum Al Bu Falasah Bani Yas, and Abu Dhabi's Sheikh Zayed Bin Sultan Al Nahyan Al Bu Falah Bani Yas – would be vital to the UAE's establishment.

Khalaf Ahmad Al Habtoor was one of the fortunate few Emirati nationals to have become a friend and confidante of both these statesmen. Each was a larger-than-life leader of a kind that comes along but once in a generation, if that. While the two of them proceeded to carve out increasingly impressive geopolitical and commercial niches for their respective emirates and the UAE as a whole on the world stage, Dr Al Habtoor commenced early on to do what he did and still does best: build and build and build. He did so at what often seemed a feverish pace, as though he were in a race against the clock – until the UAE's infrastructure became recognized for what it is and has remained; of world-class dimensions and seemingly forever in the mode of reinventing itself. The emirate, thanks in no small measure to Khalaf Al Habtoor's and others' manifold contributions and accomplishments, is a marvel in the Lower Gulf region that, but a few decades earlier, had been one of the more forgotten corners of Arabia. Stand in the middle of Dubai, turn slowly around, and what one will notice in practically any direction is one or more buildings that were the result of the design, engineering, materials procurement, and construction skills of a unit within the Al Habtoor group of companies. No small feat.

It would be hard to overestimate what Khalaf Al Habtoor and numerous among his fellow Dubai construction magnates were able to achieve, the results of which still endure. In providing much in the way of the bricks and mortar, the development skills and the commercial acumen that distinguishes the UAE from arguably all the world's other developing economies, he helped enable the UAE not only to be catapulted onto the regional and global stages economically and financially, he also was a principal actor in assisting it to become globally renowned for a public and private sector atmosphere that has long been exceptionally conducive to doing business. Not to put too fine a gloss on it, Khalaf Al Habtoor's life and works are monuments unto themselves. They provide a window onto how the UAE, for more than four and a half decades and counting, stands not only as the oldest and most successful confederation among the League of Arab States' 22 members, it also stands as something else, too: the single longest and most successful experiment in sub-regional integration in modern Arab history.

That someone of Dr Al Habtoor's many talents and responsibilities in the development of his country could and would find time to be a philanthropic contributor to educational, charitable and other worthy causes, and also share his analyses and assessments on some of the most pressing issues of the day, has to be recognized for what it is: yet another of his living legacies. Among his fellow citizens and the readers of his articles, essays and popular autobiography the world over, Dr Al Habtoor's writings are increasingly acknowledged for the fact that they provide additional evidence of his testimonial contributions to helping people understand, from his up-close perspective, some of the many fascinating features of the extraordinary life that he has lived and experienced. What he has penned can also be likened to signposts along roads that lie ahead in the form of national and international policies, positions, actions and/or attitudes not yet adopted, endorsed or taken by the world's leaders.

From his having been blessed to witness firsthand most of the vast changes that have so radically altered the landscape of his small polity in the middle of the southern reaches of the western side of the Gulf, it will be readily apparent that many of his projections of what future developments might look like have been prescient. He has also spoken at major events in cities around the world to provide an Arab perspective on key issues impacting the Middle East and beyond.

In *Is Anybody Listening* Dr Al Habtoor recounts his warnings to world leaders about the ramifications and implications of Western Great Power foreign policy errors and failures, as well as Arab limitations and shortcomings. He warns that the greatest threats facing the world today are largely due either to inaction by policymakers, or to their mistaken decisions and the scarred landscapes that have been the result. But one of many highlights that he underscores for its tragic consequences in this collection of his articles is, in his view, "the US' lack of decisive action against one of the most ruthless criminals of our century – Syrian President Bashar Al Assad ... and the empowerment of Iran, the patron of terrorism in our world". As his readers will attest, Dr Al Habtoor's thoughts, proposals and pronouncements on policy-related matters are refreshingly original in much of what he has to say. Like former US Congressman Paul Findley – a 23-year veteran of Congress before being effectively targeted for defeat by the Israel lobby, and whose exceptionally popular books Dr Al Habtoor enabled to be translated into Arabic and sold in bookstores throughout the Arab World – he is courageously outspoken in what he has to say. Of particular interest and value are the realistic solutions he offers for some of the largest and most complex issues and the sound advice he gives to global leaders to help make the world a better place.

Of particular note, amid the challenging backdrop of developments in the region addressed by Dr Al Habtoor, are the events of the past few years when the world witnessed the fall of numerous Arab leaders. The causes in many instances were similar – often in reaction to governments' harsh repression of individuals who despaired of hope and the prospect of peaceful and effective change in support of their legitimate needs, concerns, interests, rights and aspirations. It started with Tunisia in December 2010 and spread to countries like Egypt, Libya and Yemen. Periodic outbreaks of violence also erupted in Bahrain, Iraq, Jordan and, to a lesser extent, Kuwait. Leaders who had been in power for decades fell, including those in Tunisia, Egypt, Yemen and Libya. Protests spread to Syria on what quickly proved to be by far the largest scale. The prolonged violence, death and dislocations of millions of Syrians have constituted the worst human tragedy of our time.

Parts of Arab civilization have been destroyed beyond repair. It is Armageddon-like in too many areas of the region, with millions seeing little reason for hope or the prospect of easy or early solutions – or, in many cases, even humanistic abatement – in the foreseeable future. Little wonder why, with many beyond the exceptionally blessed six GCC countries believing that deep-rooted, massive and pervasive poverty, together with the inability of millions of disillusioned youth to obtain meaningful and gainful employment in order to be able to marry, begin to raise a family and have access to affordable housing, lie at the root of the manifold economic, social and psychological tragedies being witnessed.

But undergirding, laminated on top of, and seemingly chipping away nonstop at these material maladies are the primary political sources and stimuli. Indeed, chief among the phenomena beneath, above and throughout the expansive and continuing malaise that afflicts the countries noted and numerous others – and that shows no signs of vanishing anytime soon – is the Palestine problem. For more than six decades and counting, Israel's continuing colonization of Palestinian and Syrian land, water and other life-sustaining resources and assets – prolonged, facilitated and subsidized by the United States – lies front and centre of what is America's, and by extension numerous other Western countries', ongoing moral Achilles heel.

No amount of media and special interest narrative spinning can hide what, in the heart of every Arab and Muslim, remains the single largest, oldest and most extensive source of region-wide malaise. The absence of the requisite statesmanship and political, physical and above all moral and humanistic courage to bring an effective end to this blatant, patent and ongoing injustice is hardly without horrendous cost. It tears at the shrouds of a seemingly seamless cloak of mourning. It rips to shreds the metaphorical sinews of Western action and inaction related to what is right and what is wrong. It idles at the intersection of that which is true and that which is false. Its continuance lies at the heart of catastrophic failures among the world's leaders.

Such failures remain rooted to this day in the inequities and calamities inflicted upon the Palestinian and Syrian people. These failures are what planted and nurtured the most fertile seeds for the virulent and violent extremism, organized militancy, anti-Western feeling and especially anti-Americanism that – apart from the structures of governance and systems of political dynamics that characterize the six GCC countries – typify the Arab centres of despair noted. Lest there be doubters of the poignancy of this portraiture, it is instructive to note that in this part of the world, prior to the US-facilitated dispossession of Palestinians pursuant to the creation of Israel in 1947–48, America had not one enemy, nary an adversary, scarcely a critic. It was upon the anvil of this issue more than any other that the Muslim Brotherhood and its offshoots and variants in the form of Al Qaeda, Hamas, Hezbollah, Jabhat Al Nusra, the Quds Force – the hardest of the hardcore Iranian Revolutionary Guards of the Islamic Republic of Iran, together with the latter's militias, proxies and wholly owned subsidiaries – and the so-called Islamic State of Iraq and Syria (Daesh) all found a formative platform and cut their anti-Western teeth. Among the sharpest of teeth, in the eyes of Dr Al Habtoor, are those of revolutionary Iran with its expansionist ambitions and continuous meddling in what he and many others view as quintessentially Arab affairs.

As Dr Al Habtoor writes from his perspective near to the vortex of action, reaction and interaction in Arabia and the Gulf: "Daesh has morphed from an Al Qaeda-related insurgency in Iraq into a self-proclaimed state in swaths of Syria and Iraq. It is more brutal and more effective than Al Qaeda ever was, and the group is posing one of the biggest threats to our region, and to the West. Nowhere is safe. Well-funded through oil, and tech savvy, the terror group is seeking to establish a caliphate across Syria and Iraq, and sadly it is making ground. In a matter of a few years, Daesh has built a network of capable individuals spanning the globe. It is now a well-known brand with its distinctive black flag that is arguably more recognizable than the flags of many nations."

"I have no doubt in my mind," Dr Al Habtoor continues, "that failings by word leaders have empowered this fanatical mob hell-bent on a reign of terror, using the false cover of religion. The scenes of extreme brutality we are witnessing, from obscene torture to mass rape and beheadings make what we saw from Al Qaeda pale in comparison. Daesh, which has been fuelled by the US-led invasion in Iraq and the multisided Syrian civil war, has taken the glorification of terror to the next level, attacking ordinary people in the most brutal of ways. And unless action is taken soon, I fear for all our futures. It is time world leaders stop dawdling and delivering false promises. They need to tackle this growing epidemic of radicalization before it is too late. Enough sitting around hoping for miracles! The Arab World cannot rely on the West anymore. Both Muslim and non-Muslim states should stand with the GCC to fight this alien sickness that is tearing our region apart."

If this last statement does not prompt one to want to read more, then it would be hard to imagine what would.

DR JOHN DUKE ANTHONY is the Founding President and CEO of the National Council on US–Arab Relations, a non-governmental and non-profit educational organization established in 1983 and based in Washington, DC.

Preface

OVER THE PAST FEW YEARS we have witnessed the fall of many leaders
in the Middle East and North Africa as a consequence of revolution.
It started with Tunisia in December 2010 and had a domino effect in
neighbouring counties such as Egypt, Libya and Yemen. Protests spread
to Bahrain, Algeria, Iraq, Jordan Kuwait, Morocco and Sudan, but on a
lesser scale. Leaders who had had a firm grip for decades fell, including
Zain El Abidine Ben Ali, Hosni Mubarak and Ali Abdullah Saleh. Even
Muammar Gaddafi, the renowned Libyan dictator and mercurial leader,
who after more than 40 years in power succumbed to a spectacular fall
from grace.

Parts of Arab civilization have been left in tatters. Worst off is Syria,
which is witnessing the worst human tragedy of our time, not to mention
the irreversible loss of important archaeological sites and centuries-old
treasures.

It is like an Armageddon in parts of the Middle East, and there is
little hope of getting out of this quagmire, which I believe is due to the
catastrophic moral and political failures of world leaders who have enabled
the likes of Daesh, the Muslim Brotherhood and the Islamic Republic of
Iran – its militias and proxies.

I vocalized my biggest fears in a speech in Washington DC in October
2015, saying: "Right now, we are witnessing the US' lack of decisive
action against one of the most ruthless criminals of our century – Syrian
President Bashar Al Assad... and the empowerment of Iran, the patron of
terrorism in our world." (See "Call for Action", 15 October 2015 in Getting
an Arab voice heard.)

The Islamic Republic of Iran has ramped up its expansionist ambitions
right before our eyes to the detriment of our once-beautiful region. In its
quest for regional dominance Tehran's tentacles have extended their reach
to Iraq, Syria, Lebanon and Yemen, among others. I pray we can curtail its
seemingly unstoppable march before other countries bear its scars.

Meanwhile, Daesh has morphed from an Al Qaeda-related
insurgency in Iraq into a self-proclaimed state in swathes of Syria and
Iraq. It is more brutal and more effective than Al Qaeda ever was, and

the group is posing one of the biggest threats to our region, and to the West. Nowhere is safe. Well-funded through oil, and tech savvy, the terror group is seeking to establish a caliphate across Syria and Iraq, and sadly it is making ground. In a matter of a few years, Daesh has built a network of capable individuals spanning the globe. It is now a well-known brand with its distinctive black flag that is arguably more recognizable than the flags of many nations.

I have no doubt in my mind that failings by world leaders have empowered this fanatical mob hell-bent on a reign of terror, using the false cover of religion. The scenes of extreme brutality we are witnessing, from obscene torture to mass rape and beheadings, make what we saw from Al Qaeda pale in comparison. Daesh has taken the glorification of terror to the next level, attacking ordinary people in the most brutal of ways. It is time world leaders stop dawdling and delivery false promises. They need to tackle this growing epidemic of radicalization. Failure to do so comes with high stakes for us all. Daesh has been fueled by the US-led invasion in Iraq and the multisided Syrian civil war. And unless action is taken soon, I fear for all our futures. Enough sitting around hoping for miracles! The Arab world cannot rely on the West any more. Both Muslim and non-Muslim states should stand with the GCC to fight this alien sickness that is not only tearing our region apart but also posing a grave threat far beyond our borders; if left unchecked it could further divide our world.

Explanatory note

You will notice that the book has been divided into two parts. The first part focuses on Iran, which over the years has become a major focus of my endeavours. The second part looks at the Arab World, but obviously it cannot be observed in isolation and so the impact of Iran is also considered in this section of the book.

The date of publication cited after each article refers to the date it was first published in the UAE, GCC and international media. It should also be noted that these articles were composed in the context of the time in which they were written; subsequent events may have changed the situation in the countries discussed. Each article appears only once in the publication. Where it is relevant to more than one chapter, a reference to the article and chapter has been included.

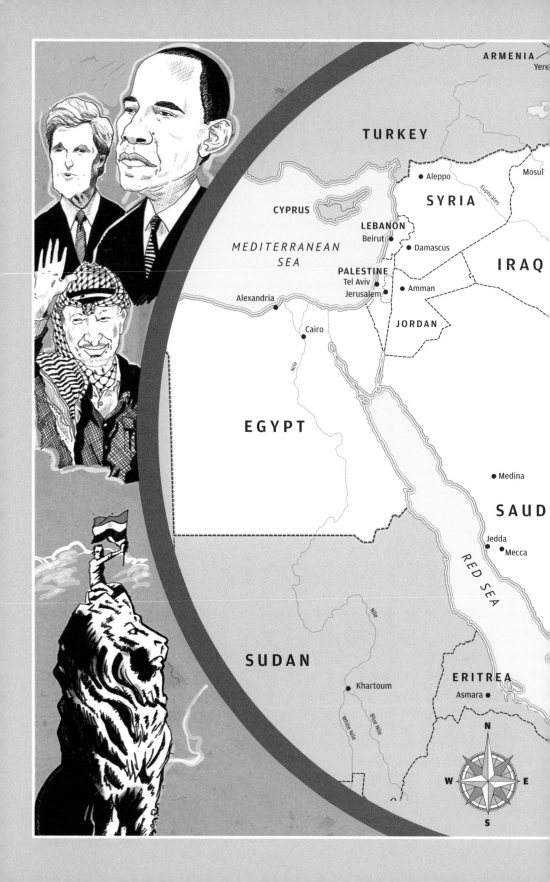

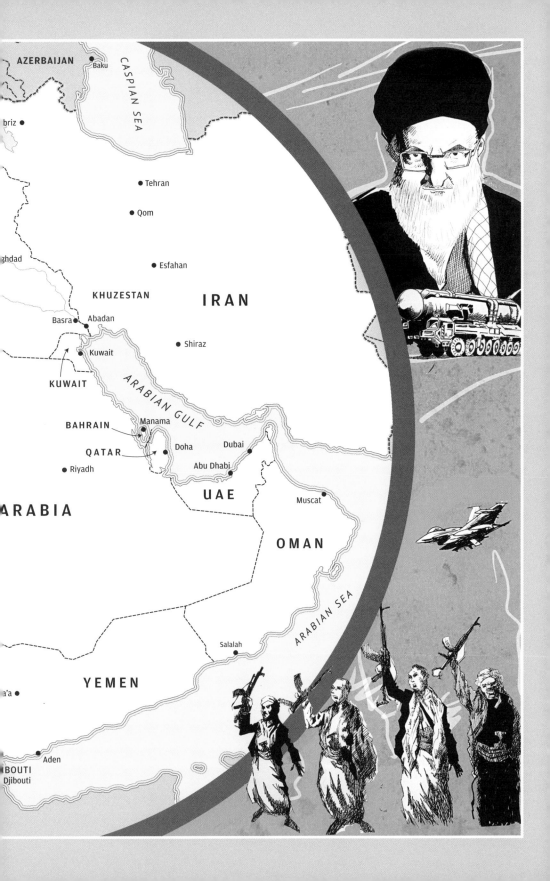

PART 1

Iran: the root of the problem

1

The dangers of Iran's manipulation of the world

Introduction

IRAN'S EXPANSIONIST AGENDA has threatened to destroy our region and continues to do so right before our very eyes. This is why I have penned more articles on Iran than any other country in the Middle East.

Ayatollah Ali Khamenei, Iran's most powerful official, has been supreme leader since 1989, making him the second-longest serving autocrat in the Middle East. The influence he and his ayatollahs have on our region is incredible. We have seen first hand how Iran has masterminded the destruction of many parts of the region – namely Iraq, Syria and Lebanon. Yemen is the latest target of interest with the Iranian-backed Houthis fighting for control of the country. More recently, the reach of Tehran's leverage has extended beyond the region. Yet the world seems to be blind to the grave threat it poses.

There are very worrying issues that can no longer be ignored. They should not be brushed under the carpet by any nation or executive who naively befriends what has been labelled numerous times: "The Axis of Evil".

Here are the facts on Iran:

- It openly sponsors terrorism around the world.
- It has proven links to the 9/11 attacks.
- It supports Syrian President Bashar Al Assad – a president leading a genocide against his own people.
- It controls the militias in Iraq.
- It is openly aggressive towards Arabian Gulf states.
- Its human rights record is an utter disgrace.
- It is responsible for the destruction of the Middle East via its many proxies.

Iran, the largest financier of state-sponsored terrorism, seems to be the favourite buzzword right now despite these very disturbing facts. In the wake of the easing of sanctions following Iran's nuclear deal struck with the US, Britain, France, Russia, China and Germany, the world suddenly wants to be Iran's new best friend. Politicians, businessmen and businesswomen are banging on Tehran's door desperate to get a piece of the pie. But, mark my words, it will come with a high cost.

Iran is – and has been for decades – the mastermind of global terrorism. The US Department of State acknowledges the fact by describing Iran as "an active state sponsor of terrorism". Even more worrying, US Secretary of State John Kerry has admitted that some of the $150bn in sanctions relief going to Iran will, in all likelihood, fund terrorism. In January 2016 he told CNBC television, "I think that some of it will end up in the hands of the Islamic Revolutionary Guard Corps (IRGC) or other entities, some of which are labelled terrorists. You know, to some degree, I am not going to sit here and tell you that every component of that can be prevented. But I can tell you this, right now we are not seeing the early delivery of funds going to that kind of endeavour at this point in time." (See *Jewish Politics News & Updates*, "Kerry admits that 'some' Iran sanctions relief will likely fund terrorism", 24 January 2016.)

Ted Deutch, the ranking Democratic member of the House Foreign Affairs Committee's Middle East and North Africa Subcommittee, was quoted as saying, "No one denies Iran's support for the world's most notorious terrorist groups. No one disputes Iran's destabilizing influence in the Middle East or role in killing Americans." He went on to say, "This deal … speeds up the enrichment of the Revolutionary Guard and the Iranian terror proxies that endanger security and stability in the Middle East." (See *The Tower*, "Leading House Democrat: White House should keep its promise on new Iran terror sanctions", 19 February 2016.)

Tehran's ayatollahs, controlling Shi'ite militias in Iraq, are more than influential with Hamas, and back the Bashar Al Assad regime in Syria. Iran's proxies must be smiling from ear to ear following the lifting of sanctions. Finances have been squeezed due to years of constraints and declining oil prices, but now the coffers are full again.

Since its inception in Lebanon in 1982, Hezbollah is an extension of Iran's foreign policy. Hezbollah's Secretary General Hassan Nasrallah uses every dirty trick he can in an effort to cement his militia's credibility within the Sunni Arab world and to justify its existence. His speeches are deliberately crafted to con Arabs, specifically Palestinians, into thinking he is the hero who will defend Jerusalem and free the occupied territories.

Among Nasrallah's rants he boasts that Hezbollah has the capacity "to cover the entirety of occupied Palestine [Israel] with missiles" adding that the militia would be the victor in any coming war with nuclear-armed Israel. He threatened to bomb a chemical facility saying that "several of our rockets combined with the ammonia storage facility in Haifa will create the effect of a nuclear weapon". (See *The Times of Israel*, "Nasrallah threatens to bomb chemical facility, kill thousands of Israelis", 16 February 2016).

Iran itself has even openly acknowledged its links to terrorism. In February 2016, an Iranian Foreign Ministry spokesman admitted that Iran is a sponsor of terrorism against Israel saying, "The Islamic Republic of Iran has declared that supporting the Palestinian nation and Palestinian

Resistance Movement is among its fixed policies." (See *The Daily Caller*, "Iran publicly admits supporting terrorism against Israel is state policy", 10 February 2016.)

It is as if we have woken up to find ourselves in a parallel universe where everything we hold dear has been reversed. Ignored are the Ayatollah Khamenei's chants of "Death to America" and "Death to Israel". Glossed over too is Iran's repression of its people and its relegation of minorities to third-class citizen status. I cannot comprehend how Iran is seemingly pulling the wool over the world's eyes.

I was astounded, in June 2016, when the United Nations Secretary General Ban Ki-moon added the Saudi-led coalition in Yemen, which includes the United Arab Emirates (UAE), to its annual blacklist. This coalition is aimed at saving Yemen from Iran's proxies – the Houthis who want control of the country. The UN has slapped Yemen's rescuers in the face and put them on par with terrorists, militia and Houthi Devils on the payroll of expansionist Tehran.

Iran's blatant manipulation of the world is a major cause of concern and if things carry on the way they are, it will have a detrimental impact on the region, and beyond. Iran has a clear agenda and the world is refusing to take a firm stand. Vested interests should not be given priority over the safety of citizens.

Iran's aggressive, interventionist and provocative policies have reached an unprecedented level. The country will not stop until its regional hegemonic ambitions are guaranteed.

We have lived too long under the constant threat of our dangerous neighbour, and have seen its influence edging ever closer to our shores. Adding fuel to the fire is Tehran's increased animosity with the Kingdom of Saudi Arabia that has intensified to a worrying level as it continues to strive for regional pre-eminence. The Gulf Cooperation Council nations will not tolerate this sabre rattling and will defend their borders from the clutches of Iran at any cost. Too many parts of the region bear the scars of Iran's foreign policies. We cannot let others share the same fate.

Oil is not a weapon

1 December 2006

WHENEVER THERE IS A CRISIS in the Middle East, fomented by the US or Israeli Arabs, streets from Morocco to Iraq reverberate with calls urging oil-producing Gulf states to play the oil card. This emotional knee-jerk reaction is understandable in the face of Israel's oppressive policies against the Palestinian people and its neighbours, as well as America's ongoing occupation of Iraq. But when viewed realistically through a 21st-century prism, the use of oil as a weapon would not only be impracticable but also detrimental to Arab interests.

When asked whether oil should be used as a weapon during the recent Israel–Lebanon conflict, the Saudi Foreign Minister Prince

Saud Al Faisal said this:"The two issues should not be mixed because oil is among the economic capabilities that countries need to meet their obligations towards their citizens. If we ignore this reality and start asking that the foundations of our life be used to enter into reckless adventures, the first to be hurt will be our citizens. And no wise government can accept this." In 2002 Adel Al Jubeir, a Saudi foreign policy advisor, told the press "Oil is not a weapon. Oil is not a tank." These sentiments were reiterated that same year by the then Defence Minister of Kuwait, Sheikh Jaber Al-Mubarak Al-Sabah, who described his country's oil as "a basic wealth for the people".

These comments may not sit well with Arabs who have legitimate grievances against the US and Israel and feel any tool that can be used to hit back is fair game. But when one weighs up all factors concerned it is clear they are right-minded and sensible.

Firstly, any use of the oil card would represent a gigantic public relations mistake. People around the world suffering from high prices at the pump, having to pay more for their air tickets and unable to afford heating bills, would be less likely to view Arab causes sympathetically.

Second, if Arab oil producers were to use this precious commodity as a bargaining chip, such an action would likely backfire hurting not only producing nations but also poor third-world countries including developing Arab nations.

It is important to highlight that it is not only the citizens of producing nations that benefit from the resource. Over the decades, Arab Gulf countries have invested billions to help their less well-off neighbours, as well as constructing hospitals, schools, mosques, housing complexes and essential infrastructure.

Since the 1973 oil embargo – imposed by the Organization of the Petroleum Exporting Countries (OPEC) to deter the US and its allies who supplied weapons to Israel during Israel's war with Syria and Egypt – the world has dramatically changed. Today, the US imports less than 20 per cent of its oil from Arab-producing countries.

The 1973 embargo caused a major global shock. Within a year the price of oil had quadrupled and the US experienced its first oil shortage since World War II. At the same time inflation was rampant, the US economy was severely shaken and the dollar weakened, which triggered a worldwide recession.

If this were to be repeated today when wealthier Arab nations are heavily invested in the West and OPEC receives its revenue in dollars, Arab economies would be thrown into turmoil. This would not only affect the citizens of producing Gulf countries but also the untold thousands of Arabs who live and work in those countries. And just as it did in 1973, such an action would have long term global economic repercussions. As a result of the '70s embargo, the West was driven to invest in hitherto untapped oil resources. Because oil prices were driven higher, far-away or difficult to access oil fields, such as the North Sea, became feasible and attractive prospects.

At the same time investment poured into nuclear energy as well as research into alternative energies and new technologies such as gas to liquids. Last year consuming countries invested $30bn in developing these new technologies. Recent years have also witnessed a resurgence of interest in coal.

One of the spin-offs from that embargo was the rise in popularity of small Japanese-made cars instead of large gas-guzzling American-manufactured limousines. Another has been calls from US leaders for Americans to conserve oil by using less. Luckily for this region, despite those trends, the demand for oil is still growing.

Moreover, since 1973, the West learnt a lesson. It was no longer going to be as reliant on uninterrupted oil supplies and so began stockpiling oil in case of emergencies.

The Bush administration, which came into power with an aggressive agenda vis-à-vis the Middle East, began hoarding oil from its early days in power. Japan and Germany hold significant reserves while China and India have embarked on a similar path.

For instance, the 26 member countries of the International Energy Agency (IEA) are able to draw on a mammoth reserve of up to 12 million barrels daily over a four-month period, thereafter reducing it to approximately nine million.

So in order for it to work, any embargo would have to be long term and would hurt the producing countries as much as, if not more than, consuming nations.

It should also be highlighted that struggling third-world countries without oil reserves would be hit hard by unavailability and rocketing prices that would thrust them into an economic wilderness for decades to come. This is especially true when an increasing demand for oil during an unstable political climate is already fuelling high prices based on market factors.

A selective embargo would not work either as oil sold to countries, considered "friendly", would simply be shipped onward to the very countries the embargo was set up to adversely affect.

In the '70s, former Saudi Oil Minister Sheikh Zaki Yamani understood this saying: "The world is really just one market." If that were true then it is so much more so today.

We should also take into account the change of "trade flow" that has evolved since 1973. Then much of this region's oil was sold to developed Western nations. Nowadays a large portion flows to South East Asia and the Far East, countries largely uninvolved with Middle East politics.

In retrospect, the 1973 embargo did a lot more harm than good in that the US and its allies continually perceive a similar threat from this region and have configured their foreign policies to avert a recurrence.

An interesting correlation is the fact that after Iraq began selling its oil in Euros, instead of dollars, it was invaded on a false pretext. Today, threats are being made against Iran, which has long planned to open an oil bourse that would cast off the petrodollar in favour of other currencies.

Michael Renner a senior analyst with the World Watch Institute said: "If the United States maintains a strong political hand in the Middle East it may be more able to convince the governments in the region not to switch over to Euro pricing and to actually stay with the dollar."

The Vice-President for Defence and Foreign Policy Studies at the Cato Institute, Dr Ted Carpenter, believes American policymakers do not understand the way oil markets work: "They (oil producers) are going to put their oil on the market regardless of who controls the political power in the capital city," he says. "And if they put their oil on the market you know that determines the ultimate price, not whether the regime is friendly to the United States or hostile."

Carpenter is no doubt correct but more and more analysts are coming to the conclusion that the real reason for America's interest in the region is more to do with power over the resource than grabbing oil for its own use.

It is ironic that while OPEC has rejected the oil card, the US wants to use the region's oil as a weapon to prevent the economic and military rise of hegemonic competitors such as oil-hungry China and India. Whether it will succeed in this aim is another matter.

The hawkish former Israeli Prime Minister Ariel Sharon famously said "the Arabs may have the oil but we have the matches". This is the real problem that Arab oil-producing nations face and will face as long as the Israeli-Palestinian conflict continues and Palestinians are left without a state.

As long as this conflict and associated conflicts are unresolved, there will be demands from people, incensed at injustice for Arabs, to brandish oil in place of the sword.

But Arab leaders must resist playing into the hands of Sharon's ideological successors, for with great wealth comes great responsibility, the most important of which is the wellbeing of the people whom God has blessed with this bounty.

Dispute over islands must be resolved

1 July 2008

THE IRANIAN GOVERNMENT is trying hard to win friends and influence people throughout this region and south Asia, to counterbalance its increasing isolation caused by the United Nations (UN) Security Council sanctions. Its officials say they want to forge strong political relationships and economic partnerships with Iran's neighbours.

But how seriously can we take Tehran's overtures when Iran still forcibly occupies three islands, to which the United Arab Emirates (UAE) has solid historical claims?

Worse, in recent months various Iranian diplomats, parliamentarians and religious leaders have deliberately ratcheted-up tensions, insisting that the islands – Greater Tunbs, Lesser Tunbs and Abu Musa – have always been Iranian and will remain so for ever more.

Iran's belligerency and intransigency on this issue was heightened in March when the League of Arab States met in Damascus and called upon Tehran to end its occupation of the islands. "The continued attempts by Iran to build settlements and conduct war-games in the territorial waters, air space, economic zones and coral reefs of the occupied islands are all acts that constitute a gross violation of the UAE sovereignty and territorial integrity," read the Summit's communiqué forwarded to the United Nations.

In response, Mohammed Khazaee, Iran's ambassador to the UN, wrote to the Secretary General Ban Ki-moon saying, "The Islamic Republic of Iran vehemently denies the UAE's unfounded claims ...", describing the islands as an indivisible part of Iran's territory. The end result is stalemate. Iran says it has historical records and documents to prove its ownership of the islands, but if this is indeed the case why does the Iranian government refuse international arbitration and reject adjudication by the International Court of Justice?

Until now, this country has displayed remarkable patience during its dealings with Tehran. Over the decades the UAE has regularly re-stated its claim in a quiet and dignified fashion without ever resorting to childish insults or offensive tones.

Our leaders have deliberately refrained from incendiary rhetoric out of a sense of responsibility towards a region that is already volatile and because the two countries are longstanding trading partners. But, sadly, it is becoming evident that Tehran mistakenly equates our patience with weakness. In reality, our case is powerful and, furthermore, it is strongly supported by the international community.

We know that as far back as the 18th century the islands belonged to the Al Qawasim (Al Qasimi) of Sharjah and Ras Al Khaimah whose sovereignty over them was recognized by the British government.

We also know that on several occasions Iran attempted to buy or lease the islands but was turned down on each occasion. These unsuccessful attempts surely indicate the islands were never the property of Iran as no country would seek to purchase or rent real estate that it already owned or believed it owned.

In his book *The Three Occupied UAE Islands*, author and consultant Thomas R. Mattair highlights 16th-century documentation indicating members of the Al Qawasim tribe controlled the islands, which they used for pearl diving and grazing land for their animals. Mattair believes the

Iranian argument is tenuous and lacks hard evidence. If the case were to reach the International Court of Justice the UAE would win, he says.

Another disagreement between the Arab World and Iran centres on whether the Gulf should be prefixed with "Persian" or "Arabian" or simply known as "the Gulf". In his letter to the UN Secretary General, Mr Khazaee called any substitution for "Persian Gulf" to be not only illegal but an act of "political chicanery".

Not so. Those clear, warm waters lap onto our shores as well as Iran's and, in any case, today there is no such country as Persia. If Iranians want maps to reflect their historical roots they can print them but they should not try to impose their diktats on others.

We prefer to adopt a more live-and-let-live approach. After all, Britain has no problem with France calling the strip of water dividing their two countries "La Manche" (the sleeve) and, likewise, France accepts that Britain refers to it as "The English Channel".

However, when it comes to our islands, the time for niceties is drawing to a close. We have been politely staking our claim for the past 37 years with no result. How much longer are we going to complain to the Arab League and how many more letters will we send to the UN?

If Iran sincerely wishes to extend its hand in friendship it must make concessions like all good neighbours everywhere and be flexible in its dealings. Simply refusing to discuss the future of the disputed islands is not good enough. Its officials should either be prepared to sit down with ours in a spirit of compromise or agree to the matter's adjudication in an international court.

In any event, the UAE should refuse to be strung along any longer. Greater Tunbs, Lesser Tunbs and Abu Musa were not barren rocks. They were inhabited by our people, several of whom lost their lives when the Shah's men used force to take them over so as to turn them into military outposts.

We need to tell Tehran enough is enough and mean it. If Iran is still uncooperative it should face diplomatic/economic repercussions, or else we might as well meekly hand the islands over, together with an open invitation to predators everywhere. At stake is more than land. Our dignity is on the line.

Let us face our suspicions

1 September 2008

A NUMBER OF FRIENDS and I were following the negotiations in Qatar to reach a settlement in Lebanon. In the company of the same friends I had followed before the tragic events in Beirut. During these successive sessions of TV news bulletins, I noticed abnormal sectarian schism scenarios raising their ugly heads in more than one part of the Arab World. I say schism scenarios hoping or believing that they will not turn into realities on the ground and that they are no more than negative symptoms that will evaporate with time.

Yes, these scenarios are being actively marketed under many banners using huge efforts of mobilization, lining up pockets, and evocation. But, I have a deep sense of confidence that these efforts will in the end give up in the face of strong realities on the ground. We have been witnessing similar efforts here and there in the Arab World for a good deal of time so far. Well it might take time, but I am sure they will retreat and leave the scene for a new coming daybreak.

Back to those TV news evenings with friends, following political developments in Lebanon. I was really shocked. I do not mean by the hateful fighting. In fact, this was a small thing when compared to the hatred expressed by many Lebanese speakers in talk shows at the time. Sectarian lines and fears were flagrant among people. Their statements and facial expressions pushed me to remember friends and neighbours from a few years ago with whom I lived without even knowing their religions. This was not only because of my belonging to a pan-Arab ideology that did not deal with people according to their religion or sectarian backgrounds, despite my strong belonging to Islam as a religion, but also because this was the situation in Lebanon in the past.

We, the people of the the United Arab Emirates (UAE), belong to Islam and we are very proud of our creed. I have never sensed any schism among us. Living on this land as one family, UAE people feel baffled when faced with newly born words such as "Sunni" or "Shi'ite". The word "Shi'ite" has never been used here before. Instead, we used to call people of this Islamic creed "Bahrani". During my early years, I and other people of my generation thought of "Bahrani" as something no more than belonging to a certain region or community. During these TV news evenings, a certain question started to occur to me. Why have sectarian attacks been so prevalent in many parts of the Arab World recently?

Is there any logic behind this? Is it because centrifugal forces are growing stronger than centripetal forces among us? Or, are there powers that want to destabilize the Arab World using sectarian arguments to start deep schisms all over our region? I will be direct and clear. There is no need for word playing. Out of belonging to the Arab Gulf and due to my Islamic belief, I absolutely refuse all of what is going now, even when the conflict does not go beyond the verbal debate and evocative statements about Sunnis and Shi'ites. Our self-awareness here in the Gulf has been built on being Muslim, and Muslims only, without being anything else.

This has been the case for us in the UAE and in the Gulf in general. Building on this belief, we had good relations and trade with our neighbours in Iran, despite the tensions resulting from Iran's occupation of the three UAE islands during the reign of Shah Mohammed Reza Pahlavi. When the Islamic Revolution overthrew the Shah, we looked to this as good news and hoped that a new era of mutual respect and friendship with our neighbours would start. This sense was reinforced among us by the new Iranian rulers' positive statements about relationships with Arab people and their commitment towards a fair settlement of the Palestinian issue, which represents a lifelong duty for every Arab man and woman. But, despite the welcoming positions expressed by Gulf states and other Arab countries towards the Iranian people and their new leadership, we found ourselves in time in the following situation:

- Iran continued its occupation of the UAE's three islands and its efforts to manipulate history by replacing "Arab" from the name of our Gulf with another name.
- The security and stability of the Gulf have repeatedly been victims of irresponsible adventures.
- The Sunni–Shi'ite sectarian fight has engulfed Iraq.
- A civil war almost happened between Sunnis and Shi'ites in Lebanon.
- A deep schism divides pro-Iran Palestinians and their compatriots who are allied to other powers.

With the exception of their occupation of our three islands, I do not mean that our Iranian neighbours are responsible for all of these developments. However, I strongly believe that they must use their political and economic influences to bridge the gap among Muslims and to support rapprochement with their Arab neighbours. Speaking on behalf of any Arab in the Gulf, I am sure that the Gulf states want to establish very strong friendships not only with the Iranians, but with all the people of the world.

Yes, every human being, as well as every society, has the right to choose whatever type of government they want, but they are not entitled to impose their choice upon other neighbouring people and countries, or to recall historic evocative ideas to spread divisions. Countries and regimes must search for factors that support rapprochements and friendships, not hateful old rivalries and historic divisions, as a way to strengthen their clout in other countries.

I hope that our Iranian neighbours will be hospitable to my good faith comments. I raise the matter to highlight the importance of building a better relationship between the two sides of the Gulf, based on respect and friendship. To show my goodwill and eagerness for a new and better chapter in the history of the Gulf, I will assume that all these sectarian divisions have been the result of bad historic coincidences, hoping that fresh winds will bring change and unity.

It is the Arabian Gulf and that is that

1 December 2009

THE GENTLE WATER that laps the shores of the United Arab Emirates (UAE), Kuwait, Bahrain, Saudi Arabia, Oman, Iraq and Iran has become a source of contention. A rose by any other name may smell as sweet but it certainly irks most people in this part of the world when outsiders invariably refer to the Arabian Gulf as the Persian Gulf. Those of us who grew up here swam in the Arabian Gulf as children and were told that the big ships we could see in the distance were sailing through the Arabian Gulf to the Arabian Sea. And, today, most tourists who flock here from every corner of the globe do not consider themselves visitors to the Persian Gulf.

It may be true that pre-1960s maps and treaties made reference to this body of water as the Persian Gulf in the same way that many ancient European maps referred to the Red Sea as Sinus Arabicus or the Arabian Gulf. But let us fast forward to the 21st century. Today, there are several reasons why the international community and its cartographers should officially recognize the "Arabian Gulf".

The first is obvious. Persia has not existed since 1935 and, therefore, does not appear on modern maps. So, by saying Persian Gulf we are implicitly attributing domination of this 24,000 sq km body of water to a long-gone era.

Secondly, the modern-day Islamic Republic of Iran is just one of eight countries that share this waterway with all the rest being Arab. Moreover, many Iranians who live near Iran's southern coastline are ethnically Arab or Arabic speaking.

Thirdly, we are living during a time when countries in the Gulf have attained unprecedented geopolitical and economic clout, which should be recognized.

Fourthly, history notwithstanding, there are numerous examples of countries, cities and seas undergoing a name change to reflect the contemporary status quo. For instance, Rhodesia is now Zimbabwe, the Gold Coast became Ghana, Burma changed its name to Myanmar and Bombay is now known as Mumbai.

You may be interested to know that the Romans called the Mediterranean "Mare Nostrum" or "Our Sea" while the ancient Greeks called the Atlantic Ocean "Oceanus", but you do not find present-day Italians and Greeks up in arms about the name change.

Unfortunately, the same cannot be said for our good friends the Iranians. They are hanging on to the "Persian Gulf" like a mother lion defending her cubs. In 2004, hundreds of organized Iranian bloggers and webmasters launched what is called a "Google Bomb" and were successful in manipulating the Google search engine so that each time anyone searched for "Arabian Gulf" up popped a spoofed Internet Explorer page that read "The Gulf you are looking for does not exist. Try Persian Gulf." Iranian hackers have also been busy hacking into Arab websites and superimposing maps of the Gulf with their own.

In 2005, the Iranian government was incensed when Qatar used "Arabian Gulf" in its official documents relating to the 2006 Asian Games and threatened to boycott them. In the same vein, Tehran has threatened to cancel the 2009 Islamic Solidarity Games planned for October because Gulf Cooperation Council (GCC) member countries, led by Saudi Arabia, have asked that the "Persian Gulf" tag be dropped from the event's promotional materials and medals. However, negotiations are ongoing and they still might be salvaged. In the past, Iran has also banned *National Geographic* publications because its World Atlas had "Arabian Gulf" in parentheses, as well as *The Economist* for using "Gulf" in connection with a map published in the magazine.

Frankly speaking, if Iranian sensitivities are that delicate then I have no problem with any name they care to give this shared body of water as long as they do not impose their terminology on anyone else. In a spirit of "live and let live" there should be no reason why they cannot continue with "Persian Gulf" while we Arabs hold to "Arabian Gulf" or, simply, "Gulf", in the same way the British say "English Channel" and the French "La Manche" (the Sleeve) when speaking of the Atlantic waters that separate the UK from France.

Just as the labels English Channel and La Manche are legally interchangeable, Arabian Gulf and Persian Gulf should be likewise in the eyes of the international community. Despite appeals from Gulf nations, as things stand, UN directives stipulate that "Persian Gulf" should be used in official documents, while the US and the UK have both endorsed "Persian Gulf" as the official term of reference. Given the close relationship that GCC countries enjoy with Washington and London, this entrenched stance on their part is uncooperative at best, offensive at worst.

Lastly, our predicament is shared by North and South Korea who have asked the UN Conference on the Standardization of Geographical Names to change the "Sea of Japan" to the "East Sea". Unlike its support for "Persian Gulf", in this case, the UN has ruled that such issues should be settled by the countries concerned.

We are just as proud of our history and geopolitical status as the Iranians are and we deserve just as much respect from our friends, especially when we host so many throughout the Gulf region. I would, therefore, ask our leaders to vigorously pursue this issue at the UN and, further, I would request our allies to look favourably upon any such a request.

Until now, Arab nations have been treating this issue with kid gloves. It is about time that we made ourselves heard. The warm waters of the Gulf will be around long after we are gone but as Theodore Roosevelt once said: "The one thing I want to leave my children is an honourable name."

Arabs should lead in fighting terrorism

14 January 2010

THE WORLD'S SUPERPOWER, the United States, has taken responsibility for combating international terrorism with help from its Western allies. Terrorism is a scourge upon the face of the Earth so, in principle, we should be grateful to Washington for attempting to make our planet safer. Unfortunately, though, until now Washington has been spectacularly unsuccessful.

Just last month, car bombings in Baghdad, blamed on Al Qaeda, robbed 127 people of their lives, while a week ago, eight were killed by explosions in a town, west of the Iraqi capital. The situation in Afghanistan is equally grim. In December, seven Central Intelligence Agency (CIA) operatives were victims of a revenge killing, while earlier this month four American service personnel and one British soldier were killed.

The death toll is mounting yet the US is no nearer its stated aims of creating a peaceful Iraq, capturing Osama bin Laden or destroying the Taliban. That may be a bitter pill to swallow but it is the undeniable truth.

After enduring eight years of the Bush administration's aggressive and biased policies, Arabs welcomed President Barack Obama with open arms. We believed his passionately-delivered promises. We trusted in his beautifully-crafted speeches. We were relieved that this Leader of the Free World was ready to listen to our concerns, as he clearly stated in Cairo. But, sadly, he has failed to translate his words into action.

Let us be frank. There are some angry people in our part of the world, eager to spill innocent blood. We cannot deny that. But Washington consistently fails to recognize that the people of the Middle East are terrorist targets too.

Instead of adopting a divisive "them and us" position by designating citizens of 14 predominantly Muslim countries as potential flight risks, America should stand shoulder to shoulder with those countries in a common cause. We are all in this together.

If the US is serious about solving this cancerous problem, it needs to take a step back. The high-profile presence of its soldiers in the region generates hatred. Moreover, most American intelligence personnel, generals and men on the ground are clueless when it comes to dealing with local people. They rarely speak local languages or bother to understand cultural norms, and, half the time, they are unable to differentiate between friend and foe. They are also often taken in by so-called "intelligence" that turns out to have been fabricated to suit someone's agenda.

We understand Middle Eastern culture, the way of thinking and the various dialects, making us the best qualified to infiltrate groups and garner intelligence. We are also able to distinguish with whom to negotiate with and whom to fight. If terrorism is spreading through the veins of our neighbourhood, then we must be our own doctors and find a cure.

Saudi Arabia should be praised for thwarting the ambitions of terrorist groups on its own soil and for driving back the insurgent Houthis of northern Yemen to the extent that they are now asking to talk. However, troublemakers who threaten the security of all countries in the region must not be rewarded with negotiation. They should be sent a message they will never forget.

To counteract the prevailing instability in Yemen, where the government is fighting terrorists and insurgents on three fronts, the entire Arab World should work with Yemeni authorities to surgically remove the contagion once and for all.

Here, I want to be clear. This does not mean League of Arab States foreign ministers should engage in lengthy debates that invariably result in a meaningless watered-down statement, and, to be frank, petitioning the UN General Assembly to vote on a condemnatory resolution is a waste of time. Instead, we should offer Sana'a as much military support as it requires. What is the point of having sophisticated armies, air forces and navies if they are only displayed trophy-like in national day parades?

Most of us in our part of the world despise conflict. We are tired of wars. But sometimes we are left with no choice. If we abandon Yemen to chaos and division, the terrorists and insurgents will infect the entire area. Stabilizing Yemen must be our first priority, and, the best country to spearhead the endeavour is Saudi Arabia with its well-trained forces and state of the art weaponry.

Successfully snipping terrorism's tentacles requires a lot more than the indiscriminate dropping of bombs from 30,000 feet or the ability to take over towns and villages. The bombs ignite fury by indiscriminately killing civilians while hard-won secured towns become vulnerable again once the foreign armies march on out, which eventually they always do.

The fact that Arabs have remained in the shadows, watching Uncle Sam manipulating an inter-factional Palestinian feud while Iran sneaks in via the back door is shameful. Just a few years ago, the thought of Palestinians allying themselves with Tehran would have been inconceivable.

Just as reprehensible is our collective apathy towards Iraq that has been invaded, occupied and virtually re-occupied by Iranian agents within Iraq's government. Our leaders should do everything in their power to keep Tehran's influence from seeping into the fabric of any Arab country. They must pull out all the stops to ensure that Iran desists from using weapons and cash as tools with which to interfere in Arab affairs.

It is time that Middle Eastern and Gulf countries became proactive instead of sitting back passively allowing others to do their dirty work. It is our duty to defend our own back garden and the sooner we embrace this duty the better. Taking a back seat in the hope that the West can magic away our problems is a cop-out, which we should tolerate no more.

Open letter to the GCC on the "Arabian Gulf"

18 April 2011

cc: League of Arab States Secretariat, UN Secretariat

DEAR SECRETARY GENERAL, I would like to remind you of a long-standing anomaly relating to the geographical name "Persian Gulf", used by the United Nations (UN) Secretariat and international bodies when referring to the 251,000 sq km long body of water flowing between the Shatt Al Arab and the Gulf of Oman that separates the Arabian Peninsula from the Islamic Republic of Iran. As most of your member countries would agree, "Persian Gulf" is obsolete.

In this respect, I would ask you to request the UN to task its Group of Experts on Geographical names to consider designating such body of water as the "Arabian Gulf". I would further propose that the Gulf Cooperation Council (GCC) becomes the Arabian Gulf Cooperation Council to set an example to the rest of the world. Indeed, when people all over world hear "Gulf countries" they automatically think of Arab states; never of Iran.

I would also call upon you to urge your American, British and European allies, as well as all international bodies, to cease prefixing the "Arabian Gulf" with "Persian", reminding them that GCC states are cooperative with the international community as opposed to being a country with hostile, isolationist policies.

The following factual arguments for bringing this case before the UN are:

The Arab coastline is longer than Iran's

Aside from Iran, which has a 2,440km shoreline on the Arabian Gulf (including the 400km coastline of the predominantly Arab province of Al Ahwaz, now Khuzestan), there are seven Arab states with coastlines bordering the Arabian Gulf. These are: Saudi Arabia (840km), the United Arab Emirates (1,318km), Qatar (563km), Kuwait (499km), Bahrain (161km), Oman (51km) and Iraq (58km). The Arab coastline totalling 3,490km is, therefore, considerably longer than Iran's. This is without adding the coastline of Al Ahwaz, an Arab province that was annexed by the Shah of Persia in 1925.

Demographics

The people who live around the Arabian Gulf on both sides are predominantly Arabs. Therefore, by sheer weight of demographics the use of "Persian Gulf" is inaccurate.

Persia no longer exists

"Persia" has existed only as a matter of historical record since 1935 when the Shah of Iran Reza Shah Pahlavi decreed his country's name should be changed to "Iran". The fact that the Ruler of Persia took his decision renders any contemporary reference to the "Persian Gulf" null and void.

Admittedly, any attempt to give the Arabian Gulf its true name has been fiercely fought by Iran. To this day, Roderick Owen's book *The Golden Bubble* (1957) is reviled by Iranian hardliners for its historically reasoned attempt to rename the Persian Gulf the Arabian Gulf. However, such name change does not affect the history of the Persian Empire in the same way that "Iran" does not negate Persian heritage.

Strategic importance to Arab states

Along the Arab coastline are such major capital cities as Abu Dhabi, Kuwait City, Doha and Manama whereas Iran's political and commercial heartland, its capital Tehran, is over 1,000km away from the cities and port towns abutting the Arabian Gulf. It could, therefore, be argued that the Gulf is of greater strategic and economic importance to GCC states than Iran.

The GCC is a political and economic force

The region's geopolitical landscape has since altered dramatically over the last half-century. Those Arab states surrounding the Arabian Gulf, in particular GCC countries, have emerged as political and economic powerhouses – jointly holding 41 per cent of the world's proven oil reserves in contrast to Iran's 10 per cent – and should be recognized as such.

Increased usage of "Arabian Gulf"

Although the UN and other world organizations are still under instructions to use "Persian Gulf" in their documentation, "Arabian Gulf" is favoured by most Arab countries. Moreover the US military based in the region uses "Arabian Gulf". Today, a number of media outlets have replaced "Persian Gulf" with "Gulf".

Apart from the core arguments as set out above, there are several other factors to be taken into consideration.

The first is political. Most nationals of GCC countries object to using "Persian Gulf" when Iran occupies United Arab Emirates (UAE) islands, has made territorial claims on Bahrain and is expanding its influence throughout the region. Iran's insistence on retaining "Persian Gulf" reinforces its expansionist plans. Attempts by Tehran to hold the world hostage, such as warning airlines not to use "Arabian Gulf" on their in-flight monitors else be banned from Iran's airspace, should not be tolerated.

The second is historical/cultural/emotional. Whereas the vast bulk of the Iranian mainland is east of the Zagros mountain range and, therefore, cut off from the waters of the Gulf, those waters, studded with Arab islands, have been a lifeline for the peoples of the Arabian Peninsula for hundreds of years.

Our ancestors were great sailors, explorers and traders who set off on wooden dhows to sell their wares in Africa and the sub-continent; they were pearl divers and fishermen. Unlike most Persians, the sea is in our blood; we could not have existed without its fruits or the cooling sea breezes that gave us respite in the days before fans or air-conditioning.

As a boy, I dove and swam in the waters of the *Khaleej al Arabi* (the Arabian Gulf) and it is my hope that with your help the day will soon come when this waterway is rightfully recognized as ours.

Respectfully yours,

Vultures circle around Gulf states

12 May 2011

FORGET THE FIERY RHETORIC, Washington, Tel Aviv and Tehran have more in common than you might imagine. All share the same aim: to control Arab states, the custodians of the world's largest oil and gas deposits, and prevent them from uniting under one powerful bloc. In earlier times, they have been co-conspirators in that endeavour. The question is whether Iran truly is an enemy of America/Israel and a natural ally of the Arab World as the Iranian leadership works hard to portray?

The rivalry between Persians and Arabs goes back 1,400 years to the Muslim conquests when Persians embraced Islam. Today, Iranians wrap themselves in an Islamic flag in an effort to lead the Muslim world yet the pre-Islamic Zoroastrian New Year *Nowruz* is still Iran's most celebrated festival. Attempts by Iranian clerics to undermine the resurgence of the Shi'ite holy city of Najaf in Iraq to retain the centre of religious gravity in the Iranian Shi'ite city of Qom exemplify Tehran's nationalistic instincts.

If Iranians were true friends of Arabs, they would not impede Arabic being spoken or the construction of Sunni mosques when Shi'ite mosques and synagogues proliferate. The Iranian government also bans parents from giving traditional Arab names to their newborns. It should be remembered too that Tehran still occupies United Arab Emirates (UAE) islands, refuses demands from the Arab population of Al Ahwaz (Khuzestan) for autonomy, has territorial claims on Bahrain and threatens airlines that use "Arabian Gulf" instead of "Persian Gulf" with being barred from Iranian airspace. With friends like these who needs enemies!

Dr Abdullah Al Nafisi, a university professor and specialist on Shi'ite affairs, says Iranians are primarily Persian nationalists who use their faith to reach Arabs via Shi'ite Arab minorities. He says Iranian officialdom from the Supreme Leader down to senior military officers, Revolutionary Guards and intelligence personnel once followed the teachings of the politician and cleric Abdollah Nouri. This former

Interior Minister maintains that all Gulf states belong to Persia and promotes Iranian retribution on Arabs for helping to destroy the Persian Empire, which may account for Iranian Arabs being treated as second-class citizens. Conversely, according to Al Nafisi, ordinary Iranians harbour no hostility towards the country's 25,000 Jews who are represented in parliament and are so well-respected that most have declined cash incentives to move to Israel.

Under-the-table dealings between Israel, the US and Persia extend back to the reign of Mohammed Reza Shah Pahlavi when Iranian oil flowed to Israel and, in turn, Israel supplied Iran with technological knowhow, missile assembly plants and military training. Iran even supplied Israel with details of Gamal Abdel Nasser's military planning according to an illuminating book by Trita Parsi titled *Treacherous Alliance*.

Following the 1979 Islamic revolution, Yasser Arafat was lectured by the Ayatollah Ruhollah Khomeini on the need for Palestinians to reject Arab nationalism and revert to their Islamic roots, Parsi says. It was clear that Khomeini was not serious in his support for the Palestinian cause. His primary aim was to lead the Islamic world, indoctrinate Arabs with his credo and bolster Arab Shi'ites.

A research paper by Xue Maior concludes Iran disseminates the principles of the Iranian revolution under anti-Israel slogans. Israel never took the "Little Satan" slur seriously and lobbied Washington to renew relations with Tehran. In 1981, Iran facilitated Israel's attack on Iraq's nuclear reactor with photographs and maps of Osirak and during the eight-year-long Iran–Iraq War, the Iranians purchased weapons from Israel with the White House's blessing, writes Parsi. In early 1986, President Reagan signed a secret memo authorizing the sale of US arms to Iran resulting in the Iran-Contra scandal.

With the signing of the Oslo Accords in 1993, Tehran saw its plan to dominate the Arab World slipping away and so began funding and supporting Islamist rejectionist groups to spoil the peace process. Despite being included in George W. Bush's "Axis of Evil", Iran offered to help strengthen the fledgling Afghan army under US supervision and in 2002 the US Department of State initiated talks with prominent Iranian political figures.

Tehran later urged Iraqi Shi'ites not to resist the US-led occupation, for good reason. Iraq – the main obstacle to Iran's access to Gulf states – had been conveniently de-fanged and was now ruled by political figures who had either lived in Iran for many years or considered it as their spiritual home. Inadvertently or otherwise, Mr Bush spent billions of American taxpayers' money and sacrificed tens of thousands of lives only to bring Iraq into Iran's sphere of influence.

Tehran has since made efforts to woo Washington so as to gain access to the International Monetary Fund (IMF), win clout in the UN and oil the lifting of anti-Iranian sanctions. It is worth noting that economic sanctions against Iran have not heavily impacted the Iranian economy, certainly not in comparison to those that crippled Iraq and were considered responsible for the death of 500,000 Iraqi children – perhaps indicating that the West is not serious about disciplining Iran.

It is curious, too, that Washington has been flexing its muscles over Iran's uranium enrichment programme since a 2006 UN Security Council resolution demanding its suspension, but despite Iran's intransigence the West has refrained from packing a punch – in dramatic contrast to its determination to punish Saddam for his non-existent Weapons of Mass Destruction (WMD). Why the double standards?

In recent decades, Iran has hardened its grip on Lebanon and expanded its influence to Syria, Iraq and Yemen as well as to Shi'ite minorities in the Gulf. Prior to the Arab Spring that may have been planned by American NGOs working with Arab youth movements – as reported in *The Washington Post* and *The New York Times* – veteran leaders kept a lid on Tehran's ambitions.

The toppling of strong Arab leaderships is an invitation to sectarian conflict, extremist organizations, secessionist groups – and civil war. I would argue that division and chaos under the banner of "freedom" will serve Iran well. It is already happening. The new Egypt has permitted Iranian warships through the Suez Canal and is preparing to normalize diplomatic relations with Tehran despite deep reservations within the GCC.

It is notable that while the US is vehemently supportive of revolutionaries in Tunisia, Egypt, Yemen and Syria and is using its airpower to attack the Libyan regime, its condemnation of Iran's repression of anti-government activists has been lukewarm. I have always suspected that the "enmity" between Iran and the US/Israel may be an elaborate act. If Tehran has covertly cooperated with its so-called enemies in the past, it is not that much of a stretch to believe that may be occurring again now.

In any case, keeping up the pretence of enmity is a symbiotic win–win situation for all concerned. Israel has a pretext to expand its nuclear arsenal and propagandize its need to put security first in the face of an Iranian existential threat. Iran uses anti-Israel slogans to increase its standing among Muslims. And the US has an excuse to maintain its military footprint in the Gulf.

What if, in the future, Washington and Tel Aviv formed an alliance similar to the one that existed at the time of the Shah? How would that impact the independence of Gulf states? It may be that such a scenario is in preparation, which would explain the West's softly-softly approach towards Iran's nuclear programme, oppression of dissidents and support of armed religious militants in Arab lands.

In conclusion, I would strongly urge GCC states to increase their military might and initiate a unified strategy to defend against threats to our land, dignity and freedom. In an increasingly unprincipled geopolitical climate where major powers are willing to dump even close allies to suit their interests we cannot rely on protection from others. We are on our own – and the sooner we face up to that fact and take care of ourselves the better.

Israeli-Iranian behind-the-door dealings

6 June 2011

A SCANDAL THAT HAS RECENTLY erupted in Israel concerning a private Israeli shipping and transport group, Ofer Brothers, that sold a tanker to Iran via a well-known Iranian front company and has been transporting petroleum products to and from Iran for a decade, heightens my suspicions that nothing is what it seems in the dirty world of geopolitics.

On the one hand, the Netanyahu government has been calling upon Washington to tighten anti-Iranian sanctions while on the other hand a company owned by Israel's richest man, the late Sami Ofer (he died on Thursday 2 June, aged 89), has been trading with Iran for years while his ships have been regularly docking at Iranian ports.

Israeli officials have denied they knew what was going on. However, conspiracy theorists are having a field day after a discussion held by members of the Knesset Economic Affairs Committee on the issue was cut short by the Defense Ministry's Security Chief who once served on the board of Ofer Brothers. Initially, the Ofer family asserted they had dealt with Iran on Israel's behalf but have since U-turned on that defence provoking speculation a deal has been done. Anyone who imagines that the Mossad and the Shin Bet have been in the dark for ten years must be naive in the extreme and for all anyone knows the Ofer revelations could well be just the tip of the iceberg.

This echoes the Nahum Manbar controversy. He is an Israeli former Israel Defense Forces (IDF) paratrooper who was accused of selling components used to make mustard gas and nerve gas to Iran. He was imprisoned for 16 years in 1997 subsequent to a trial held behind closed doors. Author and former Mossad agent Victor Ostrovsky revealed Manbar's connections with Israel's security services while other insiders suggested Israel used him as a fall guy when the transaction became known.

Manbar has always insisted his dealings with the Iranians were blessed by the Israeli intelligence community and is none too pleased that the Ofers seem to be getting off lightly. "The establishment took revenge on me while they, the Ofer Brothers, have connections in government and nobody's touching them," he said.

Last week, *Ynetnews* reported: "Israel–Iran trade ties thriving" with "dozens of Israeli companies secretly engaging in relations with the Islamic Republic through third parties". The article quotes the chairman of the Israeli-Arab Friendship Association Yehoshua Meiri saying: "Despite what is seen on the ground, the secret relations with Iran total tens of millions of dollars a year ... . Even when harsh statements are made on both sides, business thrives. Relations with the Iranian colleagues are excellent and political statements are ignored."

Just days before, Tehran's Trade Ministry had to answer to Iranian exporters/importers who claimed Israeli apples and oranges were on sale in the country's markets. It is an open secret that Israel buys marble, cashews and pistachios from Iran while Iran imports organic fertilizer, artificial hormones to boost milk production, irrigation pipes and seeds from Israel.

How can that be?, you are probably asking yourself, when President Mahmoud Ahmadinejad has been relentlessly bashing Israel since he took office? According to a recent article on *Yedioth Ahronoth's* English-language website: "Ahmadinejad's top advisor Esfandiar Rahim Mashaei stated three years ago that Iran should have 'friendly ties' with the Jewish state", a statement that was supported by his boss.

In one of my recent columns, I suggested that the mutual enmity currently displayed between the US/Israel and Iran could be part cinema, allowing Tehran to curry favour with the Arab World, enabling Israel to pinpoint Iran as a threat to its existence in order to propagate its victim status – and giving America a pretext to maintain military bases in the region.

I highlighted that although Washington and Tehran have been "sworn enemies" since the 1979 Islamic Revolution, the Iranians facilitated Israel's bombing of an Iraqi nuclear reactor in 1981 and the Reagan administration shipped weapons to Iran during the mid-1980s via Israel. Following the invasions of Afghanistan and Iraq, Iran offered to train Afghan troops under US supervision and urged Shi'ite Iraqis not to resist the US-led occupiers.

Moreover, despite Iran's failure to allay the international's community's suspicions that Iran may be developing nuclear weapons, anti-Iranian sanctions have been toothless compared to those that crippled Saddam's Iraq for ten years. On this, President Barack Obama has been sending mixed messages. Last month, he vowed to keep up the pressure on Iran but the question is "what pressure"? It certainly is not the same sort of pressure the White House heaped on President Mubarak and President Ben Ali to step down.

The bottom line is that all three military powers consider the Middle East and the Gulf as their sphere of influence and would not shed a tear if the Arabs were to lose their grip on this strategically-positioned, oil and gas-rich region.

I would urge the Gulf Cooperation Council (GCC) states' leaderships to focus on the menacing dangers and pursue political and military independence; in particular, Egypt should resist Tehran's self-serving overtures to normalize diplomatic relations. With the Israel–Palestine peace process in its death throes, storms brewing over the Arab Spring and Iran working to expand its influence, sitting on the fence and hoping for the best is no longer an option.

Open letter to GCC heads of state

24 August 2011

YOUR ROYAL MAJESTY AND HIGHNESSES, There is a mighty storm gathering over the Arabian Gulf that if we continue to ignore it will catch us by surprise with devastating consequences. However unsettling the Arab Awakening may be it is nothing compared to the real and present danger Gulf states face from a neighbour that purports to be our friend while all the time is scheming against us behind the door. To my mind, this neighbour is in many respects an even worse threat than our historic foe Israel whose enmity towards Arabs is well known and up front.

For all its denials, the Islamic Republic of Iran has expansionist ambitions, which its ruling mullahs keep close to their chests. The ayatollahs have been patient and subtle putting into motion a slow, insidious agenda to dominate the Gulf and the entire Arab region.

For years, while we Arab patriots were sleeping, Iran has been flooding Gulf Cooperation Council (GCC) states with rabble rousers, spies as well as sleeping cells, whose members use their stay in Gulf countries to increase their wealth while masquerading as our friends. Many are Arabs in name only; many have taken the nationalities of Gulf states while all the time their loyalties lie with Tehran.

Tehran is even more dangerous now that it has forged strong links with a number of formerly exiled Iraqi politicians who today hold high office within the Iraqi government, including Iraq's Prime Minister Nouri Al Maliki who lived for eight years in the Iranian capital and regularly visits his Iranian counterpart.

The current diplomatic contretemps between Iraq and Kuwait should be taken as a warning of things to come. Iraq is threatening to prosecute Kuwait over its construction of the Mubarak Al Kabir Port on Boubyan Island, which Baghdad claims will be detrimental to its shipping routes, – and will also take its case to the UN. This has frightening echoes of Saddam's era. Iraq has no right to interfere with any facility situated on Kuwait's sovereign land.

Worse, the Hezbollah Brigades in Iraq who holds allegiance to Iran's Supreme Leader Ayatollah Ali Khamenei and has links to the Revolutionary Guards' Al Quds Brigade, has warned it will use surface-to-surface missiles to target workers building the port.

It seems that Iraqis have failed to learn lessons from the 1991 Gulf War; either that or they are now dancing to Tehran's tune. It is ironic that Washington's drive to impose democracy on Baghdad has backfired on America; Iran has been the beneficiary of that ill-thought-out war without having to fire a shot.

The Iraqi Prime Minister's reaction to the Syrian regime's brutal attacks on dissenters is certainly out of tune with the rest of the Arab World as *The New York Times* reported under the headline "Iraqi leader backs Syria, with a nudge from Iran". Apparently, Mr Al Maliki has "urged the protestors not to 'sabotage' the Syrian state … ."

I fear that when all US troops have finally withdrawn from Iraq, the day will come when Iraq and Iran will form a federation whereby their collective oil and gas reserves will give their union unprecedented geopolitical clout. In that event, it is feasible that such a federation could be capable of closing our airspace, blockading our shipping lanes and preventing traffic from reaching us overland. Once we are isolated even our highly trained, well-armed militaries will be rendered ineffective.

I am saddened that Iraq's pure Arab land has been gifted to Tehran by its own political leaders and pro-Iranian militias. Our Iraqi brothers – both Sunnis and Shi'ites – who love their country, the Cradle of Civilization, are pleading with you to rescue them from Iran's tentacles. I believe it is time for you to recognize that neither Persia nor Iran has ever been our ally and, accordingly, take the decision to keep the ayatollahs' influence from our shores, beginning with the cutting of all diplomatic links and inter-Gulf consultations on a unified strategy for dealing with Iran.

Iran's instigation of Shi'ite unrest in Bahrain and also its loud condemnation of Saudi Arabia and other GCC countries for rushing to help quell the uprising at the request of the Bahraini government should be seen as a wake-up call for the GCC to take action. We must face up to the unpleasant reality that we are on our own now that so many of our Arab allies are facing problems of their own that may take decades to resolve.

In comparison to the volatility in the Middle East and North Africa, GCC states are relatively stable, which is why I believe the headquarters of the League of Arab States should be relocated to Saudi Arabia (or another GCC member country) and its Secretary General should be a Gulf national who is not afraid to take hard decisions. We can no longer afford to remain neutral during these tumultuous times and we must ensure that we have a say in everything that affects our own neighbourhood.

Sirs, our people rely upon you to preserve their independence but I would respectfully request that you, for the sake of your own children and grandchildren, act decisively before it is too late. With the Arab World in disarray, you, Your Royal Majesty and Highnesses, are the only ones who can protect the house of Ibrahim from the Persian wolf in sheep's clothing baying outside the door.

Yours sincerely,

A union of Gulf states could be a regional force for good

25 December 2011

WHEN OUR ARAB WORLD is trembling from violent shocks, this is the moment for Gulf states to assert themselves as a united force for good. This has been my message to Gulf Cooperation Council (GCC) leaders for several years and so I was pleased to hear Saudi Arabia's King Abdullah bin Abdulaziz urging his GCC counterparts "to move from a phase of cooperation to a phase of union within a single entity" to better overcome challenges and stave off growing threats. It is encouraging that the initiative has been welcomed by Gulf states, who will form a committee tasked with its study.

Personally, I would like a future union of Gulf states to have one leader – perhaps appointed on a rotating basis – with full command over such a union's army, navy and airforce in both defensive and interventionist capacities. In this ever-more-dangerous neighbourhood, we can either decide to become players or we will end up being played.

The biggest threat to our region is the devious way that Iran is disseminating its ideology, which it uses together with its oil wealth and weapons to divide the region and attract proxy states and actors. Now that the last US combat troops have been withdrawn from Iraq it will not be long before Iraq fits neatly into the Iranian sphere of influence, especially when the loyalties of senior Iraqi government figures lie with Tehran or the Iranian ayatollahs. Trouble is already looming. In past days, the major Sunni bloc has boycotted parliament and the pro-Iranian Prime Minister has authorized an arrest warrant in the name of the Sunni Vice-President Tareq Al Hashemi.

I would not be surprised if in the future Iran and Iraq formed some kind of political and military union – perhaps even a federation – that would leave Gulf states vulnerable and under siege from all corners. The window of opportunity for the GCC and its allies to keep Iraq from Persian claws is narrowing, which is why Gulf leaders should support patriotic Iraqis, both Sunni and Shi'ite, loyal to their Arab heritage and Iraq's autonomy, to ensure Baghdad never takes its marching orders from Qom. We cannot allow an enemy to form on our doorstep; we must place the security of our countries as top priority, overshadowing diplomatic niceties and the pretence of warm relations. In short, Gulf states must unite and act to avert such a scenario before it can manifest itself.

In a perfect world, the role of protecting Arab states and interests should fall to the League of Arab States but, unfortunately, this body has a history of being ineffective and is even more so today when so many of its member countries are torn from within, especially with Egypt in intensive care. I used to have great hopes for the Arab League but as we see with its handling of

Syria, it is too hesitant and weak to make a real difference. The Arab League is expert at holding summits and coming up with suggestions but as long as it does not wield a fist its efforts are wasted.

The Arab League's representatives have been urging the Assad regime to stop imprisoning, torturing and killing and to allow in impartial monitors for months, without success, and they have not managed to take a unified, tough position on Syria. Prior to the recent meeting between the League and the GCC in Cairo, I asked two senior GCC leaders what it is that the GCC needs to do in order to save the Syrian people from their own president and his cohorts. I was told that Algeria, Sudan, Lebanon and Iraq are putting up obstacles to the implementation of hard decisions.

Lebanon can be partially forgiven because it is a tiny country bordering Syria and has a government dominated by one of Syria's proxies. Likewise, Iraq borders Syria and its Prime Minister Nouri Al Maliki is under orders from Iran's Supreme Leader Ali Khamenei to keep Assad's government afloat. Khartoum has military ties with Tehran and is currently seeking closer cooperation. I am, however, surprised at the stance adopted by Algeria. President Abdel Aziz Bouteflika lived and enjoyed the UAE for 6 years – and now he stands against those who once supported him who are keen to show solidarity with their Syrian brothers and sisters.

As long as Iran pulls the strings of some Arab League members the organization is unable to do its job. It has taken the organization months to get Assad's signature on a piece of paper promising an end to the crackdown on an unarmed and defenseless population, political reform and permission for Arab League peace monitors to enter the country. But on the same day the agreement was signed with great fanfare some 150 Syrians were killed.

Clearly, from the Syrian government's perspective, this agreement is nothing more than a time waster, a sham designed to keep the League from making good on its threat to send the Syrian file to the United Nation (UN) Security Council. It was disappointing to hear the Prime Minister of Qatar say Assad's tenure is a matter for the Syrian people. Assad has lost all credibility when more than 6,000 have been killed, over 100,000 are behind bars and so many men, women and children have been tortured – and when mercenaries are flooding into Syria from Iran and Iraq and the government is using *Shabiha* militias to ruthlessly murder its citizens irrespective of gender or age. In any case, the large demonstrations all over the country show that the Syrian people have already spoken.

This is an emergency. If the Arab League does not make good on its threat to send Syria to the Security Council, then the GCC's rapid reaction force partnered with the Jordanian military should "encourage" President Al Assad to step down.

We the descendents of Abu Bakr Al Siddiq, Omar bin Al Khattab, Othman ibn Affan, Ali bin Abi Taleb and Khalid ibn Al Walid have a duty to make a stand against repression and injustice. We have been bystanders in our own neighbourhood for too long. We must lose our attitude of *w'ana mali?* (What has this got to do with me?). We should feel repelled by the sentiments encapsulated in the Arabic saying "If my camel and I are safe, I do not care about my friends." We must remember the days of Gamal Abdel Nasser when Arab honour and dignity was paramount. If the GCC transforms into a union of Gulf states, it will be powerful enough to protect its own as well as to shine its light throughout the entire Arab World.

To the leaders of GCC states I would say just one thing: join your hands together and make your people proud!

GCC should balance diplomacy with increased military power

27 January 2012

THE FACE OF OUR ARAB WORLD has changed beyond recognition in less than 12 months. At least four autocratic regimes have been unseated by popular uprisings. On the face of it, this should be a time for celebration. But, as I have predicted over and over again in my newspaper columns, such sudden widespread change has led to uncertainty, instability, insecurity and disunity among states, weakening the Arab region as a whole.

On Wednesday 25 January, Egyptians flocked to their squares to mark the first anniversary of their revolution but the mood was hardly celebratory. Getting rid of former President Hosni Mubarak was no magic bullet. Discontent runs through all sectors of society. The youth say their revolution has been stolen by the military and Islamist parties. The Muslim Brotherhood and the Salafists dominating parliament are pushing the Supreme Council of the Armed Forces (SCAF) to transfer power to a civilian government. The poor do not care who is in charge; they want jobs and an end to spiraling prices.

Early on, when most political commentators were responding emotionally to the revolution, I wrote of the dangers. As long ago as 5 February 2011, in a column titled "Egypt's youth revolution has been hijacked" I warned that the Muslim Brotherhood was well organized and artfully portraying itself as moderate while secularist parties led by Mohamed ElBaradei and Ayman Nour had little following.

In "A worrying turn for Egypt's revolution" (6 April 2011, see earlier in the chapter) I wrote of warming relations between Egypt and Iran and of my worries that should the Muslim Brotherhood dominate politics, "it could become a conduit for Iranian influence in the heart of the Arab World". I note with concern that a new Egyptian movement calling itself the Egyptian Revolutionary Guard that has replaced the eagle on Egypt's flag with the Ayatollah Khomeini has since emerged. During a speech delivered in Bahrain, Dubai's Police Chief Lieutnant General Dahi Khalfan Tamim went as far as to equate the threat to the Gulf from the Muslim Brotherhood with that of Iran.

I was not far off the mark in my other articles on Egypt published last year: "The fine line between freedom and anarchy", published 1 March 2011, "Egypt's economic recovery is in the balance" (23 May 2011), "An impatient majority holds Egypt hostage" (24 July 2011), "Only God's mercy can save Egypt" (6 August 2011) and "Egyptians require saving from themselves" (14 October 2011). (See earlier in this chapter.) In those, I reiterated that no state can flourish under mob rule and asserted the importance of strong governance and law and order allowing the economy to grow. I foresaw a revolution of the hungry. That has not happened yet but when the country's foreign currency reserves have been halved, the stock market volatile and the government is reluctantly pursuing an IMF loan and may have to devalue the Egyptian pound causing rampant inflation, the hungry will make their voices heard sooner rather than later.

Given that Egypt is in no fit state to re-adopt its rightful role as one of the Arab World's leaders and the League of Arab States is divided and ineffectual, I have been urging the Gulf Cooperation Council (GCC) to forcefully take the leadership reins. In my column "Moment ripe for firm GCC union," I seconded the call from Saudi Arabia's King Abdullah bin Abdulaziz urging GCC states "to move from a phase of cooperation to a phase of union within a single entity to better stave off growing threats".

Lieutenant General Tamim has recently put US policies atop his "threat list" ahead of Iran. In his speech, he blamed America for being insincere, exporting revolution and handing Iraq to Iran. I think the Iranian regime is far more dangerous but I broadly agree with him and as I wrote in my column "GCC grapples with Iranian threat", published 14 March 2011, the US operates entirely out of self-interest. This is why it is about time that the GCC took a leaf out of Washington's book. The GCC should be responsible for the protection of its lands and peoples. The GCC should develop its military might and warn its enemies that we are strong and awake as I have urged in several articles, including my "Open letter to the heads of GCC states" (27 August 2011).

I have also strongly advocated for the GCC's rapid reaction force to intervene in Syria to protect innocents in various of my writings and am grateful to the Emir of Qatar Sheikh Hamad bin Khalifa Al Thani for his readiness to deploy Gulf troops. I am also pleased that Saudi Arabia saw the Arab League monitoring as the failure it was and pulled out the Saudi observers, a move that was emulated by Gulf states. It is a good sign, too, that the Arab League secretariat is liaising with the United Nations (UN) to lend weight to its demands. It is, however, shameful that some Arab countries are erecting obstacles to progress.

Tarik Al Humaid, writing in *Asharq Al-Awsat* under the headline "Syria: KSA did it, what about you?" took the words out of my mouth when he asked why other Arab states were hesitant to help the Syrian people and again when he suggested that the GCC should join with Turkey to rescue Syria. I am also appreciative of Mr Humaid's recognition that Iraq has been gifted to Tehran by Prime Minister Nouri Al Maliki and his pro-Iranian cohorts.

Once again, I would ask the heads of GCC states not to rely on outsiders. Depend on your own power and do not be afraid to display your military capabilities to scare our enemies. Listen to your hearts, your instincts and you will do what is right. Hear the message of Surah Al-Anfal [8:60] and be guided by it when taking your decisions:

"And prepare against them whatever you are able of power and of steeds of war by which you may terrify the enemy of Allah and your enemy and others besides them whom you do not know [but] whom Allah knows. And whatever you spend in the cause of Allah will be fully repaid to you, and you will not be wronged."

Are Sunnis victims of a new "Great Game"?

24 April 2012

HOW WOULD YOU FEEL if you knew that there was a slow ticking time bomb in your neighborhood while all around you refused to heed your warnings? That is exactly the situation I find myself in these days. The bomb I hear ticking is Iran's belligerence, interference in Arab countries and growing military might. This threat is dire and if we do not take it seriously we will wake up one day to find that Iranian Revolutionary Guards have reached our coastlines.

A few days ago, I read an Arabic article by Mishari Al Thaidy published in *Asharq Al-Awsat* titled "Knocks on the Persian door" that adds grist to my fears. The writer cites the views of former Central Intelligence Agency (CIA) field operative and author of *The Devil We Know*, Robert Baer, who claims America's trust in weak Sunni, regimes is misplaced. Instead, he maintains Iran, which is more powerful and stable, is a better bet. Baer advises the US to invite Iran to the peace table without preconditions.

Al Thaidy also discusses the sentiments of Iranian-born American Middle East analyst and author of *The Shia Revival* Vali Nasr. According to Nasr: "Shias have welcomed both the fall of Sunni domination and the rise of prospects for political change. This makes them, in principal, more likely to work with the United States. Greater democracy serves Shia interests across the region, and hence Shia revival is favourably disposed towards democratic change," he writes. Although that is hardly true when Sunnis proved their thirst for democracy during the Arab Spring and are laying down their lives for pluralistic governance in Syria.

A growing number of respected American think-tanks are reaching similar conclusions to those of Baer and Nasr. If President Mahmoud Ahmadinejad has whiffed this warmer mood wafting over the Atlantic in his direction, no wonder he feels confident enough to strut around Abu Musa, a UAE-owned island under Iranian occupation. Which of our lands will he be gloating over next? Unless Gulf Cooperation Council

(GCC) leaderships wake up and smell the danger, as I have been advising over and over again, tragically we may soon know the answer.

Historically, our Arab leaders have taken the promises of Western powers at face value and have failed to read the writing on the wall. Sykes and Picot were free to carve up the Middle East with the stroke of a pen in 1916 and a year later Balfour merrily gave away Palestine that was not his to give. When it came to oil-rich Gulf states, their strategy was more sophisticated. We were not occupied in the traditional sense, but rather dominated by Great Britain and later the US.

Well, that is ancient history, you might think. But history has a nasty habit of repeating itself. We must absolutely refuse to be treated like pawns in an endless geo-strategic chess game being played out by Washington and Moscow. We must let them know in no uncertain terms that we will not be pushed around and shore up our own joint defence capability. With unified objectives and effective militaries we can avert the threat of being treated like playthings without any say in our destiny.

A few weeks ago, US Secretary of State Hillary Clinton said the US was committed to the security of Gulf states but the truth is that America is only committed to securing its own interests. Washington's Middle East policy is always focused on retaining US regional hegemony using the tried and true method of "divide and rule".

America fancies itself as a puppet master manipulating client/compliant states. During the presidential tenure of George W. Bush when newly democratic Russia was hesitant to flex its muscle, the US had free rein to invade Iraq and Afghanistan – and set up military bases throughout the Gulf and the Caspian Sea.

However, contemporary Russia is a different creature. President Vladimir Putin regrets his former conciliatory position and is set on countering America's regional ambitions by taking Iran and Syria under his country's wing. Russia has played an important role in Iran's nuclear development and is currently using its clout to keep Syria's ruthless Assad regime in power.

The game of who controls the Middle East and the Gulf may not be what it seems. Superficially, the US and Iranian governments are sworn enemies but this may be a ploy as highlighted by author Trita Parsi in his book *Treacherous Alliance*. It is no secret that Britain and America were behind the ousting of the Shah and the installation of the Ayatollah Ruhollah Khomeini. Since, Iran's mullahs have actively cooperated with Washington to rid Afghan-istan of their mutual foe the Taliban and they have leant their support to the US-led invasion of Iraq, now sheltered under an Iranian umbrella.

There is a credible school of thought that Washington's long-term agenda revolves around luring Iran into its camp on the premise that Arab Shi'ites would follow. This is one instance when the US and Israel, which perceives Iran as a threat to its existence, differ. Should the US succeed in bringing Tehran on side, Russia would be edged out of the picture and Israel's security would be assured. There is a precedent. Under the presidency of Gamal Abdel Nasser, Egypt eschewed the West in favour of the Soviet Union but the US wasted little time in courting his successor Anwar El Sadat, the man who forged the Camp David peace treaty with Israel.

In theory, Washington would like to appoint a powerful entity like Iran as its proxy regional caretaker, just as the Shah was until he suffered delusions of grandeur. But first of all, it would be obliged to throw predominately Sunni states under a bus. America's aim is and has always been to divide Arabs by keeping Sunnis contained in manageable small pockets while empowering Shi'ites, a policy that it has successfully achieved in Iraq.

Think about it! With so much sectarian violence in Iraq there is still a strong possibility that the country could be divided up into two or three states. Western hands were behind the slicing of Sudan into two warring entities. And their part in the downfall of Muammar Gaddafi has resulted in residents of Libya's second city in the east Benghazi demanding autonomy. Yemen is also splintering under the weight of splits in the army, secessionist demands in the south, Houthis wreaking violence in the north and Al Qaeda poisoning the mix. In each case, Sunnis are the losers.

Strangely, the Alawite, pro-Iranian Assad regime appears to have been given a license to kill as long as United Nations observers are taking a tally. Moreover, the US and Europe seem to have entered some kind of accommodation with Iran over uranium enrichment during recent P5+1 talks in Istanbul bringing a scowl to Benjamin Netanyahu and an optimistic grin to the faces of UN Secretary General Ban Ki-moon and EU Policy Chief Catherine Ashton. Forget President Barack Obama's harsh anti-Iranian rhetoric, designed to placate Tel Aviv and America's pro-Israel lobby! He is certainly oiling this fledgling détente behind the scenes.

We should not wait for a nasty surprise. Western powers will always compromise with and join hands with powerful countries able to protect their interests, while the weak and those without sufficient gumption to preserve their honour will be squashed under foot.

Moreover, the Israel writer Yaron Friedman predicts that new post-Arab Spring political realities will spark sectarian clashes between Sunnis and Shi'ites. He believes the main arena of conflict will be the Arabian Gulf. We must pray that he is wrong while remaining alert to prevent any such violent eruptions.

If only GCC governments and peoples would open their eyes to these new geo-political trends before citizens of Gulf states are herded into Gaza-type pens wishing we could turn back the clock. We must protect our dignity that rests in our countries' sovereignty over our land and borders. And GCC states must set aside selfish interests and petty disagreements to form a seamless united front. Then, and only then, there is hope.

Is anybody out there listening?

GCC leaders should not attend NAM Summit

16 June 2012

IRAN'S PRESIDENT MAHMOUD AHMADINEJAD is not lacking audacity. He has extended invitations to Gulf Cooperation Council (GCC) leaders to attend the 16th Non-Aligned Movement's (NAM) summit, scheduled to be held in Tehran from 26–31 August. For a number of reasons, it is my hope that GCC leaders not only politely decline but also decide not to send even a low-level representative in their stead.

Let us not keep up the charade any longer. It is no secret there is no love lost between GCC countries and the Islamic Republic of Iran when Tehran is behind the Shi'ite uprising in Bahrain on which it has made territorial claims in the past. Iran's president has been lambasting Saudi Arabia on various issues and recently rubbed salt in the UAE's wound over his country's occupation of UAE-owned islands by making a provocative visit to the smallest island Abu Musa that was vehemently condemned by the Abu Dhabi, Riyadh and Manama. The UAE recalled its ambassador from Tehran over that incident. Instead of inviting our leaders to the NAM Summit, if the Iranian government wants to mend fences it should immediately return our islands, stolen by the Shah in the 1970s.

Firstly, the differences between the GCC and Iran go much deeper than that. Gulf Arabs do not appreciate that Iraq has been virtually turned into an Iranian satellite or that non-state actors are ruling Lebanon at Tehran's behest using Iranian cash and weapons to do so. Moreover, the Iranians are currently using their wealth to court Egypt's Muslim Brotherhood, currently dominating Parliament, into their camp, which, in the worst case scenario, could ensure that Cairo never regains its status as an Arab World leader; on the contrary it would become an object of suspicion for Western powers who would waste little time placing Egypt on their hit lists.

So why keep up the buddy-buddy pretence with Tehran? Iran is no friend of ours and we should not be afraid to admit it or take a stand for what we believe is right. Our leaders should refrain from sitting at the same table as those working against us or shaking hands with people whose own hands are soiled.

Secondly, Iran, along with Russia and China, is staunchly defending the Syrian President Bashar Al Assad whose army has been slaughtering, dismembering and torturing Syrian men, women and young children for over a year. Everyone's seen horrific pictures of the ongoing destruction and carnage and GCC member states are rightly united in the wish to take action to stop this humanitarian tragedy by any means – or support action, approved by the League of Arab States and the United Nations (UN). It goes without saying that President Al Assad has also received an invitation to the NAM Summit, which is another reason Gulf leaders should think twice before attending. Photo-ops of our heads of state – or their envoys for that matter – with the blood-stained Syrian dictator would send the wrong message to our peoples and the world.

Thirdly, I am not sure that NAM is one that the GCC should be associated with. The Movement's very name is a misnomer as it gives the impression that each is geopolitically independent, while, in fact, its 120 member countries are aligned with each other primarily against Western powers when it suits their own interests. In any event, it has not lived up to the ideals outlined by Fidel Castro in 1979 that were to assure "the national independence, sovereignty, territorial integrity and security of non-aligned countries" struggling "against imperialism, colonialism, neo-colonialism, racism and all forms of foreign aggression, occupation, domination, interference or hegemony as well as against great power and bloc politics".

Although NAM's member states represent some 55 per cent of the world's population, the Movement was ineffective in preventing the invasions of members, such as Afghanistan and Iraq. Indeed, certain NAM members provided either troops or ancillary support to the coalition, such as Azerbaijan, the Dominican Republic, and Hondurus, thereby breaching NAM's own set of principles, including "mutual respect for each other's territorial integrity and sovereignty", "mutual non-aggression" and "peaceful co-existence". Likewise, Azerbaijan and Bangladesh (both NAM members) supplied armed forces and naval vessels respectively to attack a fellow member Afghanistan in 2001. The fact is that countries that purport to have adopted the principles on which NAM was founded are not non-aligned at all; certainly not in the way that, say, Switzerland has proved to be.

When considering whether or not to accept Iran's invitation, I would only advise the leaders of the GCC to think upon these wise words written by Aesop: "A doubtful friend is worse than a certain enemy. Let a man be one thing or the other, and we then know how to meet him."

Gulf states are pawns in a new "Great Game"

17 October 2012

THE PIECES OF THE JIGSAW are slowly coming together and from the perspective of Gulf states and Arab Sunnis the emerging picture is not pretty. The Cold War between Russia and the West has been resurrected by President Vladimir Putin who regrets the break-up of the Soviet Union, Russia's loss of superpower status and, in particular, his passive compliance with George W. Bush's invasion of Iraq that cost Moscow dearly from both economic and geostrategic standpoints. That war hit Russia's pocket to the tune of $8bn in unfulfilled deals and resulted in the mushrooming of US military bases throughout the Middle East, the Caucasus and Central Asia. Driven also by the encroachment of the

European Union (EU) uncomfortably close to its territory, the Bear has not only broken out of his cage he is on the rampage.

In his determination to muscle back into the region, Putin has few scruples about forging unholy alliances with anti-Western countries on the basis of "the enemy of my enemy is my friend" as well as mutual interests and shared ambitions. Unlike most of the world, Moscow has little fear of a nuclear-armed Iran. Indeed, it is one of Tehran's major weapons suppliers and over the years has provided Iran with nuclear and missile technology as well as hardware. Today, it actively supports Iran's nuclear programme with knowhow plus nuclear reactor components, and benefits from trade deals amounting to more than $4bn annually.

Russia constantly warns the West that striking Iranian nuclear sites would be disastrous. And, in August, the Russia Foreign Ministry warned the US not to impose unilateral sanctions against Iran with this message on its website, "Washington should understand that our bilateral relations will suffer considerably if the American restrictions affect Russian economic entities cooperating with partners in the Islamic Republic of Iran in strict compliance with our legislation and UN Security Council resolutions."

Furthermore, Moscow has set itself up as a buffer against any attempt by the international community to use UN sanctions or military intervention to halt the carnage in Syria and actively props up Iran's closest ally President Bashar Al Assad, a genocidal monster, responsible for the deaths of over 30,000 of his own people and the destruction of huge swathes of Syrian towns and cities, levelled by Russian-made tanks and attack helicopters. Keeping Assad in power is essential to Iran's ambitions for regional dominance when pro-Shi'ite Syria acts as a supply route for Iranian proxies.

In this game of one-upmanship between Russia and the US, Putin can now add another notch to his belt – Iraq. This supposed free and democratic nation has been gifted by Western allies to Iran – and, by extension, to Moscow. It is no secret that the Shi'ite-dominated Iraqi government is made up of Iran's puppets, men who make few decisions without a green light from Tehran or Qom, which is why Iraq is one of just three League of Arab States member nations that objected to the League's appeal for the Assad regime to step down.

America's finest political and military minds would have been unbelievably naive to expect gratitude from Iraqis. But I doubt they predicted that the Al Maliki government would leap aboard Russia's ship with such alacrity. Iraqi Prime Minister Nouri Al Maliki's recent visit to his Russian counterpart Dmitry Medvedev was sealed with the restoration of bilateral cooperation in numerous fields, including diplomatic, military, aviation energy and trade.

The ninth of October signified an even higher watermark in the blossoming relations between Moscow and Baghdad. On that day, Russia announced the signing of a $4.2bn arms contract to include MI-28 attack helicopters and Pantsir-21 surface-to-air missile systems. Since Iraq and Iran are virtually joined at the hip – I have long warned of the potential for an Iranian-Iraqi federation – this move is another nail in the coffin of Gulf states' vulnerability. Mark my words! There will come a time when those weapons will be aimed at us. Together, Iran and Iraq could endanger our very shores.

Iran is becoming ever more belligerent. It has revived an old, debunked territorial claim to Bahrain, has bullied airlines to use the term "Persian Gulf" rather than "Arabian Gulf" and made threats to Gulf oil fields and the Straits of Hormuz. So I was not surprised at media reports, quoting an Iranian Foreign Ministry spokesman, indicating Iran was mulling cutting diplomatic ties with the United Arab Emirates over the UAE's legitimate demands for the return of three islands – Abu Musa and the Greater and Lesser Tunb – forcibly occupied by the Shah in 1971.

My initial thought was *What kind of joke is this? Does Iran expect the UAE to roll over and accept its stolen islands are gone forever in return for its ongoing "friendship" and trade relations with Iran?* In the first place, Iran is not our ally and never has been; secondly, with Iran's economy and currency wilting under UN, US and EU sanctions, it needs us – one of its main trading partners – substantially more than we need it. Clearly, somebody high up in the Iranian government thought the same. A day later, the Iranian Foreign Ministry swiftly went into damage control mode by dismissing the reports as untrue.

True or untrue, it is time that we proved to Iran that the days when it felt free to trample on our dignity are over. What are we waiting for? We should immediately close the embassies of GCC countries in Tehran, bar Iranian aircraft from entering our airspace, instruct our banks to freeze the accounts of Iranian officials and ban all forms of commerce and trade. We should also prevail on our friendly Arab neighbours to do the same.

Such steps would not only be in keeping with the sentiments of the majority of United Nations (UN) Security Council member nations towards Iran, anything that contributes towards Iran's international isolation will assist in bringing about the ayatollahs' downfall from inside. Indeed, recent anti-government demonstrations, triggered by the dramatic currency slide, indicate Iran's business community is already disillusioned with Ahmadinejad and his government.

Until the Iranian people decide to free themselves from the yoke of oppression and return their country to the community of freedom-loving nations, the GCC should have nothing more to do with this dangerous pariah state. As I have said time and time again, Gulf states must unify under a Gulf-wide federation, fortify their joint sea/air/land borders and create a single powerful military capability so we can stand up as main players instead of mere pawns.

No mercy for terrorists and conspirators

2 January 2013

THE ENLIGHTENED THOUGHT, sweat and sheer hard slog that has gone into making the UAE the near-Utopia it is today is incalculable. Together we have created a harmonious multi-cultural, peaceful society offering bright individuals unlimited opportunity. Our country is beautiful from the inside out, a place where innovation and creativity can flourish. Success has not come easy. I know. I am old enough to remember the hard times we faced. I shared our nation's struggles from its inception in 1972 and watched with pride as we overcame each obstacle with flying colours.

Emiratis are arguably the most privileged on earth. We enjoy a better standard of living than the so-called developed world and the same is true for most Gulf Cooperation Council (GCC) countries whose citizens are provided with financial assistance, homes, inexpensive utilities – and the highest standards of education and healthcare – at home and abroad. Nobody here is forced to sleep on the street or worry where their next meal is coming from, unlike the wealthiest countries on earth where even middle-class individuals down on their luck are queuing outside soup kitchens. In the United Nations' Human Development Index, the United Arab Emirates (UAE) ranks first in the region for "very high human development" in terms of health, education, income and gender equality. We have so much to be proud of.

So hearing that UAE security authorities in coordination with Saudi Arabia had arrested "an organized cell" (consisting of Saudi and Emirati nationals) planning to carry out actions against the national security of the UAE, Saudi and other Gulf states, set my blood boiling with rage.

I thank God that the UAE has a sophisticated intelligence and security apparatus capable of interrupting such unthinkable plans. Intelligence officials deserve our utmost respect for their great efforts. But even the idea that there are people out there plotting to do us harm is a cause of distress. The question is why? What is that drives some of our own citizens to destroy rather than build? What kind of creatures are these? A report by Emirates News Agency, WAM, on the arrests was non-specific, mentioning only "a deviant group". It is not unlikely that they are part of a rogue state like Iran and its allies.

"The only conspiracy that Emiratis should worry about is that of the government to stamp out any and every semblance of dissent," said Sarah Leah Whitson, Middle East Director at Human Rights Watch, following the arrests, while asking "Just how many Emiratis does the government intend to jail for expressing political opinions?" I would respectfully ask Ms Whitson to either get her facts straight or mind her own business. They were detained for committing crimes that harm state security and for having affiliations with groups harbouring foreign agendas, according to WAM, and not for expressing political views.

Whoever were involved in this latest plot are failures, men with weak, dysfunctional minds that have either been brainwashed or paid by outside entities, those same entities that are causing upheaval in Bahrain and Kuwait. They are traitors who no longer deserve to be called Saudis or Emiratis. They should be made an example of. No punishment is too severe for people whose agenda includes the spilling of innocent blood and threats to our safety and security. We must never allow our soil to be polluted by even one drop. Our police forces and intelligence communities must remain vigilant to keep these diseased ideologies far away from our shores. And every patriot in the UAE and the GCC should be alert to any hint of this poison among us before it begins to flow through our society's veins and becomes unstoppable.

Forget the complaints of human rights organizations with nothing to lose and who care more about the rights of terrorists than safeguarding populations. Terrorists and troublemakers do not have rights, end of story. The day they begin assembling bombs or planning to bring down buildings, they forfeit their membership of the human race. They contend that they are true Muslims, an obscenity when Islam is a peaceful and tolerant faith. The UAE and the GCC governments and citizens abide by the pure teachings of Islam and its laws without distortion. We are guided by the legitimate interpretation of Islam every waking hour by showing respect to the beliefs of others and reaching out a hand to the needy irrespective of the recipients' faith, race or colour.

If I sound intolerant, so be it. I cannot and will not tolerate anyone seeking to make my beloved homeland a hell on earth, whatever the pretext, and worse, doing so while using Islam as their banner. They are nothing less than traitors and blasphemers and I would urge the UAE, Saudi and other GCC authorities to crush their cells with an iron fist. There must be no freedom for those who will stoop to heinous acts to rob us of ours.

We only have to cast an eye at the mayhem all around us to realize the urgency of cleansing our countries from the enemy within and of protecting our borders from enemy infiltrators, especially Iranian-backed sleeper cells with a malicious agenda. Those groups patiently waiting to take advantage of the slightest opportunity are an even bigger danger than Islamist organizations. The loyalties of GCC citizens working with Iran in any capacity should be evaluated by intelligence authorities. Iran's surrogates, intent on our downfall, are the most lethal and poisonous of all because their aim is to place us under Tehran's boot as an Iranian province like predominantly Arab Ahwaz is today.

I do not know which Holy Book those bent on our ruin adhere to, but for certain it is not the Holy Quran that states the killing of one person – other than someone who murders or spreads mischief in the land – is akin to the slaying of all humanity. Moreover, numerous references in the Quran enjoins Muslims to be unified, such as Surah Ali 'Imran [3:103]: "And hold firmly to the rope of Allah all together and do not become divided."

These are some of the most worrying times in our nation's history requiring each one of us who loves his country to support our government's efforts to protect all that we have worked for and keep us safe.

GCC must act decisively to halt Iran's ambitions

12 June 2013

"IF YOU ARE OUT to describe the truth, leave elegance to the tailor," said Albert Einstein. So get ready for some straight-talking on what I believe is the greatest threat our region currently faces. I'm not a man who pulls any punches and, certainly, during a time of grave danger, I am not prepared to skirt around the issues with diplomatic-speak. The indisputable fact is that our neighbour, the Islamic Republic of Iran, which has territorial ambitions towards Gulf states, is set on dominating the Arab World via its Shi'ite proxies and is actively proselytizing its extremist ideology throughout the area. In short, Iran is no friend.

Until now, we have tolerated Iranian threats to set Gulf oilfields alight, closed the Straits of Hormuz to shipping and barred airlines using the term "Arabian Gulf" in its airspace. And we have failed to react in any meaningful way when the Iranian President Mahmoud Ahmadinejad trampled on Emirati sensitivities by paying a controversial visit to Abu Musa – one of three United Arab Emirates (UAE) islands forcibly occupied by the Shah in 1971 – following a 2012 statement from his country's Foreign Minister to the effect that Iran's "ownership" of those territories was "definitive, permanent and non-negotiable".

We have virtually turned a blind eye to Iran's rabble-rousing of Bahraini Shi'ites to rise up against the government but at least Saudi Arabia had the wisdom to step in at Bahrain's invitation to thwart Iran's plot to exert control over a Gulf Cooperation Council (GCC) member state on which it has had the audacity to make territorial claims in the past. We have been ineffective in saving Lebanon from the ayatollahs' de facto rule. But we cannot and should not forgive or ever forget Tehran's role in supporting a vicious Syrian war criminal's grip on power amid rivers of innocent blood. On this, Iran has crossed an indelible red line and must be halted in its tracks.

Forget diplomacy! Forget half-hearted compromises! Can talk be effective with a nation defying the international community by seeking nuclear weapons with which to blackmail the region and supply fighters and missiles to enable a barbaric despot to murder its own people? We are only deluding ourselves if we believe a string of back-to-back conferences will deter Iran from pursuing its "will to power" agenda.

It is time that we take charge of our own destiny while we still can. If, God forbid, Syrian President Bashar Al Assad rides to victory on the guns of revolutionary guards and Hezbollah's military wing, his political longevity will be owed to Tehran and he, along with every other Syrian, will remain under the Iranian/Russian thumb. Every Syrian town and

39

city will be flying Shi'ite flags and hoisting posters of Ayatollah Khomeini. Hezbollah will be empowered and non-Shi'ites in Syria and Lebanon will be treated as second-class citizens; that is if they manage to escape bloody sectarian reprisals.

It is useless to rely on intervention by the US, Britain or France; they have talked the talk but have stood by watching the killing of 90,000 Syrian men, women and children and the displacement of one-and-a-half million from their homes while hundreds of thousands have sought refuge in Turkey, Lebanon, Jordan and elsewhere. I strongly suspect that the US and Israel have decided "better the devil they know". Assad has been unwilling to take on Israel even in response to its bombing of Syrian military sites. So much for their stated commitment to humanitarianism and democratization; principles that seemingly apply only when they suit their interests!

Should Syria fall to the regime and its masters, Iran and its proxies will be emboldened with oil-rich Gulf states; their ultimate prize. Iran's spies and sleeper cells are already entrenched in our countries waiting for an opportunity to strike. Until now, many have held to the belief that the US and its allies would step in to prevent such an eventuality. The thought may help us sleep better but how can we count on Washington for protection when the Obama administration has obliquely criticized Saudi Arabia for intervening in Bahrain and is still pondering whether or not to arm the Syrian opposition? Likewise, the Europeans have lifted the EU's arms embargo but still have not come up with the goods. In truth, despite its harsh anti-Iranian rhetoric, the West has given Iran free rein to spread its tentacles around Lebanon, Syria, Iraq, Bahrain and Yemen. History tells us that fuelling destabilizing Sunni–Shi'ite sectarian conflicts is at the core of America's divide-and-rule strategy, a tactic inherited from the British Empire.

To counter the Iranian menace, I would urge GCC leaders to consider the *immediate* implementation of the following steps:

- Gulf states should acknowledge that we're on our own and take responsibility for the fate of our citizens.
- Diplomatic relations with Iran should be cut and its ambassadors and diplomats sent packing.
- All trade and commerce between GCC countries and Iran should cease forthwith.
- The GCC should lend material support to the Syrian opposition in terms of manpower, weapons and intelligence.

The balance is tipping in favour of Assad and his gangs. With Hezbollah's assistance, his forces have been making strategic gains, most recently the town Qusayr on the Lebanese border, which served as a supply route for opposition forces. The Syrian President is boasting about gaining the

upper hand as he sends his army to take back Aleppo. I, therefore, appeal
to Gulf rulers to take action now, within days, because, we no longer
have the luxury of time for endless, inconclusive debates and discussion.
Closing our eyes and hoping for the best or fooling ourselves into believing
Syria is not our business, simply is not an option. There is an old adage
that says: "Don't fear the enemy who attacks you … . Fear the fake friend
who hugs you." When dealing with Iran, it is one that all Gulf states and
predominately Sunni Arab states should heed.

Is the US plotting regional mayhem?

9 October 2013

SOMETHING IS COOKING in the White House and the aroma drifting
towards Saudi Arabia, the Gulf states and Egypt is far from pleasant.
America is one of our closest Western allies, or so we are meant to believe.
Recent disclosures suggest otherwise. The Obama administration's policy
vis-à-vis the Middle East and the Gulf lacks transparency and is marked by
contradiction and confusion – perhaps deliberately so. This column aims at
giving you a clearer picture.

One of my biggest fears may be close to realization. For years,
I have been warning, in numerous articles, about a future unholy alliance
between the United States and the Islamic Republic of Iran to the
detriment of Gulf Cooperation Council (GCC) states. Under the title
"Are Sunnis victims of a new 'Great Game'?", published in April 2012
(see earlier in this chapter), I wrote: "There is a credible school of thought
that Washington's long-term agenda revolves around luring Iran into
its camp on the premise that Arab Sh'iites would follow … . In theory,
Washington would like to appoint a powerful entity like Iran as its proxy
regional caretaker just as the Shah was until he suffered delusions of
grandeur. But, first of all, it would be obliged to throw predominately
Sunni states under a bus."

A year ago, when Iranian President Mahmoud Ahmadinejad was
still spouting his unhinged rants, some readers may have found the
above analysis hard to believe, even though a US rapprochement
with Iran has long been promoted by various US think tanks as well
as prominent American writers, analysts and politicians, including
Secretary of State John Kerry. You will recall that President Barack
Obama pledged to reach out to Iranians during his first term, saying the
US wanted to end the strained relationship. That approach failed, mostly
because a US president cannot engage in photo-ops with a Holocaust
denier without locking horns with the pro-Israel lobby.

Then along comes Hassan Rouhani who worked his treacle-coated
magic when, hey presto, he makes history as the first Iranian leader
to have a phone conversation with a US president since 1979. Obama's
National Security Adviser Susan Rice says normalization of US-Iranian

relations could ensue. King Abdullah of Saudi Arabia is not amused while Israel's Prime Minister Benjamin Netanyahu is practically foaming at the mouth calling Rouhani a wolf in sheep's clothing.

Not only is Obama alienating his traditional allies with his bearded new best friend, he has astounded Egyptians by showing support for the Muslim Brotherhood and condemning the interim government for arresting its leaders. There is a belief among Egyptians that the US President funded the Muslim Brotherhood's campaign prior to last year's elections in connection with some kind of deal. Conspiracy theory! I thought so until I read an article in the *World Tribune* some days ago quoting former US Joint Chiefs Chairman General Hugh Shelton, who revealed to Fox News that the Obama administration had been working towards destabilizing Egypt and Bahrain for the last two years.

"Had General Al Sisi not deposed Morsi, Egypt would have today become another Syria and its military would have been destroyed," Shelton is quoted as saying. As for Bahrain, he explains that "America thought Bahrain was an easy prey that would rather serve as a key to the collapse of the GCC regime and lead to giant oil companies controlling oil in the Gulf." He says the plot was foiled by the Bahraini King Hamad bin Isa Al Khalifa when he invited Saudi Arabia to assist in quelling the mutiny. If true, this is outrageous and cannot under any circumstances be forgotten or forgiven, especially when US intervention has placed Iraq under Tehran's sway and bequeathed Libya to feuding militias while leaving Iran's minion Assad free to continue his genocidal war against non-Shi'ites.

His Majesty King Hamad may be taking General Shelton's words seriously. An article by Zuhair Centav maintains the US has put pressure on the King to remove the Prime Minister, Sheikh Khalifa bin Salman Al Khalifa, from office in keeping with the demands of Shi'ite insurgents, thus handing the rabble rousers – and by extension Iran – a victory.

It is notable that last Saturday the Bahraini Prime Minister was enthusiastic about the formation of a Gulf Union while urging Gulf states to close the door on foreign interference. Just days before the Prime Minister's announcement, King Hamad visited Egypt for talks with the interim President, Adly Mansour to "foster coordination and consultations among Egypt, Bahrain and the GCC". The King underlined his support for Egypt in various fields and an agreement was reached on a comprehensive strategy for Arab national security via military and security panels.

Is the picture becoming clearer?

I have said it before and I will say it again and again. GCC leaders must wake up to the looming danger. The countdown has started; the US/Iranian plan is about to be implemented. A serious plan of action is urgently required.

Firstly, together, GCC states are strong enough to stand alone, both economically and militarily, and should not permit foreign powers to make decisions for them.

Secondly, the GCC should diversify its weapons with purchases from different countries, rather than be vulnerable to the whims of one that is rapidly losing trust and conduct international relations like business ventures, with confidence, vision and planning.

Thirdly, Gulf states should take a leaf out of Iran's strategic book by offering material support to the Iranian opposition, not just the Ahwazi Arabs but also Iranians seeking freedom from oppression. Give Iran's government a taste of the same turbulent medicine it metes out to its neighbours. Internally weakened, its attention will be diverted from mischief-making abroad and hopefully it will implode from within.

Fourthly, the GCC must cease following Western diktats. We should only accept "advice" we consider beneficial and which syncs with our own national interests. If we do not display self-confidence and strength, no nation will respect us.

Lastly, GCC rulers should encourage their peoples to have a say in decisions that affect their future and feel they are being respected as patriots loyal to the country they love. When governments and citizens are one hand, no foreign plot can succeed in driving a wedge between them.

In the meantime, accusations of US plots should be thoroughly investigated and guarded against. As an old Scottish saying goes "False friends are worse than bitter enemies."

Do not insult our intelligence, Abdullah Gul!

12 June 2014

TURKEY, WHICH IS currently out of favour with several of its traditional Arab allies, is now apparently cozying up with Iran, despite differences over the Syrian conflict, as evidenced by Iranian President Hassan Rouhani's recent state visit to Ankara, marking the first by an Iranian head of state in 18 years. Frankly, if they have decided to kiss and make up that is their own business, but what really rankles with me is their leaders' sheer hypocrisy vis-à-vis Gulf states, disguising plots with sweet words. I think I speak for almost all Gulf nationals with this message: "Sorry, but we're not falling for your flowery rhetoric because the facts speak for themselves."

A senior advisor to the Turkish Prime Minister Recep Tayyip Erdoğan disclosed to the London-based daily *Asharq Al-Awsat* that during his talks with Rouhani the Turkish President stressed upon the importance Ankara places on Gulf security, saying Turkey is "committed to the security, welfare and aspirations of the Gulf Cooperation Council (GCC) states, without any country's interference in their internal affairs".

How reassuring! Now, we in the Gulf can all sleep better at night knowing Turkey has our back. But unfortunately for Turkey's spin doctors, we are just not that gullible. Aware of how negatively Rouhani's red carpet welcome would be perceived in our part of the world, President Gul disingenuously went out of his way to show the GCC how much his country cares in order to preserve bilateral trade and goodwill. Relations between Turkey and Saudi Arabia, in particular, have been dented over Erdoğan's persistent cuddling of the Muslim Brotherhood and a slew of insults he has thrown at Egypt's government and military, including announcing that as far as he is concerned, former President Mohamed Morsi is still the President of Egypt, Saudi Arabia's King Abdullah bin Abdulaziz has made it clear that attempts by foreign nations to undermine Egypt's progress is, for him, a red line.

But let us suppose for a moment, let us stretch our imaginations to assume Prime Minister's Gul's sentiments are, in fact, genuine. In answer to that admittedly far-fetched hypothetical scenario, I would respectfully tell him that we can look after ourselves, thank you very much. We are not anyone's responsibility except our own and our leaders are more than capable of protecting our people, our land, our borders and coastlines. For a leader of a foreign country – and especially one outside our region who has no Arab antecedents – such pronouncements are disrespectful of our independence and territorial sovereignty.

Instead of worrying about our security – or pretending to do so – Turkey should quit protecting terrorists and conspiring with the international Muslim Brotherhood to bring down Egypt. Surely Erdoğan and Gul have enough on their plate at a time of increasing civil unrest at home due to alleged high level corruption, human rights abuses and a crackdown on freedom of expression?

Not so long ago, Erdoğan was admired for being at the forefront of a system of political Islam that brought stability and prosperity. But now we understand that all along he was an extremist in sheep's clothing and a man who will swipe down anyone who dares challenge his chair. Now we see that his self-control mechanisms have broken down as evidenced by his slapping of a bystander during the miners' protests, while his aides brutally kicked another.

The idea of such a loose cannon setting himself up as the chaperone of Gulf states is, for me, abhorrent and totally unacceptable – and, likewise, his new best friend Hassan Rouhani, for all his personal charm, is also a person who should be viewed with a huge dollop of distrust. He is billed as "a moderate cleric" whereas the man who was actually in charge, Ali Khamenei, the heir to the Ayatollah Ruhollah Khomenei, is sitting in Qom. Who knows what plots they were hatching against Arabs behind closed doors.

Like Turkey, the Islamic Republic of Iran is another country whose leaders talk from both sides of their mouths. The moderate picture they are currently attempting to draw for an international audience has one aim – to get crippling UN, US and EU sanctions lifted.

Even as Rouhani is courting the P5+1 countries during negotiations over Iran's uranium enrichment programme, just days ago Ali Khamenei spoke to a gathering of political and military officials, some holding banners with the words "America can't do a damn thing." Khamenei used the occasion to imply that President Barack Obama is a coward without the guts to take on a fight, adding, "The Great Satan's" efforts to bring "Iran to its knees" have failed. This is the country with which the US and other world powers are working towards détente? What will they do next? Give the murdering Syrian President Bashar Al Assad a medal of honour?

Khamenei has lately been pushing for closer ties with Gulf states, or rather to repair relationships made frosty by a laundry list of Iranian meddling in Arab affairs, from its support of Shi'ite insurgents in Bahrain out to overthrow the monarchy to its backing of Shi'ite Houthis in Yemen, its domination over Lebanon via its proxy Hezbollah and the presence of Hezbollah fighters and Iranian Revolutionary guards fighting alongside Assad's troops in Syria. Less publicized is Iran's continued persecution of Ahwazi Arabs who have been treated as third-class citizens, stripped of rights since the days of the Shah and subject to the eradication of their Arab culture, including being banned from giving their children Arab names. Instead of shaking hands with Iranian envoys, GCC leaders should stand up for those abandoned people.

Iran's hostility to the Arab nation is an historical fact and if more proof was needed then the failure of Hassan Rouhani to attend the inauguration of Egypt's new president, Abdel Fatah El Sisi but merrily showing up days later in Ankara, speaks volumes. Whatever the Turks and the Iranians may be cooking is not my concern but whatever it is, then please leave us out of it!

The West is not duty-bound to solve Arab problems

8 November 2014

WHILE IT IS TRUE that Western powers cannot claim to have clean hands in the Middle East, Arabs do not either. Most of the Arab leaderships have consistently shrugged off their responsibility to defend their own people. For decades, Arabs have looked to Baba America and its allies for protection, knowing full well that US foreign policy is geared solely towards its own security and geopolitical interests.

During my latest visit to the US to join President Jimmy Carter in announcing a new Israeli-Palestinian peace initiative at Illinois College, I had the opportunity of meeting up with old friends as well as several high-ranking officials and executives. I have a fondness for the American people. Many have been unfailingly kind to me. But US policy is another matter entirely; it knows no friends, only interests. Former Central Intelligence Agency (CIA) Chief and Defence Secretary Leon Panetta spelled that out clearly in his book *Worthy Fights*. I do not object to that; it is beyond time that we took a leaf out of America's book.

Moreover, even if, for the sake of argument, the US was committed to having our back, it is hardly result-oriented. As Ambassador Charles (Chas) W. Freeman writes, "We [the US] are trying to cope with the cumulative consequences of multiple failures. Just about every American project in the Middle East has now come a cropper." The Ambassador rightly points out that US "policies have nowhere produced democracy. They have instead contrived the destabilization of societies, the kindling of religious warfare, and the installation of dictatorships contemptuous of the rights of religious and ethnic minorities."

Washington is a good friend when its interests happen to coincide with ours or when there are coveted natural resources at stake. Heaping blame on the West for directly or indirectly triggering our woes has become an unproductive mindset throughout the Arab World. We are wrong to blame the US for hesitating to come to our aid. America has its own economic and security priorities. We should respect that reality, appreciate all the goodness that has come our way from the West and refrain from condemning any country that looks out for its own interests. Our region would be well-served if Arab governments and peoples spent less time bashing America and more time learning how best to depend on ourselves.

For as long as I can remember, I have been writing articles appealing to Arab governments to deal proactively in ending regional conflicts and to become more diplomatically assertive. We have well-trained armies, sophisticated intelligence apparatus and advanced weaponry; all it takes is enough will and determination to shake off our victim mentality inherited from the Ottoman era, Western imperialism and security treaties with European powers. What will it take for Arabs to wake up to the fact that those days are long gone, and now we stand alone?

In truth, this column is in response to readers who have expressed their opinions on this topic, which accord with my own. A post appended to my column recently published on Al Arabiya, 7 September 2014, titled "World leaders should hang their heads in shame as ISIS marches on" reads in part: "Stop crying to the US to save you; stop crying that the US is to blame …. Save yourselves." Another reads: "Why don't the Arabs … send in their armies to sort out Assad and ISIS?" There are several in a similar vein including a few that are unprintable. It is extraordinary that readers get it when Arabs do not, cannot – or purposefully won't.

It is not the duty of the US or the UK to clean up our neighbourhood and in light of regional conflicts, terrorism and a growing menace from Iran that openly boasts that its proxies now control four Arab capitals – Beirut, Damascus, Baghdad and Sana'a – my argument is far from being merely academic. We have enemies without and within plotting to invade our homes. We must protect our own borders. We cannot sit back relying on empty pledges from Western leaderships currently attempting to enter into some kind of Grand Bargain with Iran's ayatollahs.

GCC states are particularly sensitive to Iranian domination and sick ideologies distorting the pure message of Islam, which is why I've called upon GCC member countries to take fast action over and over again, not only via my articles but also during face-to-face discussions with high officials. Do we still imagine Uncle Sam will send in the cavalry? If so, we should think again.

From the perspective of US policy-makers, oil-rich Arab nations may have outlived their usefulness. President Barack Obama's decision to pivot foreign policy away from the Middle East is well known and is evidenced by his reluctance to remove the Assad regime and his token gestures towards eradicating Daesh in Syria and Iraq. This sway away is partly due to the fact that the US is now not only energy self-sufficient but has a surplus. American production of shale oil has surpassed the outputs of Saudi Arabia and Russia's crude. Today, America is the world's number one producer of gas and, next year, is set to take the top oil producer's slot.

The West's thirst for Arab oil is already diminishing along with our global influence. However, extracting shale oil is expensive, so several oil-exporting Arab countries have been driven to reduce their prices hoping to hang on to remaining bargaining chips. Ambassador Freeman correctly reminds Washington that even though oil and gas production is booming in the US, what is happening in the Middle East should still matter. This, he explains, is because the Gulf "is where international oil prices are set" and "without stability in West Asia, the global economy is also unstable".

However short-sighted it may be for the West to turn its back on its traditional allies, we can no longer live like ostriches burying our own heads in the sand, pretending Washington, London and Paris are concerned with the safety of our peoples or working to further secure and stable societies. Their efforts at enforced democratization failed when Islamist parties grabbed the reins, sectarianism opened the doors of hell and terrorists were only too happy to step in. And now that our oil has lost its shine amid rivers of their own oil supplies, the underlying message from Western capitals is basically: "Thanks a lot; it was nice knowing you." I will not be surprised to wake up one day to find the Iranian Supreme Guide has been tapped to be our de facto governor, just as the Shah was until he became too big for his boots.

I am no longer interested in Western promises. My concerns rest with what we plan to do when Daesh is on the rampage against Sunnis. What steps are we going to take to thwart the takeover of Yemen by Shi'ite Houthis knocking on the gates of Saudi Arabia and Oman? How much longer will we give the Assad regime a free pass to continue its cancerous rule which, a few years ago, could have been cured with a dose of chemotherapy before its metastasis?

That said, what is past cannot be undone. We can apportion blame from here to eternity to no effect. We can lay out our concerns before the UN

General Assembly; again to no avail. Only our future trajectory is alterable. We can shape tomorrow, and we must, else the tears of our children and grandchildren will be our legacy of shame.

Hezbollah sleeping cells in Kuwait are a wake-up call

18 August 2015

KUWAIT'S DISCOVERY OF a massive secret weapons cache, including rocket launchers, machine guns and grenades, in the hands of one of Hezbollah's sleeping cells allegedly plotting to overthrow the government should be viewed as a harbinger of Tehran's future malicious intentions. An immediate response, beyond mere verbal condemnation, is needed from Gulf Cooperation Council (GCC) states.

Apparently such cells have been in existence for 16 years awaiting the moment to strike. The *Arab Times* reveals that all 25 Kuwaiti, Lebanese and Iranian suspects were trained in Lebanon and reports that a foreign intelligence service had warned the Ministry of Interior almost a year ago of an upcoming terrorist plot "against Kuwait by a sleeper cell belonging to Hezbollah".

Together, Gulf states make up one interlocking body formed on the basis of geography, common history and ties of blood. When one of its extremities is injured the others are more vulnerable. Therefore, all GCC member states must take the toughest measures possible to protect their borders and to use every available tool to root out those who would harm us.

Guest commentators on the Al Arabiya channel expressed their surprise at Kuwait's lack of decisive action to thwart these kinds of threats, and I could not agree more, given Iran's destructive meddling in Bahrain, Yemen, Syria, Lebanon and elsewhere.

Iran is the mastermind behind many regional troubles, but Hezbollah is the implementer. Kuwait needs to get tough but its democratic system of governance and constitution may be restraining the authorities. Kuwaitis tend to treat their constitution with reverence but it is not a Holy Book. If its civil liberties provisions endanger the country, it should be changed to give the government a free hand to deal with individuals or parties having dubious links to foreign governments and organizations.

Muna Al Fuzai, a Kuwaiti journalist, hit the nail on the head when she wrote it is imperative to "put an end to the intervention of pro-Iranian parties in Gulf States, whether in Kuwait or other states and those who support them ... ."

Indeed, if democratic freedom means opening up ones house to enemies, however they are disguised, then who needs it! Let us not be fooled by the illusion of Western-style democracy. In my view, Kuwait's parliament is holding the country back from political stability, economic growth and from adopting stringent security policies. The democratic process permits infiltration by parties covertly serving an Iranian agenda.

Years ago, some Kuwaiti lawmakers displayed their loyalty to Hezbollah during visits to Lebanon, appalling when one recalls Hezbollah's multiple attacks on targets and assassination attempts in Kuwait during the 1980s. Kuwait should purge parliament of treasonous representatives too cosy with Iran.

Kuwait was one of the first countries to declare Hezbollah terrorist, yet the organization still manages to remain active on Kuwaiti soil. No citizen should be allowed to jeopardize Kuwait's national security and anyone who does so should face the death penalty.

Kuwait's experiment with democracy needs fine-tuning. In the meantime, I would ask GCC member states, in particular Saudi Arabia and the UAE, to respectfully urge Kuwait to call for a State of Emergency in the first instance. Moreover, every Gulf state must be on alert for Iranian plots.

Most of this region's troubles are rooted in Iran's thirst for hegemony. That is known! So the Obama administration's portrayal of Iran as a benign entity insults our intelligence.

We are not safer just because Iran's nuclear ambitions are curbed for ten years; on the contrary, the ayatollahs will soon be flush with $80bn to fuel Tehran's troublemaking regional proxies and affiliates. Here is the evidence straight from the horse's mouth: "The Islamic Republic of Iran will always support the current resistance front and of course, with the nuclear agreement, it will have more power to side with its friends in the region," said Ali Akbar Velayati, a high Iranian official who is also the Secretary General of the World Assembly of Islamic Awakening.

Iran and its Iranian satellite Hezbollah have a single goal, ideological and physical domination of the Arab World; its prime target being oil-rich GCC states. Why do Gulf countries maintain diplomatic relations with a country that has boasted of its control of Arab capitals and used proxies to attempt to overthrow our leaderships?

The call by Qatar's Minister of Foreign Affairs Khalid Al Attiyah for a dialogue between the GCC and Iran, was backed by Oman but rightly met with deep reservations from Saudi Arabia, the UAE and Bahrain. Iran is not seeking reconciliation but rather supremacy and Gulf states should not engage with its game that amounts to a PR exercise for Western consumption.

The GCC should cut all diplomatic and economic ties with Tehran and Beirut starting with the withdrawal of ambassadors from both Iran and Lebanon, which has recently benefited from billions in aid from the countries Hezbollah is attacking. Its ingratitude is astounding!

Kuwait dodged the bullet this time. Together, our leaderships must do all in their power to ensure there will not be a next.

Corbyn's anti-Arab agenda

3 October 2015

WHEN I HEARD Prime Minister David Cameron's reaction to the new leader of the Labour Party, I dismissed it as a scaremongering tactic designed to undermine his rival. "Labour are now a serious risk to our nation's security, our economy's security and your family's security," he warned.

But after scrutinizing this former backbencher's record and listening to his speeches, I share Mr Cameron's concerns. Should Jeremy Corbyn ever make it to Number Ten, Britain's stature will be diminished globally and its relations with the US, the European Union (EU), Saudi Arabia, Gulf states and Egypt will be strained to breaking point.

Great Britain would be reduced to an inconsequential island, a fringe state, without its membership of North Atlantic Treaty Organization (NATO) and its Trident nuclear capability, not to mention powerful allies willing to come to its defence.

At first glance, the idea that this slightly dishevelled-looking dyed-in-the wool socialist activist, with a knack of coming across as a genuine do-gooder out to set the world to rights, seems preposterous. After all, he has succeeded in charming the party faithful during the recent party conference with self-effacing humour and he elicited standing ovations for his championship of the workers and poor families.

Since his election Labour has garnered over 60,000 new members drawn mostly from the working class, keen on strengthening the unions, increasing welfare payments and upping the minimum wage rather than being interested in foreign policy.

The old guard among his party's establishment are chafing at the bit. They want him gone now. His refusal to sing Britain's National Anthem "God save the Queen" was an embarrassment; likewise were his crony appointments of his former mistress and close friend to high positions in his shadow cabinet.

Worse, Corbyn has alienated the United States with a public announcement that 9/11 was manipulated as a pretext to invade Afghanistan and at one time he said he mourned the death of Osama bin Laden.

Labour's centrist old guards are so appalled that it is believed they are cooking up a leadership challenge but are forced to bide their time until his popularity wanes. The question is what if it does not?

He is no politician. He is an extreme left-winger with some very unsavoury friends and associates, among them the leaders of Iran as well as those of Hezbollah and Hamas whom he was once "honoured" to invite to Parliament. He is even alleged to have supported the Irish Republican Army (IRA) while it was engaged in killing British soldiers and, on one occasion, he handed one of his assistants money destined for IRA operatives fleeing justice.

In August this year, he was scheduled to speak at a conference hosted by a Muslim Brotherhood British-based mouthpiece *Middle East Monitor* where he would have shared a stage with Brotherhood propagandist Anas Al Tikriti, Hamas figures and one of the runners-up in Iran's Holocaust denial cartoon contest.

He only cancelled because of the scandal surrounding an announcement by the publication's senior editor blessing the practice of stoning to death. Regularly interviewed by another Brotherhood rag *Middle East Eye*, he told the Egyptian President that he was unwelcome in London because of his country's imprisoning of its failed Brotherhood president Mohamed Morsi.

One established daily wrote this before the election: "If Jeremy Corbyn wins, Labour will be in the extraordinary position of having a leader with the most extensive links in Parliament to terrorists."

The Iranian ayatollahs are jubilant at the success of their best British buddy. This headline in *The Telegraph* says it all: "Iran hails Jeremy Corbyn for shaking the British ruling class."

According to the article, an aide to Iran's Supreme Leader Ali Khamenei, Syed Salman Safavi "has lavished praise on Mr Corbyn" for lauding Iran's ability to "bring peace to the Middle East" and for his drive to pull Britain out of NATO.

Naturally, a toothless Western country without diplomatic clout or the nuclear weapons capability that assures its place among the big five United Nations (UN) Security Council members, would serve Iran's purposes.

And as for Safavi's statement that Iran – the region's prime aggressor in Syria, Lebanon, Bahrain and Yemen – could bring peace to the Middle East, well, that is nothing less than a bad joke when Khamenei has sworn to up his support for "the resistance".

Corbyn has hosted a political call-in chat show in the absence of its regular host George Galloway, on the Iranian English-language channel Press TV that continually spews out anti-Saudi and anti-Bahraini propaganda and which has been removed from the UK's airwaves. Last year, he visited Iran and was pictured sharing a warm handshake with the country's foreign minister Mohammed Javed Zarif.

He used his speech at the annual Labour Party gathering to attack Saudi Arabia and Bahrain on their human rights record and called upon Cameron to prevent the Kingdom's authorities implementing a death penalty, as though any British leader has the right to interfere in the affairs of a sovereign country.

Al Bawaba, a news and media website in Amman, rightly asks, while pointing out that GCC countries are heavily invested in the UK: "Should Gulf investors worry about Jeremy Corbyn?" If he ever becomes prime minister, I would answer a resounding yes given his anti-Arab rants as well as his ideological vendetta against the rich, whom he proposes taxing to the hilt.

Jeremy Corbyn looks humble and sounds authentic yet look carefully and you will see that his belligerence against the Gulf precisely echoes that of Press TV and other Iranian media outlets. His chances of getting the top job may be slim because the British media has his measure, but I would caution investors from this part of the world to be alert for a surprise upset.

I have no message for Mr Corbyn; his views are too entrenched. How can anyone trumpet concern for human rights with any authority when they cuddle a regime like Iran that subjugates its own people and treats its minority populations as second-class citizens whose political and cultural rights are trampled upon?

Why does he ignore the dozens of imprisoned opposition party members, journalists and activists or the children awaiting their end on death row? Instead, he celebrates the Iran deal as a triumph for peace. The man is a hypocrite!

I would ask the British people to see through the façade and moreover I would stress that his attacks on Saudi and Bahrain have no foundation. Both countries threatened by Iran and its proxies have the right to handle their security and deal with bad apples in the best way they see fit.

The peoples of the Gulf enjoy the highest standards of living anywhere. In July, a premature newborn died because the local authorities in Poole, Dorset, refused temporary shelter to its homeless parents. That is a tragedy that does not happen here.

Our people are looked after; their needs taken care of and those are the most important human rights of all. Corbyn is an extremist, a defender of terrorists and terrorist regimes, in sheep's clothing. I can only second David Cameron's warning and urge the British electorate to beware!

Saudi Arabia and the UAE, the "Shield of the Gulf"

6 December 2015

OUR REGION IS WAR-TORN and fractured. We are facing multiple threats of multiple kinds. This is the most dangerous era I have ever lived through, surpassing the 1991 Gulf War when we came together to defeat a single enemy.

While almost the entire world is shining a spotlight on the so-called Islamic State in Syria and Iraq, Gulf Cooperation Council (GCC) states must not take their eyes off our neighbourhood's greatest threat – the Islamic Republic of Iran and its militias in Lebanon, Syria and Iraq.

It saddens me to observe some Arab countries claiming to stand with us whereas in reality they are either straddling the fence or are covertly in the ayatollahs' pockets.

It is imperative that transparent Gulf states stick together and be very wary of fair-weather friends, especially at a moment in time when there are those doing their utmost to split us apart and scatter us in different directions to render us vulnerable.

Unfortunately, those enemies are using slick propaganda for the purposes of making us doubt one another. They speak of rifts between the Kingdom of Saudi Arabia and the United Arab Emirates (UAE) when there are none.

The relationship between the Kingdom and the Emirates is based on a shared history, culture and bloodlines. It is unbreakable. Threats to Saudi Arabia are the same as those that threaten the UAE. Iran's ultimate goal is to seize our territories, strip us of our natural resources and take control of the Holy cities of Mecca and Medina. Rest assured that nothing will come between these two brotherly nations who have always worked as one to hoist the standards of the Muslim and Arab World high.

Thanks to the Saudi-led Arab coalition, which has successfully stemmed the march of Shi'ite Houthis across Yemen's border with Saudi Arabia, that route has been blocked. But, recent news reports suggest that Iran may now be pursuing its Plan B from a different direction. As I write, highly-trained, battle-hardened pro-Iranian Shi'ite fighters from Lebanon and Syria are heading to Iraq to further destabilize Iraq in support of their Iranian masters.

And according to a report published in *Al Quds Al Arabi*, hundreds of thousands of Iranians are crossing into Iraq via its ports without passports stamped with entry visas, ostensibly to visit Shi'ite holy sites. Is this mass relocation being carried out in preparation for Iran to launch a surprise? The fear is the Iranians (perhaps with a green light from Moscow) are positioning Iranian Revolutionary Guard forces, Iranian foot soldiers and Shi'ite militias in preparation for a terrorist attack.

Russia's goal is to become the dominant regional power and to further his endgame President Vladimir Putin is throwing his country's weight behind Iran. During his meeting last month with Iran's Supreme Leader, he presented Ali Khamenei with a replica of Russia's oldest handwritten Quran. The commentator Jamal Khashoggi rightly notes the irony of Putin's gesture of respect to Islam while in Iran even as he slams the Turkish President Recep Tayyip Erdoğan for Islamicizing Turkey.

Turkey's shooting down of a Russian plane has provided Russia with a pretext to go on the warpath against parties within the US-led coalition, accusing several of cooperating with Daesh and other terrorists. Russia's semi-official *Pravda* newspaper is being used by Moscow as a propaganda tool. Its columns are filled with direct threats against Turkey, Saudi Arabia and Qatar for "their involvement in terrorism"! Kashoggi highlights a report from the the Echo of Moscow, Russia's most famous radio station, quoting a former advisor to President Putin calling for attacks on military and oil installations in Saudi and Qatar.

Putin, who has never recovered from the disbanding of the mighty Soviet Union, is on a roll following his illegal annexation of Crimea, a move met with little more than a slap on the wrist from the US and its allies.

Emboldened, he is calling the shots in Syria as though he is that country's leader while ingratiating himself with the world's greatest terrorist funder, Iran, which due to its murky affiliations has escaped becoming a target of terrorism. Of course, even terrorists do not bite the hand that feeds them!

Far from providing geopolitical balance in the area, President Barack Obama's policy of leading from behind has left a void permitting Russia to fill it as a dangerous aggressor that is not only hand-in-glove with Iran but one that has knives out for Sunni Arab states.

As I have warned again and again in my columns, we must remain alert and prepared for anything. That does not mean we should merely wait and watch. No, the snakes' heads must be cut before they slither to nest on our own soil. We were burned by the overthrow of the elected government in Yemen by the emissaries of Tehran and if we do not stem the growing threat in Iraq, we will have only ourselves to blame.

In order to defend our borders, our coalition must be strengthened and enlarged. If we imagine we can place our trust in global powers, that strove to empower and enrich Iran via a nuclear deal, we are mistaken because they are driven solely by self-interest. And neither can we rely on other Arab countries to defend us for two reasons.

Firstly, those far away from Iran's reach by reasons of geography have different priorities; theirs is to eviscerate Daesh. Secondly, there are countries suspected of harbouring Iranian or Russian sympathies (or both) that must be weeded out or, at the very least, told to come clean on their loyalties. Our destiny cannot rest with fence-sitters or pretend friends. It is time for all to be open about their allegiances and interests.

The only significant forces in the GCC are those of the UAE and Saudi Arabia. We are the shield and the sword of all Gulf states and we are ready to partner with Arab countries proven to be on the same page. It is time for all regional leaderships to be transparent, and those suspected of playing both sides or of hiding their true intentions should be banished behind a virtual Trump-style wall.

Hezbollah's role in 9/11 goes under the radar

18 March 2016

IRAN'S PROXY IN LEBANON Hezbollah works hard to promote itself as the Lebanese resistance against Israeli encroachment and as a political organization representing all Lebanese citizens. In reality, it is anything but. It began life as an Iranian arm on the Mediterranean operating under the pretence of standing against Israel to justify its terrorist activities against Arab and Western interests.

Hezbollah's concern for Palestinian interests is nothing but a front to attract recruits. The conflict it unwittingly unleashed with Israel in 2006 with its kidnapping and killing of Israeli soldiers caught its Secretary General Hassan Nasrallah by surprise; he was later to admit that if he had known the abductions would result in a full-scale conflict, he would not have given the orders.

Hezbollah's terror operations, hostage-taking and assassinations going back as far as the 1980s are well known, but the fact that a US District Judge has ruled that Hezbollah colluded with the perpetrators of the 11 September 2001 attacks on the Twin Towers and the Pentagon is not deemed worthy of front page news in the United States or Europe.

The story has been picked-up by *Asharq Al-Awsat* and the *Jerusalem Post* but has almost been ignored by the Western media whose governments are actively pursuing lucrative deals with Tehran now that its coffers overflow with more than $100bn following the lifting of sanctions.

Given the emotional trauma experienced by the American people on that fateful day, which still haunts many, especially the victims' loved ones, the relative silence of the Western media on the case is peculiar – and that is an understatement. Even stranger is that the US has erased both Iran and Hezbollah from its terror threat list in spite of overwhelmingly evidence to the contrary. If the American people were polled as to their knowledge of this, I predict there would be very few who have any inkling at all.

Moreover, President Barack Obama has displayed his displeasure at measures taken by Saudi Arabia and other Gulf Cooperation Council (GCC) states to brand Hezbollah terrorist, to halt aid to the Hezbollah-infiltrated Lebanese Army and to issue travel advisories warning citizens not to visit Lebanon.

On 15 December 2011, Judge George Daniels ruled that Iran and Hezbollah materially and directly colluded with Al Qaeda to attack America on its own soil and, thus, they are responsible to pay compensation to the families of victims.

He did not pick his findings out of thin air. His judgment against Iran's Supreme Leader, its former President Ali Rafsanjani, Iran's Revolutionary Guard Corps and Hezbollah was supported by 53 pages of evidence as well as testimony given by three Iranian defectors, three members of the 9/11 Commission, CIA operatives and investigative journalists.

In summary of the Judge's findings:

- Iran assisted the Al Qaeda terrorists by permitting them to travel freely from Afghanistan to other countries via Iran where their passports were not stamped to permit ease of entry into the United States.
- Terrorists fleeing the US-led invasion were given sanctuary in Iran along with their families.
- A witness testified that Iran procured a Boeing 757-767-777 flight simulator using front companies to facilitate the training of the hijackers' pilots.

- An Iranian government memorandum proves that Iran's Supreme Leader knew in advance of the impending attacks.

- The official 9/11 Commission states that "a senior Hezbollah operative" identified as Imad Mughniyah, coordinated Al Qaeda's activities and either he or one of his henchmen were on the same Beirut to Tehran flights taken by the hijackers.

- Hezbollah aided the hijackers in planning and advised them on the mechanics of the attacks.

Hezbollah likes to take a back seat in a futile attempt to prove to the Lebanese people and the world that it has eschewed terrorism, which is why it partners with other groups behind the curtain.

However, that curtain has opened to expose Hezbollah's collaboration with its Saudi affiliate to strike the Khobar Towers residential complex and with Al Qaeda to bomb US embassies in Africa as well as the *USS Cole*.

In 1992, Hezbollah instructed Islamic Jihad to bomb the Israeli embassy in Buenos Aires in retaliation for the killing of its former Secretary General Abbas Al Moussawi.

More recently, an Egyptian court has indicted Hezbollah operatives for illegally entering Egypt for the purpose of colluding with other groups to release their terrorist buddies from prisons during the 2011 revolution.

Last week, the US court ordered Iran to pay $11bn to the victims' families who were plaintiffs in the case as well as $3bn to various insurance companies. The families concerned are delighted but without the support of the Obama administration, which has refrained from pointing any finger at either Iran or Hezbollah for 9/11, their chances of receiving damages for their pain and suffering are close to nil.

As reported by *Asharq Al-Awsat*, intelligence from Argentina, Mexico and Canada has revealed that Hezbollah is expanding its nefarious activities, which with support from Iran are being expanded in Venezuela, Mexico, Nicaragua, Chile, Colombia, Bolivia, Ecuador and the area between Paraguay, Argentina and Brazil.

An individual, linked to Hezbollah, who was arrested by Mexican authorities after being caught with fake papers and drugs at the border with the US, has exposed the presence of Hezbollah units around the world under orders to pinpoint potential targets.

An intelligence, report compiled by Sid Blumenthal, a close friend of Hillary Clinton, is particularly revealing. Upon information drawn from Israeli intelligence sources, it accuses Hezbollah of setting up a base in Cuba to mastermind terrorist attacks throughout Latin America.

In the meantime, even as the US government is soft on Iran and Hezbollah, on Thursday, Saudi Arabia announced it will freeze the bank accounts and seize properties of anyone suspected of belonging to Hezbollah or of being a sympathizer. Other GCC countries are deporting Lebanese expatriates with known links to the organization.

Whatever cloak of innocence Hezbollah wraps around itself, it can never be big enough to hide its criminal acts. President Obama may not wish to acknowledge how dangerous Hezbollah is to Lebanon, the region and the world, but with the clock ticking on his tenure, I can only hope that the eyes of America's next president are open wide.

2

Iran's domestic policy
and persecution of minorities

Introduction

FOLLOWING IRAN'S 1979 REVOLUTION, Tehran introduced a new ideology in the country. The *Wilayat al-Faqih* rule brought in by Ayatollah Ruhollah Khomeini meant the clergy became the country's major political figures. Today, Supreme Leader Ayatollah Ali Khamenei, the country's commander-in-chief, is the single most powerful individual in the regime. He exerts ideological and political control over a system dominated by clerics. Both foreign and domestic decisions require his stamp of approval. The President, Hassan Rouhani, is the second-most important leader. He is considered the public face of the government.

The Islamic Revolutionary Guard Corps (IRGC), created by Khomeini in 1979 and intended to maintain internal order and protect the country's Islamic system, functions today as both the primary internal and external security force. The IRGC is the country's premier security institution. There are believed to be up to 150,000 active troops divided into land, sea and air forces. This is in addition to the 200,000-strong regular army. The Guards are also key players in the country's political system as well as the economic stratosphere. They are said to control about one third of the country's economy. The force, acknowledged by the outside world as a terrorist entity, is used internally to crack down on the opposition by suppressing dissidents and reformists while keeping the ethnic minorities in check.

Iran's abuse of its own people amounts to a humanitarian catastrophe. To this day the rights of all minorities are severely trampled on. They are discriminated against, denied their basic human rights, and not allowed express their culture in public.

Deprivation is sadly the norm for Iran's ethnic minorities and the world is seemingly oblivious to the fact. This persecution seems to have been brushed aside by Western nations in favour of making a fast buck. The religious minorities are doomed, living under the Iranian regimes of atrocious oppression where they face discrimination, abuse, oppression and arbitrary detention – or worse.

The United Nations' Special Rapporteur on the situation on Human Rights in Iran, Ahmad Shaheed, said in a 2014 report that violations of human rights and oppression of minorities and women have worsened since President Hassan Rouhani took over in 2013, despite his intentions to improve them. He wrote that he was "deeply concerned about the human rights situation facing religious minorities in Iran".

The report, to the United Nations Human Rights Council (UNHRC), focused on a wide range of violence including that faced by minorities like Baha'is, Christians, Sufi and Sunni Muslims. Since the report was issued Dr Shaheed has not been allowed back in the country.

Among the minorities discriminated against are an estimated eight million Ahwazi Arabs who are sadly forgotten to the world. The territory of Al Ahwaz – known as Khuzestan in Iran – encompasses almost 187,000 sq km, stretching, stretching between the Zagros Mountains to the north and the east, Iraq to the west and Kuwait to the south. Its main cities are the capital, Ahwaz, and Abadan. Ahwaz is blessed with vast deposits of oil and gas as well as fertile agricultural land, yet its Arab population is overwhelmingly poor and illiterate, lacking modern educational and medical facilities.

Despite the vast natural resource wealth, the province is plagued with severe socio-economic deprivation. Tehran has discriminated against the Arabs of Ahwaz since their homeland's occupation and annexation by the Shah Reza Shah Pahlavi in 1925; they are being treated as third-class citizens who endure primitive living standards without even the basic political rights enjoyed by the Persian relocated minority who refer to the indigenous Ahwazis as "gypsies".

If you cannot treat your own people with the respect and dignity they deserve, what hope does the rest of the world have?

The persecution that the Ahwaz and Iran's other struggling minorities face on a daily basis will not stop in the foreseeable future. The world has ignored their plight for too long, but now that Iran is considered "open for business" by Western nations following the nuclear agreement, perhaps it will help put the spotlight on the Iranian regime's systematic human rights abuses of its own people and potentially energize a debate.

In his 2015 report, the UN's Ahmad Shaheed said the nuclear deal and the lifting of certain economic sanctions on Iran "can potentially have a beneficial multiplier effect on the human rights situation in the country". He added that the nuclear deal "presents opportunities for advancing human rights".

I pray that some good will come out of the nuclear treaty and improve the conditions of the millions of people suffering oppression in Iran. But I doubt it will filter down to those that need it most.

The Iranian statement of aggression needs a clear response

1 November 2008

OUR REGION WAS the cradle of civilization and the place where the world's three monotheistic faiths originated. Unfortunately, this region has been the battlefield for endless conflicts. Conflicting ideologies, competing regional aspirations, the strategic interests of world powers and efforts to get their hands on the region's natural resources by many players are some of the reasons behind this perennial situation of struggle. Despite being relatively small, Gulf Cooperation Council (GCC) countries are rich ones and attractive for any ambitious adventurer. Today, our survival as nations is at risk and we need to formulate real alliances to fend off potential aggression.

In a rosy world, every nation wants to live in peace with its neighbours. Still, a responsible head of a household must do something to rectify things when rubbish is thrown on their doorstep by a neighbour. A nation is obliged to defend itself against any act of aggression. A rosy world where you can sleep in peace believing that everybody around you is full of goodwill is a fascinating dream. However, in a world of ever-diminishing resources, we cannot expect such a world.

Iran's threatening manoeuvres must be stopped. Let us quit playing with words of diplomacy. Like it or not, it is a fact that we all must recognize: the probability of the region succumbing to Iran's military dominance is increasing day by day. To reach this end, Iran has been slowly implementing a carefully devised process. And in this context, the Iranians managed to persuade the GCC leaders that they have no hidden agenda or expansionist policy, but only friendly wishes for their Arab neighbours. However, we cannot rest on the superficiality of such assurances.

On 26 July, Iranian Deputy Foreign Minister Manouchehr Mohammadi questioned the legitimacy of GCC states, predicting their demise. "The next crisis predicted to cover mainly the 'Persian Gulf' is the crisis of legitimacy of the traditional systems, which considering current circumstances cannot go on living," said Mohammadi.

Such a statement can be interpreted at least as an offensive act. It can also be interpreted as threatening. And in any case, it cannot be made by someone who pretends friendship.

Gulf Cooperation Council Secretary General Abdurrahman Al Attiyah immediately slammed the Iranian official's statement. "GCC states are very disappointed by, and deeply concerned at, such irresponsible remarks and they expect an immediate clarification from Iran of its deputy foreign minister's statement. Such suspicious comments do not at all help build trust among states of the region. They can only stoke conflicts and drag the region into a cycle of dangerous crises," he said.

I appreciate Mr Al Attiyah's words. However, voices of our leaders must be loud and affirmative this time to support the Secretary General's statement. We are facing a prominent Iranian official who made an unprecedented and unjustified attack against our governments and their legitimacy.

The silence maintained by major policy makers in Tehran regarding the statements of their Deputy Foreign Minister would by all means let us conclude that the offence was approved by their leadership.

Our governments must show now a strict and clear stand vis-à-vis Iran. Every time they abstain from answering such an offence, Iran's behaviour will be more aggressive. Who knows where Iran will extend its reach next time, after it has established its strong grip in Iraq, Syria, Lebanon and Gaza?

Talking to the world with a unified voice will not be sufficient for GCC member states now. They must work to have a clear definition of their allies' position regarding all disagreements between Iran and the Arabs, including Iran's continuing occupation of the United Arab Emirates' three islands.

Many GCC member states have worked closely with the US in its War on Terror during the last few years. These states did so to help a so-called ally. However, such a relationship is not supposed to be a one-way street. Is it not the right time for the US to recognize the Arab Gulf and not the "Persian Gulf"?

In 1935 the world was asked to say "Iran" instead of "Persia". And in 1979, the country was renamed the "Islamic Republic of Iran". So why does Iran insist on using the "Persian Gulf" and not the "Iranian Gulf"? Does the word "Persia" have an imperial resonance?

In fact, the majority of GCC member states have no problem with the Iranians naming the Gulf in the way everyone wants, in the same way England and France use different names for the body of water separating them. It is the "English Channel" in England and "La Manche" in France. However, Iran has seen in such a thing a fundamental issue and mobilized all its media institutions to support its cause.

Our governments must stop their policy of self-restraint that has been in place for a long time. Instead, we must tell Iran that while we are striving to build a friendly and peaceful relationship with our neighbours on the other bank of the Gulf, we will not accept being pushed to the margins. Yes, on an individual level we might be small countries. But as a block, we are strong and influential. And we have strong allies with whom we have important mutual interests.

Friends might come or go, but neighbours will stay with us. The region's nations must understand this fact well and work to serve the interests of the region's people and their shared bonds developed down through history.

Al Ahwaz will always be Arab

31 March 2011

IN AN ERA when citizens throughout the Middle East and North Africa (MENA) region are asking for political change, Iran's systematic oppression and discrimination against an estimated eight million Ahwazi Arabs should not be allowed to continue unchallenged.

The territory of Al Ahwaz – known as Khuzestan in Iran – encompasses almost 186,479 sq km, stretching between the Zagros Mountains to the north and the east, Iraq to the west and Kuwait to the south. Its main cities are the capital Al Ahwaz, Abadan and Mohammerah. Al Ahwaz is blessed with vast deposits of oil and gas as well as fertile agricultural land, yet its Arab population is overwhelmingly poor and illiterate, lacking modern educational and medical facilities.

Tehran has discriminated against the Arabs of Al Ahwaz since their homeland's occupation and annexation by the Shah Reza Shah Pahlavi in 1925; they are being treated as third-class citizens, who endure primitive living standards without even the basic political rights enjoyed by the Persian relocated minority who refer to the indigenous Ahwazis as "gypsies".

In June 2005, the Director of the Ahwaz Education and Human Rights Foundation, Karim Abdia, spelled out the Ahwazi plight before the United Nations (UN) in Geneva, explaining that the Ahwazi population suffers from a shortage of drinking water, electricity, plumbing, telephone and sewage. Fifty per cent of these people live in absolute poverty, he said, while 80 per cent of their children are malnourished.

The dispossessed Ahwazi Arabs are grossly underrepresented in Parliament and are rarely posted to government positions. They accuse the Iranian government of having racially-based political and economic prejudice, which is why some groups are calling for Al Ahwaz to be liberated from Iran and for the United Nations to recognize them as an independent Arab group with their own state.

However, the government is attempting to pull the rug from under their demands by setting up self-contained farming settlements and bringing in Persians to work with them as part of a planned strategy to alter the area's demographics.

According to Amnesty International: "Land expropriation by the Iranian authorities is reportedly so widespread that it appears to amount to a policy aimed at dispossessing Arabs of their traditional lands. This is apparently part of a strategy aimed at the forcible relocation of Arabs to other areas while facilitating the transfer of non-Arabs into Khuzestan ...."

It is believed that the government is pursuing a strategy of enforced assimilation by trying to eradicate the Ahwazi Arab culture. For instance, the Iranian authorities will not register birth certificates to Arab newborns unless they assume Persian names.

Schools in Al Ahwaz have been instructed not to teach Arabic, which is also banned from being spoken in Parliament and government ministries. Arabic media is forbidden in the territory. The Ahwazi consider their Mesopotamian Arabic dialect, shared with southern Iraqis, to be their mother tongue. However journalists who write against this cultural barbarism are routinely imprisoned.

In 2007, six Ahwazi Arabs were subjected to kangaroo courts and put on death row on charges of converting to Sunni Islam, giving their children Sunni names, flying the all-white Ahwazi Arab flag, and as "enemies of God" constituting a threat to national security.

Those and similar rigged trials resulting in executions have been condemned by the European Council, the EU Parliament, the UN and numerous human rights organizations including Human Rights Watch and Amnesty International.

Besides their very real human rights and economic grievances, the historic claim of the Ahwazi Arabs to their Arab homeland is rock solid. Al Ahwaz was a thriving province of Mesopotamia for centuries, rich from sugarcane plantations. It also proved fertile ground for Muslim scholars, poets and artists.

From the mid-7th century until the mid-13th century its people were ruled variously by Umayyad and Abbasid caliphs, their numbers swelled by itinerant Arab tribes from the Arabian Peninsula. A Mongol invasion led by Genghis Khan devastated most of Al Ahwaz that was later occupied by the founder of the Timurid Empire, Tamerlane and his successors until the early 16th century when it fell under the domination of the Persian Safavid Dynasty.

Al Ahwaz came to be known as the semi-autonomous region of "Arabistan" towards the end of the 16th century when it received an influx of Arab tribes from southern Iraq as well as a clan of the powerful Bani Kaab whose origins lie in Central Arabia.

Under the leadership of Sheikh Jabir Al Kaabi the Bani Kaab fought to stave off British and Ottoman invasions. Sheikh Jabir was a wise governor of the province who established law and order and turned the coastal city of Mohammerah into a bustling free port.

At the cusp of the 20th century, oil was discovered around Mohammerah when the British wasted no time in founding the Anglo-Persian Oil Company and entering into an oil exploration treaty with the late Sheikh Jabir's son Khaz'al. The UK guaranteed Arabistan's security and agreed payments to both Sheikh Khaz'al and the Shah of Iran

What should have been a blessing for the Ahwaz Arabs was, in fact, a curse. When Sheikh Khaz'al realized that Shah Reza Shah Pahlavi's ambitions extended to Arabistan and its oil wealth, he allied himself with the Shah's opposition and asked the British to defend the Ahwazi people and back the area's rightful separation and independence from Persia as an Arab state.

Forced to choose between Arabistan and Tehran, Britain reneged on its treaty with Khaz'al and supported the Shah, mainly because London wanted Iran on-side as a pro-Western bulwark against the spread of Soviet communism.

Betrayed by duplicitous Albion, in 1924 Khaz'al put his case before the League of Nations but without the UK's support it was rejected. Given that Persia's membership of the League of Nations was prior to its annexation of Arabistan, and Tehran was, therefore, bound by that body's rules prohibiting invasion, that unfair decision should be reconsidered.

A year later, the Shah ordered Sheikh Khaz'al abducted, imprisoned and killed. With Britain's help Shah Reza Shah Pahlavi gained absolute control over the oil-wealthy territory when he changed the five-century-old name Arabistan to Khuzistan. The period between 1928 and 1946 witnessed nine unsuccessful uprisings on the part of the Ahwaz and since numerous secessionist groups have emerged, they have been written off by the Iranian government as troublemakers or stooges of foreign countries.

Today, Al Ahwaz produces four million barrels a day – 87 per cent of Iran's oil production – but the indigenous population profits little from its revenue in terms of employment, infrastructure and welfare. Only 15–20 per cent of workers in the petroleum industry are Arabs holding mainly blue collar jobs.

Eight million Ahwaz Arabs may have been issued with Iranian documents but they are not Persians. They have as much Arab blood flowing through their veins as those of us privileged to live in Gulf Cooperation Council states. I would, therefore, request Arab countries to call upon the League of Arab States to study their case and put their right of self-determination before the UN Security Council. Their abandonment is nothing less than a stain upon the Arab Nation to which the Arabs of Arabistan proudly belong.

Tehran's new face on same old murky policies

19 June 2013

IF ANYONE SERIOUSLY believes that Iran's President-elect Hassan Rouhani will be empowered to make a difference, they are dreaming. The media refers to this conservative Khomeini loyalist cleric as a reformist or a moderate. When compared with Mahmoud Ahmadinejad, who is bordering on lunatic, then yes. But it is naive in the extreme to suppose that Iran's Supreme Leader Ali Khamenei, whose iron grip over the Iranian people has endured since 1989, would permit a man with liberal persuasions to even run for office.

In reality, anyone with the potential of being a populist rival to Khamenei, such as former President Ali Akbar Hashemi Rafsanjani, was excluded from the race by the Guardian Council's vetting committee, along with candidates from the genuinely reformist

Green Party, which goes to show that the poll lacked legitimacy. Out of 680 candidates who registered, only eight were approved to run.

Frankly, I am amazed at the effusive reaction to Rouhani's triumph. The United Nations (UN) Secretary General Ban Ki-moon offered his congratulations and Britain's former Justice Minister Jack Straw says he is a man with whom the UK can do business. Vladimir Putin sent the new President a message of confidence that Rouhani would promote the prosperity of a friendly Iran and further strengthen Russian-Iranian relations. Gulf Cooperation Council (GCC) leaders have also sent him a congratulatory missive expressing their wish for improved ties. King Abdullah of Saudi Arabia wishes "greater progress and prosperity for the people of the brotherly Islamic Republic of Iran" at a time when Saudi-Iranian relations are at an all-time low over Syria.

I get that phrases used in diplomatic protocol should not necessarily be taken seriously. But let us get something straight. There is nothing brotherly about Iran from the perspective of Gulf states as I have highlighted time and time again in my columns, while strongly urging Gulf leaders to cut diplomatic and trade relations with Tehran and expand the GCC's military capacity to defend our lands against Iran's territorial and ideological ambitions.

Brothers do not steal from one other, as Iran did when in November 1971 it forcibly grabbed three United Arab Emirates (UAE) islands, which until today it refuses to give back. And Tehran's plotting to overthrow the Bahraini monarchy shows that it cannot be considered a friend by any stretch of the imagination. So, when I read that the GCC seeks better relations with its Persian neighbour all because the man who will shortly hold the title of President is considered to be a reasonable man, my heart sank.

We should not permit the ayatollahs to pull the wool over our eyes and neither should the Iranian people who have been celebrating in the streets. Make no mistake! The old guard is still in charge and has cleverly consolidated its power with a crafty PR coup. Ahmadinejad was unpopular, hot-headed and unstable. Rouhani is well-educated, well-travelled, well-connected in diplomatic circles and charismatic. He is tapped into the pulse of the public – currently angered over surging inflation, high unemployment and a freefalling currency – and knows how to craft his rhetoric to suit. But whoever lands the title President knows that it is largely cosmetic when it comes to issues that matter. Rouhani will serve as a valve to reduce the tension in a pressure cooker of discontent at home and anti-Iranian sentiment abroad. He has ignited false hopes and is giving the world the fake impression that Iran is poised to turn a new page.

Whether or not Hassan Rouhani is seen as a breath of fresh air in an oppressive country that stifles personal freedom and discriminates against non-Shi'ite minorities is neither here nor there. He is a proficient diplomat, making all the right noises, promising nuclear transparency and steps to reduce tension with Western powers – which is all very well, but can he deliver? The answer to that is well known. With all the will in the world, he will have little say over Iranian foreign policy, which is strictly the province of the Supreme Leader – and as recent history has taught us, anyone who challenges that authority is gone.

Rouhani will be free to change the tone of his dealings but not the substance. He may be more amenable than Ahmadinejad to dialogue with the West on Iran's nuclear file, but the decision to cease uranium enrichment is not his to make, even if he were disposed to do so. In fact, he is known to be proud of his nation's technological achievements. He is keen to get economically crippling UN, US and European Union (EU) sanctions lifted, but unless he gets the go-ahead from his master to make concessions, that aspiration is dead in the water.

The President-elect says he wants improved relations with the US and Saudi Arabia. The real test will be his stance on Syria. Flowery words will get him nowhere as long as Iranian Revolutionary Guards and Iran's proxy in Lebanon, Hezbollah, are flouting the will of the League of Arab States and the majority of United Nations member states by fighting on the side of a pariah engaged in the destruction of his own country.

In the final analysis, the Iranian leadership is undeserving of our congratulations and certainly does not warrant diplomatic niceties from our leaders as long as it persists in killing our true brothers and sisters in Syria – and neither does its partner in crime, Russia, that keeps Bashar Al Assad's forces supplied with missiles and vetoes anti-regime sanctions in the UN Security Council. In the meantime, let us not be willing dupes to the new guy's sweet words that cannot be backed up with action. In many ways Rouhani is more dangerous than his predecessor. Ahmadinejad wore his aggression and hostility on his sleeve; whereas Iran's new president could emerge as the Great Deceiver. I can only appeal to GCC member states to remain alert.

Iran's agenda consolidates while the Arabs are distracted

25 September 2014

TO SAY OUR REGION is in imminent peril is an understatement. Threats are emerging from all directions in many different guises. Most derive from warped ideologies that mask a will to power and territorial domination. Today, the US, together with its Western and predominantly Sunni Arab allies, has finally woken up to the danger posed by Daesh, a danger I have been warning about for over a year, and has deployed its military resources to eradicate this lethally toxic group in northern Iraq and around the Syrian city of Raqaa where those killers are headquartered.

This intervention is long overdue. Unfortunately, it took the beheading of Western hostages to grab the attention of the international community, which failed to be galvanized by the mass slaughter of Iraqi men, women and children. But while all eyes were on Israel's devastation of Gaza and the horrors perpetrated by Daesh, Tehran, arguably a far greater menace to the security of the Middle East and the Gulf, is quietly achieving its hegemonic goals, unimpeded and unnoticed.

If I had to prioritize the respective threat levels of Daesh and Iran on a scale of one to ten, the former would be way down the scale because an estimated 35,000 fighters cannot hope to beat back the combined might of a 50-member-strong international coalition. Granted, purifying the earth from this disease isn't going to happen overnight and, sadly, many more innocents are destined to lose their lives in the process. Overall this evil parody of a caliphate will be nothing more than a footnote in tomorrow's history books. Halting the ambitions of Iran's ayatollahs is a far greater challenge, which is not being addressed. On the contrary, Iran has been afforded an aura of respectability by US efforts at détente once differences over the Iranian nuclear programme have been bridged. The fact that Iran is one of the biggest sponsors of terror hasn't figured in the US equation.

What are those ambitions? There is no need to speculate, the answer is known beyond a shadow of a doubt. Iran is out to export its brand of Shi'ite ideology to as many regional states as possible, either directly or indirectly, with the use of proxies, with the goal of replacing Sunni governments with Shi'ite regimes. I've been aware of this for decades and I've appealed over and over again to Gulf Cooperation Council (GCC) member states and our Arab allies to clearly acknowledge this problem and do all in their power to ensure our grandchildren don't end up speaking Farsi.

The message is clear. I can only hope they will hear the words coming right out of the horse's mouth, spoken by Alireza Zakani, an Iranian lawmaker and confidante of Iran's Supreme Leader Ali Khamenei. In short, he exposed the mullahs' box of tricks during a recent parliamentary speech. Iran is currently going through a stage during its "Great Jihad" that requires a particular strategy and a cautious approach, he said while boasting that: "Three Arab capitals are now in Iran's hands and affiliated to the Iranian Islamic Revolution," adding that the Yemeni capital Sana'a is well on its way to becoming the fourth with at least 14 out of 20 Yemeni provinces coming under Houthi control. He did not name those Arab capitals but I assume he is referring to Damascus (Shi'ite Allawite regime), Beirut (under the sway of the Shi'ite militant organization Hezbollah) and Baghdad, whose constitution ensures the Prime Minister must be drawn from the Shi'ite community. And, yes, Yemen – a country considered the birthplace of the Arab nation – has fallen into the hands of Shi'ite Houthis, former separatists turned terrorists no longer content with striving for part of the cake, they now seek to consume all of it.

Due to the hesitance of our governments to stand alongside the Yemeni government against these terrorist Iranian puppets, we've enabled their aspirations. Yemen's President Abdrabbuh Mansour Hadi has been coerced by their violent seizure of much of the capital into signing a deal with the Shi'ite rebels resulting in Houthis being appointed as political advisors as well as other concessions. Hadi has described the deal as "historic". I call it a disastrous error of judgment reluctantly agreed to by a man with his back up against the wall. A stroke of his pen has made him complicit in this crime. He has sold his country to Iran for the price of quiet but instead of honouring their pledge to withdraw from Sana'a, the Houthis are demanding even greater concessions.

It doesn't surprise me that Houthis are celebrating their victory with firework displays and revenge attacks on their enemies. But what's truly shocking is that the United Nations (UN) has blessed this agreement. Even more mind-blowing is that some Arab leaders have congratulated the Yemeni government on this step towards "reconciliation". What are they thinking? Houthis due to their proximity, sheer numbers (approximately eight million) and their reputation for barbarity are more hazardous to the security of Gulf states than even Hezbollah. This entire scenario feels like a nightmare in which I'm running for my life chased by a hideous monster, while everyone around me is smiling and chatting even as the creature breathes fire, scorching their hair.

No wonder Alireza Zakani is self-satisfied! Before the Islamic Revolution there were two main components to the US axis in the region – Saudi Islam and Turkish secularism – he notes. Now, he says the political balance has altered to benefit Iran. "Today we are at the peak of our strength and able to impose our will and strategic interests throughout the region," he said, claiming that Iran was responsible for keeping the Assad regime in power and saving Baghdad from Daesh. In truth, Iran is destabilizing and divisive and through Hezbollah has paralysed Lebanon. It still escapes my comprehension why the Western nations, including the US, have sought to brand only the group's military wing "terrorist" when the political and military wings have a single leader.

And now I would really like GCC leaderships to pay attention. The Iranian plot doesn't end with Yemen. "Certainly, the Yemeni revolution will not be confined to Yemen alone," says Zakani. "After its success, it will reach the territory of Saudi Arabia, given the long Yemeni-Saudi border – two million organized armed men are in Yemen – and it won't be long before it is Saudi Arabia's turn." And yet, I read that Riyadh and Tehran are experiencing a thaw in relations! We are indeed very vulnerable. GCC states from Saudi to Oman are surrounded on all sides by hostile Shi'ites under Tehran's sway, whether Iranian, Iraqi or Houthis, but instead of acting to shore up our defence, we are patting Houthi terrorists on the back, turning a blind eye to Hezbollah's crimes and hugging Iranian officials.

I can only cling to the hope that now some of our countries have been galvanized to act against Daesh, our armies and air forces will extend their operations to take back Syria, Iraq, Lebanon and Yemen before the Sunni Arab World is reduced to shadow in a darkening Persian night. We must hold our GCC flag high and show the plotters around us that we see through their game, which is one they will not be allowed to win.

Arab paralysis oils Iran's regional domination

18 March 2015

FOR MANY YEARS, I've appealed to the Arab World, in particular, Gulf leaderships, to rescue both Iraq and Yemen from falling into Iranian hands. Today, like Syria and Lebanon, those once proud Arab heartlands are virtually under the control of Iran's Supreme Leader. That's no exaggeration. There's not only a wealth of factual evidence to back up my conclusions, prominent Iranians have actually admitted as much. And their ambitions don't stop there.

Earlier this month, Iran's former intelligence minister and current advisor to the President for ethnic affairs and religious minorities, Ali Younesi, had this to say in a public forum: "All of the Middle East is Iranian... ."

Decades ago, I might have dismissed those words as laughable wishful thinking, but there's little to laugh at now. Iranian-backed Shi'ite Houthis have succeeded in taking over most of Yemen, and according to reports, Tehran is not only openly flying in weapons, the government has pledged a year's oil to its Yemeni proxy as well as a study on the feasibility of constructing power stations. Yemen now constitutes a direct threat to security and stability on the borders of Saudi Arabia.

Meanwhile, the Iranian Revolutionary Guard Corps (IRGC) – that together with Hezbollah fighters are hand-in-hand with Syria's Assad regime battling opposition groups – has turned its attention to Iraq. Senior Iranian Revolutionary Guards are in country orchestrating the Iraqi army that's partnered up with Iraqi Shi'ite militias to liberate the Sunni-majority province of Anbar from Daesh terrorists.

One of Iraq's paramilitary leaders, Hadi Al Amari, among those fighting to take back former President Saddam Hussein's hometown Tikrit, told CNN that he is proud to declare to the world that "we have Iranian advisors", adding, "Anyone who puts their faith in the international coalition to liberate Iraq is putting their faith on a mirage." Moreover, the Governor of Kirkuk, Dr Najmaldin Karim, told CBS News: "If Iran is helping with whatever way I don't see how you can say no to them."

And do not for a minute imagine those Iranian "advisors" – or Iranian troops – will pack up and go home once the job is done, as the

Iraqi Prime Minister would have us believe. He cannot be trusted. Read what Ali Younesi has to say on the subject: "At the moment Iraq is not only the bastion of our civilization, it is also our identity, culture and capital and this is true now as in the past … . The geography of Iran and Iraq cannot be divided."

Ali Larijani, Iran's National Security Advisor, tried to sweeten the pill. He told a Kuwaiti television channel that Younesi's message had been misinterpreted, contending that "he had only raised the issue of cultural harmony". Unfortunately for Larijani, that weak re-jigging of meaning will not wash.

Here I would quote an extract from one of my own columns published in September last year: "The message is clear." I can only hope they will hear the words coming right out of the horse's mouth, spoken by Alireza Zakani, an Iranian lawmaker and confidante of Iran's Supreme Leader Ali Khamenei. (See "Iran's agenda consolidates while the Arabs are distracted," 15 September 2014.)

In short, he exposed the mullahs' box of tricks during a recent parliamentary speech. "Iran is currently going through a stage during its 'Great Jihad' that requires a particular strategy and a cautious approach," he said while boasting that "Three Arab capitals are now in Iran's hands and affiliated to the Iranian Islamic Revolution," adding that the Yemeni capital Sana'a is well on its way to becoming the fourth with at least 14 out of 20 Yemeni provinces coming under Houthi control.

I must admit to having been mistaken on one point. America is not distracted, it is complicit. In early March, the Chairman of the US Joint Chiefs of Staff General Martin Dempsey actually said Iranian intervention in Iraq might be a positive thing.

Saudi Arabia and its Gulf allies have at last woken up to the threat. A few weeks ago, the Saudi Foreign Minister, Prince Saud bin Faisal bin Abdulaziz Al Saud, asked US Secretary of State John Kerry for ground forces to take on Daesh in Iraq on the grounds there was a risk that Iran would "take over Iraq".

Prince Saud's fears have gone unheeded. President Barack Obama knows there is no appetite among American voters to see their country get involved in any further Middle East wars and he is in no mood to upset the Iranians while delicate talks on limiting Iran's nuclear programmes are ongoing. Basically, the US has reneged on its responsibilities to the country George W. Bush broke in 2003 and has instead farmed out those responsibilities to its long-time foe, Iran. It is so outrageous, you could not make it up.

In a nutshell, Tehran has been given free rein to further its ideological and territorial strategy of placing the entire Middle East under Iran's red, white and green flag. A new Persian Empire is being solidified under our noses. Syria, Iraq, Yemen and Lebanon are now little more than Persian vassal states, while Bahrain is still one of Tehran's prime targets.

Larijani is now in the process of trying to woo Gulf states to accept Iranian hegemony, beginning with Kuwait. During a recent meeting with the Kuwaiti Emir in Kuwait City, he stressed the two nations' "enormous cultural and historical ties". From there, he travelled to Qatar to urge closer parliamentary ties. I can only hope the leaders of these states don't fall for it. Appeasement is not the right way to go.

Any international legitimacy Iran might receive if the P5+1-Iranian negotiations prove fruitful, resulting in the lifting of sanctions and the restoration of full diplomatic relations, will only serve to bolster Iran's coffers, confidence and geopolitical clout.

And now we learn from John Kerry that the US has given up the ghost when it comes to freeing Syria from the most oppressive and brutal regime in its history. So much blood spilled; so much suffering, gone to waste. Why? Because, according to Kerry, the Obama administration is ready to reignite peace talks, this time to include Iran's partner-in-crime, the Syrian president himself!

Sorry, but Arabs shouldn't be left off the hook in all this. We have the weapons, the air power, the finances, the intelligence apparatus and the men to defend our own lands. We in the Gulf are especially vulnerable. As I've warned repeatedly in my columns, the day will surely come when Iraq and Iran will amalgamate into one massive Shi'ite nation with its eye firmly turned towards Gulf Cooperation Council states.

Just a few years ago, Iran threatened to close its airspace to any airline using the term "Arabian Gulf" and to close the Straits of Hormuz if it were attacked. If those threats were carried through and also implemented by an Iranian-controlled Syria, Iraq, Yemen, Gulf Cooperation Council nationals and residents would be held hostage, unable to fly.

What happened to us? We used to have pride; our hearts used to burst with Arab patriotism. Are we waiting for Iranians to occupy our land too? Will we wait with tied hands until our dignity and the sanctity of our homes are stripped from us?

We cannot go on cowering indefinitely in the face of a burgeoning Greater Iran. We must be honest, instead of being afraid to come out and say who our enemies truly are. We must muster our determination and use all our power to cut the head off the snake.

On 23 March the League of Arab States Summit is expected to place the idea of a joint Arab military force to conduct missions of emergency intervention at the top of its agenda. I've long been calling for such a force, but there is no time to waste. It will be of little use once the Iranian horse has bolted. This is our opportunity to send a unified message to Qom that the Lion of Arabia has opened its eyes and bares its teeth.

Arab Ahwaz must be liberated from Iran

28 March 2015

WHENEVER THE ARAB WORLD is discussed, forgotten are the eight million Arabs struggling to survive under the Persian yoke in an Arab region bordering Iraq and the Arabian Gulf, rich with oil and gas. Once an autonomous area, separated from Persia by the Zagros mountain range, under the governance of Sheikh Khazaal bin Jaber whose family had ruled for over a century, it was grabbed by Shah Reza Shah Pahlavi in 1925 with a nod and a wink from Britain eager to preserve its relationship with Iran due to its oil interests.

Formerly known as Arabistan, the Iranian occupiers wasted no time in changing the name of this new Iranian province to Khuzestan, rejected by its Arab residents even today. Arabs and Persians have little in common and as Sir Arnold Wilson, a British colonial administrator, once said: Arabistan is "a country as different from Persia as is Spain from Germany".

Although Arabistan provides Iran with 80 per cent of its oil requirements as well as half of its gas, its sons are exploited and oppressed; their human rights tramped upon, their very identity in danger of being obliterated. Iran's policy of ethnic discrimination combined with its Persian resettlement endeavours has resulted in turning the Ahwazi Arabs into an economic and social underclass.

Numerous Arab villages are without schools and those "lucky" enough to attend school are educated in Farsi. Some 80 per cent of Ahwazi Arab women are illiterate as opposed to 50 per cent of Ahwazi men. Over thirty per cent of the under-30s are unemployed in this heavily industrialized region, primarily because Persians receive priority and jobs are often advertised outside the governorate.

Thousands are without access to drinking water, because rivers have been diverted to arid Persian provinces. Their streets are open sewers; many are deprived of electricity and gas. In 2013, Arabistan's capital, Ahwaz, was classed by the World Health Organization (WHO) as the most polluted city on earth partly due to desertification and industrial smog. Arab farmers are regularly stripped of agricultural land and although there has been loud international condemnation of Israel's separation walls, there have been no media headlines about the segregation walls hiding squalid Arab ghettoes from wealthier Persian settlements and glossy new towns.

It is no wonder that Ahwazi Arabs are now driven to protest against such blatant discrimination. According to the Ahwaz Studies Center, "increasing joblessness and rising poverty is creating a humanitarian crisis among Ahwazi Arabs that threatens to lead to widespread unrest ... ." The authorities use a heavy hand against demonstrators and rights activists.

However, one of the central reasons behind the Ahwazis' discontent is their evaporating sense of who they are; the erosion of their roots, their language, their Arab identity. That was brought home to me a few days ago as I watched a video of Iranian security forces attacking Ahwazi football fans for wearing traditional Arab dress while celebrating the triumph of the visiting Saudi Al Hilal team against the local Foolad Khuzestan side. In truth, the video touched an emotional chord in me.

The authorities were alerted when Ahwazis referred to the Saudi players as "their Arab Brothers" and welcomed them to "Arab lands". The forces attempted to move the Arabs away from the cameras, provoking resistance. The crowd responded by destroying posters of Iran's Supreme Guide, Ali Khamenei, in the face of Iranian Revolutionary Guards, and threw stones at police. This resulted in arbitrary arrests when peaceful protestors were also swept up. "Iran will never be able to smother our voice and our Arab identity," say the demonstrators.

For me, this was emotional because despite all Iran's measures to choke the Ahwazi's inner being and stifle all dissent over the past 90 years – even to the extent of forcing them to give their babies Persian names – they remain proud to be Arab.

It also saddens me when I remember that those Arabs, our own people, have been abandoned to fend for themselves. Why isn't the United Nations taking up their cause? Why are those Western countries, endlessly trumpeting human rights to the Middle East, not only turning a blind eye but actively wooing Iran's ayatollahs? Most importantly, we can no longer stay silent when eight million Ahwazi Arabs equates to a population three times bigger than that of Gaza?

Here I would call on Arab countries – especially Gulf Cooperation Council (GCC) states and their allies – to stand tall with our Ahwazi brothers so as to empower them on their journey to freedom. Apart from the fact that this is our moral duty, it could also offer strategic benefits at a time when Iranian officials boast of a new Persian empire that includes four Arab capitals.

Help Arabistan gain its independence and Tehran can kiss goodbye to its oil exports and the revenue it uses to fund its terror proxies. Iran's meddling in Arab countries is rife and unrestrained. Yemen is just one example and I'm gratified that Saudi, partnered with GCC states, Egypt, Sudan, Jordan and Pakistan, has launched a military intervention to free this historic Arab heartland from Iranian-backed Shi'ite militias; this action is one that I've long called for. Iran deserves to be treated in kind.

The first step towards freeing the people of Ahwaz is a vigorous and determined campaign by GCC leaderships to undermine the Iranian fist on this dear Arab land involving billions of dollars in direct financial aid to support the development of Al Ahwaz.

Secondly, the League of Arab States and/or the GCC should bring the forgotten truth that Al Ahwaz is, indeed, Arab territory to the international spotlight so as to raise awareness.

Thirdly, the file should be lodged with the United Nations Security Council for investigation with the aim of procuring a resolution to the effect that Ahwaz has been and is under illegal occupation and, thus, has a right to self-determination. Such applications have been lodged by Ahwazis previously but haven't been taken with the seriousness they deserve. The GCC should use its power to ensure the Ahwazi cause can no longer be swept under the carpet.

Just a year ago, I would have had little hope that this appeal would be heard. But, thankfully, GCC states and its Arab friends have at last resolved to be proactive in defending Arab peoples and lands. Operation Decisive Storm in Yemen is just the beginning, signalling Iran's hitherto clear path towards regional domination is now strewn with roadblocks.

I still bristle when I recall a conversation I had many years ago with former US ambassador Richard W. Murphy, who informed me that America was now responsible for Gulf security. When I asked him on what authority, he answered without flinching, saying the Brits handed the region to us. What are we, sheep? I remember thinking. Today, we are emerging as lions. We are standing with our Yemeni brothers in distress and proving to the Islamic Republic of Iran, its militias and proxies that we will never be parcelled off to any country's hegemonic ambitions ever again.

The Iranian regime nears its sell-by date

5 May 2015

A S IF IT WASN'T CONTEMPTIBLE enough that Iran's ayatollahs have been oppressing religious and ethnic minorities ever since they took power in 1979, they are currently attempting to strangle the entire region with their medieval ideology. Worse, they have resorted to threatening neighbouring countries and funding terrorists and proxy militias to overturn governments.

The Quran stresses upon the unity of Muslims in numerous verses and the Hadith tells us that the Prophet Mohammed (PBUH) said: "Stay with the group (of righteous Muslims), for the wolf eats the sheep that strays away from the herd." [Ahmad and Al-Tirmidhi]

In essence, the ones issuing proclamations in Qom are acting in ways that are the very antithesis of the Quran's edicts by fomenting divisions and sectarian hatreds, "And if two factions among the believers should fight, then make settlement between the two. But if one of them oppresses the other, then fight against the one that oppresses until it returns to the ordinance of Allah. And if it returns, then make settlement between them in justice and act justly. Allah loves those who act justly." Surah Al-Hujurat [49:9]

The regime, created by Ayatollah Ruhollah Khomeini, was born out of a revolutionary climate and his own will to power. The inherently political Shi'ite Islam that claims to champion resistance against tyranny and subjugation was used by the Ayatollah Khomeini as a tool to attract the poor and the disenfranchised onto his bandwagon.

The irony is that there is no country on earth, with the exception of North Korea, which squashes its population underfoot, both politically and socially, while keeping over almost 11 million illiterate and 15 million struggling below the poverty line, in addition to 24 per cent of the country's youth being unemployed.

The late Iranian thinker and writer Ali Shariati described this trajectory perfectly relative to his homeland years before the West turned its back on the Shah: "A religious regime is one in which, instead of the political figures, religious figures take up political and governmental positions. In other words, a religious regime means the rule of the clerics. One natural consequence of such a regime is dictatorship, because the cleric views himself as God's representative who carries out his orders on earth, and therefore, people have no right to express their opinions, or criticize and oppose him." He expressed his belief that under such a regime, followers of other religions are considered deviants from "the true path" whose oppression is "God's justice".

Shariati's words turned out to be prophetic. Iran's human rights record worsens year upon year. President Hassan Rouhani goes out of his way to present himself as a moderate reformist but statistics contradict his rhetoric. According to the United Nations, on Rouhani's watch, executions have risen, women's economic opportunities are diminishing and his government's influence over the media, civil society, political organizations and the judiciary has expanded.

It is only a matter of time before the Iranian pressure cooker explodes. Eighty million human beings can only be trodden upon for so long before they rise up en masse. Many will be galvanized due to Iran's repressive policies; others will react to the dire economic situation.

Signs are that more than eight million Ahwazi Arabs in Iranian-occupied Arabistan – an oil-and-gas-rich region bordering the Arabian Gulf – are readying an Intifada against Persian discrimination and economic neglect. Likewise, Turkmens, Baluchis, Kurds as well as Sunnis in the Iranian provinces of Kurdistan, Kermanshah, Khorasan and Sistan, are angry at being treated as second-class citizens. The internet and satellite television has afforded young Iranians a glimpse of what 21st-century freedom looks like; they will soon rebel against subjugation.

Whether it takes one year or 10, the future of Iran will rest in the hands of peaceful Iranians seeking prosperity, not those arming and funding terrorists around the globe. These are the people the US, which never fails to trumpet its own values and works to export "democracy and freedom", should be helping. Instead the Obama administration may be about to sign a pact with the devilish Mullahs in Iran, biding their time to turn the Middle East into a fireball as a precursor to what they believe will be the appearance of the 12th Imam, Al Mahdi Al Mountathar.

And one day, the veil will be lifted from the eyes of Lebanese Shi'ite supporters, nay slaves, of Hezbollah that turned this once peaceful

Mediterranean haven into a paralysed state operating under a democratic façade plagued by conflicts and internal violence.

Musa Al Sadr is widely credited as being the Lebanese Shi'ite's first power broker. Born in Qom, he became a cleric upon his coming to Lebanon when he wooed the underclass. In 1967, he headed the newly-founded Supreme Islamic Shi'ite Council, which set out to dominate Lebanon militarily, economically, politically and socially through the use of Shi'ite theology to politicize the Council's goals.

In 1974, Al Sadr launched a movement called the Harakat Al Mahrumin (the Movement of the Dispossessed) that bore a militia, the Amal Movement, a year later. Following his mysterious disappearance, Iran's mullahs were quick to see an entrée into Lebanon on the pretext of resisting the 1982 Israeli invasion when Hezbollah came into being. However, an article published in the *Weekly Standard* titled "The secret history of Hezbollah" has a more accurate take: "It's an Israel-centric myth that makes the Jewish state Hezbollah's motivation and prime mover. In reality, the story of Hezbollah's origins is a story about Iran, featuring the anti-Shah revolutionaries, active in Lebanon in the 1970s years before Israel's intervention .... There we find that, contrary to the common wisdom, Hezbollah did not arise as a resistance movement to the Israeli occupation. Rather it was born from the struggle between Iranian revolutionary factions opposed to the Shah."

Iran's aim to control Yemen, via the agency of Shi'ite Houthis, was thwarted by a Saudi-led Arab coalition. Syria is close to being liberated from rule by the Allawite minority Shi'ite sect responsible for the death of over 200,000 Syrian citizens. Furthermore, Iraqi Shi'ite militias that take their marching orders from Tehran will not survive in the short-to-medium term. Those traitors to this great Arab country should flee to their true home, Iran, and the same goes for Iran's conspirators in Lebanon and elsewhere in the Arab World.

Arab Shi'ites, mesmerized by their propaganda, should repent and be forgiven. But there must be no forgiveness for Hezbollah that's crippled Lebanon for generations or for the leaders of the pro-Iranian Houthis in the pay of Tehran. There can be no pardon for Iraqi militias directed by Muqtada al Sadr or the pro-Iranian Badr Organization, headed by Hadi Al Amiri, or the Islamic Supreme Council of Iraq, led by Ammar Al Hakim. And Iraqi Prime Minister Nouri Al Maliki, who gave those thugs free rein, should not get a free pass either. There can be no negotiations with anyone whose hands are blood-soaked, just a single address – the International Criminal Court in The Hague.

Iran's vision of a new Empire will not manifest. Arab states are coming together in an unprecedented way to slice its roaming tentacles and are increasingly wary of foreign allies seemingly engaged in playing a double-faced game. We Arabs want to live in peace and security. We don't crave Empire but we will be our people's rescuers and protectors of our faith and our culture.

Evidence is mounting that the mullahs and their terrorists are in for a mighty fall; their masks are off, their hypocrisy and lies cannot be hidden. I long for the day when those deceivers get their just reward. I pray for the day when we can reclaim our authority over our lands. And I believe deep in my heart and soul that those days of celebration won't be long in coming.

Iran's open aggression demands a harsh response

5 January 2016

THE GLOVES ARE OFF. Not content with boasting that it controls certain Arab capitals and using militias to destabilize others, the Islamic Republic of Iran has passed the point of no return by directly interfering in Saudi Arabia's internal affairs.

The Kingdom is a country of laws that must be respected by all, regardless of their sectarian affiliations and, in a region fraught with danger, Saudi's zero tolerance for terrorists and those inciting people to violence regardless of whether they are Sunni or Shi'ite, should be applauded.

Nimr Al Nimr, a Shia cleric, admitted his crimes and is seen on videos whipping up violence and sedition. He was tried in a court of law and sentenced just as others who received the same fate. There was no sectarian bias involved when the other 46 individuals were Sunnis.

Condemnation from Tehran rings hollow when it has been accused by human rights groups of being on a hanging spree. Just last month, a woman was sentenced to death by stoning. Since the so-called moderate President Hassan Rouhani took office over 2,000 prisoners, including Sunnis, have been hanged (700 last year alone).

Many are cruelly pulled up by their necks on cranes where their bodies are left dangling for all to see and there are reports that some have taken up to 20 minutes to die. In March, 33 Sunni men were on death row and six were executed for "enmity of God", a charge Amnesty International says was fabricated.

As the Saudi Minister of Foreign Affairs Adel Al Jubeir revealed in a press conference on Sunday 3 January 2016, the Iranian authorities organized shifts of thugs to storm and torch the Saudi embassy in Tehran and its consulate in the Iranian city of Mashad ignoring repeated requests from Saudi diplomats for protection.

This flies against all diplomatic norms and proves once again that Iran is a pariah state and an unfit partner within the community of nations. Iran's lawless character has not changed since the days of the American embassy siege that endured for 444 days during 1979 when authorities stood by as a mob attacked the British embassy in Tehran in 2011.

This blatant infringement of Saudi sovereignty was compounded by rhetoric from Iran's Supreme Leader Ayatollah Ali Khamenei who arrogantly tweeted "Divine revenge will seize Saudi politicians" as though he believes he is God's mouthpiece; in itself blasphemous. Only the

Prophet (PBUH) was honoured with the task of revealing God's will. Iran's Foreign Ministry warned the Kingdom would pay a high price for its actions, a threat that cannot go unanswered.

Such vicious statements and behaviours can be construed as an act of war. For sure Khamenei has encouraged Shi'ite communities in Iraq, Lebanon and Bahrain to take to the streets in protest and galvanized his Lebanese puppet Hezbollah's Secretary General Hassan Nasrallah to spout fiery anti-Saudi rhetoric amid chants of "Death to the Al Saud". I am sad to say that this incident raises questions as to where the loyalties of Arab Shi'ites lie. Is their prime allegiance to the countries which bore and fed them or to the ayatollahs in Qom?

With the future of our countries at stake, we can no longer tolerate Iranian sympathizers, whether residents or visitors, in our midst. Anyone who pays allegiance to Iran and its proxies is welcome to join his Iranian masters. We must put out a sign "backstabbers not wanted".

It has long been suspected that Iraq's leadership is under Tehran's boot and now it is confirmed. Iraq's Prime Minister Haider Al Abadi accuses Saudi of "violating human rights", which will have repercussions "on the security, stability and the social fabric of the peoples of the region". Doesn't he know that people in glass houses should not throw stones; Iraq post-Saddam leadership has caused the Sunni–Shi'ite divide while spawning terrorist groups with its unjust treatment of Sunnis.

Any Arab country that fails to quell anti-Saudi demonstrations and attacks on Saudi interests will either be viewed as being in agreement or fearful of Iran's retribution. Either way, they should be held responsible for their people's crimes.

I have long warned that Iran is the greatest threat to Gulf states and I was reassured that Saudi Arabia acted firmly and decisively to cut diplomatic relations and all other ties with Iran. Adel Al Jubeir hinted that others should do the same. I could not agree more. Now is the moment for all GCC states (and Arab allies, in particular Egypt and Jordan) to show their solidarity with a member country when times are rough.

I cannot count how many columns I have written urging the GCC to take strong action in response to Iran's continuous aggression and I am relieved that message has finally hit home. There should be no backtracking or forgiveness. The enemy is at the door. Our self-defence demands that we must continue along this path by implementing the Joint Arab Force and firming-up the Saudi-led anti-terrorism military coalition involving 34 predominately Muslim states.

Our ultimate goals should include the liberation of Al Ahwaz (Arabistan) from Persian occupation and its Arab majority's release from repression, poverty and denial of religious freedom. This long-suffering population of millions, deprived of water and fuel in a region rich with oil and gas, and criminalized for giving newborns Arab names, are crying out to be saved from the mullahs' fists.

Furthermore, Iraq and Lebanon should not be abandoned to Iranian flunkies who make obeisance to the Ayatollah Khamenei. Saudi Arabia has donated billions of dollars to strengthen the Lebanese armed forces yet no amount of fighter jets or weapons can be a substitute for courage and love of country. What kind of army allows an armed militia to lead its country by the nose? Put simply, we must do our utmost to cleanse the Arab World from the destructive Persian contagion – and there is no time to waste.

Lastly, I would reiterate my call to the decision-makers within the GCC and beyond to cut diplomatic and trade relations with the region's biggest sponsor of terrorism and its Arab proxies. Any country spewing threats or trying to teach us how we should deal with terrorists, posing a grave danger to our peoples and our very existence, is an enemy that must be shunned and isolated on every level. Let us have the courage to prove to the Saudi government and people, with more than mere sympathetic words, that they are not alone.

3

Iran and the nuclear threat:
the danger of new alliances

Introduction

I COULD NOT BELIEVE MY EARS when I heard that world powers
had lifted Iran's sanctions after years of "economic isolation". Iran's
ayatollahs have played their cards well. I have to give them kudos for
that. They have managed to convince first-world nations that Tehran
has complied with the terms of what is officially called the Joint
Comprehensive Plan of Action (JCPOA) between the E3+3 and Iran.

In July 2015, Iran and a group of six countries known as the E3+3 or
the EU+3 – France, Germany and the United Kingdom from Europe, along
with China, Russia and the United States – reached the JCPOA, entrusting
the International Atomic Energy Agency (IAEA) with verifying and
monitoring Iran's nuclear programme.

Essentially it is a deal in which Tehran has agreed to curb its nuclear
ambitions. Seriously? Do world leaders really believe that it will stop
developing nuclear weapons based on its word? If so they are more gullible
than I thought.

US President Barack Obama made an historic mistake by succumbing
to Iran's whim. That mistake has dire repercussions that will be
widespread and felt throughout the world, but they will be particularly
detrimental to Arab interests and security.

At its core, this has little to do with nuclear weapons and all to do with
facilitating the emergence of Iran as a regional power, in league with
Washington to exert control over Arab states, in particular Saudi Arabia
and Gulf states, and to rebalance regional power in America's favour.

I am convinced there is much more to this narrow deal than meets the
eye. I transmitted my concerns of a potential "Grand Bargain" in a report
to Gulf leaderships in June 2013 and I have laid out my fears in numerous
columns since. If I was concerned then, I am deeply disturbed now. This is
one time I hate to be right.

However, faced with this fait accompli, the Arab World must join forces
to shore up its defences. Thankfully, there are concrete moves in that
direction. Saudi Arabia has woken up to the dangers following Iran's direct

interference in its internal affairs, not to mention its use of proxies in Syria, Bahrain and Yemen. I am somewhat relieved that a Joint Arab Force is on the table and that a Muslim anti-terrorism coalition has been formed with the participation of 34 predominately Muslim states.

· I know there is an ulterior motive on the West's part. It comes down to power, money and oil – and perhaps a feather in outgoing US President Barack Obama's hat – but what a dangerous game it is playing. Tehran sugar-coated the deal with an extra surprise by releasing five American political prisoners – including *The Washington Post* reporter Jason Rezaian – as part of a prisoner swap, which saw the US pardon three Iranian-Americans in return. How considerate!

So Tehran and Washington are friends again. Financially that is great for Iran as billions and billions of US dollars' worth of the country's assets will be unfrozen. No wonder the country's President Hassan Rouhani hailed "Implementation Day" as a "golden page" in Iran's history book. "The nuclear deal is an opportunity that we should use to develop the country, improve the welfare of the nation, and create stability and security in the region," he said. There were smiles all around following the "landmark" moment, which was officially sealed mid-2015 by Iran and the six countries listed on the previous page. That agreement, on 14 July, took more than 20 months of negotiations, and was the result of more than a decade of careful diplomacy.

Iran is back in business. But I am compelled to say this again – maybe this time I will be heard – if you look at what Iran has achieved with sanctions, just imagine what it will be capable of with sanctions lifted. Money will flood into the country as the world clamours to access Iranian oil. The world will be feeding terrorists and Iran's future nuclear capabilities with an endless pot of money. It will have blood on its hands.

Everyone – including the United Nations (UN) and the IAEA – seems to have short memories, or to have been brainwashed. The Vienna-based nuclear watchdog said in a statement in January 2016: "Iran has carried out all measures required under the [July nuclear deal] ... to enable Implementation Day to occur." No sooner was the ink dry than the US formally lifted sanctions. The European Union (EU) swiftly followed suit. In my view they have well and truly opened Pandora's box.

Tehran has long claimed its nuclear ambitions were for "peaceful purposes". The world did not believe it then, so what has changed? Iran has the world's fourth largest oil reserves. Are we that desperate for oil that we would sell our souls to the Devil?

It amazes me that all Iran had to do to get the world back on its side was to "limit" its nuclear activities ... not halt them completely. In return it has been awarded with the scrapping of decade-old sanctions.

So, what does it mean? Well, let me tell you in plain English. An economic boom like no other for Iran. But I am surer than sure it will not go to the millions of hungry Iranians living in squalor. Do not forget Iran's supreme leader, Ali Khamenei, had already amassed a huge fortune worth tens of billions of dollars before the nuclear deal, while the majority of his people live in poverty and destitution. The new money flooding in will be used to further fund terrorism in the Middle East.

While I understand that this newly opened market offers multi-billion dollars' worth of opportunities, it worries me that people are being blinded by dollar signs.

An unprecedented number of business delegations have flocked to Tehran, and Iran has wasted no time in courting international trade. Iranian state-related bodies, backed by billions of dollars in unfrozen assets, have been quick to capitalize on the lifting of most sanctions. The Iranian President Hassan Rouhani has been on roadshows to Europe striking deals with companies left, right and centre – including Airbus, Peugeot and others.

What amazes me more than anything is the lack of understanding about the danger of Tehran by Western nations. They are delusional. US Secretary of State John Kerry was quoted saying, "Today, as a result of the actions taken since last July, the United States, our friends and allies in the Middle East, in the entire world are safer because the threat of a nuclear weapon has been reduced."

United Nations Secretary General Ban Ki-moon said he was heartened by the lifting of sanctions. "This is a significant milestone that reflects the good faith effort by all parties to fulfil their agreed commitments," he said in a statement issued by his spokesman.

UK Secretary of State for Foreign Affairs Philip Hammond concurred saying the deal "makes the Middle East and the wider world a safer place".

Those words were echoed too by the EU foreign policy head Federica Mogherini who said the nuclear deal would help improve regional and international peace – and security. Has the world gone mad?

While Western nations roll out the rhetoric that safety has been instilled, Iran's neighbours in the Gulf certainly will not be hoodwinked into believing it, that is for sure. We have experienced first hand the country's capabilities, which I have outlined throughout this book.

At least the Israeli Prime Minister Benjamin Netanyahu understands the continued threat that Tehran poses. He was quoted as saying "Even after signing the nuclear deal, Iran has not relinquished its ambition to obtain nuclear weapons, and continues to act to destabilize the Middle East and spread terror throughout the world while violating its international commitments." Bravo Mr Netanyahu, but unfortunately your words are falling on deaf ears.

I almost had to laugh out loud when I heard what Rouhani said in a live broadcast to counter the Israeli Prime Minister's concerns. "The friends of Iran are happy and its competitors need not worry, we are not a threat to any government or nation. We are a messenger of peace, stability and security in the region and the world."

Iran, a messenger of peace? Someone must be playing a joke on us. The money will go to the Islamic Revolutionary Guard Corps without a doubt. It will be used to increase Iran's ability to play puppeteer in the region, and allow terrorism to flourish throughout the world.

I am not convinced that Iran's nuclear deal will stick. I fear that we will once again be threatened with the possibility of a nuclear armed Iran right on our doorstep. But until that day comes, the money will continue to flood into Iran courtesy of the lifting of certain sanctions, and end up in the hands of terrorists hell-bent on creating further destruction around the world.

When will the West stop meddling in our affairs? It is playing an incredibly dangerous game and we are right in the centre of it. Western nations are so far from reality that they have helped enable terrorism with Iran by their side. They have thrown fuel in the fire once more, and we are the ones who will have to bear the dire consequences. We live in a world where we no longer know our friends from our enemies, and where allies become foes at a moment's notice. I fear for our future and the future of our children.

Time to react to open Iranian threats

1 January 2012

HOW MUCH LONGER are Gulf states going to remain in denial? It may be a bitter pill to swallow but we cannot go on pretending that the Islamic Republic of Iran has friendly intentions when it is becoming increasingly hostile to its Arab neighbours. Now is the time for the Gulf Cooperation Council (GCC) to shore up its common defence capabilities and engage with its allies to guard the sovereignty and security of its member countries. How much more proof do our leaderships require before they are willing to shed diplomatic niceties and put their cards firmly on the table? Forget supposition! We can have no more illusions when the facts are so damning.

As if it was not bad enough that Tehran has been inciting the Shi'ite minority in Bahrain to launch violent anti-government protests, in recent days it has been showing off its military muscle throughout the Strait of Hormuz and the Gulf of Aden during an exercise ominously dubbed "Velayat" – a Farsi word that means "supremacy". If this is not a clear message to the world and the region, I do not know what is. Actually, there is no room for misinterpretation; no reason at all to give Iran's leaders the benefit of the doubt.

The Commander of the Iranian Navy Habibollah Sayyari has spelled out his country's motive in conducting war games on our doorstep. "Displaying Iran's defensive and deterrent power", "relaying a message of peace and friendship" and showcasing "the county's power to control the region as well as testing new missiles, torpedoes and weapons", were the reasons he gave.

The operative phrase is of course "power to control the region" with peace and friendship ridiculously thrown in for good measure. Someone should inform the Commander that friendship cannot be cemented at the barrel of a gun. A number of the missiles test-fired were advanced short-range. No prizes for guessing which countries they are ultimately destined to hit; certainly not Iran's allies Syria and Iraq or the Caucuses that fall into Russia's sphere of influence – and neither are they meant for nuclear-armed Pakistan.

Those missiles have the names of GCC states virtually etched on their casings. Well, if that is how they want to play it, a dangerous old-fashioned game with echoes of the Cold War, Gulf states should send a similar message by exhibiting their own military hardware and capabilities that are far more sophisticated than Iran's. There is a saying in Arabic that translated says "Show your strength else people might mistake your calm and quiet exterior as weakness."

Some may be tempted to believe that our United States ally will protect us against Iranian aggression; that may be true but it is not something we can rely upon absolutely. We should have learned our lesson. When the Trucial States, the forerunner to the United Arab Emirates (UAE), were still under Britain's protection, the Shah was not deterred from grabbing the islands of Abu Musa and Greater and Lesser Tunbs. Major world powers do not have friends, only interests. They could sell us out any time that suits them which is why with the help of God we must get in the driver's seat and take control of our own destiny.

Compounding an already volatile climate was an Iranian threat to close the Strait of Hormuz to shipping in the event Washington imposes sanctions against Iran's oil industry exports. Once again, Habibollah Sayyari did not hold back. He said his country has "comprehensive control over the strategic waterway" – the conduit for 15 million barrels of oil daily. Sealing it with vessels would be a "very easy" task for Iranian forces, he somewhat arrogantly believes.

If that warning has substance and is not just empty rhetoric, as US Department of State spokesman Mark Toner seems to think, its manifestation would have a negative effect on GCC economies and send oil prices soaring, shattering global efforts to stabilize currencies and markets.

A spokesman for the Pentagon has responded, describing the waterway as an "economic lifeline" and adding that "interference with the transit or passage of vessels through the Strait of Hormuz will not be tolerated". He has wagged his finger at Tehran alright, but what is it that the United States proposes to do about it? Washington's done years of finger-wagging over Iran's uranium enrichment programme in concert with major European capitals, but that is still ongoing with some experts holding to the belief that Iran is close to building a nuclear bomb.

As for the UAE, its diplomatic links with Iran run hot and cold but the two countries have maintained strong trading relations. That is until now.

According to Iranian media, Tehran has banned the extension of letters of credit relating to imports from the UAE and has announced its intention to suspend trade between the two countries. One Iranian politician has warned the UAE "to resist the meaningless pressure imposed by arrogant powers so that they can continue their economic relations with the Islamic State". He is dreaming. Iran is the pariah country suffering economic sanctions, not the UAE, which translated means "they need us a whole lot more than we need them". No wonder subsequent statements out of Tehran sounded conciliatory.

What are we waiting for? I have said for a long time that the UAE must cut diplomatic relations with Tehran and should ban all trade with Iran. Yes, our merchants would incur losses but within a very short period those could be covered by new trading partners. We cannot go on compromising our souls for a fistful of Persian Rials.

The rules of the game changed while we were not looking. These new rules need bold decision-making, innovative lateral thinking and the courage to take pre-emptive steps to thwart the ayatollahs from checkmating us all.

Arabs must tackle Iranian threats head on

14 August 2012

FEW WOULD DISPUTE that the Islamic Republic of Iran is actively engaged in expanding its military capabilities, developing its nuclear potential, arming and funding Shi'ite minorities and disseminating its ideology throughout the region. As each month passes, Tehran becomes more powerful and influential. Chances are that we may wake up one day to find it has become a nuclear-armed state on our doorstep despite denials from the ayatollahs. If and when that happens, Iran will be empowered to dictate terms and unless the international community is willing to risk nuclear Armageddon, the Gulf will be enveloped in the same Shi'ite flag that currently flies over Iraq, Lebanon and Syria.

Iran's tentacles have spread far and wide. Last month, two Iranian agents were arrested in Kenya after they had been spotted casing the Israeli embassy, the British High Commission and a golf course as potential targets in an alleged bombing plot. Iran is courting Algeria and is currently seeking political and economic relations with Egypt's new government along the lines of those it enjoys with Sudan and Eritrea.

In Morocco, the mullahs have been funding "Tashyeeh" institutes for the purpose of converting Sunnis; in Yemen they have been arming Houthi rebels. A non-state actor, an Iranian surrogate, dominates Lebanese politics while Syria has witnessed a marked increase in Iranian "pilgrims" who also happen to be military advisors or Iranian Guard, inserted to lend support to Assad's crimes against humanity.

Moreover, according to the author of *A Time to Betray*, Reza Khalili, a former CIA operative who successfully infiltrated Iran's Revolutionary Guard: "Iran has expanded its terror network and now has tens of thousands of agents in Latin America." Khalili quotes a member of the Supreme Council of Cultural Revolution in Iran as saying this on Iranian state television: "We must get ready for global operation .... Our fellow fighters are present in all five continents of the world ... an international jihad must be provoked; we must fear no one."

When the pieces of the Iranian jigsaw are fitted together a disturbing big picture emerges. The danger it portends for my part of the world has been clear to me for years. I have penned numerous columns warning Gulf Cooperation Council (GCC) leaders and Arab governments about this but it seems to me that no serious steps have yet been taken. I have also expressed my suspicions, supported by certain facts, that Israel and Iran have been cooperating in various areas under a US umbrella. But, again, no reaction from Western authorities, no attempt to contradict my thesis.

Superficially at least, the US and its premier ally in the Middle East – Israel – are Iran's sworn enemies. Both Washington and Tel Aviv have vehemently condemned Iran for its terrorist activities and its insistence on enriching uranium. If the Israeli media is to be believed Prime Minister Benjamin Netanyahu is contemplating bombing Iran's nuclear sites later this year, but he is beginning to sound like the boy who cried wolf.

The Obama administration has, indeed, been relentless in instituting anti-Iranian sanctions on banking and the country's oil sector knowing full well that their impact will be minimal as long as major powers such as Russia, China and India along with Iran's main trading partners find ways of circumventing them. Europe is even considering lifting some of its sanctions against Iran in light of the P5+1 group's so-called fruitful negotiations with Tehran on the nuclear issue. And it is well known that Western banks and corporations have been working with Iran via intermediaries to market Iranian oil and launder its proceeds.

The US and Europe are good at talking the talk when it comes to the atrocities being perpetrated on Syrian civilians by their own government. They have organized "Friends of the Syrian People" conferences, attempted to censure the Assad regime in the United Nations (UN) Security Council, and have provided humanitarian assistance to Syrian refugees. But when it comes to walking the walk, they have consistently buckled.

I am appalled by their lack of action, especially when they were so swift to bypass the UN and invade Iraq on false pretexts only to gift that Arab heartland and cradle of civilization to the ayatollahs. If this is "the New American century" it certainly is not the one envisaged by George W. Bush's neoconservatives. The US can no longer be considered a superpower when it is so easily intimidated by the likes of Russia and its partners in crime Iran and Syria. Obama's credibility is eroded when he applauds popular uprisings in Arab republics while ignoring the struggles of the Iranian people who also seek freedom from the oppression and poverty that quashes the dreams of the 85 per cent of Iranians subsisting below the poverty line.

Of course, the US Secretary of State Hillary Clinton gives a good impression of being actively involved. Her latest "amazing" discovery was so impressive I could not help laughing. She says Hezbollah is engaged in assisting Assad within Syrian territory. So much for her intelligence sources; I could have told her that. I hope I am wrong but America's inaction has forced me to consider whether the US is coordinating with Russia and Iran on Syria.

Kofi Annan, who was appointed as the UN's envoy to Syria, was so fed up with the Security Council's paralysis that he resigned. Word is that he is being replaced by 78-year-old Lakhdar Brahimi, a former Algerian Foreign Minister, favoured by UN Secretary General Ban Ki-moon. A strange choice given that Mr Brahimi takes a dim view of peace prospects; even stranger is the fact that the UN's Under-Secretary General for Political Affairs Jeffrey Feltman invited the Syrian ambassador to the UN to deliberate on Brahimi's appointment.

Such ineffectual rearranging of the deckchairs as a substitute for action might be amusing if it were not for the continuous spill of innocent blood. Sadly, the League of Arab States is no better. Its member countries include well-intentioned GCC states that want to do something tangible but they are thwarted by countries under Iran's thumb or some are too caught up in their own internal problems to go out on a limb for the Syrian people.

Where did our famous courage go? What happened to our dignity? Why have we become so complacent that we will not defend ourselves against Iran's hegemonic ambitions let alone protect our brothers and sisters in Syria? Our ancestors, from the Prophet Mohammed (PBUH) to the Rightly Guided Caliphs Abu Bakr, Umar, Uthman and Ali, and one of the greatest of all leaders Khalid ibn Al Walid, were brave men who never hesitated to battle on the side of right and, with God's help, were always victorious. They never shirked their duty to rescue anyone who asked for their help even those far away in Bilad Al Sham, the Iberian Peninsula or parts of Asia. They would be ashamed of their descendents who lounge on their sofas doing nothing but helplessly shake their heads, watching the corpses of Syrian women and children pile up before them on their TV screens.

Enough meetings, enough conferences, enough delegations and envoys! Enough pretending to ourselves that the Iranian threat to our region will magically fade away! Enough clinging to our comfort zones! We need action!

America's dalliance with Iran alienates Middle East allies

24 October 2013

A MERICA'S CLOSEST REGIONAL allies are reeling from a series of shocks undermining their national security and interests, delivered by the Obama administration. Reports in the mainstream media indicate Saudi Arabia may have concluded "with friends like that, who needs enemies?"

Saudi Arabia's intelligence chief Prince Bandar bin Sultan is quoted as saying his country is making "a major shift" away from the US, a mutually beneficial partnership that has endured since 1932 when full diplomatic relations were forged. Repercussions could involve Riyadh shopping around for alternative weapons supplies, curtailing US oil privileges or liquidating its US Treasury bonds and other US investments.

Supported by most Gulf states, Saudi Arabia has lost patience with President Barack Obama's "Jekyll and Hyde-type" foreign policy missteps and U-turns during his second term, which have eroded trust in America's will to cooperate with the Kingdom and its Sunni allies.

Secretary of State John Kerry refutes the existence of any such rift. He is clearly in denial unlike global markets that are taking the news seriously. Oil prices climbed to six-month highs within hours of the news breaking. Unfortunately for the US, the Kingdom's fury over America's deal with Russia on the disposal of Syria's chemical weapons, lending legitimacy to the Assad regime, cannot be wished away.

Obama has missed the point. Death is just as tragically final whether innocents are victims of chemical weapons, machine guns or airstrikes. What is the use of Syria giving up its sarin gas that has snuffed out the lives of hundreds when over 120,000 have been slaughtered by conventional means? This deal with the Devil was made to save the US President's face without a thought for the millions of refugees facing a cruel winter under canvas or those risking being drowned in the Mediterranean en route to European shores.

Saudi Arabia's rejection of a revolving seat on the United Nations (UN) Security Council over its "double standards" and ineffectiveness on working towards a Palestinian state and peace in Syria could be construed as a poke in America's eye. Kudos to the Kingdom for taking a strong position against the international community's impotence and for rightly demanding a shake up of the Security Council, a call echoed by the League of Arab States, the Organisation of Islamic Cooperation (OIC), the Gulf Cooperation Council (GCC) and Turkey. The Saudi authorities did well not to participate in a charade to keep up the Council's numbers when the Security Council can be paralysed by any one of its five veto-holders.

Washington has been hammering nails in the coffin of US–GCC relations since it failed to support Saudi–Gulf military intervention in Bahrain to thwart a violent Iran-backed insurgency. Its punitive measures against Egypt's army, pitted against Muslim Brotherhood rioters and terrorist groups in Sinai, has been seen as another slap to Saudi Arabia, the UAE and Kuwait, morally and financially invested in the most populated Arab country's security and stability.

Without question, the most destructive nail of all has been the US administration's flirtatious advances towards its supposedly "sworn enemy" Iran whose leadership has been fluttering its eyelashes westwards to get crippling UN, US and European Union (EU) sanctions lifted. Americans abroad have a reputation for being wide-eyed and naive, but how is it possible that the US President's national security advisors can be so easily conned by a silky-tongued mullah desperate to salvage Iran's free-falling economy? There is a lot more at stake here than haggling over the price of a Persian carpet.

It stretches belief that both sides are clamouring to forgive and forget almost overnight; there must have been back-channel discussions going on in secret for months. Talks between Iranian negotiators and a group of six world powers known as P5+1 have been hailed by the EU's Catherine Ashton as "substantive and forward-looking". Even so, since when does Iran deliver on its promises? Has mistrust over Iran's nuclear intentions not been the issue from day one?

Iranian détente with the West is swift-moving. The UK and Iran are already restoring full diplomatic relations; the US is poised to do so providing nuclear talks pan out. "If they're ready to go, we are ready to go," said a senior White House official. Once again, the West concentrates on the detail while ignoring the substance. Iran's nuclear programme is only one side of a multi-faceted coin.

Accepting Iran into the community of nations will empower Tehran's territorial ambitions while increasing the vulnerability of Gulf states. It will energize its Lebanese proxy Hezbollah, currently fighting alongside Iranian Revolutionary guards in Syria and bolster Iraq's Shi'ite-dominated government. A blind-eye will be turned towards Iran's material support of Yemeni Houthis and its lesser-known ties with Al Qaeda, whose operatives – Saif Al Adel, Abdullah Ahmed Abdullah, Sulaiman Abu Ghaith and Abu Hafs Al Mauritani – were afforded safe refuge in Iran.

Israel's Prime Minister Benjamin Netanyahu gets it and is lobbying the US not to fall for President Hassan Rouhani's sweet-sounding duplicitous words but his fears are being written off in Washington as the hysterical rants of a spoiler. On this matter, Uncle Sam is turning a deaf ear to his worries in favour of his about-to-be new best friend. The question is why?

America's faithful friends in the region are astonished and dismayed by this latest turn of events. Regular readers of my columns know that I saw this coming. I have been warning the Gulf Cooperation Council to protect against these eventualities for years, via newspaper articles, letters, reports and face-to-face meetings. Now that Saudi Arabia has woken up to the danger, finally there is hope. The time for relying on others is over. United and independent, with God's help, we will stand strong.

Obama's flirtation with Iran raises suspicions

4 April 2015

EVIDENCE IS MOUNTING that the Obama White House cannot be trusted to preserve the interests of Gulf states or their Arab allies. Were an Arab country perceived to be hostile to the US or the international community, it would be attacked without hesitation. On the other hand, this administration is treating its "favourite enemy" with a silk glove instead of the iron fist it deserves. This sure feels like a pro-Iranian administration.

US-prompted negotiations with Tehran to limit its nuclear enrichment programme have borne fruit. Both sides have displayed exceptional commitment and now a nuclear framework agreement has been agreed. It is easy to understand Iran's willingness to make concessions when sanctions have bit hard. But why the Obama administration has made supreme efforts to shake hands with America's long-time foe is perplexing.

US Secretary of State John Kerry behaves as though he is on his life's mission, even as Iran's Supreme Leader Ali Khamenei still calls "Death to America" while negotiations are underway. Far from being perturbed, Kerry is seen linking arms with his Iranian counterpart, Mohammed Javed Zarif as though he is reuniting with an old school pal.

Added to this love-fest was a video greeting from Obama to the Iranian people on the occasion of the Persian New Year. Iran should seize this moment marking "a new chapter in the history of Iran and its role in the world", he urged. It is not so much Iran's "role in the world" I am concerned about but rather its energized role in the Middle East region with a view to recreating a new Persian Empire.

Then, last month, both Iran and its Lebanese arm Hezbollah were mysteriously omitted from the US National Intelligence terrorism threat report – and this at a time when Iranian Revolutionary Guards and Hezbollah fighters are hand-in-glove with the Assad regime in Syria and while Iranian-backed Shi'ite Houthi militias are on the rampage in Yemen!

Most astonishing of all, is the news that US airpower is currently giving cover to an Iranian-led assault on Iraq's Sunni heartland Tikrit to rid the city of Daesh terrorists. *The Daily Show's* Jon Stewart nailed this anomaly on the head, saying, "Iran is … I don't want to say our ally, let's go with battle buddy." It was a battle directed on the ground by Iran's Quds Force commander General Qassem Suleimani, said by *The Guardian* newspaper to be "secretly running Iraq".

I find it extraordinary that President Barack Obama is bulldozing ahead seemingly unfazed by the legitimate concerns of America's friends in the region. Israeli Prime Minister Benjamin Netanyahu is practically tearing his hair out trying to prevent what he terms "a bad deal", which, he says, should be conditional upon Iran changing its aggressive behaviours. While I have no love for the Israeli Prime Minister, in an accident of fate,

Israel and Sunni Arab states find themselves on the same page vis-à-vis the Iran threat.

Netanyahu does enjoy support from some members of Congress; a few are coming up with extreme solutions. Senator John McCain, for instance, is openly advising Israel "to go rogue" – to bomb Iran and force the US to come to its defence. The letter signed by 47 Republican senators warning that President Obama's term is drawing to an end and, moreover, any agreement signed without Congressional backing could be ripped up by his successor, further evidences Republican discontent.

Saudi Arabia and its Sunni Arab allies are similarly piqued that they have been left out of the loop on the details of this potential détente. The Saudi Foreign Minister, Prince Saud Al Faisal, recently spelled out the Kingdom's stance. "It is impossible to give Iran deals it does not deserve," while accusing Iran of conducting "aggressive policies, and interfering in the countries of the region ... ".

In response Obama has launched a charm offensive to persuade the Gulf Cooperation Council (GCC) to come on board. He called the Saudi Monarch, King Salman bin Abdulaziz, and Sheikh Mohammed bin Zayed Al Nahyan, Crown Prince of Abu Dhabi and Deputy Supreme Commander of the UAE Armed Forces, to invite GCC leaders to discuss the deal with Iran at an upcoming Camp David Summit. This invitation should have been forthcoming before the preliminary negotiations were finalized, not after the fact.

We are Iran's neighbours in the potential firing line, not the US or the Europeans. If they were truly our allies, they should have prioritized our demands; beginning with the West's recognition of the term "Arabian Gulf", instead of the "Persian Gulf", when the coastlines of Arab states cover 80 per cent more area than Iran's. The GCC is being treated as an afterthought instead of a main player and partner, which is not only insulting but dangerous.

Should the GCC leaders accept Obama's invitation, I would urge them to show a united front by appointing just one head of state to represent all at Camp David. I reject the idea that the US President can just click his fingers; our kings, emirs, sheikhs and sultans are not at his beck and call. Moreover, whatever the approach the GCC decides to take to protect our interests, its resolve should be absolute and immovable. While it is my hope that Congress succeeds in blocking this foolishness, if that does not happen, we should be given the right to appoint our own Arab weapons inspectors to observe the work of the nuclear watchdog, the International Atomic Energy Agency (IAEA).

So, let us analyse what is really happening.

The Obama administration is ready and willing to seriously antagonize not only Israel, but also its major Arab allies, as well as a significant chunk of Congress, in order to conclude a pact that would leave Iran a threshold nuclear weapons state in ten years, when the agreement is set to expire. On a cost/benefit analysis, the US has more to lose than it has to gain. Could we be missing something here?

When the pieces of the puzzle are put together, a picture emerges giving credence to what was once mere speculation – the idea that a geopolitical "Grand Bargain" is being cemented to the detriment of predominantly Sunni states, which President Obama is throwing under a bus, one by one.

If George W. Bush handed Iraq to Iran, Obama has gift-wrapped it with a pretty bow. It is the same story with Syria. US assistance to the largely Sunni opposition is starting to look like a major bluff when, just last month, John Kerry announced that he would be willing to talk face-to-face with Assad. Until recently, the White House almost treated Egypt, battling terrorism in its cities and on the Sinai Peninsula, as a pariah state, while continuing to cuddle the Muslim Brotherhood.

It is no secret that during the start of Obama's presidential journey, sections of the US media were raising the possibility that President Obama, whose Kenyan father and Indonesian stepfather were both Muslims, might not be a Christian. Well, a few days ago, I watched a guest on an Arab television station argue that the US President is secretly a Shi'ite. I certainly would not go that far, but what I would say is that the White House's Middle East policies look like they have been lifted straight out of the ayatollahs' playbook.

We are used to dealing with administrations that are more respectful to their Arab allies, while this administration is headed by individuals, such as John Kerry and Vice-President Joe Biden, who have both been defending Iran's case for decades. Obama pledged to talk to the Iranians when he was still on the campaign trail so it is perhaps natural that the President would select like-minded senior figures.

The President's faith is not at issue. Islam respects Christians and Jews as the Peoples of the Book. And please do not mistake my words as an attack on Shi'ite Arabs; they are our brothers who share the same home. My criticism is reserved for individuals with allegiance to trumped-up human beings in Qom and especially those who connive to topple our governments.

The bottom line is this: Arab leaderships must be alert to plots and should use their best endeavours to seek political and military independence, along with new alliances. A Joint Arab Force, currently under discussion, is a good first step when our security and territorial integrity is under threat from a terrorist-supporting would-be hegemonic power that gets a White House red carpet.

Relying on the US for security is a mistake

21 May 2015

AT A PASSING GLANCE, President Barack Obama's meetings with the leaders of the Arab Gulf states have borne fruit in terms of furthering mutual respect and as a building block to closer cooperation. But when one digs beneath the flimflam and the verbal pledges – with the exception of a joint missile defence system and a promise that deliveries of US weapons would be fast-tracked – the recent Camp David Summit delivered few tangible benefits.

Indeed, more than a few commentators have described the meet as a US-hosted arms bazaar, one that will fill the coffers of American weapons manufacturers with billions of dollars. Plus the P5+1-Iranian nuclear deal is set to enrich and empower Tehran once economic sanctions are lifted.

Obama says Iran's newfound wealth will be used to improve lives rather than end up in the treasure chests of Hezbollah, the Shi'ite Yemeni Houthis or other troublemakers under the Iranian wing. Sorry, but to me that smacks of naivety at best, snake oil at worst.

According to a *Daily Telegraph* investigation, Iran's Supreme Leader controls "a financial empire" estimated to be worth $95bn, more than even the grandiose Shah had managed to accumulate. That alone should tell Mr Obama that Iran has no intention of prioritizing the needs of its people over its regional mischief-makers.

The question is whether the leaders of the Gulf Cooperation Council (GCC) countries should rightly feel secure from Iranian aggression now that the US President has promised to come to their defence, militarily if deemed necessary. Naturally, that assessment would be made by the White House, not by the threatened states. Without a signed and sealed security pact and in light of Obama's track record of hesitancy in ending regional conflicts or eradicating terrorism, I don't think so. Are we seriously to believe that the US would declare war on Iran were we to be menaced?

Obama's rhetoric spoke otherwise when he told *The New York Times* that internal threats to Gulf states are "bigger than Iran" and, at Camp David, he warned his guests not to "marginalize" Tehran. And even if Obama's undertaking was rock solid, his term expires in just over 18 months. What happens then?

In any case, while there is nothing wrong with cementing better relations with the US, we must not on any account rely on its protection or that of any other world power. Yemen proves that we are able and willing to protect ourselves and our allies and when the proposed Joint Arab Force comes into play, our capabilities will be strengthened. We have no need of guardians or bosses in foreign capitals. We have strong, well-equipped armies and air forces. We are not helpless, underage youths pleading to be defended, as characterized by sectors of the media.

I would urge GCC heads of state to put Camp David under a microscope to ascertain whether it was a genuine attempt on Obama's behalf to induce closer ties or merely a public relations exercise to bring Gulf states on board; a bad deal rewarding Iran for its hostility, regional interference and its backing of terrorists.

In my opinion, trusting the Obama administration to rein in Iran would be a huge mistake. US engagement with Iran was exactly the legacy Obama was after even before he moved into the Oval Office. And to that end he surrounded himself with pro-Iranian officials, such as Vice President Joe Biden, Secretary of State John Kerry and Deputy Secretary of State Bill Burns, who have all been championing détente with Iran for many years.

Obama's personal advisor and family friend, Valerie Jarrett, grew up in Iran, speaks Farsi, and was a main player along with Bill Burns in US-Iranian secret talks to pave the way for official negotiations. The President's National Security Council Director for Iran, Sahar Nowrouzzadeh is a former employee of the National Iranian-American Council, a pro-Iranian lobbying organization.

The President's own behaviour with regards to America's long-time sworn enemy was suspect since the beginning. He has been sending the Iranians video *Nawrus* (New Year) messages and letters to Iran's Supreme Leader. This year, Obama actually celebrated the Persian New Year at home with his wife and daughters!

Just as strange was Obama's silence concerning Iran's crackdown on street protests following elections. And if he condemns Tehran for its human rights abuses and lack of civil liberties, he must be whispering, because all we hear from him is condemnation of predominately Sunni Arab states on those issues.

Stranger still, while Obama comes across as the ayatollahs' new best friend, just days ago, the Ayatollah Khamenei attacked the US as "the greatest supporter and plotter of terrorism" and accused Washington of pursuing its own interests making the region insecure, while branding America as the enemy of both Shi'ite and Sunni Muslims. Far from committing to stay out of Arab affairs, Khamenei stressed that his country would continue supporting "the oppressed people of Yemen, Bahrain and Palestine in every way possible".

Are we really going to place our trust in America's Commander-in-Chief when he claims to be backing the Free Syrian Army (FSA) against the Syrian regime partnered with Iran and Hezbollah, even as his air force provides air cover to Iran's Quds Force and pro-Iranian Shi'ite militias in Iraq's Anbar province? This rabble with blood-stained hands – officially known as Popular Mobilization Forces (Al Shaabi) – has been deployed by Prime Minister Haider Al Abadi and is directed by the commander of Iran's Quds Force Qassem Soleimani. What is worse is that Iran is poised to send in ground troops as soon as it receives the go-ahead from the government.

And what does Mr Obama say about the shocking news revealed by *The Times* and other papers to the effect that the government in Baghdad is turning away tens of thousands of desperate Sunni refugees fleeing the city of Ramadi, recaptured by Daesh? Nothing much as far as I can tell! Iraq families with nowhere to go are being treated worse than foreign foes, barred entrance into their own capital city unless they happen to have a local "guarantor". This is a plan to reduce the Sunni population by sending them into the fray to die; there is no other explanation.

In reality, Saudi Arabia's towns bordering northern Yemen are under direct threat from Houthis, while Iran, close to being literally under the Iranian boot, constitutes a grave threat to Gulf states. Does the Obama administration plan to wait until the horse has bolted before acting? The Iranian plot to dominate the region is taking shape before our eyes. We are being surrounded. Yet the US President asks us to play nice with the plotters.

The bottom line is we did not get what we asked for. Obama's commitment to intervene in Syria to stop the regime's killing spree was off the table along with a joint defence pact along the lines of those the US has with Israel, Japan and South Korea. Moreover, he has turned down the Saudi request to purchase state of the art F-35 Joint Strike Fighters to maintain Israel's qualitative military edge over its neighbours.

And we certainly did not get what we need. Most importantly, any final agreement with Iran should be negotiated with the participation of Gulf states and co-signed by our leaders. Such agreement should not be limited to nuclear issues, but should be conditional upon Tehran's commitment to quit meddling in the affairs of Arab countries, notably Syria, Lebanon, Iraq, Yemen and Bahrain, whether directly (in the case of Iraq and Syria) or via its armed proxies (Lebanon and Yemen).

We should not trust any other countries but our own. We must not await instructions from the White House on how to pursue our own interests, as it is well known that US friendship is not proffered without strings. We must proceed with our mission to free Yemen of the Houthi rabble, continue with our efforts to destroy Daesh and lend every support to that sector of the Syrian opposition fighting for a democratic, inclusive state – as opposed to terrorist groups that seek to drag Syria back to the Middle Ages.

Lastly, we should insist upon the stringent terms outlined above. And if those terms are not put in writing, the GCC should work to weaken the Iranian regime once and for all, beginning with material support for the oppressed Ahwazi Arab citizens of Iranian-occupied Arabistan – a region Iran now calls Khuzestan – which supplies the country with most of its oil and gas.

I fear that Camp David was a well-timed bluff and its weapons bounty no more than candies to sweeten the pill. I trust and believe that our leaders understand the score and will maintain independent strategies to counteract threats to our very existence. We cannot gamble with tomorrow on the words of one man, even if that man is the President of the United States.

Our region has been burned many times before. If the past is a good predictor of the future, we should recognize that ultimately we must become the masters of our own destiny, which is far too precious to be handed to the safekeeping of fair-weather friends.

Iran deal goes from risky to farcical

23 August 2015

WHEN I FIRST LEARNED from Fox News that the International Atomic Energy Agency (IAEA) had signed a secret agreement permitting Iran to self-monitor at least one of its major nuclear sites, I shrugged off the news as a figment of someone's heated imagination. It is inconceivable that the world's nuclear watchdog, known for its professionalism and stringent monitoring, would sign off on something so bizarre – or so I initially believed.

Iraq, whose nuclear activities, both civilian and military, were dismantled following the Gulf War, certainly did not get off that lightly. Even after years of intrusive inspections, the IAEA under the directorship of Mohamed ElBaradei declined to present Iraq's deserved clean bill of health to the United Nations (UN) Security Council prior to the US-led invasion.

Yet the Islamic Republic of Iran, that has been spinning thousands of centrifuges to enrich uranium beyond accepted civilian levels and has refused to come clean on its past activities in this sphere, is trusted to inspect itself!

The IAEA cannot be accused of lacking innovation. Perhaps we will soon see drivers suspected of being under the influence allowed to test their own substance levels. Moreover, given the ayatollahs, whose mantra is "Death to America" are suddenly considered trustworthy, years of negotiations could have been avoided. A simple affidavit signed by the Supreme Leader would have sufficed just as well. Something does not smell right here.

Just as fishy is the Obama administration's claim that the US was not a party to this joker's agreement specific to the Parchin Military Complex – known as Separate Arrangement II – when it was approved by all P5+1 countries.

A White House spokesman has confirmed the administration is "comfortable" with the terms of the confidential side agreement between Iran and the IAEA. Are we to suppose that the IAEA took this dangerous, lackadaisical approach off its own bat?

According to a leaked draft of this "Separate Arrangement" divulged by the Associated Press, Iran is bound to provide the IAEA with photographs and videos of the various locations within Parchin, together with environmental samples. The question remains, how can those photos, videos and samples be verified as relating to the Parchin complex – and even if they are legitimate, who is to know whether or not they have been cherry-picked?

President Barack Obama's assurances that Iran's activities would be subject to "unprecedented verification" sound ever more hollow. The IAEA has been barred from this site, suspected of carrying out tests related to nuclear weapons, since 2005 and, now it has assented to being locked-out for the duration, which is out of character.

This surrender on the part of the IAEA leads me to believe that like so many other UN bodies, the IAEA is politicized; in this case, it has shaped its usual rock-solid strategies to suit political goals. However it is spun, this does not amount to "the most robust inspection regime" ever, as touted by the Obama administration.

The Associated Press report has been slammed by the IAEA as "misleading". However, the agency's Director General Yukiya Amano has not disavowed the draft's published content. He insisted that the arrangements are in conformity with long-established IAEA practices, while emphasizing that he has "a legal obligation not to make them public". One is left wondering why the public, not to mention US lawmakers, are being left in the dark.

As my regular readers would know, I have been against this unsatisfactory arrangement since day one, primarily because of its narrow remit. An acceptable deal would have been conditional upon Tehran ceasing its trouble-making and attempts to topple governments throughout the region.

My view broadly reflects the opinions of many of Iran's neighbours, rightly fearful that the lifting of sanctions will see Iran's coffers overflowing into the hands of its armed proxies.

President Obama has repeatedly countered our concerns on the grounds that curbing Iran's nuclear ambitions for ten years is better than no deal. I did not find his arguments credible then, but now the existence of secret side agreements have come to the fore, my suspicions that Iran is being deliberately empowered to fit a geopolitical end-game are heightened.

I would love to know why this entity that has been hostile to Western powers and their allies since its inception in 1979 is being rewarded for its terrorist associations and its regional will to power. Or is this animosity with the West just a farce to fool us?

European capitals are eyeing up lucrative trade deals and planning to reopen their embassies in Tehran. Iranian-Russian trade is set to expand exponentially. Iran's oil industry is gearing up to expand production of crude to pre-sanctions levels, which could see already depressed oil prices spiralling to new lows making the US fracking industry uncompetitive.

Obama's hard-sell campaign is not working, despite his frequent appearances on US news networks to plug the deal for all he is worth and his furious lobbying of Congress. He has even resorted to pleading with the American people to press their Congressional representatives to vote "yes", but is making little headway. A recently released CNN/ORC poll indicates that 56 per cent of Americans want Congress to reject the deal.

Just about every Republican presidential hopeful – with the exception of Jeb Bush who is on the fence – vows to undo the deal and re-impose sanctions; most of their Democratic rivals are trying to distance themselves from the topic.

Congress has 60 days to put the issue under a spotlight and is set to vote early next month on a "Resolution of Disapproval". If the vote fails to go in the President's favour, in theory, Congress could prevent him from lifting sanctions against Iran. Obama has threatened to use his veto, risking putting the White House and Congress on a war footing. In the unlikely event that two-thirds of Congress is opposed, requiring Democrats to jump camp, his veto is automatically overridden.

President Obama has been browbeating and bribing America's Middle East allies, appealing to the American people and playing the heavy with Congress to seal his deal, to the point of being unseemly. At stake is his legacy. It is my hope that America's lawmakers will rise to the occasion to ensure that we in my part of the world are not doomed to pay the price.

Europe's unseemly haste to embrace Tehran

27 August 2015

THE INK HARDLY DRIED on the Iran nuclear deal before European countries were racing to seal trade deals and reopen embassies. The mullahs have gone from zero to hero in the blink of an eye. Forgotten are Tehran's links to terrorists, attempts to overthrow Middle Eastern governments and mass gatherings organized to hurl insults and threats at the West.

Cast aside are concerns about Iran's suppression of minorities, its dismal human rights record or its practice of stoning women. Iran has made no statements to the effect it is willing to change. On the contrary, its message throughout has been one of defiance. It has not been required to denounce terrorism let alone its participation in terrorist acts.

Iran's crimes are suddenly of no consequence to Europe's democracies; they have purposefully put their blinkers on and are literally queuing with their hands out to beat down Tehran's golden doors. All they see now are flashing neon dollar signs. The Islamic Republic of Iran, soon to be flush with an $80bn-plus bonanza, is destined to become Europe's latest cash cow.

I was extremely disappointed and saddened at Britain's rush to reopen its Tehran embassy that has been closed for four years subsequent to coming under mob attack in November 2011. I have always had great respect and admiration for the UK that I consider as my second home, based on my homeland's historic ties and the principled stances taken by great leaders like Winston Churchill and Margaret Thatcher, who kept the "Great" in Britain, politically, militarily, industrially and economically.

I cannot imagine that those prime ministers, whose names remain engraved on world history to this day, grovelling before a country that five minutes earlier was their enemy, just to get their clutches on a fistful of dollars.

The UK's Secretary of State for Foreign Affairs, Philip Hammond, has been beating a track to Tehran since 2003. Naturally, he arrived with a trade delegation and took the opportunity to stress the "huge appetite" shown by British business to invest in Iran as well as the readiness of British banks to finance deals.

As the Iranian network Press TV has reported, Iran has recently hosted "a delegation of government ministers from Italy", who signed a Memorandum of Understanding to fund industrial, construction and infrastructure projects worth over €3bn. This comes on the heels of a visit by Germany's Minister for Economic Affairs and Energy, Sigmar Gabriel, with a team of manufacturers, as well as visits from Austrian, Serbian, Swiss and Azerbaijani government officials. Spain is also champing at the bit to board the gravy train.

Moreover, President Hassan Rouhani has been invited to visit Rome "in the coming weeks". Rouhani's red carpet travel schedule is getting fuller by the day. Following a visit to Tehran by France's Minister of Foreign Affairs and International Development, Laurent Fabius, accompanied by business leaders, he has been invited to visit the Élysée Palace in November. Russia and China, who have always been cosy with Tehran, are waiting in the wings with lucrative energy and weapons contracts at the ready.

No doubt President Barack Obama is rubbing his hands together awaiting his turn to get in on the action, delayed by pesky lawmakers who refused to take his word that his deal is the best thing that has happened since the invention of the wheel.

Iran and its Lebanese proxy in Lebanon, Hezbollah, have not changed. Nevertheless, America inexplicably saw it fit to remove those entities from its terror threat list even as Iran is fighting to preserve Syria's Killer-in-Chief and supporting a Houthi takeover of Yemen.

At least one senior Iranian official has gleefully announced his country's continued support for "resistance" groups, which translated means their armed minions and spies targeting Arabian Gulf states. Who can blame Iran's Arab neighbours for being rattled when a massive cache of weapons was recently discovered in Kuwait in the hands of a Hezbollah cell poised to create mayhem and bloodshed!

Where are Human Rights Watch and Amnesty International that relentlessly point fingers at Arab states for taking measures to protect their peoples? They have become so politicized that it appears they are willing to give Iran a free pass so as not to spoil the party.

I am starting to wonder whether there is more to the nuclear deal, which permits Iran to carry out self-inspections of its suspect Parchin Military Complex, than meets the eye – especially when there are other secret agreements between Iran and the International Atomic Energy Agency (IAEA), which the nuclear watchdog is legally bound not to disclose, even to the US and the other P5+1 countries. Believe that if you will!

In this case, one can only speculate about the existence of other secret arrangements between Iran and the Obama administration that has displayed unprecedented determination to ensure the deal passes muster with Congress and has gone to extreme lengths to persuade America's longstanding Middle East allies to come on board, including invitations to the leaders of Gulf states to weekend talks at Camp David. Likewise, President Obama is trying, unsuccessfully, to bribe the Israeli Prime Minister Benjamin Netanyahu into silence with a massive "military compensation package".

The Shah of Iran may have sat on the Peacock Throne, but it is my bet that Iran's Supreme Leader Ali Hosseini Khamenei is strutting around like a peacock these days, his feathers plumped up by European sycophants and endless praise from US officials. He is getting everything for nothing. Iran's nuclear infrastructure remains intact, uranium enrichment will be ongoing. Opening up some of the country's nuclear facilities, barring military sites, to intrusive inspections for 10 years is just a mere inconvenience, paling by comparison with the glittering rewards.

I warned again and again of the potential of a "Grand Bargain" being struck between the West and Iran many years ago and now it is unfolding before our eyes. I recall President Obama saying the nuclear deal could possibly lead to normalization of relations with Iran way into the future provided it sticks to its commitments. What is happening now makes a mockery of those cautious words.

Here is another prediction. Those Western leaders prostrating themselves before the Iranian leadership will live to rue the day. Enriched and emboldened, it is only a matter of time before Tehran strikes at their countries interests because its ideology and hatred for all things Western are immutable.

The Arab World, in particular Iran's closest neighbours, the Arabian Gulf states, must not only be alert to the coming danger, but should take a leaf out of Donald Trump's book by erecting an impenetrable wall in terms of military, surveillance and intelligence capabilities, to keep Iran, its mercenaries and proxies far from our shores. If we are not careful, the West's lust to bolster their failing economies will leave us hung out to dry.

America's gifts should not be understated

28 October 2015

SETTING ASIDE WASHINGTON'S woeful Middle East policies, it is worth reminding ourselves that the United States of America is one of the greatest nations on the planet. A world in which America did not exist would be poorer in terms of technology, space exploration, medical advances, entertainment and life-changing inventions.

Moreover, the fact that the US is such a stable country given the mix of religions and ethnicities is miraculous. Americans are us, all of us.

With the exception of Native Americans, their genes are our genes. This potpourri of 320 million individuals, whose ancestors escaped poverty and persecution to follow their dreams, has succeeded in uniting all with fierce pride and patriotism under one flag.

During my recent visit to the US I was privileged to be asked to deliver the keynote speech at the 24th Annual Arab–US Policymakers Conference in Washington DC before a huge audience. I spoke on many topics but focused primarily on the relationship between the US and the Arab World, our joint security and our historical friendship.

At the same time, I was critical of President Barack Obama's embrace of Iran, his lack of commitment towards a Palestinian state and his failure to intervene in order to save the Syrian people sandwiched between regime bombs and terrorists. That I was able to speak my mind on what I consider to be a country's mistakes on its own soil means that America is confident enough to hear constructive criticism unlike so many other countries that pay lip service to free expression.

America-bashing has become a popular pastime in many parts of the world, not least my own. We have come to the point where if anything does not work, we conclude it is all Washington's doing. We relish in anti-American conspiracy theories and accept them as the unvarnished truth no matter how ridiculous and embellished they seem. There is no nation without fault and no person without fault. Just as we are quick to fault America, we should also celebrate its blessings.

American administrations have blundered through the Middle East over the past 14 years. Few would deny that US interventions in Afghanistan, Iraq and Libya have been costly failures or that American mediation in the Palestinian-Israeli conflict has not worked. But we should accept that like every world power – Russia, China and the European Union (EU) – the US acts according to its interests.

Whether they like us, are with us or against us that is their prerogative as a sovereign nation whose sole responsibility is to its own citizens. We who have been affected by US actions also have the right to be transparent when airing our views of America's wrongdoing within our region.

Because America's global reach is so vast and as is often said "When Washington sneezes the rest of the world catches a cold", part of my keynote speech was devoted to next year's presidential election. Unfortunately, George W. Bush and his neoconservative advisors were a disaster for my neighbourhood. President Obama, who began his presidency with a warm reach-out to Muslims, turned out to be as bad, if not worse.

"Some might say that the presidential election is an American matter, and as an Arab I should not interfere," I told attendees at the Arab–US Policymakers Conference. "Allow me to correct them. The choice of a president and his policies will affect the whole world," I said.

Both during my speech and in a column published on 5 August, I endorsed the property magnate Donald Trump as the best candidate for president on the grounds that the career politicians are likely to repeat the same mistakes as their predecessors because they share similar mindsets. A businessman might not.

Obama is a great intellectual able to see all sides of the argument and view issues in shades of grey rather than black and white. Those can be assets in daily life or in the legal profession from which he is drawn, but in a leader they make for paralysis and indecision. Obama has proven the old adage, "he who hesitates is lost".

Thankfully, there is a new page for the United States in the offing. Polls indicate that voters seek a fresh face with fresh ideas, which is why Trump is still surging ahead despite his straight-talking that some consider offensive. Too rich to need campaign donors, he will not be under the heel of wealthy individuals, corporations or lobbying organizations.

He says what he thinks and goes with his gut, no matter what anyone else thinks. He may not have a complete grasp of all the issues yet, but he speaks truth as he sees it. His statements are only shocking to people who are not used to politicians coming out with the truth even when it hurts. His latest outpouring dominated headlines. He has verbalized what just about everyone in the Middle East and Gulf knows – the world would be a 100 per cent better place if Saddam Hussein and Muammar Gaddafi were still in power.

"I mean, look at Libya. Look at Iraq. Iraq used to be no terrorists. He [Saddam] would kill the terrorists immediately, which is like now it's the Harvard of terrorism," he told CNN. "If you look at Iraq from years ago – I'm not saying he was a nice guy, he was a horrible guy – but it was a lot better than it is right now. Right now, Iraq is a training ground for terrorists. Right now Libya .... Nobody even knows Libya. Frankly there is no Iraq and no Libya. It's all broken up. They have no control. Nobody knows what's going on." None of the so-called experts, retired generals or politicians, wheeled out to express their opinions, have ever come out with that gem of pure truth.

As of now, it looks like Trump and Hillary Clinton will be facing off at the finish, which is good news. America will choose between a strong and determined successful businessman and one of the toughest women in politics, whose composure before a Senate Committee investigating the attack on the US mission in Benghazi was outstanding. The lady looked presidential and even under vicious personal attack she remained cool, calm and collected.

This time Americans are spoilt for choice. But whether it is Trump or Clinton, or a combination of both, there is a good chance that Americans – and hopefully, the peoples of the MENA (Middle East and North Africa) region – will be the winners.

Saudi Arabia, a target of hypocrisy and double standards

8 January 2016

To MY ASTONISHMENT and dismay Western powers, human rights groups and international institutions have ganged up against the Kingdom of Saudi Arabia alleging "human rights abuses" over its execution of 47 terrorists, tried and sentenced for their crimes following lengthy transparent trials.

Rather than salute the Kingdom for its policy of zero tolerance of terrorists, many of Saudi Arabia's so-called allies seek to undermine its efforts with scurrilous statements and condemnatory rhetoric. Such criticism not only has little basis in fact in many cases it is spewed by some of the biggest human rights abusers on the planet.

No country has the right to interfere with another's domestic affairs let alone criticise its laws or judicial process. Every state must protect its people and state institutions from those who would do harm in the best way it sees fit – and this is especially pertinent in a region splintered by violence and conflict.

Firstly, Saudi Arabia, that borders war-torn Yemen and Iraq and is being openly threatened by Iran, is particularly in a sensitive situation, which is why it cannot afford to turn a blind eye to snakes within plotting its downfall no matter their religious persuasion.

Secondly, the Kingdom is the victim here when its embassy and consulate in Iran came under state-sponsored mob attacks; their computers and documents stolen even as diplomats called upon authorities for help, which went unheeded. Yet, instead of condemning the Iranian government for once again breaching diplomatic norms, the United States, the United Kingdom and the United Nations are blaming Saudi Arabia for executing a Saudi Shi'ite cleric who organized violent demonstrations against the government, supported terrorist cells and used his sermons to call for the overthrow of the state.

Thirdly, this is a case of people in glass houses. Take the US whose invasion of Iraq spawned Daesh and was the prime mover of the sectarian divisions Iraq and its neighbours now face. When we remember Guantanamo, Abu Ghraib, renditions, torture and the ongoing extrajudicial assassinations, clearly President Barack Obama's staff have taken courses in hypocrisy 101.

White House Deputy National Security Advisor Ben Rhodes has urged the Saudi government to show respect for human rights while senior administration figures slam Riyadh for "an apparent absence of due process" and "negligent disregard" for acting in ways that destabilize the region.

If there is one country to be blamed for inflaming the area, it is the United States that removed Saddam Hussein, a buffer between Iranian expansionism and Gulf states, toppled Muammar Gaddafi abandoning Libya to armed militias and stood aside as Daesh swept over great swathes of Iraq and Syria. Those errors of judgment were compounded last year by Obama's nuclear pact with a devil.

And how can anyone take US critics seriously when the country's presidential candidates call for all Muslim visitors to be banned along with vetted refugees including orphans as young as five years old? What moral right does America have to wag its finger at others over the death penalty when 31 of its states variously hang condemned prisoners, place them before a firing squad, subjected them to electrocution, gas them or finish them off with lethal injections that often go wrong? Last year a death row inmate Joseph Wood suffered one of the longest executions in US history taking two hours to die from a botched lethal injection.

Since 1976, the US has executed 1,422 convicts, 28 this year and 35 in 2014. Analysis undertaken by legal experts in Michigan and Pennsylvania found that 4.1 per cent were victims of a miscarriage of justice. Kudos to Obama for issuing an executive order related to gun control, but his tears for the victims of gun crimes merely echoed US double standards when it is the world's greatest supplier of lethal weapons.

The European Union (EU), which never fails to jump to Washington's command, has issued a statement asserting the execution of Sheikh Nimr Al Nimr raises "serious concerns regarding freedom of expression and the respect of basic civil and political rights". That complaint rings hollow from countries with refugees fleeing bombs and terrorism stuck in the freezing cold on their borders, without food, pleading to be allowed entry when it is their duty to give them asylum under international refugee conventions.

As for basic civil and political rights, France rightly banned demonstrations in response to terrorist attacks while deploying the army to patrol its streets. When a country is threatened – as France was and Saudi Arabia is – it tightens its security to ensure its people's safety.

Britain's comments have been fairly low key for which Prime Minister David Cameron is being criticized. However, the Foreign Office reiterated the UK's opposition to the "death penalty in all circumstances" as undermining human dignity. That view is Britain's prerogative, but why is the government singling out Saudi Arabia when its closest ally, the US, is high on the death penalty statistics list in company with Iran, Iraq and North Korea?

The same can be said for the United Nations (UN). Its Secretary General Ban Ki-moon has cited concerns over the nature of the charges and fairness of the judicial process, while urging Saudi Arabia to commute all death sentences. Who is he to judge the fairness of Saudi trials when he was not present – and why does he not address similar remarks to the governments of China, Iran and the US? The UN would do well to concentrate on its own problems when its peacekeepers are being investigated for the sexual exploitation of underage girls and women in the Central African Republic, Democratic Republic of Congo, Liberia, Haiti, Liberia and South Sudan.

Criticisms from the leaderships of Iraq would be laughable if the matter was not as serious. "Violating human rights leads to repercussions on the security, stability and the social fabric of the peoples of the region," stated Iraqi Prime Minister Prime Minister, Haider Al Abadi. Well, he should know! His Shi'ite-dominated government is one of the biggest violators of human rights and the greatest conductor of oppression and sectarian bias having sold out the Iraqi people to Tehran. When Arab country after Arab country is breaking off relations with Iran, his Foreign Minister Ibrahim Al Jaafari was in Tehran genuflecting before his masters.

Naturally, human rights organizations have jumped on the bash-Saudi Arabia bandwagon with enthusiasm. Human Rights Watch, accused of being a revolving door for the Central Intelligence Agency (CIA), accuses Saudi Arabia of discriminating against Shi'ite citizens, notwithstanding that Al Nimr was the only Shi'ite among 46 others. Reprieve urges the UK not to "turn a blind eye to such atrocities". What atrocities; the execution of terrorists? Amnesty International, which prioritizes the rights of terrorists over their victims, stated the carrying out of dozens of executions on the same day marks "a dizzying descent to yet another outrageous low for Saudi Arabia". Would it have been acceptable if the executions had been stretched out over a year as they are in the US?

It is strange that these groups are focusing on the Kingdom whereas over 700 individuals have been hanged by Iran this year alone (many of them Sunnis), a female cartoonist is on trial for the "crime" of shaking hands with her lawyer, a woman was sentenced to be stoned to death as recently as last December and poets and writers are being rounded up and tried.

In short, countries with blood on their hands should mind their own business. Saudi Arabia and its Arab allies have had enough of foreign interference and are resolved to stand against Iranian plots whatever it takes. We will no longer listen to states that contributed to our dangerous neighbourhood. The reaction of Saudi Arabia's fake allies is both disappointing and eye-opening. At least now we know which states to trust and which we cannot, a lesson I pray has been well learned.

Obama's historical mistake has dire repercussions

19 January 2016

THE DEED HAS BEEN DONE. The International Atomic Energy Agency (IAEA) has confirmed Iran's compliance with its obligations under the nuclear deal, the key to the lifting of anti-Iranian sanctions.

Iran's parliamentarians are hugging one another; most US Republican lawmakers are highly sceptical if not downright enraged at what they perceive to be a deal with the Devil. President Hassan Rouhani says Iran "has opened a new chapter" in respect to its relationship with the world while hailing the sanctions-lifting "a glorious victory".

It certainly is a victory for Iran, especially when the IAEA has stated its nuclear weapons ambitions were shelved nine years ago. Not only does it stand to receive its frozen assets worth in the region of $100bn, global corporations, including major oil giants, are queuing to negotiate lucrative deals. Moreover, word has it that Iran has been stockpiling oil to flood the market; this at a time when there is a glut that has driven down prices.

President Barack Obama has sought to silence the deal's critics asserting that Iran's implementation of the agreement "marks a fundamental shift in circumstances with respect to Iran's nuclear program". This is nothing but a red herring. Vice President Joe Biden and Secretary of State John Kerry were pushing for a US-Iranian détente long before they took office.

In fact, I predicted this dark day – so detrimental to Arab interests and security – would come years ago. At its core, this has little to do with nuclear weapons and all to do with facilitating Iran becoming a regional power in league with Washington to exert control over Arab states, in particular, Saudi Arabia and Gulf states, and to rebalance regional power in America's favour.

Iranian-born American academic and author Vali Nasr warned of an upcoming showdown between Iran and Saudi Arabia in his book *The Shi'a Revival* claiming that Iran's growing strength and reach makes it a preferred US partner because it is too strong to destroy and should be brought onside with engagement rather than confrontation.

Obama's former Pentagon chief Chuck Hagel was quoted saying: "the United States must find a new regional diplomatic strategy to deal with Iran that integrates our regional allies, military power and economic leverage".

I am convinced there is much more to this narrow deal than meets the eye. I transmitted my concerns of a potential "Grand Bargain" in a report to Gulf leaderships during June 2013 and I have laid out my fears in numerous columns since. If I was concerned then, I am deeply disturbed now. This is one time I hate to be right.

However, faced with this fait accompli the Arab World must join forces to shore up its defences. Thankfully, there are concrete moves in that direction. Saudi Arabia has woken up to the dangers following Iran's direct interference in its internal affairs, not to mention its use of proxies in Syria, Bahrain and Yemen. I am somewhat relieved that a Joint Arab Force is on the table and a Muslim anti-terrorism coalition has been formed with the participation of 34 predominately Muslim states.

Sad to say that among our sister nations there are those enjoying close relationships with Iran in a less-than-transparent way. We know that behind the scenes they have been furthering Iranian interests during its years of virtual isolation. Now they are no longer needed, it is only a matter of time before Iran turns on them too. They need to be cautioned by the GCC and if they continue their pro-Iranian policies, then we have no choice but to build a Trump-style wall between us and them.

Most importantly, Saudi Arabia and Gulf states can no longer rely on mere verbal assurances from their US ally purporting to be their protector when President Obama and his Secretary of State celebrate the release of billions of dollars to the biggest supporter of terrorism in our times. Obama has admitted that there are no guarantees that a portion of those billions will not go to advance Iran's ideological and territorial ambitions within the region.

Hezbollah, which the US has generously removed from its terrorist blacklist, will continue its killing spree in Syria and Iraq with impunity and will be free to transform Lebanon into an Iranian province. Iran's efforts to grab control of Yemen and Bahrain, upon which it has made successive territorial claims, will be strengthened by mega sums of cash. Obama is aware the money will be spent on terrorism and the further destabilization of the Middle East and in particular the Gulf, but has ignored the concerns of America's friends in his rush to seal a narrow agreement that fails to take Iran's crimes into account.

Obama has tried to placate GCC countries with an invitation to heads of state to meet with him at his Camp David retreat. Just last week, US Secretary of State John Kerry met with Saudi Minister of Foreign Affairs Adel Al Jubeir to persuade him there is nothing to worry about, which according to press reports he is not buying, especially since the Obama administration expressed its "dismay" over the execution of convicted terrorist Nimr Al Nimr while seeming less dismayed over the torching of the Kingdom's embassy and consulate by a rabble suspected of being in the regime's pay.

Fact is the US must put its money where its mouth is. Sweet words partnered with yet more offers of weapons sales will not provide us with a good night's sleep. Basically, our governments must receive clarification from Mr Obama as to whether the US is with us or with Iran. We must demand that the White House proves it genuinely has our interests at heart by leaning on Tehran to comply with the following measures:

- The official severing of Iran's relationship with Hezbollah, which is strangling Lebanon and has chosen the wrong sides in both Syria and Iraq.

- An end to Iran's arming and financial support of Shi'ite Houthis in Yemen.

- A commitment from Iran's Supreme Leader Ali Khamenei to dismantle its terrorist cells within Gulf states and to quit their infiltration with spies.

- Tehran's agreement to negotiate the independence of Arabistan, renamed Khuzestan following Iran's seizure, so that the Ahwazi

Arab population, reduced to third-class citizens, can regain their independence, their natural resources and their dignity.

- Iran's acceptance that the body of water it refers to as the "Persian Gulf" is henceforth to be known as "the Arabian Gulf" given that 85 per cent of the population of countries surrounding the Gulf (including Ahwazi Arabs) are Arab.

I must point out that I have nothing against the Iranian people of whatever faith or sect. They have all been oppressed socially, economically and politically since 1979 when Ayatollah Ruhollah Khomeini turned up to send the country back to the Middle Ages. Despite its wealth, 55 per cent of urban Iranians live below the poverty line. People there live in fear in a country where women are stoned, men hung from cranes in public places and even poets and songwriters are jailed and lashed.

Given that the US, that fought hard for the deal, is now Iran's prime benefactor, the Obama administration should find ways to ensure the billions of dollars released are used to build the economy, improve infrastructure and create jobs and must tie any future rapprochement to an improvement in Iran's miserable human rights record.

I look forward to the day when the Iranian people reject their fanatical regime and reclaim the freedoms and prosperity they enjoyed under the Shah. Only then should Iran be welcomed into the community of nations – and in that event I will be celebrating too.

Western powers shamefully kowtow to Iran

30 January 2016

IRAN'S TREASURY IS OVERFLOWING. President Hassan Rouhani, touring European capitals on a shopping spree, is being treated like royalty. Italy was so keen not to offend the sensitivities of their guest that white panels were placed around ancient statues in a museum, and it was rewarded for its hospitality with deals totalling over $18bn. France's government welcomed Rouhani promising a new beginning in relations prior to the mutual signing of 20 lucrative agreements worth billions.

They say money talks. This time it is shouting loud, trumping Europe's so-called values and the interests of the continent's tried and true friends. Forgotten is Iran's shocking human rights record along with its terrorist proxies, aggression towards Saudi Arabia and Gulf states; concerns regarding Tehran's partnership with the Syrian butcher conveniently shelved. Ignored are the Ayatollah Khamenei's ongoing chants of "Death to America" and "Death to Israel". Glossed over are its repression of the Iranian people and its relegation of minorities, such as the Ahwazi Arabs, to third-class citizen status.

It was left to ordinary citizens who went to the streets of Paris and Rome as well as children in the bombed-out Syrian city of Aleppo to vent their disgust at Rouhani's grand European tour. "Ask Iran to stop killing us in our country" read the children's posters. But Italy and France had more important priorities. This was not the moment for finger-wagging in their view when the Iranian President was poised to sign on a whole host of dollar-illuminated dotted lines.

It is as if we have woken up to find ourselves in a parallel universe where everything we hold dear has been reversed. Iran signed up to abandoning a nuclear weapons programme it had binned in 2009 according to the nuclear watchdog the International Atomic Energy Agency (IAEA), and was promptly welcomed into the international's community's fold like a long-lost favourite son flush with a bonanza of up to $100bn and the opening of doors to oil, gas and trade deals.

As if the sight of European heads of state bowing and scraping, clutching begging bowls to gain the favour of a representative of a country considered an enemy state a mere few months ago, is not humiliating enough, the once mighty United States is accepting Iranian insults and slaps with a virtual "Thank you, Sir!"

First we hear that Iran detained 10 US naval personnel whose vessel "accidentally" strayed into Iranian waters. They were made to kneel with their hands behind their heads on the deck of their own ship before being paraded on Iranian State TV to offer apologies. Quite a propaganda coup for Iranian authorities and the hordes of anti-Western hardliners! And even as Iran was milking their captives' humiliation for all its worth, the White House assured Americans thus: "We do not see this as hostile intent. They have been well treated."

And now we read the headline "Iran warns US warship to leave waters near the Strait of Hormuz" followed by a report beginning: "Iran navy warned a US warship on Wednesday to leave waters in the Sea of Oman near an area where the Islamic Republic was performing military drills." The US vessel beat a hasty retreat even though it was in international waters and was later accused by Iran's fleet commander of spying on Iran's activities.

The question now for Saudi Arabia and Gulf states, who have been assured by President Barack Obama that their security is paramount, is how can the US cooperate with us against Iranian plots when its own navy appears to be running scared and its Commander-in-Chief hails the new détente and makes excuses for Iran's shameful behaviour?

How much abuse is the most powerful country with the strongest military on earth willing to swallow and why is Obama doing his utmost to keep the ayatollahs sweet? It is hard to believe that the US that has always flexed its muscles to save a single American citizen is now making prisoner swap deals with their kidnappers to release seven dual nationals.

A top Iranian commander disclosed that an amount of $1.7bn was paid in exchange for their freedom. The State Department issued a statement to the effect the amount was paid in relation to a pre-1979 case related to a sale of military equipment plus $1.3bn in negotiated interest. That is a pretext to cover America's long-held policy of not paying rogue states or terrorists to avoid encouraging further abductions. When the payment was purportedly due in the 1970s, only a simpleton would neglect to ask "Why now?"

It is little wonder Rouhani's smile is wide these days when billions are pouring in courtesy of the Obama administration that initiated the sanctions-lifting and the unfreezing of Iranian assets, a hefty portion of which will no doubt be spent on bolstering Iran's military capability and that of militias and spies on Arab lands.

Iran's policies towards the West and its meddling in the affairs of Arab states remain unchanged. Its leaders' rhetoric may have softened temporarily because they are desperate to revitalize their country's aviation industry with new airplanes and spare parts, not to mention securing buyers for its oil and other commodities. They must be chuckling seeing the haste with which major European states are racing to re-open their embassies in Tehran while showering the Iranians with praise and invitations to arrive on state visits.

Let us face it, Iran the global midget has gained the upper hand merely because it has agreed to more intrusive IAEA monitoring for a ten-year period and has put a percentage of its centrifuges to bed. Obama and Secretary of State John Kerry have robbed the American people of their pride. They have greatly diminished the international status of their great nation that not so long ago inspired respect and instilled fear in the hearts of its enemies.

Obama has been widely accused of leading from behind on foreign policy. No so today! He is the one who is being led and if GCC member states fail to recognize how the Obama administration is wittingly or unwittingly altering the regional order, I am afraid we may be being led to the slaughter.

It seems an age ago since the Muslim world was excited hearing Obama's promises made during a visit to Cairo University in 2009. He called for a new beginning between the United States and Muslims. He pledged to give Iraq to the Iraqis whereas it is a de facto province of Iran. He pledged to pursue a Palestinian state with patience and dedication, which has now been scrubbed off his "to-do" list. He later stepped back from rescuing the Syrian people but he was instrumental in toppling Muammar Gaddafi before abandoning that country to armed militias and terrorists. Adding insult to injury, he is complicit in furthering Iran's territorial and ideological ambitions.

I can only respectfully ask GCC heads of state to take a long hard look at the big picture and take decisions accordingly. If America continues to bend to Tehran's diktats perhaps it is time to re-evaluate our relationship with Washington. A friend who plays both sides is no friend at all.

Obama's anti-Arab views confirm suspicions

22 March 2016

JEFFREY GOLDBERG'S APPRAISAL of the "The Obama doctrine" that has caused a furore in response to the President's scathing views on America's Arab allies has done us a favour. Now we know beyond question where we stand in the US global pecking order, which appears to be way down the scale of the Obama administration's priorities.

Barack Obama no longer believes that the Middle East is "terribly important to American interests" but insists that the Saudis need to share the region with their Iranian foes in the form of a "cold peace". Of great concern is his failure to disagree with his interviewer's observation that he "is less likely than previous presidents to axiomatically side with Saudi Arabia in its dispute with its arch-rival Iran".

That makes sense when he has evidently forgiven the past sins of both Iran and its Lebanese proxy Hezbollah. It comes as Iran has been legitimized and enriched by the US-initiated nuclear deal.

I strongly second the published rebuttal of HRH Prince Turki Al Faisal headed "Mr Obama, we are not 'free riders'"… "You add insult to injury by telling us to share our world with Iran, a country that you describe as a supporter of terrorism and which you promised our king to counter its 'destabilizing activities'" was his message to the US President.

Prince Turki rightly highlights that Saudi Arabia initiated the meetings that resulted in the coalition fighting Daesh, offered ground troops, is assisting Yemenis to reclaim their country from pro-Iranian Houthi rebels, and has established a coalition to help eradicate terrorists from the planet.

I too was appalled at Obama's disrespectful opinions, especially those related to Saudi Arabia, but not surprised because they correlate with his actions and non-actions within the region. Rather than the "free riders" and "oppressors" he allegedly considers Saudi Arabia and other Arab states to be, it is beginning to look like we are the ones who have been taken for a ride.

In his much celebrated 2009 reach-out to the Muslim World at Cairo University, he called upon Muslims to join with the US in "a new beginning" based on mutual respect. He was flattering, acknowledging the contributions of Muslims to civilization while admitting many of his own country's mistakes. He commiserated with Palestinian suffering and was later to pledge that the creation of a Palestinian state was a goal he would actively pursue. He dropped that pledge at the first hurdle and it appears respect has become a one-way street.

It turns out the Cairo address was a con. When Goldberg asked Obama what it was meant to achieve, he said: "My argument was this: let us all stop pretending that the cause of the Middle East's problems is Israel … I was hoping my speech could trigger a discussion, could create space for Muslims to address the real problems they are confronting – problems of governance, and the fact that some currents of Islam have not gone through a reformation that would help people adapt their religious doctrines to modernity." So it was not a reach out at all; it was a lecture dressed in sweet-smelling roses.

According to Goldberg, the day he stepped back from his own red line on Syria's use of chemical weapons was "the day he defied not only the foreign-policy establishment ... but also the demands of America's frustrating, high maintenance allies in the Middle East" – countries, he complains privately to friends and advisors, that "seek to exploit American 'muscle' for their own narrow and sectarian ends".

On the contrary, Mr Obama, it was America's unwarranted muscle in Iraq that fuelled the sectarianism that bore Daesh, and it was your intervention in Libya that helped create the armed militias and the feuding tribes, creating a chasm between Benghazi and Tripoli that is being filled by Daesh fighters fleeing Syria. Bringing down the Syrian dictator, who has murdered hundreds of thousands of his own people and caused over half the population to flee their homes, would have been a just war, but you turned your back on the Syrian people.

As for America's "high maintenance allies", I would remind you that Arab troops were on the frontlines of Desert Storm and fighter jets from Saudi Arabia and other Gulf Cooperation Council (GCC) states were in the air. A report by the Rand Corporation tells us that the Kingdom paid over half of the costs of that war to liberate Kuwait, and, as you well know, without Arab military purchases running in the billions of dollars, the coffers of US arms manufacturers would dramatically shrink.

Let us not forget too that America's generosity to less wealthy Arab countries comes with strings. One must also question why you rapped Egypt on the knuckles for bombing Daesh in Libya if you are keen to see Arabs sort out their own problems.

Obama's insults come fast and furious. He says his insistence that Arab and European states took the lead in striking Muammar Gaddafi's Libya was to prevent them from "holding our coats while we did all the fighting". He has questioned "the role" played by "America's Sunni Arab allies in fomenting anti-American terrorism", and blames Saudi Arabia and Gulf states for Indonesia's conservatively religious status.

Yet, he was one of the Muslim Brotherhood's greatest cheerleaders in its quest to transform Egypt into an Islamist theocracy, overlooking anti-American statements by its leadership including this from the mouth of its jailed former Supreme Guide Mohamed Badie, who described the US as an infidel that "does not champion moral and human values and cannot lead humanity".

Saudi Arabia and Gulf states have been close allies of the United States since 1945 when King Abdulaziz Al Saud joined President Franklin D. Roosevelt on board an American cruiser off Egypt's shores to sign an oil agreement. Apart from a few minor hiccups, the relationship has always been warm and mutually beneficial.

However, when Obama was asked whether he considered Saudi Arabia a friend, he answered: "It's complicated." That certainly wasn't the impression he left with GCC heads of state and high officials who accepted his invitation to Camp David where they accepted his assurances over the Iran deal!

In a world beset by increasing dangers, we need the US to retain its role as the global power as long as its policies are applied fairly and justly within our neighbourhood. President Obama will be packing up to leave the White House in less than nine months. There will be few tears shed in my part of the world; he has let us down.

I can only hope that the coming Leader of the Free World will be more appreciative of our efforts to battle against terrorism and bring stability to the region. I trust that he or she will see Iran bathed in its true colours, assist us to free the downtrodden Arabs in occupied Ahwaz, release Iraq from its Iranian puppet government, Lebanon from Hezbollah's stranglehold, and treat the Israeli-Palestinian peace process as a priority. In short, America needs a president that leads from the front, not from behind – and so do we.

Saudi Arabia must stand firm against US insults and threats

19 April 2016

CONGRESS IS HURLING DAGGERS at Saudi Arabia, America's staunchest Arab ally since 1933. Several presidential candidates, including Hillary Clinton and her rival Bernie Sanders, have positioned their own darts ready to strike. Some 15 years have gone by since Al Qaeda attacked the United States for which Afghanistan and Iraq paid, and are still paying, a terrible price.

Yet, Congress has chosen to regurgitate this issue with a bill permitting the Kingdom to be stripped of its sovereign immunity so that lawyers acting for the families of 9/11 victims eyeing massive pay-outs can drag the Saudi government through US courts alleging Saudi participation.

Those lawmakers championing the passing of this scurrilous law designed to entrap Saudi Arabia in lengthy litigation are not only casting unacceptable slurs on the integrity of the Saudi royal family, they are risking the serious erosion of already frayed US relations with the Kingdom, Arabian Gulf states and their Sunni allies.

According to a report in *The New York Times*, they are also placing America's economy at grave risk, the ripples from which could negatively impact the global economy. It does not help that there is another bill working its way through Congress aimed at curtailing weapons sales to Saudi Arabia due to its intervention in Yemen on behalf of the legitimate Yemeni government.

The Saudi Foreign Minister Adel Al Jubeir has warned that to avert the risk of his country's treasury securities and assets in the US being frozen by courts, the Kingdom would be obliged to sell up to $750bn of its holdings. Bernie Sanders is yelling "blackmail". "Saudi Arabia is one of the most powerful and wealthiest families of the world; that's why they can threaten to withdraw hundreds of billions of dollars from our economy," he said. What he fails to understand is that there is no attempt by Saudi Arabia to threaten. Which country on earth would leave that amount of money vulnerable to the whims of American politicians on election campaigns!

If this measure goes into effect it could well be the straw that breaks the camel's back. It comes on the heels of revelations by Jeffrey Goldberg writing in *The Atlantic* that President Barack Obama considers Saudi Arabia and other Sunni Arab states as "free riders" and when asked "aren't the Saudis your friends?" he responded saying: "It's complicated." Adding insult to injury, he expressed his belief that Saudi Arabia must learn to share the neighbourhood with Iran.

On Wednesday, Obama is scheduled to arrive in Riyadh on a charm offensive; he will need every ounce he can muster, especially when he is responsible for rearranging the regional geopolitical deckchairs with a deal with Iran, the largest sponsor of terrorism, whose main target is destabilizing the security of Gulf Cooperation Council (GCC) states, which is why Saudi Arabia has formed a 34-nation Muslim anti-terror coalition and has given its blessing to a Joint Arab Force.

Admittedly, Obama is greatly opposed to the Congressional bill and is furiously lobbying against it, but he is doing so solely because he is concerned about its potential diplomatic, military, intelligence, legal and economic repercussions and is right to be so concerned, particularly if all GCC member states decided to follow suit by liquidating and repatriating their own US bonds and other assets. Furthermore, a precedent would be established encouraging Iraq, Afghanistan and Pakistan to sue the United States for the deaths of hundreds of thousands of soldiers as well as for the civilian victims of drone strikes.

Hillary Clinton and Bernie Sanders, however, support it, saying they stand with the 9/11 families notwithstanding that Congress approved a $7bn compensation fund for the families of the fallen, the average payout over $2m. Sanders has accused Saudi Arabia of spreading a "horrific fundamentalist ideology", going so far as accusing Riyadh of supporting Daesh and other terrorist organizations. In addition, Clinton told ABC News: "Obviously, we've got to make anyone who participates in or supports terrorism pay a price ... ."

Enough is enough! The Obama administration has done all that it can to undermine the forward trajectory of Egypt since its Muslim Brotherhood friends were removed from power and now Congress has launched an offensive against Saudi Arabia, which, unlike Iran, was not indicted in the 9/11 Commission Report that reads "no evidence" was found "that the Saudi government as an institution or senior Saudi Arabia officials individually funded the organization" or conspired with or funded the attackers.

That same report did, however, evidence that there was increased contact between Iran and Al Qaeda and confirms that several of the 9/11 terrorists were allowed to travel through Iran without receiving the usual stamp in their passports. More recently a US federal court entered a ruling to the effect Iran and its Lebanese sidekick Hezbollah "materially and directly supported Al Qaeda" in the attacks on America and are responsible for paying damages to stricken families. Are those lawmakers who cooked up this bill implying that regional foes and rivals, Saudi Arabia and Iran, were in collaboration? That is not only insulting, it laughable.

It is true that many of the hijackers were Saudi nationals. Then again, many of the suicide bombers and shooters involved in the attacks on Paris and Brussels were Belgian and French nationals, so are we to conclude that the Belgian or French governments were pulling their strings? Of course not! Likewise, several of Daesh's decapitators are British. Is there anyone stupid enough to take the UK government to court? As a matter of fact, a substantial number of Americans have long asked US governments for greater transparency on events surrounding 9/11 but to date their questions remain unanswered.

I would love to know the real reasons why Congress is ignoring the established Iranian connection to go after Saudi Arabia. Why is the Kingdom the preferred target? I have found it hard to believe that US politicians of all political stripes are out to weaken GCC states and other majority Sunni countries, but the proof is building daily. The Iranian President gets bouquets and billions. Saudi Arabia gets slanders and snubs. Such double standards can no longer be brushed under the rug.

Some of the blame for the circumstance in which we find ourselves should fall to us Arabs and Gulf nationals. We have been far too quick to forgive and too willing to be convinced that the mighty US is our forever friend and has our interests at heart. Now, more than ever, we need tangible proof that Washington is on our side or else we should study alternative options. President Obama will be treated with courtesy and hospitality during his visit to Riyadh this week. But this time his red carpet should not be strewn with flowers but with hard truths.

PART 2

The Arab World: the real and present dangers threatening to destroy the Middle East

4

The devastation of the Cradle of Civilization: Iraq's downfall

Introduction

THE MIDDLE EAST has had more than its fair share of war, foreign invasion and occupation over centuries. Foreign interference has exasperated this already turbulent region, and I fear that if it continues then the entire Middle East will be under threat.

Look what has happened to Iraq – the Cradle of Civilization. Destroyed beyond repair by foreign interference. The US and its allies are directly to blame for the destruction of the country.

The West only intervenes militarily when such interventions suit its geopolitical interests. It has made some serious foreign policy mistakes in the region and the consequences have been dire.

It is no secret that the US and its allies have vested interests in this part of the world, and many of their decisions have been made out of self-interest.

Today, Iraq has been devastated economically, socially and physically due to the decision of one man – former US President George W. Bush – who invaded the country under false pretences. His decision marked the beginning of the end of Iraq, and gave Iran the access to the region it always craved.

By Bush's side was his ally, Britain. The long-awaited Iraq Inquiry report by Sir John Chilcot, released in July 2016, strongly criticized the way former British Prime Minister Tony Blair took his country to war in Iraq in 2003 on the basis of "flawed" intelligence with inadequate preparation at a time when Saddam Hussein did not pose an "imminent threat".

Lord Prescott, the deputy prime minister at the time of the invasion, said the Iraq War was "illegal". Prescott said the Chilcot report was a "damning indictment of how the Blair government handled the war – and I take my fair share of blame". (See *Independent*, "Chilcot report: John Prescott says Iraq War was illegal", 10 July 2016).

In its heyday, under the reign of former President Saddam Hussein, Iraq acted as a shield protecting the Sunni world from the Iranian Shia crescent and its expansionist plans. Iran should have been the one coming under fire from the West, not Iraq. The biggest threat to peace in the region is – and always has been – Tehran.

Saddam Hussein took power the same year as the Islamic Revolution in Iran, in 1979. The then Shah was replaced with the radical regime of Ayatollah Ruhollah Khomeini, who had just returned from years of living in exile. Relations between the neighbouring countries became increasingly tense, and one year later, in 1980, Iraq invaded Iran, resulting in a costly eight-year war that impoverished the country. During this time Iraq's relations with the West were warming. It was not until 10 years later, when Iraq invaded Kuwait, that things turned sour with the West and resulted in the Gulf War. This was a nail in the coffin for both Saddam and his country.

Following Iraq's dramatic fall, it was inevitable that other Arab nations would follow. The Arab World's buffer was destroyed.

Bush's actions spread well beyond Iraq. While I understand that as Leader of the Free World he had to do something, his methods were questionable and the ramifications beyond repair. He should have looked for the real problem instead of using Saddam Hussein as a scapegoat and destabilizing the region. Former British Prime Minister Tony Blair has to accept his share of responsibility too. Although I have to give him a certain amount of kudos for publicly admitting his mistake. (See *The Guardian*, "Tony Blair makes qualified apology for Iraq war ahead of Chilcot report", 25 October 2015.) In an interview with CNN Blair said: "I apologise for the fact that the intelligence we received was wrong.... I also apologise for some of the mistakes in planning and, certainly, our mistake in our understanding of what would happen once you removed the regime."

The pretence of bringing so-called democracy to Iraq has had dire consequences on the country and wider region. Large parts of Iraq have since fallen under the rule of the Islamic State in Iraq and the Levant (ISIL), or Daesh. The rest of the country is fast being divvied up between Iran's mullas and ayatollahs thanks to foreign meddling. Iran has played a clever game and the fruits of its labour are paying off to the detriment of many. The consequences are a direct result of the US, which dismantled the Iraqi army, weakened the Sunni and Shi'ite Arabs and strengthened the dormant militias with Iranian loyalties. This, in my view, is the biggest and most catastrophic failure in Iraq. Sunnis have become refugees in their own country.

The land grabs by the jihadists operating in Iraq have been unprecedented. Daesh took much of the world by surprise when it claimed Iraq's second-largest city of Mosul in June 2104. It marked the biggest strategic victory for the group – as well as being a symbolic win. City after city fell into their hands, including Fallujah, one of the largest cities in Anbar province. The extremist group has since ruled its territories with a brutal legal system where residents live in fear; women's rights are restricted, flogging is commonplace, crimes are counteracted with draconian punishments, and shrines and Shi'ite mosques destroyed.

World leaders must eradicate Daesh in Iraq and Syria as quickly as possible and ensure it does not emerge in an even more virulent form. As the organization gains more ground it gains more prominence. It operates its own bureaucracy and even publishes textbooks for schools; it collects taxes and enforces its own laws. (See the *Middle East Institute*, "Outside views on the U.S. strategy for Iraq and Syria and the evolution of Islamic extremism", 2 February 2016.) With each passing day it is growing stronger while the international coalition that is trying to "degrade and destroy" it is making little headway. The US-led coalition and Iraqi government forces are working together to tackle Daesh, but they are a long way off from driving out the jihadis.

Daesh has caught the world's attention – but not for the atrocities and devastation it has caused to the Middle East – instead for instilling fear through international terrorism; targeting civilians in Paris and downing a Russian passenger plane in Egypt. The Western world has paid little attention to the obliteration of Syria and Iraq. It only woke up once Daesh was present on its shores. That is the sad reality.

If Daesh had been prevented from making a home for itself in the Middle East, it would not be the beast it is today. Daesh has emerged as a consequence of the Iraq War.

Tony Blair concurs. He told CNN he saw merit in the view that the Iraq War was to blame for the rise of Daesh. "I think there are elements of truth in that," he said when asked whether the Iraq invasion had been the "principal cause" of the rise of Daesh.

The fact is, under Saddam Hussein's rule Iraq was a much safer place than it is today. Irrespective of whether you liked him or not, business and the country's economy were chugging along quite nicely, although I admit accurate data is hard to ascertain given economic data was considered a state matter under Saddam's rule. Let us not forget though that Iraq was flourishing in the 1970s and '80s – even while it was at war with Iran. There was universal healthcare and a solid education system. During Saddam's time literacy levels rose significantly and the country had one of the best educational performances in the region.

The former Iraqi leader made some very big mistakes during his long tenure. The Kuwait invasion in 1990 being one of them. The sanctions that followed took a huge toll on the Iraqi economy, but the "illegal" US-led invasion in 2003 – on the pretext that Iraq was developing Weapons of Mass Destruction (WMDs) – was one of the biggest political mistakes ever made by the West. The US went in despite no strong evidence of WMDs.

Daesh has capitalized on Iraq's demise and inadequate security post-Saddam Hussein's fall. Stratfor – a geopolitical intelligence firm that provides strategic analysis – says that the territories of Iraq and Syria that are controlled by Daesh are perhaps "the most volatile conflict today".

A United Nations (UN) report, released in early January 2016, (see *The New York Times*, "U.N. quantified the suffering in an Iraq divided and under attack", 19 January 2016) says that nearly 19,000 people have been killed in Iraq between January 2014, around the time Daesh began seizing territories, to the end of October 2015. It said a further 40,000 had been injured – mostly at the hands of Daesh. The report went on to say that more than three million had been displaced from their homes during that time. The UN described it as a "staggering level of violence" in the country. The 40-page dossier details the human suffering ignored by the world; unlawful killing, abduction, bombings, mass graves, untreated illness and malnutrition, as well as abuse by government forces. How Iraq can ever recover from the mess it is in today I do not know. This is the hard reality, and mark my words we will see other countries follow if the world does not act.

Sons of Abraham ... beware

1 April 2006

IN AN INTERVIEW on the BBC programme *Hardtalk*, the presenter Stephen Sackur asked the cultural editor of the infamous paper *Jyllands-Posten* if it would publish, under the slogan "Freedom of Speech" that led it to insult the Prophet Mohammed (PBUH), a caricature of a Jewish Rabbi killing a Palestinian child while holding a Nazi emblem. The editor answered very rudely: "No, because there are limits that should not be exceeded."

Although it is difficult to be logical under circumstances where our Prophet (PBUH) was so gravely and disgustingly insulted, I did choose to look at the issue and study it objectively, beginning with this query: Why does the West insult a person regarded by 1.3 billion Muslims as the most important being after the Lord?

While trying to answer that question, I remembered a piece of news reported by most international radio stations. It was about the arrest of British writer David Irving in southern Austria on 11 November last year on charges that he denied the existence of the Holocaust. He received a jail sentence of three years. However, Austria is not the only European country that enacted laws that regard the denial of the Holocaust as a grave crime that must be penalized. Nine other European countries, including France, Switzerland and Germany, have enacted such laws.

The Holocaust is not my subject here. What I wish to stress is that those advanced countries respect the feelings and sentiments of 14 million Jews in the world, while deliberately ignoring those of 1.3 billion Muslims.

The offending caricatures were published in September 2005. London's *The Guardian* newspaper reported that the same Danish paper that published them had, in April 2003, refused to publish caricatures drawn by Danish caricaturist Christopher Zoeler about Jesus Christ. This proves that the paper was acting in bad faith and that it deliberately insulted Muslims. Danish Muslims and Arab ambassadors attempted to avoid any worsening of the situation but, obviously, the Danish government felt that there was nothing to fear and decided not to apologize for the insult.

The only reason was our weakness as a Muslim nation and as Arab Muslims. If any consideration had been given to the Arabs in general or Muslims in particular none of this would have happened.

Who benefits from the after-effects of the insult?

First: the European extremist right-wing parties that call for restricting Muslim immigration to Europe and for stricter immigration laws. They will use the Muslim reaction as a reason to accuse them of violence and claim that Muslims do not believe in dialogue. This will limit Muslims' ability to immigrate into Europe and their absorption within European communities will be delayed.

Second: Israel and the United States were extremely put out by the Arab-European rapprochement because, many times, Europe hindered US plots in relation to Iraq and Israeli plots in relation to Palestine. We must also take into account the European Union's support of the Palestinians. Doubtless, the evil act of the Danish paper will cast a dark shadow over our relationship with the Europeans for a long time, especially if Europe continues to take an indifferent stand towards the Arab and Muslim sentiment on that issue, which is a grave one for us.

What should we, as Arabs and Muslims, do in the face of that offence?

I want to stress here that our religion has instructed us to respect all religions. Any response to insulting our Prophet (PBUH) must be expressed in a civilized manner, far away from violence and agitation, to reflect the true face of our religion which is based upon justice and peace. The Holy Quran is very clear: "We make no distinction between any of His messengers." Surah Al-Baqarah [2:285]

Therefore, we must reaffirm that offending any of the heavenly religions, apostles, temples or rites is a red line that we will not cross, regardless of how grave the offence or challenge.

The tolerance of Islam is historically proven and its attitude towards other religions should be a model for us. I will mention here the story of Caliph Omar bin Al Khattab when he entered Jerusalem and was received by Patriarch Sophronius in the Church of the Holy Sepulchre. When prayer time came, Omar asked the Patriarch where he could pray. The Patriarch answered: "Right where you are." But Omar said: "Never. Omar will not pray in the Church of the Holy Sepulchre, for Muslims after me would say that Omar prayed here and would build a mosque in this place."

Therefore, as Muslims and as Arabs, here is what I think we should do:

- Establish Islamic and Arab information centres all over the world, where professionals can clear any ambiguity related to this great religion or to the Prophet Mohammed (PBUH).

- Conduct high level civilized dialogues with European and other countries to convince them to enact laws that prohibit offending any religion or insulting any prophet, especially Mohammed, Jesus and Moses (PBUT).

- Carry out a public boycott of products from Denmark, Norway and other countries that were insolent towards our Prophet (PBUH). This would put their governments under pressure from big companies and would make them pay for their indifference and force them to prevent any such future incident.

It is of utmost importance that we uncover the truth about ourselves. The truth that makes others view us without any consideration. Let us compare ourselves to the Israelis: only 14 million strong, but respected and even feared by all nations because of their economic, political and academic influence.

At the Islamic Summit Conference held in Putrajaya in 2003 the Prime Minister of Malaysia, Dr Mahathir Mohamed talked, rightly, about the heavy influence enjoyed by the Jews. We need an honest review of ourselves. And for that I suggest that a forum be established so we may listen to our foremost intellectuals from all over the world. They must lay down an integrated plan that allows us to catch up with advanced nations. Then, I am sure no one would dare even to think of abusing our Prophet (PBUH).

Finally I would like to call on all our Arab brothers, Muslims and Christians alike, to stay away from violence. Let us learn from the tolerance of the Prophet (PBUH) himself when the non-believers from Qureish and other tribes insulted him. He would maintain his tranquillity and peacefulness by learning from the Holy Quran. There, God says:

"You will surely be tested in your possessions and in yourselves. And you will surely hear from those who were given the Scripture before you and from those who associate others with Allah much abuse. But if you are patient and fear Allah - indeed, that is of the matters [worthy] of determination"
Surah Ali 'Imran [3:186]

Islamophobia must be stemmed

1 December 2006

CERTAIN WESTERN POLITICAL and religious leaders along with members of the media are guilty of stirring up public opinion against Islam. Whether this is intentional is beside the point. It is happening and must be stemmed if Samuel Huntington's "clash of civilizations" is to be prevented.

The latest onslaught appeared in an op-ed published by the French paper *Le Figaro*. Penned by Robert Redeker, the article accused Islam of "exalting violence".

But the problem goes much deeper. Anti-Islamic currents have been simmering since 11 September 2001. This disturbing trend emanates from three separate Western strata: political (governments, intelligence agencies and think tanks) as well as from certain members of the clergy and influential members of society (arts and media).

The chasm began with what was presented as an innocent slip of the tongue. When Muslims reacted angrily to George W. Bush's September 2001 use of the word "crusade" they were considered over-sensitive. If the word had not come from the lips of a devout born-again evangelical he might have been afforded the benefit of the doubt.

The US President apologized and all was well until the Reverend Franklin Graham, a preacher close to the White House, jumped into the fray calling Islam "a very evil and wicked religion".

Ignoring outrage from prominent Muslims, the US television preacher Pat Robertson poured fuel onto the embers by describing Islam as a "violent religion". Then in the autumn of 2002, Jerry Falwell, an evangelical minister, appeared on the CBS show *60 Minutes* calling Prophet Mohammed (PBUH) "a terrorist".

In 2004, the Dutch columnist and director Theo van Gogh released the film *Submission* showing verses from the Quran painted on women's bodies. Shortly afterwards he was assassinated. The result was a public backlash against Muslims in Holland, hitherto known for its religious tolerance.

In 2005, the attacks on Islam continued with cartoon depictions of the Prophet (PBUH) published in the Danish newspaper *Jyllands-Posten*. Howls of protest ensued but these did not deter 143 international newspapers from reprinting the offensive material.

Five years on from that terrible day in September 2001 the attacks on Islam continue unabated.

On 10 August 2006, George W. Bush issued a reminder to the American people that "this nation is at war with Islamic fascists". Did he forget the controversy caused over his use of "crusade" or did he no longer consider the feelings of Muslims important?

A renewed attack on Islam came just a month later from an unlikely quarter, Pope Benedict XVI. The Pope's followers feigned surprise that Muslims would be hurt by anti-Islamic quotes delivered by a theologian, known to be one of the Catholic Church's foremost intellectuals. The Pope, they said, was taken aback by Muslim outrage. It is doubtful that his predecessor Pope John Paul II would have been so oblivious.

Responding last September to a leaked US National Intelligence assessment that suggested the Iraq War has led to a mushrooming of jihadist ideology, Tony Blair had this to say: "Look, 9/11, which is the worst terrorist act in world history, happened before the wars in Iraq and Afghanistan. And if you go back to this movement founded on a warped and perverted view of Islam, the roots of it are deep."

Mr Blair just does not get it (or pretends not to). Muslim anger is generated by ongoing Palestinian suffering and the dissemination of Iraq, as numerous official reports suggest. The British Prime Minister, however, prefers to blame what he calls an "evil ideology", in the hope of getting himself off the hook.

The above represent just a small selection of the insults heaped on Muslims since 9/11: numerous reports allege that US prison guards have disrespected the Quran. Muslims are regularly being ousted from airplanes due to nervous passengers who object to the wearing of a T-shirt printed in Arabic or the sight of fellow passengers sporting Islamic dress or beards.

Muslim charities have come under suspicion, which has led to a drop in charitable donations even though zakat (giving a proportion of one's wealth to the poor and needy) is the third pillar of Islam. Islamic banks have had their funds frozen while under investigation. Mosques and Islamic bookshops are being monitored by security services.

Islamic schools and their textbooks are likewise being scrutinized. The wearing of the hijab was forbidden in French public schools forcing some devout Muslim girls to drop out.

The British Home Secretary John Reid visited East London in October in an attempt to persuade British Muslims how to raise their children. "Look for the telltale signs now," he said. "Talk to them before their hatred grows and you risk losing them for ever." One can only imagine the screaming headlines if Reid had sought to wag his finger at a primarily Jewish or Christian group.

Western intellectuals often view the attacks on Islam through the prism of free speech. They contend that nothing is above criticism or discussion and seek to paint Muslims who object to insults against their core beliefs as unreasonable reactionaries, troublemakers or even the favoured mot de jour "terrorists".

Nobody can or should attempt to condone violence or assassination in response to words spoken in ignorance, but it must be understood that Islam is an emotive issue with most Muslims. Islam is more than a religion. It is not something that is practised one day each week. It is a way of life and being.

Critics should also take into account the heightened sensitivities of Muslims at a time when their countries are occupied by Western powers that seek to redesign the Middle East in their own image, and when Muslims are being abducted, incarcerated and tortured.

Moreover, when it comes to the issue of free speech, we must consider this. Would the rights of those who condemn Islam and insult the Prophet (PBUH) be upheld with such fervour in the West were similar offensive statements being made against Judaism rather than Islam? If we're being honest we already know the answer to that one.

Free speech is a wonderful thing but even in the West it has its limits as anyone who cried "fire" in a crowded theatre, publicly called for the elimination of the President or denigrated the Holocaust would soon discover to their cost. Surely those who wilfully set fire to inter-religious harmony are equally as guilty.

In fairness, Muslims should help to repair the damage. While keeping a wary eye on orchestrated political machinations, Muslims should take into account East–West cultural differences. The type of religious slurs that hurt Muslims to the core would not necessarily have the same effect on Americans or Europeans.

To avert a widening chasm between the world's 1.4 billion Muslims and the rest of the planet, Muslim leaders must use any reasonable means to deter the snowballing of anti-Islamic assaults sanctioned by governments.

Their silence is in part due to the current political and military vulnerabilities of some Muslim states. It is doubtful whether the terms "fascists" or "evil ideology" would be used by contemporary Western leaders in relation, say, to China or Russia.

In the same way that Britain's Queen Elizabeth II is officially "Defender of the Faith" (in this case the Church of England) rulers of Muslim nations should see themselves in a similar light. For if they are not willing to defend their peoples' faith, dignity and security, then who will?

It is interesting that upon his succession to the throne Prince Charles wants to be Defender of all Faiths – a fine sentiment worthy of being emulated by all.

America bashing has gone far enough

1 May 2007

YOU CANNOT TUNE in to an Arabic channel nowadays without coming across analysts, former politicians and ex-generals moaning and groaning about America and the West. Their views almost always paint the Middle East as a terminal victim of neo-imperialism, corporate greed and raw aggression.

In the world of the professional pundit we are always the innocent bystanders. The conflicts besetting this region are not of our making, they say. Everything is America's fault. Few ever come up with viable solutions.

To be fair the US government deserves much of the anger directed towards it for its ill-thought-out Middle East policy.

A recent BBC poll, that sought the opinions of 26,000 people in 25 countries, indicated 49 per cent feel the US plays a mainly negative role in today's world. Surprisingly, attitudes in Germany, France and Indonesia were least favourable.

But here is an interesting snippet. Some 57 per cent of Americans disapprove of the way their government handled the Iraq War.

Ok. So we know that Washington has blundered over Iraq but this should not mean that everything America and its allies propose is automatically perceived as negative.

This trend has become so bad there is now a situation of "them and us", which has led some Arab nations to cool relations with the West and cast around for new friends.

A 25 January Reuters report was headlined "Gulf states seen shifting away from US assets". The fact is we must be careful what we wish for because it just might happen.

Let us ask ourselves these questions. Do we really want to sever or water down our alliances with the world's superpower? And if we were to do something that foolish what might be the economic, political and strategic consequences?

With regards to the Gulf Cooperation Council (GCC) states it would be nice if we could emulate stand-alone, neutral Switzerland. The problem is we cannot. Our countries are blessed – some might say cursed – with the world's most coveted resource – oil. Everyone wants a stake in it and we need to protect it. In truth, we cannot do this alone.

So, like it or not, we need to cooperate with a friendly foreign power at least until such time as we are set-up militarily and technologically to stand on our own two feet.

Imperfect as it is, the US is the only superpower in town. There are pretenders, countries that aim to muscle out the West and which are currently out to woo us. But their challenges are fragile and, in any case, their world view, ideologies and agendas are not ours.

To be painfully frank, if America and the West were to dump us we would soon be saying "Come back, all is forgiven."

If we no longer had the benefit of US satellites, for instance, our communications would be cut. If the West stopped supplying spare parts, our planes would be grounded; our hospital equipment left to rust.

Moreover if we work towards harming the US economy, in the end we will only be harming ourselves since our own economies are inter-related and inter-dependent and especially since our currencies are pegged with the dollar.

I believe the time has come to stop the anti-Western rhetoric, and work with the West instead of against it.

With a sincere will, together we can strive towards a peaceful Iraq, which does not discriminate along sectarian lines. Together we can help Lebanon heal its war wounds and divisions. And together we can concentrate on bringing a Palestinian state to fruition.

This requires a massive change of heart on our side. We are hurt, rightly so, and it will not be easy but it is worth remembering this: in January 2009, the White House is due to receive new tenants. Whether these will be Republican or Democrat there will be a change in policy.

The US public proved their eagerness for a new direction in the November 2006 mid-term elections and presidential candidates are reflecting this new mood in their pre-campaign speeches. One after the other they speak of the need for diplomacy and a new hearts and minds approach vis-à-vis this part of the world. In this case, we must not burn our bridges.

In the meantime it is worth reflecting on the good things the US has done in the world and put the last few years into perspective as an out-of-character aberration.

Realistically speaking we need each other, so let us be courageous enough to offer Washington the hand of friendship. We need to transparently and professionally convey our concerns and requirements while emphasizing that any new way of dealing with each another cannot be a one-way street.

With our region imperilled and the future of our children at stake the road ahead demands an adult and sensible approach, not one based on revenge and grievance.

The nub of the issue is this. How do you envisage the future of your country? Do you want to live in a free economy that offers you the freedom to choose your own lifestyle?

If so, then the West is indispensable. And that is the bottom line. We are at a crossroads. There are hard choices to be made. The responsibility lies with all of us to choose wisely and well.

Talk is cheap; the Middle East needs results

1 May 2008

IN RECENT YEARS, Washington excelled in talking the talk but failed when it came to walking the walk. As far as I can remember I've admired the United States for being a strong and just nation, operating on fine democratic principles. And I have been blessed with loyal American friends and business associates. But good friends should tell each other the truth as they see it.

The fact is American foreign policy is flawed. It just does not deliver promised results and in some cases actually makes the prevailing situation ten times worse.

Take Iraq, for instance. The 19th of March marks the fifth anniversary of the US-led invasion of Iraq, which we were promised would quickly be turned into an envied free and democratic nation. Five years on and the reality belies the seductive rhetoric of the war merchants.

Turkey is carrying out military operations in the Kurdish north; the south is under the ideological sway of Iran, while Baghdad and its surrounding regions are still suffering insurgent attacks. Yet, despite all evidence to the contrary, the US goes to great lengths to convince us that Iraq is on the brink of peace and an economic renaissance. The surge has worked say the American officials in Baghdad from behind the walls of the secure Green Zone.

In this case I cannot help wondering why the US President's visits to Iraq are still cloaked in secrecy, while Iran's President Mahmoud Ahmadinejad announced his arrival in advance, was driven under American protection from Baghdad Airport to the city and was welcomed by President Jalal Talabani as though he was a long lost brother.

The Iraq War and subsequent invasion has cost up to one million Iraqi lives and over 4,000 Coalition military personnel have been sacrificed, while $3tn has been expended, as mentioned in the book by Joseph Stiglitz and Linda Bilmez – *The Three Trillion Dollar War*. In addition, it has harmed America's credibility. How could Washington's foreign policy strategists and think tanks have got it so wrong when the country arguably boasts the finest minds on the planet? So much has been sacrificed, and for what?

They have got it wrong in Palestine too. Two months after the death of Palestinian President Yasser Arafat, in 2004, Mahmoud Abbas was elected President of the Palestinian Authority. Abbas was considered someone with whom the US, Europe and Israel could do business.

But instead of strengthening the position of Abbas, the Bush adminis-tration banged its "New Middle East" drum and insisted Palestine held free and fair elections. After congratulating the Palestinian people, as we now know from leaked US Department of State documents, Washington plotted to overthrow the people's choice of political organization – Hamas.

In the April 2008 issue of *Vanity Fair*, David Rose writes, "After failing to anticipate Hamas's victory over Fatah in the 2006 Palestinian election, the White House cooked up yet another scandalously covert and self-defeating Middle East debacle ... touching off a bloody civil war in Gaza and leaving Hamas stronger than ever."

Now that it has been confirmed that a foreign power deliberately engineered their split, Hamas and Fatah should find a way to put aside their differences.

The Gaza Strip is in lock-down and under Israeli military siege, Israeli settler colonies are expanding and Palestinians are divided. But all this does not deter Secretary of State Condoleezza Rice from smiling sweetly and promising a two-state solution by the end of this year.

Foreign powers are also the cause of disunity in Lebanon, which has been unable to elect a president since former Lebanese President Emile Lahoud stepped down last November.

As the country bleeds politically and economically, the Lebanese people are split between the Hezbollah-led pro-Syrian/Iranian 8 March alliance and the pro-Arab and Western 14 March coalition.

The White House has loudly and repeatedly verbalized its backing of Prime Minister Fouad Siniora. Ms Rice and State Department officials frequently fly into Beirut with a fistful of promises. But talk is cheap. During the 2006 Israel–Lebanon war Siniora pleaded with the US to push for a ceasefire and was rebuffed in favour of Israel's demand for more time to do its worst.

Washington further promised the government substantial financial aid, but much of this was contingent on Siniora being able to push through economic reforms, which he has been unable to do because the government is in disarray.

Conversely, Iran has reportedly bolstered Hezbollah to the tune of $1bn enabling Hezbollah to begin post-war reconstruction even as the government was flying around in search of cash. Every home rebuilt by Hezbollah served to consolidate its power base.

Currently, most of the Bush administration's threats target Iran. The more they threaten, the more popular Mr Ahmadinejad becomes. The more UN sanctions Washington contrives to put in place, the more the moderates in Iran are undercut. In the end, the only ones hurt by such sanctions are ordinary people struggling to do business and make a living.

It is unbelievable that the White House has learned nothing from its mistakes. What is even more unbelievable is that many nations in this region still believe in the power of America to deliver peace, prosperity, democracy and freedom, even as American warships head for the coast off Lebanon.

Hopefully, the next administration will reject false promises and empty threats in favour of brokering genuine dialogue, which, in the end, is the only route to the long-term security we all crave. If not, we can only trust that our leaders have learned to be less gullible.

After all, as former US Secretary of State Henry Kissinger is quoted as saying: "America has no friends, only interests." Perhaps it is time the Arab World heeded his words and adopted a similar approach.

War criminals evade international justice

30 July 2010

WHY IS A COURT tasked with dispensing justice to those alleged to have committed war crimes, crimes against humanity and genocide wherever they are in the world only pursuing non-Westerners? Since its inception in 1998, the International Criminal Court (ICC) in The Hague has only opened investigations into "situations" on the African continent in Uganda, the Democratic Republic of the Congo, the Central African Republic, Kenya and the Sudanese region of Darfur.

In a world where so many innocents have been killed, maimed, wrongly imprisoned, tortured, displaced or forced into starvation with the perpetrators seemingly immune from prosecution, it is clear that the court's mandate should be broadened and its powers increased. For international justice to be meaningful it must be one size fits all. Anything less is a mockery of the principles on which the ICC was founded. Either the ICC should be empowered to try all those suspected of committing crimes within its remit or it should close its doors.

Former United Nations Secretary General Kofi Annan once said that he hoped the court "will deter future war criminals and bring nearer the day when no ruler, no state, no junta and no army anywhere will be able to abuse human rights with impunity".

Those hopes have been dashed. In practice, the ICC is toothless when it comes to landing big fish and relentless in its pursuit of weaker fry. I am amazed by the lack of outrage over such blatant inequality exercised by a court that is supposed to protect the rights of victims wherever they may be. An international court should stand as an example to national courts. Imagine the public outcry were the British government to decide that London's Central Criminal Court, the Old Bailey, could only try nationals of certain countries allowing all others to walk free.

On 12 July the ICC issued a second arrest warrant for the President of Sudan Omar Al Bashir alleging that he bears individual criminal responsibility for genocide committed in Darfur in addition to war crimes and crimes against humanity. In recent days, the court's Chief Prosecutor Luis Moreno-Ocampo has asked members of the United Nations (UN) Security Council to ensure President Al Bashir is arrested and brought to trial. The Prosecutor's enthusiasm for his job is commendable but why does his zeal not extend to other leaders who may have blood on their hands?

The fact is the hands of Mr Moreno-Ocampo and his colleagues are tied because the ICC can only open an investigation under one of these three conditions: the accused is a national of a member state; the alleged crime was committed on the territory of a member state or the case is referred to the ICC by the UN Security Council.

In effect, those conditions constitute a straightjacket for the court, whereby nationals of most big powers are excluded from its jurisdiction. For instance, three of the five permanent Security Council members, China, Russia and the US, have declined to become ICC member states (the US signed the Rome Treaty but never ratified it) and can, therefore, use their powers of veto to block their nationals – as well as nationals of allied nations – being referred to the ICC.

That is the main reason President George W. Bush and others in his administration were able to evade accountability for their role in the deaths of up to one million Iraqis during a war waged on cooked-up pretexts. I am appalled that someone could wreak so much devastation – and preside over a crippling global economic downturn – without facing any consequences whatsoever.

In a published letter dated 10 February 2006, the ICC Prosecutor admitted that war crimes may have been perpetrated in Iraq but those allegedly committed by nationals of member states were not serious enough to warrant investigation. In other words, the ICC does not have jurisdiction over crimes committed by Americans on the soil of a non-member country. This does not, however, explain why the ICC refrained from investigating Britain's former Prime Minister Tony Blair, whose country is a member state.

Blair shares culpability with Bush for the destruction of this ancient Arab nation. Furthermore, evidence is emerging from the Iraq Inquiry, currently underway in London, that Blair deliberately hyped up the threat from Iraq's weapons and was aware that the invasion was illegal in the absence of a UN Resolution authorizing force. Proof is also emerging that under Mr Blair's watch, Britain's MI6 was complicit in the rendition, torture and illegal detention of insurgents. Yet since his resignation from office Blair has been rewarded with high-profile positions and lucrative speaking engagements.

The restrictions placed upon the ICC evidences what most of us already know. International law is of little relevance to major powers and their friends. While President Al Bashir is liable to be arrested should he venture out of Sudan, Israeli war criminals are treated with kid gloves in Western capitals fearful of landing up in Washington's bad books. Israel's former Prime Minister Ariel Sharon "the Butcher of Beirut" was found by an Israeli tribunal to have been indirectly responsible for the massacre of Palestinians in Lebanon's Sabra and Shatila camps yet he was subsequently feted in the US and elsewhere.

In recent times, the British government has tipped off high profile Israelis intending to visit the UK that they were liable for arrest in relation to private prosecutions. Last year, an arrest warrant for Israel's former Foreign Secretary Tzipi Livni, for war crimes, issued by a British court, was dropped due to pressure from the Brown government. Today, Britain's new coalition government is attempting to change the law of universal jurisdiction so that Israeli criminals get a free pass. "We cannot have a position where Israeli politicians feel they cannot visit this country," said Britain's Foreign Secretary William Hague.

Naturally, those concerns do not extend to President Al Bashir who is the leader of an Arab country. Arab leaders are fair game as we witnessed when the occupiers cheered the kangaroo trial that sent Saddam Hussein to the gallows. If the Arab World does not stand with President Al Bashir, then we can only wait to see which Arab head of state will be the next to feature on the ICC's wanted list.

Such biased attitudes were highlighted when the Goldstone Report recommending the UN's referral of certain Israelis to the ICC for war crimes and crimes against humanity in Gaza was ignored by the Security Council, which has also turned a blind eye to Israel's attack on a Turkish aid vessel in international waters as well as its continuing illegal blockade of Gaza.

There is only one law that governs the international community: might is right. To pretend otherwise is nothing but hypocrisy. I will not be happy to see the Sudanese leader flown to The Hague unless seats are booked for Bush, Blair and Benjamin Netanyahu too. If the author Jonathan Swift was right when he wrote "Laws are like cobwebs which may catch small flies, but let wasps and hornets break through," those laws and the system of justice that applies to them must be changed.

Time to heal post-9/11 wounds

11 September 2011

TEN LONG YEARS have passed since 19 ruthless criminals used passenger planes to attack symbols of US power. Little did those of us watching in horror as the World Trade Centre Twin Towers dissolved into dust realize that September 11th 2001 would forever be known as the day our world changed; sadly, not for the better.

The repercussions of that dark day in America's history are still being felt in Afghanistan and Iraq, countries that would not have been bombed and invaded if 9/11 had never happened. Unfortunately, in his haste for retribution, George W. Bush squandered the Muslim world's post-9/11 goodwill enflaming anti-American sentiment, which served to recruit new batches of Al Qaeda clones. As Commander-in-Chief he had to react to the attacks but his methods did not bring the success he craved.

Mr Bush did not succeed in smoking Osama out of his cave, he was not able to eradicate the Taliban and his efforts to democratize Iraq resulted in an Arab country, the Cradle of Civilization, being dished up to the Iranian ayatollahs. Those blunders could have been avoided if his administration had characterized 9/11 as the work of criminals, cooperated with Arab and Muslim leaders on intelligence and used Special Forces to hunt Bin Laden in the way that President Barack Obama did earlier this year.

Bush's approach – in particular the rounding-up and incarceration of 5,000 Muslims in America during the 9/11 aftermath, and the closing-down of Islamic charities – led the right-wing US media to tar the world's 1.5 billion Muslims with the same brush as the perpetrators who could not have been believers when Islam teaches us that killing one person is as great a sin as killing all mankind.

Muslims were suddenly being asked to distance themselves from terrorists who do not differentiate between Muslims and people of other faiths when they strap on their bomb belts or drive vehicles packed with explosives into buildings. Law-abiding Muslims were cast under suspicion to the extent that many ordinary Americans were afraid to travel on the same airplane with people reading the Quran or wearing an Arabic-emblazoned T-shirt.

Fox News contributor Michelle Malkin called for all American Muslims to be interned in camps like Japanese-Americans were during World War II. Terry Jones, a Florida preacher announced a "Burn the Koran Day" and thousands protested against a proposed Islamic Centre a few blocks away from Ground Zero in Manhattan. There was a moment when a clash of civilizations seemed inevitable. But, thankfully, the world has dodged that bullet; our kinship as members of the human race has ultimately prevailed.

Now we must put old hurts behind us and move on. Governments and the media have been commemorating 9/11 every year for a decade but in order to heal and repair the gap between the US and the Muslim world we should not keep opening up old wounds or dwell on sorrow that can so easily derail our coming together.

One definition of "evil" is ignorance. The idea that west is west and east is east and never the twain shall meet should be discarded. We must teach our children that we may hold different beliefs, follow different traditions and wear different clothes but we are all citizens of one shrinking global village. We must explain to them that the Peoples of the Book – Muslims, Christians and Jews – are all children of Abraham and his sons Isaac and Ishmael.

We share a belief in many of the same prophets such as Adam, Noah and Moses (PBUT), while Muslims revere Jesus as a prophet and hold his mother Mary, whom we know as Maryam (PBUH), in the highest esteem. People should understand that these three great religions all worship the same One God even if He is known by different names.

The secret to greater tolerance and understanding is education. We must remove our blinkers and open our minds. Both sides must cast aside their ingrained fear of the other for the sake of peace. I am trying to do my bit towards interfaith understanding by opening up Jumeirah's Al Farooq Mosque and Islamic Centre – my gift to the people of Dubai – to non-Muslims so that they can read about Islam in the Centre's library, ask questions of the Imam and observe us at prayer.

The past cannot be changed. The victims of 9/11 should be remembered always and lessons must be learned. However, the only road open to us is forward; I pray that we will take that journey to a better tomorrow in unity and harmony. As a new World Trade Centre tower reaches for the sky as a symbol of a new dawn, surely now we should respectfully close the book on 9/11 and its painful aftermath once and for all.

Why holding an Arab League summit in Baghdad is a bad idea

7 February 2012

THE WORD "BAGHDAD" was once a symbol of Arab culture and nationalism. Iraq was the beating heart of our Arab World from the 7th-century rule of the Umayyad Caliphate. The capital Baghdad was built by the Abbasids and its population was acknowledged to be the most learned during Islam's Golden Age. And say what you will about Saddam Hussein, as brutal as he was, he was a champion of Arab causes until he stupidly sent his army to invade Kuwait – a decision that crippled his country and left it vulnerable to foreign jackals.

Saddam knew that the greatest threat to Arabs was Iran, which until today has had ambitions to dominate the Gulf. In September, 1980, he went to war against Iran for several reasons that included the liberation of oppressed Arabs in the oil-rich Iranian province of Khuzestan (Arabistan) and the return of islands to the United Arab Emirates that were occupied by the Shah in the early 1970s.

I do not wish to defend Saddam's numerous shortcomings and mistakes; he was, indeed, a strong-arm dictator, but with all his faults, his soul was that of a fearlessly proud Arab, supporting the Palestinians and opening up Iraq to Egyptian workers. Unfortunately, I cannot say the same about the current rulers of Iraq who appear to have sold their souls to the neighbouring Islamic Republic of Iran.

As just about everyone will agree, the 2003 US-led invasion of Iraq was a failure on many levels. American combat troops were recently withdrawn leaving sectarian divisions and terrorist attacks in their wake. Moreover, Iraq's Sunni population has been politically marginalized by the exiled Shi'ite-dominated government which appears to be more interested in aligning itself with Tehran rather than Arab states.

The Iraqi leadership has been cozying up to Iran for years to the detriment of its fellow Arabs, which is why I consider the decision by the League of Arab States to hold a summit in Baghdad next month to be madness – and especially when Iraq's government is purposefully siding with Tehran against the Arab's League's majority will.

Firstly, Baghdad is actively supporting Iran's ally in Syria, the Assad regime that is being loudly condemned by most of the League's member countries for its bloody crackdown on a helpless freedom-seeking civilian population. There is no excuse for the Iraqi government's stance when Iraqis have experienced life under ruthless dictatorship and therefore should not hesitate to defend others who now find themselves in similar circumstances.

Baghdad is even prepared to fall out with its main trading partner Turkey whose government has taken an unshakeable position against Assad with whom it formerly enjoyed friendly relations. Turkey's leadership has called upon Assad to step aside and is hosting camps for Syrian refugees near its border. I, therefore, suspect Iraq's Prime Minister of bowing to the wishes of Iran where he spent several years in exile and to which he has since made numerous official and private visits.

Secondly, Iraq's leadership is thwarting international anti-Iranian sanctions designed to prod Tehran into relinquishing its uranium-enrichment programme to avert looming war clouds on the horizon. Baghdad has no intention of complying with US and EU sanctions, and in any case its long border with Iran means infringements of sanctions will be almost impossible to police. Iran is presently Iraq's second largest trading partner to the tune of $10bn annually and is currently developing greater industrial and economic cooperation. For instance, Tehran and Baghdad have signed an agreement for the establishment of jointly owned transport companies facilitating ease of passenger and goods traffic between the two neighbours. Personally, I believe the potential for some kind of future Iranian-Iraqi political alliance/federation that would pose a direct threat to Gulf states is not that far-fetched.

Given that Baghdad appears to be more loyal to Tehran than Arab governments and is undergoing a period of instability and insecurity, I am appalled at the Arab League's decision to hold a summit there. I'm not the only one. According to *Al-Hayat*, the Arab League Secretary General Nabil Elaraby and several Arab League member nations may decline to attend the Baghdad meeting in protest at Iraq's position on Syria. Moreover, Elaraby has confirmed that he has personally passed on those countries' objections to the Iraqi delegation attending the recent Cairo summit.

Our beloved Iraq is slowly turning into Tehran's creature, which must be devastating for those Iraqis, both Sunni and Shi'ite, who are proud to call themselves Arabs. Instead of feuding against each other, they should remember how close they once were and together turn their attention on their quisling leadership. Iraqis, all Iraqis, must decide either to rejoin the Arab World or to cast aside thousands of years of history to permit their homeland to become an Iranian satellite.

I would, therefore, request the rulers of Gulf Cooperation Council states not to attend or send representatives to the March summit in Baghdad or any future meeting scheduled to be held there until Iraqis decide which side of the fence they want to stand on – and when both Sunnis and Kurds are allowed an equal platform with Shi'ites in decisions of state.

The GCC must do all in its power to keep Iraq from falling into Iranian hands; it must support Iraqis desperate to save their country from a pseudo-Iranian occupation via Iraqi puppets in power. I long for the day when "Baghdad" is once again a byword within the Arab World, representing the best of our culture and heritage. But as long as Arab governments continue closing their eyes to the ugly truth, sadly, that day will never come.

Enough trusting others to keep us secure!

5 April 2012

ON SATURDAY 31 MARCH, United States Secretary of State Hillary Clinton told the foreign ministers of Gulf Cooperation Council (GCC) states that America's security commitment "to the people and the nations of the Gulf is rock-solid and unwavering". She advocated taking "practical and specific steps to strengthen our mutual security, such as helping our militaries improve interoperability, cooperate on maritime security and missile defense, and coordinate responses to crises".

Her words may sound reassuring to some in our region; others may sleep better at night in the knowledge that Washington proposes to cushion us with a missile shield. What is there to object to when the superpower wants to take Gulf states under its mighty wing, you may ask, especially at a time of heightened threats? However, in my view, those people should think again.

Mrs Clinton's statement had an affect on me, but not the one she intended. Far from feeling grateful or comforted, my overwhelming emotion was one of "Here we go again" annoyance. My mind immediately transported me back to the 1990s when I met with former US Assistant Secretary of State Richard Murphy, then a US Special Envoy, for a game of tennis; we had played several times before.

On this occasion Mr Murphy was accompanied by the US Ambassador to Jordan Roscoe Seldon Suddarth. While we were resting between games, our conversation turned to America's relationship with Gulf countries; something Murphy said on this topic left me quietly seething. He somewhat proudly disclosed that "'we' [the US] have assumed responsibility for the protection of the Arabian Gulf from the British".

Once I had digested his message I asked him "Who gave you that authority?" He responded that the UK had handed the Gulf region over to America. "Strange that we the people who live here are the last to know," I retorted, asking whether the region's rulers had given their permission for such handover, even though I was certain they had not.

Almost two decades later, I had hoped things had changed. GCC states are economically sound; they enjoy stable governance, are blessed with a wealth of expertise and are militarily strong. I support our collaboration with big powers, but we should not allow them to control our future. Such powers are fickle; they operate out of self-interest as we witnessed when Britain allowed the Shah of Iran to rob the UAE of its islands. We have seen how this White House and the last have delivered Iraq to a pro-Iranian regime that classes Iraqi Sunnis as second-class citizens. If Iraq, one of the larger Arab countries with regards to territory and population, was parcelled up this way, who knows what our fate could be if we abandon it to others' self-serving hands!

A great friend of mine who happens to be a US diplomat once said to me: "We don't care who rules in the GCC as long as the oil is flowing our way." Of course, it is a little more complex than that nowadays when the US imports only 16 per cent of its petroleum from the Arabian Gulf; today, the US government is out to control regional oil exports to keep energy-hungry competitors like China and India under its heel.

Have we, the peoples and governments of the Gulf, not learned any lessons from the US-led invasion and occupation of Iraq, which we were powerless to prevent? Besides being humiliating, there is danger in relying on another country, even an ostensibly friendly country, for our defense. What happens if and when we disagree in the future? We will either have to bury our principles and bend our heads – or be vulnerable to a protector-turned-foe.

First it was Britain, now it is the US. If we accept the principle that our peoples and land can be "bought and sold" who knows what boss we will get next time. The Iranian ayatollahs perhaps! You may smile, but just look at what is happening in Bahrain where Tehran has planted poisonous seeds capable of spreading to neighboring states if it were not for the determined stand of the Bahraini government aided by Saudi Arabia.

GCC states must unite and reinforce a common defence capability, not only to keep our people safe but also to take charge of our own neighbourhood. It is good that Saudi Arabia and Qatar are taking a diplomatic leadership role on the world's stage but that is not enough. In a perfect world, the GCC should be equipped to step in to save Syrian civilians, men, women and children who are being butchered by Bashar Al Assad and his gang daily. Just like the Americans, the Europeans and the Turks, Gulf leaders are verbally holding the regime's feet to the fire but still the killing goes on. The Syrian opposition requires more than mere words. They need weapons and military advisors. Syria is our house, our Arab house, and we should not wait for Russia's and China's approval before we take action.

I will repeat what I have written in many of my previous columns. We have to quit being our own worst enemy. If we do not get a grip on Syria, if we allow this humanitarian tragedy to continue unabated, this fever will reach our area via Iran's proxies in Iraq and Lebanon. This is more than simply freeing Syrians from dictatorship; it is also about rescuing GCC states and Lebanon from Iran's long penetrating arm.

As a citizen of the GCC, I would ask our leaders to consult with their people; not only those within their inner circles but also others who love their nation's soil and will protect it with their blood. I talk to Gulf nationals regularly on this topic. I know that deep down they are greatly concerned about Iran's intimidating announcements, war games, missile tests and naval exercises on their doorstep even if they try not to show it. And where is our answer to those threats? Where are our displays of power? Are we waiting for the Pentagon to launch military exercises on our behalf?

I can only hope that our leaders assess the volatile climate and come up with an urgent plan of action. I pray that their hearts will be brave enough, their minds focused enough and their resilience unbreakable enough to propel our heads high and afford us the security we crave. From my own perspective, there is only one thing I would like to say to Mrs Clinton. "Thanks, but no thanks!"

GCC must react to the Pentagon's "total war on Islam"

4 June 2012

I USED TO BELIEVE that the Obama administration had a policy of reaching out to the world's 1.6 billion Muslims in an effort to mend fences incinerated by George W. Bush's wars. I was gratified by his efforts because, like many Muslims and Arabs, I have been working to bridge the gap between east and west and in a small way have striven to bring all of the Prophet Ibrahim's (PBUH) children together in peace; notably with my gift to Dubai the Al Farooq Omar Ibn Al Khattab Mosque and Centre that welcomes visitors of all faiths and the Khalaf Al Habtoor Leadership Center at Illinois College as well as through many other efforts. Just recently, I hosted one of the college's students in Dubai – his prize for coming second in an essay competition I sponsor – and he later wrote that his negative preconceptions of Arabs had been replaced with admiration.

The leaders and peoples of the Gulf Cooperation Council (GCC) states consider America to be a friendly nation with coinciding interests. So I was astonished and appalled to learn that US military commanders and officers had been attending a year-long course at the Joint Forces College in Virginia taught by Lieutenant Colonel Matthew Dooley advocating "Total war with Islam".

This abomination that is surely a recipe for Armageddon was exposed by the media some weeks ago in a strangely low-key fashion. An American friend confirmed that "mainline American news media barely made mention of this story"; he expressed his concern that "such gross ignorance about Islam" should find its way into any classroom, civilian or military. It was given so little air-time and prominence in the press that, unlike the burning of Qurans in Afghanistan, it has escaped the radar of most Muslims too. I cannot rid myself of the question, is America merely posing as our friend while working against us?

Dooley based his instruction on the premise that there is no such thing as "moderate Islam." "This barbaric ideology will no longer be tolerated," he said. "Islam must change or we will facilitate its self-destruction." His solution included nuclear attacks on Mecca and Medina without any regard for civilian lives.

The course advertised on the Pentagon's own website was cancelled but, shamefully, Dooley has retained his job. Chairman of the Joint Chiefs of Staff General Martin Dempsey called a press conference to slam the course as "objectionable" and "academically irresponsible". However, it has since emerged that a similar course was being taught in another military college complete with anti-Islamic slides that were approved by former Central Intelligence Agency (CIA) Director James Woolsey and two three-star generals.

Moreover, the Federal Bureau of Investigation (FBI) has been driven to vet its own course materials when it was discovered that counter-terrorism agents were being taught that "American Muslims are likely to be terrorist sympathizers" whose charitable donations equate to a "funding mechanism for combat". FBI materials refer to the Prophet Mohammed (PBUH) as a "cult leader".

Likewise, as revealed by *The New York Times*, the New York Police Department (NYPD) has been infiltrating mosques and Muslim community centres. The department's officers were shown a docu-mentary, in which the NYPD's chief participated, called *The Third*

Jihad, which contended that the Muslim leadership in the US harbours ambitions to "infiltrate and dominate." The film was also endorsed by New York's former mayor, Rudolph Giuliani.

In the Arab World we have become used to dismissing crimes perpetrated by US soldiers in Iraq, Afghanistan and Pakistan as "mistakes" that run counter to official US policy. Indeed, when I contacted a few of my American friends in the know to ask their views on the offensive courses, their responses were broadly the same, i.e. that any anti-Islamic vein that may exist in the Pentagon, US intelligence services and law enforcement is the work of renegades and does not reflect the views of the US government. I am sure that my friends are sincere because as American nationals anything else is too horrendous to contemplate, but with my full respect to them, I am far from being convinced.

I have a hard time accepting that those courses were unauthorized when they appeared on the Pentagon website, were taught in military schools, were signed off by generals as well as a CIA director and are somewhat mirrored within the FBI and the NYPD. The idea that the US government knew nothing about this philosophy of hate sounds like the most fantastical fairy story. It is imperative that President Barack Obama launches an investigation, apologizes to Muslims everywhere and explains to America's predominately Muslim allies how such dangerous propaganda, designed to infect commanders with hatred for Muslims that would trickle down the ranks, went unchecked for so long.

We need answers from the White House, the Pentagon and Congress. These latest exposés could merely constitute the tip of the iceberg. Just how deep does the contagion go? Soldiers who burn holy books, humiliate Muslim detainees or urinate on Muslim corpses can hardly be blamed if their officers are advocating using nukes to wipe Muslims from the face of the earth.

In one of my recent columns titled "Enough trusting others to keep us secure" 5 April 2012, I quoted Hillary Clinton telling GCC foreign ministers that America's security commitment "to the people and the nations of the Gulf is rock-solid and unwavering". She advocated the strengthening of "our mutual security, such as helping our militaries improve interoperability... and coordinate responses to crises". But how can we coordinate with a military whose officers are instructed to wage total war on Muslims?

As I have been urging time and time again, the GCC can only rely on itself for its military defences. Surely, the neoconservative's "Project for a New American Century" paper, whose authors became leading figures in the Bush administration, should have raised suspicions as to Washington's true geopolitical goals. How hard do we need to be hit on the head before we get the message?

Given the turmoil in Arab countries ostensibly in pursuit of American-style democracy that was partly instigated by US non-governmental organizations (NGOs), the potential for slicing apart of Iraq and Libya in the same way that Sudan has been split, and the possibly orchestrated divisions between Sunnis and Shi'ites (to the detriment of Sunnis), it is possible that the US has a clandestine policy of inciting Arabs to destroy each other as a continuation of imperialist Britain's "Divide and Rule". After all, that was effective in tearing Syria, Jordan and Palestine asunder. If that is the case, then I suspect that the Assad regime, Hezbollah, the Iraqi Badr Brigades, Al Sadr Militias, and even the Al Maliki government are complicit in America's plan of reducing numbers of Muslims by killing Sunnis; they may even be commissioned by the US to commit murder by proxy in accordance with America's policy of hate towards Muslims, reflected by the invasions of Afghanistan and Iraq that resulted in up to one million deaths. If they are not endorsed by the US, then why does not Washington act to prevent civilian massacres in Syria and lean on Hezbollah's military wing, an army outside state control, to relinquish its weapons? I sincerely hope I am wrong.

For our own self-preservation, the GCC must unite, become a federation and build an independent, powerful military capability. We cannot rely on fair-weather friends to protect our peoples. Sleeping while our enemies pretend to be our friends even as they plot our destruction is no longer an option. If our leaders fail to take "Total war on Islam" with the seriousness it deserves, we are doomed.

To those attempting to put a lid on this disturbing news, I would quote Abraham Lincoln who once said: "You can fool all of the people some of the time, and some of the people all of the time, but you cannot fool all of the people all of the time." I, for one, refuse to be fooled any more.

America's muddled priorities and double standards

21 November 2012

I AM STUNNED at the banquet Washington's political establishment and the US media have made out of the personal indiscretions of a couple of four-star generals past their prime. General David Petraeus was leaned on to resign due to his suspect relationship with his biographer Paula Broadwell. General John Allen, the commander of the North American Treaty Organization (NATO) in Afghanistan, has been treated less harshly for sending flirtatious emails to Jill Kelley, a Florida woman whom Broadwell suspected of getting her hooks into "her man". Allen's appointment as NATO's commander in Europe has been put on hold. This maybe the kind of titillating scandal that feeds reality show viewers but, in the great scheme of things, it is inconsequential. It is incomprehensible that the White House and the Pentagon have hyped what should have been personal matters into a national issue dominating headlines. It should have been buried as soon as it was leaked by the media with a simple "no comment".

Conversely, the real news barely gets a front-page mention primarily because the American readership is disinterested in what their military has perpetrated in Afghanistan and Iraq in their name. How many bother to look behind the propaganda? How many care that hardly a week passes without car bombs exploding in Iraqi cities? Or that the lives of thousands of their troops were sacrificed under democracy's standard when, in reality, Iraq has fallen into the open arms of America's arch enemy Iran? Where is the anger within the US over up to one million Iraqi lives lost and the waste of more than one trillion of their tax dollars squandered to rid Iraq of a toothless dictator on a pack of lies?

Let us not kid ourselves that the Americans and their allies have achieved anything positive in Afghanistan either. They ostensibly went there to get Osama bin Laden but as it turned out he had fled early on to Pakistan. They destroyed the country's Al Qaeda training camps, true. But Al Qaeda is alive and well throughout the Middle East, the subcontinent and Africa; Al Qaeda fighters are actively engaged in the Sinai Peninsula and Yemen. For eleven years, the US and NATO have been battling to destroy the Taliban who ironically are now being courted by the governments of Afghanistan and Pakistan.

Just days ago, Pakistan released eight Taliban commanders from its custody, including one who enjoyed close links with Osama bin Laden, at the behest of the Afghan government that is seeking reconciliation. According to Pakistani newspapers, the Taliban are gleeful over the public disgrace of Petraeus, the man who engineered "the surge". No doubt Taliban leaders are rubbing their hands in anticipation of 2014 when the Americans are scheduled to leave; they are looking forward to business as usual. If the American people expect gratitude from the Afghans they are in for disappointment. Anti-Americanism is rife partly because of indiscriminate drone attacks that have destroyed entire villages.

Is there not something seriously wrong with America's priorities? General Petraeus has been severely punished over his love life yet those American military personnel known to have tortured detainees in Bagram, Abu Ghraib and Guantanamo were characterized as "a few bad apples" and were let off with little more than a ticking off or demotion or short jail terms. They and their commanders were the ones that blackened America's name, not Petraeus or Allen who are guilty of foolishness. Moreover, if any Arab country had acted even remotely like the US, kidnapping individuals from the streets of European capitals to be rendered to third countries for torture, or had incarcerated Western citizens in gulags for years without charge or trial, they would have been labelled terrorist states; they would have been sanctioned, bombed, perhaps even invaded.

It is puzzling how so many Americans are bewildered at how far respect for their country has dwindled throughout the Arab and Muslim world. I have dozens of fine upstanding American friends and I used to look up to the "Land of the Free and the Brave" as being the most wealthy and powerful nation on earth, a dynamic repository of knowledge, science and invention – and a bastion of human rights. I usually avoid stereotypes but, in my experience, Americans are some of the most friendly and likeable people anywhere. I believed they had a right to be proud of their achievements. They do have much to be proud of but, at the same time, they should be ashamed of their governments' bullying foreign policy that treats non-Americans as inferior and other country's leaders as pawns to be pushed around in game of global hegemony. How do they sleep at night when so many of their fellow citizens live in virtual shanty towns, homes made of cardboard, sleep with their children in cars, rely on food stamps or have to mortgage their homes to get medical treatment? There is a wretched underclass in America as exposed by Hurricanes Katrina and Sandy, people for whom the American Dream is unattainable. I know that Americans and Europeans tend to look down on us Arabs. In many disciplines they are, indeed, light years ahead of us. Yet, even their finest minds have not succeeded in combating economic crises or rocketing rates of unemployment engendering violent civil unrest.

We, who are privileged to live in Gulf Cooperation Council (GCC) states, do not claim to know more than our Western counterparts, quite the opposite. Our children study in their schools and our sick are tended to in their hospitals. We have benefitted from their experience and skills that we have used to boost our economies. It is notable that GCC member countries recovered from the global downturn much faster than others. The difference between them and us rests in our unity and the fact that we always shun anything that threatens our security, stability and prosperity. We do not permit corporations or individuals to negatively impact our countries, which is common in the West.

Our leaders will not tolerate troublemakers bent on hurling the GCC into turmoil, for which they have been wrongly criticized by human rights groups. I thank God that they are protecting the status quo and prioritizing the safety and well-being of their citizens, providing them with homes, education and medical treatment. Caring for those less fortunate at home and abroad is not something we learned from the West. That is a staple of our religion, Islam.

You, who chastise us for neglecting human rights when our people enjoy enviable lifestyles and high per capita incomes should take a long hard look at your own countries, places where prisons are full to bursting, drug addicts and criminals make the streets unsafe and there are long queues for welfare handouts. Why do you not visit one of your own tent cities and speak about human rights. Or if you dare, go to Afghanistan or Iraq and ask the people there, the millions of widowed, orphaned and maimed, about their human rights. Unless the US and its Western allies admit their mistakes, sadly, the days when they deserve our admiration are numbered. The silly Petraeus affair that has been blown out of proportion is just another nail in that coffin.

Tagging Sunnis "moderate" or "extremist" is offensive

29 June 2014

THE WESTERN media no longer reports hard facts in its coverage of the Muslim World, but rather seeks to shape the perceptions of its viewers or readers by using blanket adjectives, especially when reporting on Sunni Muslims. US administration figures, including the President, are also guilty of stereotyping and using words like "moderate" or "extremist" in an attempt to pigeonhole believers. I have been seriously annoyed by this hurtful "classification" trend for a very long time, but now Nathan Lean, the Research Director at Georgetown University, has taken the words right out of my mouth.

Writing in the *New Republic* under the headline "Stop saying 'Moderate Muslims' you're only empowering Islamophobes", he accuses *Newsweek*, *NPR*, the *Wall Street Journal*, *Reuters* and *Time* among others for using "moderate" to "describe Muslims who fit a certain preferred profile". Lean contends that, "The idea of a 'moderate Islam' or 'moderate Muslim' is intellectually lazy because it carves the world up into two camps: the 'good' Muslims and the 'bad' Muslims, as Columbia University professor Mahmood Mamdani noted." Such categorization infers that until proven good – or in this case moderate – all Muslims are perceived as bad or potentially extreme.

In reality, terms like "moderate" or "extremist" cannot be applied to Sunnis that make up almost 90 per cent of the world's Muslim population. There is no such thing as progressive Islam and Islam's tenets cannot be watered-down to fit contemporary lifestyles or cherry-picked to suit personal preferences. The Quran, as the word of God, is unchangeable. Therefore the term "moderate Muslim" is patently false as those applying it know only too well. It is being used as a euphemism for "non-threatening" or to label a Muslim embracing Western values i.e. someone who won't cause any trouble.

"That's the problem with this 'moderate Muslim' nonsense," says Nathan Lean. "It empowers anti-Muslim activists by implying that the degree to which a Muslim digests their religious faith is indicative of their status as a potential terrorist. Thus, 'moderately' subscribing to the teachings of the Quran is OK, but should they cross over into the world of daily prayers, Friday afternoons at the mosque, and, God forbid, Ramadan, they're suddenly flirting with extremism."

In a nutshell, there are no moderate Muslims; there are only Muslims. And there are no Muslim extremists, only power-hungry terrorists using their own distorted version of Islam to fire-up a bunch of wild-eyed losers into strapping bomb belts around their waists. The question is whether or not those are grass-root aberrations or are their strings being pulled by unseen hands?

Is there a secret white paper locked in someone's drawer in Washington strategizing how to weaken or divide up Muslim countries into toothless entities? Is this the implementation of long-held US plans to break up Iraq into three, leaving its neighbours to fall, one by one, like skittles? As the award-winning author, Professor Michel Chossudovsky, points out, the chaos in Iraq could be by design, with the goal to break-up the country. "Washington's intent is no longer to pursue the narrow objective of "regime change' in Damascus," he writes. "What is contemplated is the break-up of both Iraq and Syria along sectarian-ethnic lines." He maintains that there is a carefully orchestrated US military intelligence agenda at play and says the US is supporting both sides. "America's military occupation of Iraq has been replaced by non-conventional forms of warfare," he writes. "Realities are blurred. In a bitter irony, the aggressor nation is portrayed as coming to the rescue of a 'sovereign Iraq'."

Worse, the categorization – moderate or extremist – has been politicized and is mainly being applied to Sunni Muslims as opposed to Shi'ites. Until Sunnis became victims of foreign interference/ occupation, for example in Palestine, Syria, Iraq and Iran they lived peacefully within their communities, coexisting with people of other faiths and exemplifying the Quran's message of tolerance. The anger displayed by Sunnis in Syria and Iraq, for instance, has nothing to do with religion but all to with oppression, marginalization, disenfranchisement and state brutality, leaving them vulnerable to those who would manipulate their distress for their own ends.

While the US Department of State is cosying up to the Iranian President, discussing the future of Iraq behind closed doors, and Britain's Foreign Office is planning the re-opening its Tehran embassy, Shi'ite cleric Muqtada al Sadr has called-up his disbanded Shi'ite militia, vowing his supporters will "shake the ground". That guerrilla group has bloodstained hands, yet I do not hear the White House complaining that its firepower represents a state within a state or labelling its members as extremists. There is a Shi'ite group holding a sword over Lebanon's government – and others working to overthrow the Bahraini monarchy, propping-up the Assad regime's killing machine and scheming against Yemen and Saudi Arabia – which manages to escape being tagged "extremist". On the contrary, they have been embraced by suspiciously backed human rights groups.

It was shocking to learn that the US Secretary of State's remedy for the Iraq crisis is to enlist "moderate" Syrian rebels – it is unclear whether he means the Free Syrian Army (FSA) – to fight Daesh in Iraq, when their main priority should be to rid their own country of a dictator who has slaughtered, imprisoned and tortured hundreds of thousands of his own people. "Obviously, in light of what has happened in Iraq, we have even more to talk about in terms of the moderate opposition in Syria, which has the ability to be a very important player in pushing back against ISIL and to have them not just in Syria, but also in Iraq," he told the leader of the Syrian opposition Ahmad Al Jarba. On Saturday, Kerry announced that the US has now deployed drones in Iraq, which will, no doubt, end up killing not only Daesh fighters but also Sunni civilians as they are intermingled in heavily populated areas, and distinguishing between the two will present an impossible challenge as it is in Pakistan, Afghanistan and Yemen.

This is just another example of the US getting others to do their dirty work, others who will apparently be the recipients of $500m if President Barack Obama can convince Congress to release the funds. Does this indicate that the White House prioritizes Iraq over Syria and is content for Assad to remain on his soiled throne while using Sunnis to assist the unpopular Shi'ite Iraqi Prime Minister to pacify a Sunni uprising in which Daesh is only one component?

Sunnis have been slandered for far too long without speaking out loud and clear in response. Given the dangerous environment in which we now live, we must put our hands together and stand tall. We should completely reject being branded by those who know nothing at all about our faith or who we are. Be proud and strong! Muslims have been reaching out and endeavouring to be understood, fearful of being judged, but we must stop apologizing for things we had nothing to do with and people we have never met. It is about time we rejected pandering to those self-appointed judges in Western capitals and began delivering a few judgments of our own.

Why are we spectators as terrorists threaten our homes?

3 July 2014

First they came for the Palestinians and I did not act – because
I was not a Palestinian.
Then they came for the Lebanese and I did not act – because
I was not a Lebanese.
Then they came for the Syrians and the Iraqis – and I did not act because
I was not Syrian or Iraqi.
Then they came for me – and there was no one left to defend me.

ISIL, ISIS, IS OR DAESH, who cares what this group of a few thousand sick killers calls itself! Today, this depraved following are celebrating their "Caliphate", stretching from eastern Iraq to Aleppo and led by Iraqi national Abu Bakr Al Baghdadi who is demanding that all Muslims pledge their allegiance to him. This is nothing but sacrilege smearing the four Rightly-Guided Caliphs – Abu Bakr, Omar bin Al Khattab, Uthman and Ali bin Abi Taleb – whose wisdom created Islam's Golden Age. Al Baghdadi is nothing but a criminal who is ruthlessly using the romanticism associated with a caliphate to attract new recruits from a global swamp of weak-minded losers out to translate violent video games into real life.

Daesh is the black sheep of the Al Qaeda franchise and so are all the other terrorist gangs in Syria, Libya, Yemen, Egypt and Lebanon, desecrating Islam to grab power, wealth and territory. They may be small in number, but together they present the biggest threat to the stability and security of our region.

I have been raising this issue with Arab leaderships for years in the fervent hope that they would act to stem this disease before it took root. And now when those bloodstained fanatics are knocking on our doors and infiltrating our shores, they are finally opening their eyes to the danger.

It is a tragedy that with all the Arab World's combined military might, airpower, intelligence capabilities and influence, we have stood back allowing those infidels hiding under the banner of Islam to proliferate and organize sleeper cells in our own countries. It is beyond belief that mere thousands of sword-touting primitives, who think decapitating, crucifying and torturing is entertainment, can terrorize 500 million Arabs or scare the Maliki Army into running away like rabbits. If someone had predicted this state of affairs a few years ago, I would have laughed in their face.

Some perspective is needed. I believe there is more to this than meets the eye. As regards Iraq, there is more than enough blame to go round beginning of course with the US invasion in 2003 that led to one mistake after another on the part of the US occupier, such as the disbanding of the army, the ousting of Baathists from government positions and the Lebanization of the political sphere, which placed the country in the hands of an Iranian puppet.

Iraqi Prime Minister Nouri Al Maliki had free rein to implement sectarian policies as soon as he waved goodbye to the last of the coalition forces, leaving the Sunni population oppressed, marginalized, deprived of rights and opportunities – and humiliated. Out of concern for his seat – and no doubt with the blessing of his masters in Tehran – he deliberately weakened the army and air force, which were stuffed with inexperienced Shi'ites and starved of airplanes, helicopters and equipment.

What is occurring now is in reaction to this tyrant's small-minded selfishness. This is a Sunni uprising involving tribes and former Baathists, who not so long ago assisted the government in ousting Al Qaeda, but now sick of broken promises and Iranian interference, are taking advantage of the firepower wielded by Daesh to take down their enemy in Baghdad. Once Daesh, operating as a mercenary force in Iraq, has served its purpose, Iraq's Sunnis will send the terrorists packing, just as they did with Al Qaeda and as the Free Syrian Army (FSA) is doing in Syria by taking on Daesh and another of Al Qaeda's spawn, Jabhat Al Nusra, there. Daesh may be bloodthirsty but it is not nearly as powerful as its effective propaganda machine would have us believe.

Predictably, the Iraq crisis has triggered calls to divide the country into three, which was the plan of neoconservatives advising George W. Bush in 2003, a plan to de-fang this once powerful Arab country to reshape Israel's environment that was set out in a white paper titled "Clean Break: a New Strategy for Securing the Realm". Echoing that was Benjamin Netanyahu's recent support for an independent Kurdish state – and, by the way, the Kurds are already selling oil that belongs to all Iraqis to Israel. When will the Arab World devise a strategy for securing our realm? With Daesh announcing they will soon be expanding into Saudi Arabia, Jordan and Kuwait, what are we waiting for?

Time for some plain speaking! How was it that the War on Terror became a terrorist incubator, not only in Iraq but elsewhere? Is there a plot to destabilize Arab states to prevent the rise of Arab nationalism, to ensure the longevity of US bases in the area, to keep Israelis sleeping peacefully while all the time keeping control over regional resources? Are we to imagine that the mighty superpower and its Western allies are impotent? Should we believe that the US and NATO are too feeble to quash Daesh and its cohorts underfoot like ants if they so willed? Satellites pinpoint their exact locations; drones can send them to hell without risk to pilots. Some are happy to oblige TV reporters with interviews, so I really have to wonder whether they are being left alive for the express purpose of threatening our existence.

I have no concrete answers but I do know this. We in the Gulf Cooperation Council (GCC) must take responsibility for our neighbourhood, beginning with a clear definition of who constitutes an enemy and who is a friend. We should erase the words "diplomacy" and "diplomatic courtesy" from our dictionary when dealing with foreign nations because beneath all their sweet talk are only interests; their interests.

The Arabian Gulf states, faced with the same threats, must remain united and produce a joint agenda on ways of protecting their respective states without having to rely on Western allies that have proved to be unreliable.

I would further ask our leaders not to only rely on advisors on foreign policy, but also to consult with prominent citizens who have proved successful in building their country's future. We must put our heads together to find ways of stopping GCC states from becoming corridors through which terrorists and militias move between Arab countries and places where they hide their funds. We must bolster our respective militaries, improve intelligence sharing, and fund our own research centres, specializing in political science and military strategic planning and staffed by proven experts in their field; individuals capable of thinking out of the box on how to overcome the challenges before us. We must be empowered by solid information and analyses to make effective decisions serving our interests, instead of being blown around like straws in the wind by gusts from outside.

Lastly, I would strongly urge all GCC member states and their Arab allies, such as Egypt and Jordan, to refuse absolutely the division of Iraq into three. And in the event this plan is put into effect, then we must take all necessary political, economic and military measures to halt its implementation. Be ready and alert! Flex your muscles and show your power with military parades and the issuance of real red lines not easily erasable meaningless smudges before it is too late.

World leaders should hang their heads in shame

7 September 2014

OH, WHAT AN IMPRESSIVE show the North Atlantic Treaty Organization (NATO) is putting on in the Welsh city of Newport! Tom Jones' *Green, Green Grass of Home* is now peppered with tanks and missiles while Cardiff plays host to mighty warships. Enemies of the West must be quaking in their boots; except they are not. They must be chuckling at the hollow rhetoric coming out of the mouths of the Leader of the Free World and his European allies; empty words delivered in the presence of representatives from four Arab countries. Are they there to write a script for one of Adel Imam's famous humorous parodies on life? This situation is starting to look like fodder for one of this legendary Egyptian actor's movies.

Our planet is experiencing unprecedented man-made crises. Like me, people everywhere are asking: *What's happening to our world?* We look at those leaders and think: *If these are the people responsible for protecting our lives, then God help us.*

As unbelievable as it sounds, here is the plot. Take note please, Adel Imam!

A gang of losers seeking power, wealth and territory decide to dupe feeble-minded young Muslims with the promise of an Islamist State; a Utopian land stretching from Syria to Iraq and eventually encompassing Lebanon, Jordan, Kuwait and Saudi Arabia, where flogging, stoning, beheading, crucifying and burying children alive are accepted norms. In this "magical caliphate" women recognizable only by their eyes are barred from leaving home without a close male relative. Televisions are smashed. Schools are forbidden to teach music, art and philosophy. Smokers are lashed in public. Landmarks are painted black to match the group's fluttering flags.

This is a place where fake Imams tell followers "We will take you to Paradise, even if we have to drag you in chains on the way there." This hell on earth not only attracts educated fighters from distant shores, it holds an appeal for young Western girls eager to become brides and breed a new generation of psychopaths.

Some 10,000–15,000 masked and attired in black, of course, initially succeed in taking swathes of Syrian and Iraqi territories larger than the size of the United Kingdom, virtually unopposed. Armies run from those thugs like rabbits; soldiers caught and stripped are mercilessly executed. Tens of thousands of civilians flee to a barren mountain top where many

154

succumb to thirst. Parents weak from hunger and dehydration are forced to abandon elderly parents and young children to the sands during escapes.

In the meantime, the fanatics consolidate their state flush with "Made in America" weapons and a treasure chest overflowing with oil revenues, cash plundered from banks, kidnap ransoms and the sale of women and girls in the local slave market. Nobody can accuse them of being disorganized. They are managing civil society, overseeing public institutions, passing laws, hiring experts to advise them in various fields and doing a roaring trade in Iraq's natural resources.

No, Mr Imam, this is not a period movie set in the 10th century; it is a contemporary reflection of events happening now. What is that you say? *It lacks credibility?* Yes, I know that Egyptian audiences are not that dumb to fall for such a fantastical, unrealistic scenario ... but ...

Yesterday, while watching the most powerful men on earth discussing what to do about the so-called Islamic State during the NATO summit, I felt an impending sense of doom. What is there to discuss? Eradicating a handful of murderous criminals before the contagion spreads is surely no challenge for a superpower. The US and its allies did not hesitate in going after Saddam Hussein's non-existent Weapons of Mass Destruction (WMD) or to invade Afghanistan to smoke out a cave dweller. In truth, they must bear responsibility for this gang's rise; Daesh drew strength and popularity out of Obama's inaction in Syria to end the regime's slaughter of its own people. Its seeming success, amplified by its well-oiled propaganda machine, spawns tentacles reaching into dungeons, back alleys and tunnels, creating a complex web of danger.

Yet, in the case of Daesh, President Barack Obama and his sidekick David Cameron have ruled out boots on the ground. Even, their pledge to arm the Kurdish Peshmerga, battling to protect Irbil as well as besieged minorities, has yet to manifest. Dropping bombs on Daesh convoys will not cut it. Why, because those extremists will simply blend with local populations or head back into northern Syria to re-group. And as Obama has controversially admitted, he has no strategy to attack Daesh in Syria, where it is headquartered. Bravo David Cameron! It is so reassuring to know that the UK government is compiling evidence against Daesh fighters for crimes against humanity. I will bet those cockroaches preferring death to life are suffering sleepless nights worrying about ending up behind bars in The Hague. They deserve pest control not a panel of judges.

If the United States, Europe and NATO are too cowardly to confront this scourge they should hire mercenaries headed by former military/ intelligence chiefs to do the job for them, just as security firms like the infamous Blackwater that in 2003, terrorized populations in Iraq. The Sicilian Mafia would be more effective than Obama and Co. Perhaps the Peruvian Shining Path or the Colombian Farc could be persuaded.

However, there is one question that bugs me more than most. Where are the Arabs? This madness is playing out on our doorstep; it threatens us directly and imminently. The fact that it hides under the banner of Islam is nothing short of a sacrilegious assault on our faith. Forget the Arab World as an entity; it is disunited and in disarray! The Gulf Cooperation Council (GCC) has the firepower and expertise to militarily intervene on its own. GCC states do not need permission from Washington to protect themselves or our brothers in Iraq and Syria. Why are we not embarrassed that the Kurds are battling on our behalf? If we do not stand up to this threat and others, such as the Shi'ite Houthis bent on the destruction of Yemen, not only will history stand as our judge, so too will our great-grandchildren.

There are no heroes in this unfolding script; only rogues, wimps and fools marching us towards Armageddon. And as for Obama and Cameron, they are nothing but strutting bit-part actors in a plot that gives them the jitters. The US President appears to have stage fright, desperately seeking cues and lines from the British Prime Minister. Neither displays the presence of a leader capable of rescuing the world, like Abraham Lincoln, Winston Churchill or Dwight Eisenhower, not to mention our great Arab personalities, such as Omar bin Al Khattab and Khalid ibn Al Walid, whose word was their bond, and whose bravery was beyond reproach.

In this B-rated film, a bunch of bloodthirsty bad guys emerge as victors. I can only pray for a different ending before it hits theatres close to all of us.

Patience has limits

3 March 2016

UAE FOREIGN MINISTER Sheikh Abdullah bin Zayed Al Nahyan spoke the truth when he placed Iraq's Hashd Al Sha'abi (Popular Mobilization) militias (along with Badr Corps, Hezbollah and the Abbas Brigade fighting in Syria) in the same terrorist camp as Daesh and the Al Qaeda-linked Al Nusra Front.

They are all driven by sectarian interests and each is as ruthless and bloodthirsty as the other. They are all different types of cancer that must be eliminated. The difference is that Shi'ite militias working with Iraq's feeble military, advised by Iranian Revolutionary Guard, are legitimized by the government of an Arab country – or rather what used to be an Arab country before it fell under the ayatollahs' domination through the agency of pro-Iranian quisling prime ministers.

The so-called Popular Mobilization militias and the Badr Corps have slaughtered untold numbers of Iraqi citizens and destroyed their homes after freeing Daesh-held areas, purely because they were Sunnis. Hezbollah and the Abu Fadl Abbas Brigade have done the same in Syria. Mosques have been turned to rubble. People forced with their children into tent cities or to take the dangerous route to Europe seeking asylum. They are, along with Daesh, two sides of the same vicious coin.

Instead of extending our hands to militias, we should be fighting them.

Iraq, a true Arab heartland, needs our support to free itself from Persian occupation. Only then, will the soil be fertile to enable this stricken land to get back on its feet. As long as it is under Iranian influence it will never be peaceful and prosperous.

The first step is to close our diplomatic missions in Iraq as long as it behaves like an enemy state. At the same time Iraqis working in Gulf Cooperation Council countries should not be made to suffer for the sins of their rogue government and its armed bands. Most left their homeland with the dream to rebuild the lives that were lost to them.

We have known this sorry state of affairs for a very long time but because of the struggles of the Iraqi people to recapture their country's equilibrium after 10 years of merciless sanctions, foreign occupation, sectarian conflicts and terrorism, we have given Iraqi governments the opportunity to lift Iraq out of its complex quagmire – and, as it has turned out, all for nothing.

Iraq's leadership has run out of chances to prove it is on the side of the people, regardless of their ethnicity or sectarian affiliations, and has done little to consolidate its place within the Arab World.

The time for coddling and diplomatic-speak is over. Kudos to Sheikh Abdullah bin Zayed for saying it like it is. Enough pretence in a turbulent region threatened by Iran's power struggle. Iraq must understand that its pretend fence-sitting will no longer be tolerated. Iraqi Prime Minister Haider Al Abadi must be challenged. Is he setting his country on a road to becoming a de facto Iranian province or will he respect its Arab roots and identity? It is probable he has already chosen.

Al Abadi wasted no time in defending his ragtag armies on Iraq's Samaria channel while accusing the United Arab Emirates (UAE) of launching "a flagrant intervention into the Iraqi affairs". Ironically, he is also asking GCC states to stand with Baghdad's anti-terrorist positions. The day that our finest young men risk their lives to fuel Iranian ambitions will be a cold day in hell!

Iraq's Foreign Ministry put out a statement reiterating: "The Popular Mobilization has come from the Iraqi components and was formed as an official body that works within the umbrella of the government and under the command of the Commander-in-Chief of the Iraqi armed forces." I would like to ask him how many Sunnis, Christians, Kurds and Yazidis are members of those government-sanctioned militias? And what kind of government relies on gunmen for its defence!

Al Abadi's message to the UAE has been pounced upon by Iraqi TV networks that have evidently been given the green light to spew insults and threats in our direction. However, such vindictiveness on the part of the government and media is not the people's; it is one that has been spawned by the Prime Minister's puppet-master, Tehran.

Those of Iraq's limbs plagued by Persian sickness must be amputated at their roots. Our hearts have been open for the Iraqis. I was deeply upset knowing that 500,000 Iraqi children died since the end of the Gulf War as a result of economic sanctions imposed on Iraq. I was distraught watching flames rise from the Baghdad skyline during George W. Bush's "shock and awe" and when coalition troops finally withdrew, I prayed that a brave new Iraq would soon emerge from the ashes.

Instead, what has arisen is a virtual Persian enclave. We can no more blind our eyes to reality. Iraq must understand that the patience we have shown was not weakness but rather tolerance for the actions of a sibling trying to get out of a maze strewn with boulders. And all we receive in return is insults!

Saddam Hussein was an Arab nationalist, fiercely proud of his country's heritage as "the Cradle of Civilization", and of its contributions to Islam's Golden Age. Most importantly, he preserved his country's Arab identity, chipped away since the US-led invasion and occupation.

The Al Maliki government's sectarian bias and oppressive tactics against Sunnis is responsible for the rise of terrorist groups, such as Al Qaeda and Daesh, where there were once none. His cleansing of experienced Sunni officers from the army to be replaced by Shi'ites loyal to his regime resulted in a force that shamefully took to its heels leaving its weapons behind when confronted by a small group of Daesh fighters in Mosul.

Prime Minister Haider Al Abadi succeeded Nouri Al Maliki, pledging to work for the benefit of all, but until now there has been little sign he is any different from his predecessor. His "Made in Iran" stamp is merely less visible.

Those days when Iraqis of all faiths and ethnicities lived together in harmony are unlikely to return because the loyalties of successive Shi'ite governments rest primarily with a foreign power. That is the bottom line in black and white. The hundreds of thousands of Iraqis martyred during the eight-year-long Iran–Iraq War must be turning in their graves.

Confirmed! Iraq was a war of aggression

9 July 2016

A BROKEN" AND "HAUNTED" MAN was *The Telegraph's* description of former British Prime Minister, Tony Blair, following the release of the Iraq War report. What I saw was a good 'poor little me' act performed to perfection in an attempt to salvage remnants of his reputation. "I didn't lie or deceive," he emphasized over and over with teary eyes while still insisting that: "The world is better off without Saddam".

He quotes from an "Iraq Survey Report" to the effect that Iraqi President Saddam Hussein was poised to reconstitute his Weapons of Mass Destruction (WMD) programmes as soon as sanctions were lifted – yet another twisting of the truth from the master manipulator.

Firstly, how would inspectors know the secretive Iraqi leader's future intentions? Secondly, Charles Duelfer, who headed the Bush administration's investigations of Iraq's weapons status, told Congressional committees that Saddam's ability had "progressively decayed" and inspectors found no evidence of any efforts to restart the nuclear programme.

Blair maintains that the 11 September attacks changed the culture. He says he was afraid that Iraq's WMDs would fall into the hands of terrorist groups, notwithstanding that there were no terrorists in Iraq pre-2003.

The Chilcot Report was no establishment whitewash like its predecessors. This time, the blame for Iraq's ruin was laid squarely at the former prime minister's feet although the intelligence services and the gung-ho Ministry of Defence, which left soldiers without appropriate vehicles and body armour, did not escape censure. But it did stop short of tarring Blair as a liar in spite of his dodgy dossiers; one listed from a student's 12-year-old thesis published on the internet.

There was another crucial omission. It failed to pronounce the war as "illegal" even though former United Nations (UN) Secretary General Kofi Annan did not hesitate to do so in September 2004, when he said the invasion was not sanctioned by the UN Security Council or the UN's Charter.

There are armies of lawyers scrutinizing the report's 6,000 pages so as to build a case against him, but it will be a mammoth challenge.

The International Criminal Court in The Hague has announced it will not investigate Blair's decision, which it maintains is outside its remit. Blair is lucky he is not African or, "even worse", an Arab. If he were, that remit would undoubtedly be stretched to accommodate. A UN-supported special tribunal is also out; it would be vetoed by the US and Britain in the Security Council.

Blair deserves to spend the rest of his life behind bars, together with his American buddies, former President George W. Bush, Vice-President Dick Cheney and Minister of Defence Donald Rumsfeld: the war's architects. Invading Iraq was on their to-do list from the get-go, along with several other Arab countries.

Blair admits that Bush's aim was regime change in Iraq and that he was on board. In one of his now declassified notes to the US President he says the war's goal is to bring about "the true post-cold-war world order", a statement smacking of neoconservative doctrine.

If truth be told, they knew full well that Iraq had destroyed its chemical and biological weapons in the aftermath of the 1991 Gulf War. The former head of Saddam's Republican Guard and his son-in-law, Hussein Kamel Al-Majid, confirmed exactly that to Western intelligence agencies when he defected to Jordan in August 1995. Dr David Kelly, a weapons expert, died in mysterious circumstances shortly after exposing holes in Number 10's case for war.

Blair's admission that regime change was the underlying goal is a hot potato. Forcible regime change is illegal under international law and violates the UN Charter. This is why they cherry-picked intelligence to suit and launched a propaganda war against "evil" Saddam, whom they armed with chemical weapons during the eight-year-long Iraq-Iran war, and who was given a wink and a nod to invade Kuwait via the former US ambassador to Iraq, April Glaspie.

They destroyed a functioning country on false pretexts. Blair's missives to Bush indicate the pair was waiting anxiously for Saddam to slip up so they could pounce. A massive troop contingent was waiting in the wings. Bush was itching to deploy it in theatre.

UN weapons inspectors asked for more time but, with or without a new UN resolution, rightly blocked by France and Russia, Bush was champing at the bit. He was getting tired of his British poodle's continual yapping at his heels demanding UN resolutions and an Israel-Palestine roadmap that ultimately led nowhere. He was ready to go it alone and gave his sycophant across the pond an opportunity to opt out with no hard feelings. But Blair had pledged in a 2002 memo to stand with Bush whatever.

This neo-imperial gang terrorized Iraqis with "shock and awe", hanged Iraq's president, dismantled its army and purged its civil service of Baathists. They are responsible for the death of hundreds of thousands of Iraqis, the displacement of more than two million and for the eruption of sectarian hatred.

They compounded their crimes with their failure to plan for the day after, leaving vacuums of governance that were speedily filled by Shi'ite militias, Al Qaeda and its "Islamic State" offshoot, which wrapped its tentacles around Syria and many other Arab countries. And they were warned that weakening Iraq would unleash its Iranian neighbour and make the way clear for the implementation of its geopolitical regional ambitions.

They threw the first stones in the pond against the advice of Middle East specialists who correctly predicted the ripples inherent in the removal of an iron fist from Iraq. Europe is paying the price in terms of terrorist attacks and hordes of Iraqi and Syrian refugees knocking on its doors. Several commentators are even pointing fingers at Blair for triggering the British public's hostility towards the political class and mistrust of officialdom.

In short, Bush, Blair and their cohorts are criminals with blood-stained hands who should be made an example of to deter others, especially the Trumps of this world who shoot first and ask questions later. But do not hold your breath!

The question that troubles me is why Iraq when the country did not have sufficient food and medical supplies and presented no threat?

On the other hand, Tehran was believed to be developing nuclear weapons, was building up its military capacity and its mullahs never stopped spewing messages of hate directed at the United States as well as threats to Israel. Not only has Iran not been targeted by the United States, it has been rewarded for its years of clandestine nuclear development with the cessation of economic sanctions while its president is courted by European capitals.

Together and separately, Bush, Blair and US President Barack Obama have upset the fragile regional balance of power, leaving Sunni states more vulnerable than they were when Saddam's Iraq was a powerful bulwark protecting Gulf Cooperation Council (GCC) member states from Iran's territorial ambitions. Was this intentional all along? Is the bolstering of Iran to the detriment of Saudi Arabia and the Gulf states America's set-in-stone foreign policy objective? Obama has been critical of Saudi Arabia, suggesting that the Kingdom must learn to share the neighbourhood with Iran!

We must never forget what was done to Iraq still bleeding from the fallout to this day. It is imperative that we know exactly who is with us and who is against us. GCC leaderships should demand honest and transparent answers from our friends in the West, not confined to mere words.

I have been warning about the potential of US-Iranian détente or some sort of Grand Bargain in my columns for many years. For many the idea was alien, even laughable. They are not laughing now.

Our allies must prove which side of the fence they sit; they can begin with an official recognition of the "Arabian Gulf" based on the fact that the coastlines of Gulf states around this body of water are 85 per cent longer than Iran's. If they refuse to comply with this comparatively minor request, we will know where we stand.

As Aesop wrote: "A doubtful friend is worse than a certain enemy. Let a man be one thing or the other and we then know how to meet him."

5

The Syrian genocide: a country destroyed by its leader

Introduction

WHAT HAS BECOME OF SYRIA? Who would have thought that this once beautiful, vibrant and peaceful country, so packed with ancient history, could be destroyed so easily? Not only has foreign meddling played a big part in the country's downfall, but worse, the country's own president, Bashar Al Assad, has had a major role in butchering his own people and allowed terrorism to flourish and completely destroy the fabric of society. I fear for the future of Syria.

A definitive death toll, since the anti-government protests broke out some five years ago, is impossible to ascertain. However, more than 250,000 innocent men, women and children have been reported killed since March 2011 according to the Syrian Observatory for Human Rights, a UK-based activist group. (See Al Jazeera English, "Almost quarter of a million people dead in Syria", 7 August 2015.) A further one million have been reported injured, and an unaccountable number of others forced to flee.

Thousands of civilians have been victims of mass shootings and gunfire between government forces and insurgents. The United Nations (UN) said more than 100 people were killed in Homs alone in one day (25 May 2012). Most were shot at close range. Half were children.

The UN, world leaders and human rights groups have condemned the Syrian regime for "alleged" atrocities including barrel bombings and chemical attacks on civilians, as well as kidnapping, torture and extrajudicial executions. In September 2015 France launched an investigation into "alleged" war crimes and crimes against humanity in the Assad regime. (See the *Independent*, "France launches war crimes and crimes against humanity investigation into Bashar Al Assad's regime", 30 September 2015.) The investigation is looking into claims of torture and kidnapping "on the basis of indications received from the Foreign Ministry".

I am tired of hearing – and having to use – the word "alleged". We know who is responsible, so why should we let political correctness get in the way?

The Syrian government has used chlorine-filled barrel bombs. Hundreds – if not thousands –were killed in a 2013 rocket attack in Ghouta, a Damascus suburb controlled by the opposition. Several rockets contained the nerve agent sarin. We saw it with our own eyes on newscasts. Was that not US President Barack Obama's infamous "red line"?

The human tragedy is unfathomable. Eleven million people – roughly half the population – have been forced to flee their homeland, putting a huge strain on other nations where they are not welcome. They are forced to live in hellish conditions, unwanted by the host nations they wish to call their new homes. Those that managed to escape, and survive the treacherous journey from Syria, do not want to be living like caged animals in other countries, they want to be safe at home. But they have little choice.

Many are unable to leave Syria. They are prisoners in their own homes. Others are living in deteriorating conditions. Famine is wide-spread in many parts of the country. Amnesty International – an international human rights group – published accounts of people trying to live on boiled water and leaves in the city of Madaya. (See CNN, "Amnesty: famine in Syria city of Madaya 'the tip of an iceberg'", 9 January 2016.) Philip Luther, the Middle East and North Africa director for Amnesty International said: "Syrians are suffering and dying across the country because starvation is being used as a weapon of war by both the Syrian government and armed groups."

According to the United Nations (UN), it will take $8.4bn to meet the urgent needs of the most vulnerable Syrians – and not even half of that aid has been raised so far.

Paulo Sérgio Pinheiro, Chairman of the UN panel investigating human rights abuses in Syria, said in a report in early 2016, "With each passing day there are fewer safe places in Syria .... Everyday decisions – whether to visit a neighbor, to go out to buy bread – have become, potentially, decisions about life and death." (See *The New York Times*, "Death in Syria", 14 September 2015.)

In an email to Reuters, Pinheiro said the UN has been in direct contact with residents inside Madaya: "They have provided detailed information on shortages of food, water, qualified physicians, and medicine," he said. "This has led to acute malnutrition and deaths among vulnerable groups in the town." (See Reuters, "U.N. war crimes investigators gathering testimony from starving Syrian town", 12 January 2016.)

The human tragedy is unforgivable. Imagine the psychological damage done to the forgotten people of Syria, particularly young, impressionable children. How will they ever forgive the world for leaving them to suffer the way they have? This casts a big shadow on all of our futures. How Assad is still in power, I cannot fathom. Five years since the start of the uprising and he has managed to do what other leaders around him failed to do. Assad remains at the helm despite being guilty of crimes against his own people. He should be handed to the International Criminal Court (ICC) and held accountable for his actions. He should pay the price for each life he has taken, and every rape and torture committed by his army of thugs.

Iran and Russia are keeping the Assad government in power – militarily and financially. With Tehran and Moscow by his side and the West doing nothing, there is little hope of Assad going anywhere.

Iran – the biggest meddler in Middle Eastern countries – is believed to have spent billions of dollars over the past five years propping up the Alawite-led government, providing military advisors and subsidizing weapons. Iran has long acknowledged sending military advisors to Syria, but continues to deny the presence of any ground forces. Despite that, media reports suggest that hundreds of Iranian troops have arrived in the country. It comes as no surprise too that Lebanon's Hezbollah movement is said to be propping up the Assad government.

Bashar Al Assad has put his premiership before his country and he is responsible for the influx of terrorists. He is the greatest war criminal of our time, and as long as he is in Russia's embrace he can sleep soundly. He is assured of immunity because, firstly, Syria is not a member of the ICC and, secondly, he is confident that the UN Security Council cannot refer him to The Hague thanks to Russia's power of veto. Russia makes a mockery of international laws and institutions set up to hold leaders to account for crimes against humanity.

Russia said it will continue to support Assad forces and back anti-Assad rebels as long as they are fighting against Daesh. In an interview with Germany's *Bild* newspaper, President Vladimir Putin countered claims that Moscow only backs the regime rather than hitting jihadists: "We support both Assad's army and the armed opposition." According to the President: "We are coordinating our joint operations with them and support their offensives by airstrikes in various sections of the front line." (See RT, "Russia supports both Assad troops and rebels in battle against ISIS – Putin", 12 January 2016.)

The simple fact is that millions of Syrians need our help. The genocide in Syria is the worst humanitarian crisis of our time, and the country is on the brink of economic collapse. It will never be able to return to its former glory. World leaders continue to sit back and watch it crumble under the pretence that their hands are tied by Syria's veto-wielding ally Russia.

But Russia and Iran are not the only ones to blame. The situation has escalated out of control because of the lack of action by world leaders, notably the United States of America, which still recognizes Assad as the President.

President Barack Obama could have and should have cut this disease at its roots while in its infancy, but he blinked over and over again. If Bashar Al Assad was dealt with in 2011, or when he used chemical weapons in 2013 against the Syrian people, then we would not be dealing with a world epidemic.

While world leaders are making plans to host refugees in their countries, all they offer is a temporary solution. But you must know that Syrians do not want to be refugees in Europe even more than Europe is reluctant to host them! What they need is to go back home to Syria. A "safe zone" should be created within Syrian land, where Syrians can have a safe shelter from the butcher Assad while a solution is being found. A safe zone protected by the North Atlantic Treaty Organization (NATO).

I said it in my keynote speech to the 24th Annual Arab-US Policy-makers' Conference in Washington DC on Thursday 15 October 2015, the best thing for Syrian refugees is to go home. I firmly believe that. Do you think that they want to be refugees? Living like cattle in fenced off areas, and suspected of being terrorists based on their religion?

The rise of Daesh

The five-year war in Syria has not only left a quarter of a million of people dead, created the worst refugee crisis since World War II and destroyed Syria beyond repair, it has also allowed Daesh – the most dangerous jihadist group of our time – to make a home for itself in Syria and vast parts of Iraq.

The size of the group may be unclear, but its intentions are blatant. It is working towards a state ruled by terror, using the cover of our holy religion Islam. The group has managed to make huge territorial gains in Syria since its formation in July 2013. Oil has played a big part in its growth. The Syrian opposition government estimates Daesh to have control of more than 60 per cent of the country's oil market giving the terror group the ability to self-finance its activities.

Daesh is responsible for the deaths of thousands of people on Syrian soil and the mass exodus of hundreds of thousands of others. It is also responsible for the lost heritage in Syria and northern Iraq. (See *The New York Times*, "Antiquities lost, casualties of war", 3 October 2014.) It has deliberately destroyed centuries-old shrines, temples and statues. Successive generations of history have been obliterated. UNESCO, the United Nations educational, scientific and cultural agency, called the demolition of the Temple of Bel in Palmyra "an intolerable crime against civilization," and a "war crime" (See *Newsweek*, "What is lost with Daesh's destruction of Syria's Temple of Bel", 1 September 2015.)

What concerns me most is how impotent the international community has become, both diplomatically and militarily. Assad's future is being used as a bargaining chip in this disgraceful geopolitical power play in which Syrian lives are considered collateral damage.

When Prime Minister, David Cameron accused Bashar Al Assad of enlisting recruits, he did not demand he leave office. (See the *Independent*, "Syria crisis: David Cameron says Assad is a 'recruiting sergeant for Daesh' – but will not call for him to stand down", 27 September 2015.) This on the slim prospect of taking part in a coalition to defeat Daesh.

Meanwhile Washington is increasing pressure on Turkey to secure its border with Syria, which has been used as a safe passage for foreign fighters aligned with Daesh. (See the *Wall Street Journal*, "Pentagon considers plan to train fighters in Syria", 12 January 2016.) In addition, the Pentagon is said to be considering a request from Ankara to help train – and equip – Sunni fighters inside Syria as part of a concerted effort to secure the border.

World leaders have to take responsibility for their role in allowing this terror group to flourish. They need to take action sooner rather than later. Look what Daesh has achieved in a few short years. Just imagine what the future will hold.

Empty talk will not save Syrians

26 February 2012

WHAT ARE THE so-called Friends of the Syrian People waiting for? Will they finally act when the Barada River flowing through Damascus turns red with blood? It is too late for conferences, toothless United Nations (UN) General Assembly resolutions and the dispatching of envoys to Damascus. Talk is cheap when every day people are dying. What use is verbal censure when the city of Homs has been bombarded for weeks?

Hama, too, is being besieged by government "occupying" forces and is now entirely cut off from the outside without telephone or internet. Civilians are huddled inside their homes, unable to shop for bread or seek medical assistance. According to activists, Syrian forces are shooting entire families, lining them up execution-style. A video posted on the internet shows the bodies of a man and a woman from a farming community along with their five children, the youngest just 10 months old. This is the kind of atrocity the Nazis committed during World War II. Who would ever have imagined that the emissaries of the Syrian government would stoop so low!

It took the deaths of two foreign journalists – *The Sunday Times'* war reporter Marie Colvin and the French photographer Remi Ochlik – whose safe house in Homs was shelled, for the world to understand that there is no refuge for the innocent as long as the Assad regime retains power. The way they died is tragic; by all accounts they were dedicated professionals devoting to getting to the truth. But unlike the residents of Homs who have nowhere else to go, they chose to put their lives at risk.

For all its sympathetic mumblings, over the 11 months since Syrians took to the streets to demand freedom from oppression the international community has done nothing tangible to prevent the regime from committing crimes against humanity. Unlike the Libyans, whose cries for help were answered, the Syrian people have been abandoned.

Given Ankara's uncompromising moral stance I had great hopes that Turkey would line up its military might to send President Al Assad packing but the Prime Minister Recep Tayyip Erdoğan's powerful rhetoric has not translated into action.

Western powers are similarly paralysed. As long as they persist in going the UN route, their hands will be tied by Security Council vetoes wielded by China and Russia, countries that are turning a deaf ear to the Syrian people's plight in favour of their own geopolitical and economic interests.

It seems that the UN wants to show it is doing something useful, so it has appointed its former Secretary General Kofi Annan as a special envoy to Damascus. What a waste of time that is! Mr Annan means well but whoever imagines he can loosen Assad's grip is dreaming. When the UN's sitting Secretary General is just a bureaucrat devoid of persuasive communication skills, what chance does Mr Annan have when his record has hardly been world-altering?

The UN can only be an effective body when its secretaries general are given real power to their elbow and when the five permanent UN Security Council member countries are stripped of their vetoes. The same goes for the League of Arab States. Its Secretary General Nabil Elaraby is hamstrung by conflicting opinions within the League; all he can do is ask the Security Council to demand a ceasefire. That is a joke when over 7,000 Syrians have been killed to date and the Syrian president has ignored such appeals from friends and foes alike.

People with real leadership qualities and the authority to make decisions, rather than clerks, should be heading the UN and the Arab League. Elaraby has proved that he lacks wisdom and judgment on several occasions. Appointing a controversial Sudanese general to head the League's observer mission to Syria was one; selecting former International Atomic Energy Agency (IAEA) chief Mohamed ElBaradei as a mediator was another guaranteed failure.

We do not need figureheads at the helm of those bodies especially when our world has become so dangerous. We need genuine leaders able to communicate well in their own language and others, especially English. We do not need males, we need men.

Bashar Al Assad has lost all credibility. There is only one route left to him and that is out. No leader can represent his people when he is killing them at the same time. He should be viewed as an occupier, subject to overthrow and arrest. For all the blood on his hands I do not want to see him killed. He should be dragged before the International Criminal Court (ICC) in The Hague, along with the rest of his corrupt gang, his cronies and his jumped-up family members, to the kind of justice he has always denied to anyone with the guts to stand up to him.

On Friday, various Western and Arab countries calling themselves the "Friends of the Syrian People" – that include representatives of the US,

Britain, France, Turkey, Qatar, Saudi Arabia and the Arab League – met in Tunis primarily to discuss the means with which humanitarian aid can reach those Syrians who need it, such as the formation of aid corridors. In the first place, I object to the location. Why Tunis when it has a brand new government with unproven credentials in dealing with high political stakes in the Middle East? Secondly, the Syrian opposition is asking for heavy weapons and a no-fly zone, not food.

My number one hero is the Saudi Minister of Foreign Affairs Prince Saud Al Faisal who backs the arming of Syrian opposition fighters and is apparently as sick of ineffective talk as I am. He walked out of the Tunisia meet due to "inactivity" on the part of their fellow delegates. "Is it justice to offer aid and leave the Syrians to the killing machine?" the prince asked. Qatar's Minister of Foreign Affairs Sheikh Hamad bin Jassim Al Thani wants an international Arab force to be formed to keep the peace in Syria, which I have been advocating for months.

Let us show those powers meddling in our affairs that we can take care of business ourselves. Were an all-Arab army to enter Syria with Arab League support, it would be welcomed by the majority of Syrians whose voices would soon drown out objections from Russia and China. This is our moment. I can only hope that Saudi Arabia, Qatar and any Arab state that is a true friend to Syria will grasp it. President Assad has closed his ears to Arab appeals and proposals but even someone as arrogant as he is cannot ignore our collective wrath.

Assad deserves to pay for his crimes

25 June 2012

A RECENT REPORT by the Associated Press (AP) that read "Britain and America are willing to offer the Syrian president Bashar Al-Assad safe passage – and even clemency – as part of a diplomatic push to convene a United Nations (UN)-sponsored conference in Geneva" was deeply disturbing.

President Al Assad does not merit mercy. He is just as brutal as former Bosnian Serb leader Radovan Karadžić and former Bosnian Serb general Ratko Mladić, on trial for committing genocide and war crimes. For more than a year, his military has been shelling homes with tanks and helicopter gunships mirroring the savagery of the Khmer Rouge in Cambodia, who had no respect for human life. His army has tortured, killed and dismembered civilians including young children. Millions have been terrorized. Tens of thousands have been forced to flee to neighbouring countries or have been displaced from their homes. Assad may be educated, well-mannered and softly-spoken, but beneath the sophisticated veneer he is even more monstrous than his father Hafez was.

Imagine the outcry were Karadžić and Mladić to be pardoned; allowing those murderers to go free would be unthinkable. How much more unthinkable would it be for Assad to be rewarded for the horrors he has perpetrated? Brutality must be entrenched in that dynastic family's genes. I still remember with a shudder how Hafez Al Assad quelled an uprising in the city of Hama during February 1982. He authorized his brother Rifaat to cleanse the area of defenders at any cost, which he did with enthusiasm, ending the lives of up to 40,000, mainly innocents, in the process.

Bashar Al Assad's ongoing ruthlessness and cruelty, his indifference to the suffering of his own people at his own hand, shames every Arab. Our brothers and sisters in Syria are crying out to the Arab World for intervention; they are pleading to be saved. Our TV screens have displayed Assad's handiwork, the tiny bodies of young children massacred by the Alawite *Shabiha* to punish their dissenting parents. Yet, until now, not a single Arab country has responded to those pleas with practical assistance, with the exception of Saudi Arabia and Qatar, who, according to *The Guardian*, are arming and helping to fund the Free Syrian Army (FSA). Unfortunately, that is not enough.

The FSA is a defensive force and no match for Assad's well-trained, well-armed uniformed henchmen. Providing them with cash and weapons is a start but it will not succeed in tipping the balance in favour of those demanding an end to dictatorship. Such gestures may go some way to salvage our conscience; they may help us sleep better at night. But let us not fool ourselves. Syria is in the worst crisis in its history. How long will Arab states continue offering its people decorative icing minus the cake?

Our inaction is nothing short of shameful. Arabs constantly complain about foreign powers meddling in their affairs but show little inclination to sort out their own problems. They may grumble behind the door but refrain from making controversial decisions or taking bold steps, preferring to show a neutral face to the world. I, for one, feel ashamed that our leaders are good at talking the talk but when push comes to shove they rarely walk the walk.

It is mystifying when we have highly intelligent politicians and strategists, effective armies, air forces and navies, the benefit of cutting-edge technologies and communications systems. We behave as though we are paralysed people sitting helplessly while anxiously awaiting Western powers to make decisions on our behalf, just as they did during the earlier part of the 20th century. Those days are long gone. Imperialism is dead. We are free and independent now... or are we? If we are no longer under the thumb of hegemonic powers why do our governments stand on the sidelines permitting the US and the UK to get involved in Arab matters? Why should they be empowered to grant an exit to a criminal responsible for slaughter on a massive scale? If we are too cowardly or weak to manage our own problems we do not deserve independence; we might as well invite our former occupiers to handle our lives for us.

I realize that I might sound cynical but, frankly, I am reaching the end of my tether. I have always referred to myself as a proud Arab, but the more I see that we are still under the heel of the West, the less pride I feel in being a son of the greater Arab nation. The only ticket out Assad should get is one-way to the International Criminal Court (ICC) in The Hague. He has forfeited his and his family's right to negotiate any political transition or participate in UN-sponsored talks. The only ones with the moral authority to show him mercy are the families of the Syrian victims. Next to him President Mubarak was saintly. It would be unjust for Assad and his fashionable wife to be spotted shopping for Louboutins on the rue Saint-Honoré in Paris while the former Egyptian leader gasps his last breath behind bars.

It is worth mentioning that in recent days, the Obama administration has denied that it is contemplating handing the Syrian dictator a free pass, but there is rarely smoke without fire. It is known that President Barack Obama is under pressure to intervene for humanitarian reasons. It is also common knowledge that he is unwilling to confront Assad's backers, Moscow and Beijing who are out to safeguard their regional interests to the detriment of the Syrian people. From Obama's perspective, permitting Assad to walk off into the sunset, in the way that Ben Ali of Tunisia did, might be a lesser evil.

Before any such seed might sprout, Arab heads of state should send Washington and London an unequivocal message: Keep out! Any dirty laundry in our neighbourhood is ours to clean, else we might as well close our eyes to the tears of Syria's children, erase the term Arab World from our minds forever more and bow our heads to our masters in Washington and London.

The United Nations: just an expensive show

7 August 2012

THE UNITED NATIONS (UN) is arguably the most worthwhile organization on earth. On paper that is. Established in 1945 with just 51 member countries, primarily to prevent a third world war, the goals encapsulated in the organization's charter are admirable. Bringing the international community together under the UN umbrella was achieved to maintain peace and security, to nurture friendship between nations on the basis of human rights, fundamental freedoms and international laws, and the self-determination of peoples.

The idea was to provide a forum for international diplomatic, social and economic dialogue and the resolution of disputes with the benefit of muscle to be exerted as a last resort under Chapter VII of the Charter that permits the UN Security Council "to determine the existence of any threat to the peace, breach of the peace, or act of aggression" and to take military action to "restore international peace and security".

No doubt UN organs such as the United Nations Children's Emergency Fund (UNICEF), the United Nations Development Programme (UNDP), the United Nations Educational, Scientific and Cultural Organization (UNESCO), the United Nations High Commissioner for Refugees (UNHCR) and the World Health Organization (WHO) undertake invaluable work within the limits of their budgets, but there is no getting away from it, the main UN body, consisting of 193 member states today, has overall proved to be a spectacular failure. It is not meeting its obligations under its own charter. A glaring example of the UN's impotence to do anything other than debate is its ineffectiveness in halting the Syrian regime's ongoing mass murder. It is good at cataloguing crimes, drafting resolutions and holding press conferences, which make not one jot of difference to Syrian men, women and children who are being tortured, mutilated, shelled and bombed almost daily.

I have been following the numerous Security Council meetings intently, hoping against hope that its five permanent and 10 non-permanent members will take decisive action to halt the killing, but all I see is squabbling, backbiting and obstruction. Most of the world agrees that something tangible must be done, and done quickly. On Friday, the UN General Assembly passed a resolution drafted by Saudi Arabia "deploring the failure of the Security Council to agree on measures to ensure the compliance of Syrian authorities with its decisions". But as the General Assembly has no power, that resolution, like so many others, is destined to be filed away and forgotten.

Kofi Annan, the envoy appointed by the UN to mediate in Syria, has thrown up his hands, announcing his resignation effective end August. "Without serious, purposeful and united international pressure including from the powers of the region it is impossible for me or for anyone to compel the Syrian government in the first place and also the opposition to take the steps necessary to begin a political process … . At a time when the Syrian people need action there continues to be name calling and finger pointing in the Security Council," Annan said.

This is not the first time that the UN has reneged on its responsibilities. The UN abandoned the people of Rwanda under Annan's watch. A report published by an independent investigatory commission led by former Swedish Prime Minister Ingvar Carlsson accused the UN of failing to stem the genocide in Rwanda that robbed the lives of some 800,000. Mr Annan in his capacity as UN Secretary General accepted the report's findings and expressed his regret while pledging to thwart a similar future disaster. That promise has turned out to be empty.

The UN has also admitted failure in its peace-keeping role by permitting Bosnian Serbs to systematically murder thousands of Muslim men and boys in Srebrenica in July 1995. Srebrenica was supposed to be a safe area under the protection of UN-led troops. "The tragedy of Srebrenica will haunt our history forever," is a quote from a self-flagellating UN report.

UN forces were insufficiently manned and if the North Atlantic Treaty Organization (NATO) had not stepped in, the Muslim Bosnian death toll would have been much higher.

Over 20,000 have been killed in Syria. Just like Rwandans, the Syrian people are crying out to the international community for protection and all they have received so far are commiserations. To be fair, neither Annan nor his successor Ban Ki-moon should be held accountable. Any UN head is virtually powerless. The way that the organization is structured with decision-making solely in the hands of the Security Council makes the UN nothing more than a house built on sand.

It is preposterous than the Big Five permanent members – the US, the UK, France, Russia and China – can veto resolutions blessed by all the other members. Russia and China have used their vetoes on three occasions to thwart resolutions censuring the Assad regime in order to preserve their respective economic and geopolitical interests. They have been loudly condemned by Washington, London and Paris but, in fact, the US does not hesitate to wield its own veto to block resolutions that justly chastise Israel or support the Palestinian bid for UN recognition of a Palestinian state with full UN membership. Moreover, whenever the US attempts to bring fellow members into line it threatens to cut its funding.

As long as individual countries prioritize their own national interests and those of their allies over the principles clearly set out in the UN Charter, the organization will continue to be a sham, a body that holds out false hope to the dispossessed and the disenfranchised. Few had much faith in the Security Council before Syria erupted but now that it has witnessed massacres of young children from the beginning of the uprising on 15 March 2011 until now and done nothing, it has been exposed as a bad joke.

I never imagined that I would agree with the sentiments of that hawkish neoconservative John Bolton, a former US Ambassador to the UN, who controversially said if the UN lost 10 floors "it wouldn't make a bit of difference". He was right. Better still, the entire bloated edifice should be demolished or turned into a museum or mall. Furthermore, those 7,750 pen pushers in the UN Secretariat and the 8,230 specially funded administrators should be sent home. The UN's annual budget currently standing at $5.15bn (2012–2013) should be put to better use such as ensuring no child dies of starvation in famine zones. I wonder how much of that budget goes on cocktail parties, trips and personal allowances. It should be investigated and audited. Its failures and accomplishments should be made public so that its usefulness can be fairly evaluated.

The UN has emerged as a tool of big powers. The body's charter is no longer worth the paper it is written on. It is lost its credibility so it should be replaced by an international organization headquartered in a neutral country like Switzerland, wherein member countries enjoy voting rights proportional to their populations – and where no one nation is empowered to lead the others by the nose.

Violence, anarchy and hunger stalk Arab lands

1 February 2013

ALL MY LIFE, I HAVE been proud to call myself an Arab. Our ancestors gave birth to great civilizations and brought knowledge to the world in the fields of mathematics, chemistry, medicine, linguistics, jurisprudence, astronomy. They were philosophers, poets and explorers, artisans, artists and builders who bequeathed magnificent buildings whose aesthetics and craftsmanship cannot be replicated today. But now it seems that Golden Age has turned to dust in countries that used to make up an Arab World that no longer exists – except in our memories and our hearts. The day when the League of Arab States headquarters becomes a museum is fast approaching.

We can no longer bury our heads in the sand. Unless we face the truth unfolding daily before us, the downward spiral will continue. Denial will bring us nothing except self-delusion. Within a region wracked by conflict, instability, chaos and poverty, Arabian Gulf states are the last bastion of reason and enlightenment but even here invisible forces via fifth-columnists are attempting to sew disharmony, which is why we must remain alert and fiercely guard all that we have achieved.

The "Arab Spring", a term synonymous with freedom, hope, renewal, failed to manifest. People of different faiths and political persuasions came together to topple oppressive leaderships but once that common goal was achieved they turned on one another. History will record that egocentricity, greed and will-to-power edged out unity. Mutual understanding was replaced by suspicion and revenge. Tolerance was cast aside for extremism and polarization, providing a breeding ground for terrorism.

When I look at the disastrous situations in Syria, Iraq, Lebanon, Egypt and Libya, I am tempted to wonder whether our area has been cursed. We have had more than our fair share of war, foreign invasion and occupation over centuries. And nowadays, so many of our Arab children are woken by explosions or wake up shivering in tented encampments or scavenge for breakfast on garbage dumps. And they are the lucky ones; particularly in Syria, youngsters have been mutilated, tortured and killed by government forces.

Is God punishing us? Is He angry that his core message of peace, brotherhood and compassion has been twisted by chest-thumping, politically-motivated false *marjaaiyas* and ayatollahs indoctrinating young minds from Tehran to Beirut, Damascus to Sana'a and filling our airwaves with hate? If we are cursed, it is because political ideologues, masquerading as religious leaders, are cheating the Creator by creating cults that distort Islam's message and stain its image. Do we not we deserve His mercy?

It hurts me to have to say this, but rot is steadily eroding our once ethical societies where family values and human dignity were once uppermost. We were born free but so many of us have become sheep without the ability to think for ourselves. The Holy Quran, the word of God received by the Prophet Mohammed (PBUH), frees us from being enslaved by anyone. The Quran enjoins us to use our brains, seek education and provides a template for making right choices.

Our forebears adhered to God's instructions and were free and united for centuries, whereas nowadays, although Muslims may read the Holy Book or even learn it by heart, they fall under the sway of religious or political leaders with un-Islamic ideologies. For instance, can someone like Bashar Al Assad be considered to be a Muslim when he has ordered the killing of over 60,000 of his own people? Are so-called preachers whipping up their congregations to strap bomb belts around their waist, destined to explode in marketplaces crowded with women and children, Muslims by any definition of the word? Why has the Middle East and North Africa (MENA) region, one of the planet's wealthiest, become inextricably associated with backwardness, violence and poverty, where innovation and progress are stifled by narrow-mindedness? It is shameful, too, that countries like Pakistan and Afghanistan where populations are devout have become havens for drug traffickers, bride-burners, rapists. The supposedly ultra-religious Afghan Taliban that torches girls' schools are funded by poppy harvests. I was recently shocked at televised reports of poppy farmers, unable to repay loans because their fields were eradicated by government forces, being forced to hand over their daughters as young as 10 to be used as sex slaves or drug-runners.

We have to admit that some of the turmoil is a direct result of interference by foreign powers who stripped Palestinians of their homeland, carved up Greater Syria, and inadvertently gift-wrapped the Cradle of Civilization Iraq to the Iranian mullahs. There is much about the US and Europe to be admired and emulated. We can learn a lot from the West and I, for one, do what I can to further inter-faith understanding. Some of my closest friends are Americans and Brits. However I do not appreciate Western interference in our business. The US and its allies are partly to blame for ruining our countries. I think I speak for the majority of Arabs when I ask you to leave us be, so that we can begin to solve our own problems unimpeded. However, blaming the West is no excuse for our failure to control our own destiny.

Yes, Egypt and Tunisia are transitioning to democracy, a process that is bound to have ups and downs. But the trajectory is far from positive. Two years on from the civil uprising in Egypt that ousted President Hosni Mubarak, no revolutionary aspiration has been achieved. On the contrary, as I write, emergency law and curfew has been imposed on three Suez Canal provinces, the air over Cairo is filled with smoke from burning buildings and vehicles mixed with teargas. And the poor are getting poorer due to rising prices, a depreciating currency and rising taxes imposed as pre-condition to a $4.8bn International Monetary Fund (IMF) loan. Authoritarianism is rearing its ugly head in Tunisia as well, a country that still suffers from chronic unemployment. There, a growing opposition accuses the government of incompetence while ordinary Tunisians complain they are no better off than they were under Ben Ali.

It is evident that Arab governance is lacking, especially when compared to Western nations and those that formerly made up the Soviet Union, countries that weathered political and economic roller coasters in an atmosphere of peace and stability. Even in the worst throes of the global economic downturn when Americans were losing homes, jobs, and, in some cases, pensions, they protested peacefully. No one tried to burn down the White House or lob Molotov cocktails over its walls like masked men in Cairo out to incinerate the Presidential Palace.

It is time for Muslims to seek the high-ground to get a bird's eye view of the current mess, the big picture if you like, before the rot destroys our very foundations. Let us get back to basics. Islam will guide us towards the light. That is provided we hold to its pillars – and deafen our ears to distorters, propagandists, extremists and cultists.

As long as we turn our guns on each other, God's forgiveness will remain elusive. The Quran exhorts Muslims to unite: Al-Hujurat [49:10] "The believers are but brothers, so make settlement between your brothers. And fear Allah that you may receive mercy." If only Muslims would heed that instruction so that we can close the book on an era that has arguably been the most destructive in living memory.

World powers cannot be trusted to save Syria

24 June 2013

BRITAIN'S PRIME MINISTER David Cameron looked like the cat that has got the cream as leaders of the world's richest countries, attending the recent G8 summit held in Northern Ireland, queued to sign a communiqué on the Syrian crisis following days of wrangling. He achieved the impossible; he persuaded his counterparts to speak with one voice. So that is it then. The most powerful leaders on the planet have spoken. Besieged Syrian civilians can look forward to being saved from a monster, an enemy of his own people, who has no right to call himself their President. I am joking, of course, although this is no laughing matter. In fact, once again, Syrians crying out for help have been mercilessly betrayed.

After hours of debate and discussion, this was their joint message: "We remain committed to achieving a political solution to the crisis based on a vision for a united, inclusive and democratic Syria … . We strongly endorse the decision to hold as soon as possible the Geneva conference on Syria." The villain who caused this ongoing tragedy, Bashar Al Assad did not even get a mention and neither did Iran or its agent Hezbollah, which remain under Vladimir Putin's protection. The communiqué should have called for Assad and the heads of his partners in crime, Iran's Revolutionary Guards and Hezbollah mercenaries, to be hauled to the International Criminal Court (ICC) for war crimes and crimes against humanity.

Instead, "the great and the good" urged both the criminal regime and the opposition to destroy organizations affiliated with Al Qaeda, which primarily translates to Jabhat Al Nusra that is battling alongside the Free Syrian Army (FSA) and other opposition forces. The communiqué is nothing but a waffle, a worthless piece of paper displaying gross impotence. Rather than appearing smug, Cameron, the summit's host, should be hanging his head in shame along with every other high and mighty participant.

Worse, US senators are actively attempting to block President Barack Obama's much overdue decision to arm the opposition, while the West's state and corporate media fails to take its governments to task, preferring to headline street protests in Brazil over bus fares, Singapore smog and the new Kardashian baby. A missing family pet or an offence committed by a single individual often warrants a media frenzy, but the fact that almost 100,000 Syrian men, women and children have been stripped of their right to life and millions more deprived of their homes, while world leaders do nothing except chat over drinks and canapés, is no longer considered newsworthy.

Evidently, the loss of Syrian life ranks low on the agendas of Western governments that permit the 21st century's most vicious criminal to continue to commit genocide before our eyes. The US and its allies had no such hesitancy before thundering into Iraq on a pack of Weapons of Mass Destruction (WMD) lies and gifting this Arab Cradle of Civilization to Iran's mullahs. They did not think twice about invading Afghanistan, ostensibly to get one criminal, Osama bin Laden, or occupying the country for 12 years to rid it of the Taliban, which, by the way, are not only going strong, but also are preparing for dialogue with the Obama administration and establishing a branch office in Doha.

Those were senseless wars, unjust wars with terrible unintended consequences. But when the US, the European Union (EU) and the North Atlantic Treaty Organization (NATO) are confronted with a genuine humanitarian disaster requiring urgent intervention on moral grounds, they do nothing except hold conferences. One is left to wonder whether some Western presidents and prime ministers secretly share the sentiments of the American right-wing radio host Glenn Beck who caused controversy saying: "We have got to stop intervening in the wars in the Middle East. This sounds awful but if they're going to kill each other, let them kill each other..."

However, while a heavy burden of guilt does, indeed, rest on the shoulders of those in Western corridors of power for paying mere lip service to supporting the Syrian opposition so as not to upset their interests, deals alliances and global strategies, the bulk of the blame must fall on us Arabs for abandoning our Syrian brothers and sisters. Why should we expect or count upon strangers to take care of our own family members? When we have reneged on our duty to heed the pleas of Syrian mothers whose children have been bombed, imprisoned, tortured or mutilated; when we have ignored the hundreds of thousands who have fled their country to live under canvas, awaiting charitable handouts or the hungry wandering around bombed-out cities hoping to find clean water or a loaf of bread, can we hold our heads high?

If the League of Arab States and the Gulf Cooperation Council (GCC) are not taking the lead in preventing Assad and his gangs from their dirty work, what right do we have to condemn President Obama and other heads of state for neglecting to treat the issue with the seriousness it deserves? When our own governments fail to take meaningful and united action to protect our own people, it is hypocritical to demand intervention from Western powers. What use are our armies, our tanks and our missiles if not to protect our own? The central role of any military is defence of the nation, in this case the Arab nation, not simply to show off its prowess, weaponry and brass bands during National Day parades.

Sad to say, the Arab League has been as ineffective as the United Nations (UN) Security Council in restraining Assad from spilling yet more innocent blood. Merely suspending Syria's Arab League membership and recalling ambassadors from Damascus are just raps on Assad's knuckles. If we close our eyes and ears to Syrian suffering, how can we expect our allies to rush to our defence if, God forbid, we were ever attacked by a hostile foreign power? Our leaderships must intervene to stop the Syrian regime's state terrorism not only because right is on our side but also as a warning to our enemies that if they cross red lines, they do so at their peril.

John Ruskin said "The strength and power of a country depends absolutely on the quantity of good men and women in it." I have appealed to our governments to act, without success, so now I ask all the good people in Arab lands to open their hearts, stand strong and say to their leaderships "We are all Syrians."

America is blind to the big picture on Syria

16 September 2013

PRESIDENT BARACK OBAMA has lost the plot on Syria to the extent his critics wonder whether he had one in the first place. If you have been following this saga as closely as I have since his "red lines" commitment a year ago, you will probably be as bewildered and confused as I am by the twists and turns of America's Commander-in-Chief. A dreadful crime against humanity was committed on 21 August. We have seen tens of videos showing children gasping for air and we have heard details of declassified evidence pointing the finger at the Assad regime. A forceful response was assured ... or so everyone believed.

Then just when it seemed the US was poised to strike, the President got cold feet. He handed his authority under the War Powers Act to one of the most bi-partisan, deadlocked Congresses in recent times, before launching a media onslaught to sell his arguments to war-weary Americans, appearing on six televised American talk shows and an address to the nation over just two days.

The American people did not buy it and neither did most lawmakers. No wonder, when the proposed strikes were billed as "short and sharp", no more than "a shot across the bow", designed to dent the regime's chemical warfare abilities. Commentators queried what a slap on Bashar Al Assad's wrist would achieve and argued that the risk of unintended consequences outweighed the administration's stated goal of ensuring the regime remained in place.

Obama was facing humiliating defeat but there was no way he could climb down from a ladder of his own making without losing face until President Putin threw him a lifeline with a proposal involving Assad turning over his chemical weapons to the international community. Assad leapt at the opportunity – and so did President Obama.

"He who hesitates is lost" is an expression Obama would have done well to heed. He boasted about American exceptionalism – a concept based on US core values empowering US global leadership – in his address to the nation. But his leadership in halting the Syrian catastrophe has been absent. Had he answered pleas from the Syrian opposition coalition for a no-fly zone, safe haven territories and heavy weapons two years ago, the Free Syrian Army (FSA) could have sent the regime packing. Instead, parts of the country have now become swamps for foreign jihadists and Al Qaeda-linked terrorists.

Moreover, his recent one step forward and two steps back has permitted Assad to evacuate military installations and hide weapons and hardware among civilian populations. The Syrian opposition, the two million refugees surviving on handouts in Turkey, Lebanon, Jordan and Iraq and over 200,000 men, women and children in Assad's prisons, many being tortured and raped, are right to feel they have been abandoned. The FSA prepared for an assault on Damascus by consolidating its battalions and handing military coordinates to US intelligence, only to find the rug pulled from under their feet.

The Obama administration is unable or unwilling to see the wood for the trees. As horrific as chemical weapons are, we should not discount the fact that over 130,000 Syrian men, women and children have been robbed of their lives by the regime's conventional arsenal. Death is final whether it results from poisonous gas or from bombs dropped by airplanes or missiles, which are equally indiscriminate. Discussions between US Secretary of State John Kerry and his Russian counterpart Sergei Lavrov on the nitty-gritty of disarming the regime of just one of its tools of war are being billed as "constructive" but those who continue to lose loved ones, limbs and homes at the hands of regime forces disagree.

The White House and its European allies are ignoring the big picture to focus on details. Western powers are increasingly being seen globally as irrelevant and unworthy of being trusted in a game of geopolitical chess in which Putin, his Syrian sidekick and their buddies in Tehran may shortly announce "checkmate". Putin contends he is not defending Assad but rather international law, but he showed no respect for legality when, in 2008, Russian troops overran Georgia.

America is keeping the threat of force against Syria on the table in the event Assad fails to live up to his pledges, but so what when Obama has no clear strategy for ending the civil war? Knocking out a few missile launchers and fighter jets will not be a game changer as long as Moscow stands ready to re-supply.

Saudi Arabia and Gulf states are eager to assist besieged Syrians but more than that, they understand what is really at stake; the importance of cutting the tail of a snake that slithers from Tehran to Damascus via Beirut. Their greatest mistake is relying on the United States to wield the axe. We, who are directly threatened by a Shi'ite military and ideological axis, must be committed to leading the charge in our own neighbourhood providing impetus to the US, France and Turkey to rally behind us. We must aim to facilitate good governance in Syria while ensuring the executioners, the torturers and those who bombed and gassed their own people face justice in the International Criminal Court.

Waiting for the US to act is futile. Obama is a ditherer, destined to be overlooked by history. He is not in the same category as Lincoln, Washington, Kennedy, Reagan or, for that matter, the Bushes, who for all their faults, cannot be accused of being indecisive.

This moment should be seized by the leaders of Gulf Cooperation Council states. No more hanging on to America's coat-tails, especially when the US is acting like a bit player who does not know his lines. If there is one thing Obama can teach us, it is "yes, we can".

US looks like a toothless tiger beyond its prime

6 October 2013

THE UNTHINKABLE HAS HAPPENED. Just when the struggling US economy was regaining its health with a positive knock-on effect for world markets, the federal government irresponsibly shuts shop over a budget wrangle. Some 800,000 civil servants have been forced to take an extended unpaid holiday; essential staff has been ordered to keep working without pay, while national parks and museums are closed impacting tourism. America's borders are now unprotected, guarded by skeleton security crews, and cancer drug trials have been brought to a halt.

Unlike the 2008 economic downturn, greedy banks and financial institutions cannot be blamed. I sympathize with low-income government workers living from pay cheque to pay cheque who fear they may be unable to pay their mortgages or keep up with car payments but blame the administration and Congress for holding its people's welfare so cheap without a thought for the rest of the world.

The US dollar's slide to a three-month low is infecting other currencies, while jittery bourses are experiencing volatility. The only winners are manufacturers of T-shirts emblazoned with messages lambasting those responsible for this mess; they are doing a roaring trade. No wonder! Americans are right to be angry. This is a deliberate man-made disaster that has arisen out of Republicans choosing to hold the nation hostage over Obamacare, passed into law almost four years ago when Democrats were the majority in the House and the Senate, which came into effect on 1 October.

The right wing's rejection of a scheme that would give millions of Americans access to health care via government-subsidized insurance is almost impossible for non-Americans to understand, especially those living in first-world democracies who look upon free health care as a basic human right. It is shocking to note that 48 million Americans (15.4 per cent of the population) are without health insurance. This translates to people who are ill being unable to visit a doctor or fill a prescription simply because they cannot afford it. A 2012 survey found that 41 per cent of working-age adults (75 million) had difficulty in paying medical bills with four million declaring bankruptcy after being harassed by debt collectors.

There could be worse to come if this impasse between the Obama administration and House Republicans is not resolved soon. Congress needs to approve a lifting of the US debt ceiling by 17 October else send the US economy – and most others along with it – into freefall. The US Treasury has announced that a failure to raise the ceiling could result in the US defaulting on its debts, which could lead to a financial crisis on par with 2008, if not worse; an analysis shared by International Monetary Fund (IMF) chief Christine Legarde who says it is "mission critical" that a new debt ceiling is agreed.

"Critical" it might be, but there is no guarantee that Republicans will heed the call. President Obama is clearly concerned. On 3 October, he told CBC's John Harwood that the street should be worried about the "suicide caucus" of the House Republicans who may decline to lift the debt limit. There is plenty of blame to go around. Republicans are blackmailing the President to ditch or delay Obamacare, or else; Obama insists it stays and is not up for discussion. Neither side is talking, let alone negotiating a way out, eliciting accusations that the President and the Republican House Speaker John Boehner are behaving like kids squabbling in a playground over a football, except at stake are the lives of millions of Americans, and millions more around the world.

Republicans are bearing the brunt of public condemnation. An ad created by the House Majority PAC, a super PAC dedicated to electing

Democrats to the House of Representatives, shows a crying baby narrated with the words "Speaker John Boehner didn't get his way on shutting down health care reform. So, he's shut down the government and hurt the economy." With House elections scheduled for November next year, Republicans are counting on short memories.

If this is democracy at work, the same democracy Americans tout as the political Holy Grail to be emulated by other nations, they can keep it. There is something fundamentally wrong with a system that leaves a country without direction, in stagnation, without a budget and potentially without the wherewithal to settle its debts. The credibility of the planet's wealthiest nation, the world's economic powerhouse that is traditionally dictated trends, has been shot – and the effects are already being felt. Faced with this crisis, Obama has cancelled his visits to the Asia-Pacific Economic Cooperation (APEC) and East Asia summits, dominated by China, which is just as well. How can he advise on Asian economies when his own may go into its death throes? US talks with the European Union (EU) over a free trade pact have also been embarrassingly postponed.

The bottom line is the buck stops with Obama; he is the man in charge. If this festering quagmire drags on resulting in the worst case scenario, he will be seen as global enemy number one. On his watch, America has bled geopolitical influence. His efforts towards an Israeli-Palestinian peace agreement are a joke. His administration is detested by Egyptians of every political colour and the Saudi Minister of Foreign Affairs, Saud Al Faisal was driven to cancel his speech to the UN General Assembly in protest against the UN's neglect and their inability to resolve the Palestinian issue "for over 60 years" and for taking Syria into a "dark tunnel of negotiations and procedures" to disarm Assad of chemical weapons even as the civil war rages on. Between the lines, the disapproving Saudi stance is targeted at the US.

Obama must get his own house in order not only for the sake of the American people, but also to retain his nation's revered top slot in the global economic and geopolitical hierarchy before the world concludes the US is just an ageing tiger without teeth.

Al Qaeda's continued existence is unexplained

27 October 2013

THE SO-CALLED War on Terror, launched 12 years ago in response to 9/11 attacks, has turned out to be as ineffective as the War on Drugs. Despite billions of dollars being poured into eradicating the terrorist disease targeting innocents going about their daily business, Al Qaeda, its associates and clones have not only survived but are flourishing in different guises.

In 2001, Al Qaeda was a relatively small group of Afghan Arabs disenchanted with US foreign policy, primarily based in Afghanistan. Now it has franchises in Iraq, Syria, Yemen, Sudan, Somalia, the Sahara,

Pakistan's tribal areas, the Egyptian Sinai Peninsula, Indonesia and the Philippines. Each franchise is motivated by a variety of localized goals but all adhere to the same core belief that the life of any man, woman or child, who does not share their extremist convictions, is disposable, as we recently witnessed when Al Shabaab sent its ruthless murderers into a Kenyan shopping mall where 68 people were gunned down in cold blood.

President Barack Obama may have patted himself on the back for assassinating the doddery, out of touch, Osama bin Laden, but he has had little success in eradicating his ideological spawn that seemingly enjoys a cockroach-like longevity, able to withstand drone attacks, bombs, advances in surveillance, communications-monitoring, facial recognition technology and global intelligence sharing.

Terrorism experts lead us to believe that most Al Qaeda founders are either dead or imprisoned; the latest "catch" was Abu Anas Al Libi suspected of involvement in the 1998 US embassy bombings, grabbed by US Special Forces outside his Tripoli home earlier this month. Bin Laden's Egyptian sidekick Ayman Al Zawahiri is still out there somewhere issuing poisonous, rambling edicts urging Egyptian Islamists to "unite against the Americanized butcher of the military coup" and jihadists in Syria to form an Islamist Caliphate. His brother Mohammed was arrested by Egyptian security forces in August, but the man said to be the brains behind 9/11 remains elusive. Where is he and who is giving him protection?

So many questions remain unanswered to this day. Where does Al Qaeda's funding come from? Where are its training camps? Who is issuing its travel documents? How are its foot soldiers able to travel around the world unimpeded and undetected when border controls are so tight? Al Qaeda's breadth of influence and activities are so extensive that it is beyond belief it is merely bankrolled by sympathetic individuals. Similarly its sophisticated intelligence capabilities suggest cooperation with insiders at the highest levels.

In the aftermath of 9/11, the West was convinced Al Qaeda was being funded by Sunni Arab sources. If that were true, then Sunni Muslims would not be among the organization's prime targets. Are there governments or powerful non-state actors manipulating Al Qaeda's strings and if so, what agenda does that support serve? Follow the money and the true maestros of death will be unearthed.

When major powers have access to satellites that can zoom in on an individual digging his garden or enable a vehicle's number plate to be read – and when those nations have the reach and the firepower to wipe terrorist organizations from the face of the earth – why do they hesitate?

Are we to conclude that the mighty US is not up to the task? Former National Security Agency (NSA)-contracted employee Edward Snowden continues to reveal America's spying on phone calls and emails, even those that are encoded, so must we assume that Al Qaeda communicates by carrier pigeon? Rather than listen in to the mobile calls of allied world leaders, does the NSA not concentrate on the phone calls and emails of known jihadists? I can only suppose that a destabilizing entity like Al Qaeda has its uses; what they are is anyone's guess.

Here is what we do know:

Superficially Iran and Al Qaeda are on opposite sides, yet the 9/11 Commission report states that in the early 1990s "senior Al Qaeda operatives and trainers travelled to Iran to receive training in explosives. In July 2011, the US accused Iran of giving safe haven to Al Qaeda operatives and assisting Al Qaeda to transit weapons, fighters and cash.

Furthermore, the fact that most Al Qaeda leaders were also members of the Muslim Brotherhood is well documented. Ousted Egyptian President Mohamed Morsi is believed to have allowed Al Qaeda and other terrorist groups to gain a foothold in the Sinai and he lobbied the Obama administration to release Omar Abdel-Rahman better known as the "Blind Sheikh", serving a life sentence in the US for seditious conspiracy in connection with the 1993 World Trade Centre bombings.

There are also unconfirmed reports that the Muslim Brotherhood was connected to the attack on the US embassy in Benghazi, yet, mysteriously the Obama administration has sought to punish Egypt for its failure to include the Brotherhood in its new political roadmap, never mind that the organization considers the interim government illegitimate and rejects any participation in the political process going forward.

The presence of Al Qaeda and other foreign jihadist groups attacking regime forces as well as the Free Syrian Army (FSA) is another mystery. How do they get there? Where do their weapons come from? Who is granting them access? One thing is certain, they have succeeded in muddying the waters; they have polluted the courageous, clean-hearted opposition making it more difficult for countries supporting Assad's downfall to supply much-needed heavy weapons to bring the civil war to a swift conclusion. At the same time, their interference "conveniently" permits Assad to claim that those fighting against his army are foreign-sponsored terrorists.

The US and its North Atlantic Treaty Organization allies have had their turn. They have expended blood and treasure but have been unsuccessful in eradicating Al Qaeda or deterring new recruits. It is about time the Arab World adopts its security obligations in this regard and takes a resolute approach to this evil threatening us all before its stranglehold on our region proves unbreakable.

Vultures destroy Syria as big powers debate

24 May 2014

I NEVER IMAGINED I would see the day when a regime that slaughters, gasses, tortures and starves unarmed civilians is free to do so with impunity. You have shuddered at videos of Syrian infants with protruding bones and distended stomachs. You have read the stories of children and elderly folk in the city of Homs forced to consume grass, leaves and beetles just to survive – and they were the lucky ones. We have all been bombarded with transmissions showing victims of chemical attacks convulsing as they fight to get air in their lungs, so terrible, they are often prefaced with "Viewer's discretion is advised." Millions – by some estimates 9.5 million – who fled to neighbouring countries are biding their time in dreadful conditions, feeling humiliated and unwanted. When will enough be enough!

In theory, this situation warrants the intervention of the United Nations (UN), founded in 1945 following the carnage wrought by World War II, to give civilian populations "freedom from fear". Moreover, UN Security Council Resolution 1674, adopted in 2006, reaffirms its responsibility to protect civilians caught up in an armed conflict. But this week, the UN lost whatever minute shred of credibility it still retained. Its headquarters is little more than an impressive building gracing the New York skyline; an expensive edifice where highly-paid officials mull the world's problems with their hands tied behind their backs.

On Thursday, a draft UN Security Council resolution, aimed at referring those responsible for committing war crimes for investigation by the International Criminal Court (ICC) in The Hague, was vetoed by Russia and China, even though 60 countries, including 13 Security Council member states, supported the text. Is there not something seriously wrong with a system that permits just two countries, both with vested interests, to hold the rest of the world hostage? China and Russia solidified their cooperation recently, sealing a $400bn gas deal, which some pundits believe is the seed of a new economic, diplomatic and military bloc set to face off against the US and Europe.

China's poor human rights record is a matter of record and Russia's government becomes more autocratic and nationalistically fuelled by the day. Both are engaged in venting their geopolitical muscles; Beijing has frayed relations with some of its Western-oriented neighbours over a territorial row concerning uninhabited islands in the South China Sea and also with Vietnam due to a Chinese oil rig positioned just 120 nautical miles off the Vietnamese coastline.

Moscow's links with the US and its European allies are hanging by a shoestring due to its annexation of Crimea and continued interference in eastern Ukraine. Their leaderships care not a jot for the suffering endured by the Syrian victims of an East–West tug of war. It is no wonder that UN/League of Arab States envoy to Syria Lakhdar Brahimi threw up his hands and quit!

The nub of the problem faced by the family of nations on Syria is undoubtedly President Putin's support of the Assad regime and its Iranian counterpart, the parent of the Shi'ite militias in neighbouring countries, that – as the intelligence services of world powers are well aware – is the source, sponsor and safe house for terrorist groups in Syria, such as Daesh and Al Qaeda, despite ideological differences, according to a report in *Asharq Al-Awsat*. It has been lately revealed that the Iranian Republican Guards are recruiting Shi'ite Afghan refugees to fight in Syria on the promise of $500 monthly plus housing and residency. Iran is severely compounding the pain, but neither the West nor the Arab World deserves to be let off the hook.

The Syrian capital Damascus and the largest city Aleppo are among the oldest continuously inhabited cities on the planet and are repositories of history, religion and culture, in danger of being lost to future generations. Even if we set aside human suffering, those facts alone should galvanize the international community to step in. Importantly, Syria is an Arab heartland; the Syrian people our brothers and sisters. Yet, what have we Arabs done to help them aside from throwing some money their way to help ease our consciences? Why do we bother to have armies, why do we bother to purchase sophisticated weaponry, if all we do is cry into our teacups watching massacres and destruction?

I still remember the time when the words "proud" and "Arabs" were twinned. But whatever our achievements, how can we feel proud when for three years we have sat in our armchairs witnessing the mass murder of 160,000 by a criminal posing as an Arab leader who is so proud of his own accomplishments he is putting himself forward for reelection on 3 June!

Syria's cities are scarred with charred shells that were once smart apartment buildings; people are without potable water or electricity and basic foodstuffs are a luxury in some areas. What does President Al Assad do in response? He campaigns to hang on to his chair. And, what is more, he is being cheered on by some Arab states under the sway of Iran and tolerated by others. At the time of the caliphs, those who captured camels or goats, let alone human beings, would be chased by armies.

So, the Arabs dispute and sigh, Western leaders wring their hands, the UN beats its chest and aid workers cry out for anything or anyone that can bring an end to this cruel war. And all the time the situation worsens; more bombed, more gassed, more displaced.

There was a fleeting moment when President Obama looked decisive but then he changed his mind and instead of acting he entered into a bargain with the Devil, permitting the killer to continue with his onslaught provided he refrained from using chemical weapons. America's weak-kneed approach reflects an absence of political will when contrasted with the US-led invasion of Iraq in 2003 that was deemed "illegal" by Kofi Annan, then the UN's Secretary General; not forgetting Washington's role in the 1990s' Balkan wars without the UN's blessing. We can only conclude when it comes to Syria that the world's self-appointed policeman has gone fishing just when he is needed most while Arab leaderships appear to be saying "wake us up when it's over".

Why is the world turning a blind eye to atrocities in Syria while reacting strongly to events in Ukraine? Could it be because there is a white paper somewhere to throw Sunni majorities in the Middle East under a bus? That is a discussion for another day, but, in the meantime, I will leave you with the thought.

Fanaticism flowers in freedom's soil

16 June 2014

PARENTS, HOW WOULD YOU FEEL if your child's teacher described himself as "an architect of minds", encouraged those in his care to pray for the release of known terrorists, spouted jihadist doctrines, banned music and drama and taught young boys that men were entitled "to rape" their wives?

This kind of dangerous indoctrination that has nothing to do with the religion of Islam is happening now – and, no, I am not talking about the *madrassas* of Afghanistan or Pakistan or those being founded in northern Syria by Daesh. It is happening right under the noses of educational authorities in Europe's multicultural, multi-ethnic European heartland – Britain.

This scandal, broken by the *Daily Mail* under the headline "Trojan horse files", has become a topic of vigorous debate between extreme leftists, unable to distinguish between the true Islam and a distorted version disseminated for political purposes, who consider the paper's report to be Islamophobic, and the majority who fear, rightly in my opinion, that their country is en route to becoming a terrorist hothouse, spearheaded by anti-immigration parties such as the UK Independence Party (UKIP).

The Muslim Brotherhood/Hamas-supporting MP for Bradford, George Galloway, who has his own talk show on the Iranian-English language channel Press TV, said "Trojan Horse-[expletive] is an Iraq War-style shock and awe attack on British Muslims complete with dodgy dossier," and vowed to "defend the immigrant families from this racist Tory attack even if no-one will". The poor man is deluded; he has been mixing with the wrong crowd for so long that he is blind to the fact that Islam is a religion of submission, moderation, tolerance and peace, which has, and is being, grossly misrepresented by his buddies and his bosses in Qom.

At the centre of the "Trojan Horse" row are five schools in the city of Birmingham that has a large Asian population. Now I am all for immigrants retaining their religious beliefs and respective cultures while, at the same time, assimilating into the society at large, but when schools incite anti-Christian chants, cancel Christmas celebrations in a Christian country, invite extremist firebrand clerics to lecture pupils and send non-Muslim teachers packing, they have overstepped their brief. Indeed, when I first glimpsed photographs of the bearded "teachers" of one of the schools, Park View, before reading the text, I thought the *Daily Mail* article was about Al Qaeda terrorists, not educators in a Western democratic country.

Park View has an Islamist curriculum and provides lessons in Jihad, advertised on the school's website. Its head of extra-curricular activities, Abid Ali, rails against the Western world on Facebook, writing: "All that occupies my mind is the reality, the hypocrisy, the mentality of the Western world" while advocating "a Muslim Khalifa" movement ... fighting to save our religion from the *zalims* (tyrants). A senior teacher, Inam Ul Haq, has celebrated the early release of "the Terrorists' Bookseller" Abu Bakr, on social media.

There are currently five ongoing government investigations into what is being described as the "Trojan Horse Plot" but, as yet, no action has been taken and the brainwashers still retain their jobs. Last week, the results of inspections of Birmingham schools were published, galvanizing Minister for Education Michael Gove to issue a statement requiring Britain's independent schools, academies and free schools to "respect British values" while announcing that consultations are ongoing to enforce new rules designed to ensure "all schools actively promote British values". This may be too little too late. Britain's extremists and wannabe jihadists are naturally up in arms screaming racism and bigotry.

Successive British governments have turned a blind eye to religious fanatics for too long – and one day, their neglect may come back and bite them, just as it did on 7 July 2005 when home-grown terrorists launched suicide attacks on the London transport system, killing 52 and injuring 770. You would think they had learned an indelible lesson from that terrible tragedy, but, just the opposite. In recent years, the UK has become a magnet for members of the Muslim Brotherhood, branded "terrorist" by Egypt and Saudi Arabia, who created a global nerve-centre above an abandoned kebab shop in north London that is now being relocated to Austria following a government investigation, aided by MI6 and MI5 and supervised by Whitehall officials, into their activities. It goes without saying that the Brotherhood's well-oiled propaganda machine has gone into overdrive, issuing heavily couched threats partnered with avowals of innocence.

British soil is also being used by hard line extremists as *the* place to launch satellite TV channels airing inflammatory sermons from preachers; one such as the Birmingham-based, misnamed Peace TV, owned by Dr Zakir Naik, who is quoted as saying "Every Muslim should be a terrorist". Takbeer TV, broadcasting from Nottingham, has been agitating against the Ahmadi sect describing adherents as suffering from a disease or having monstrous intentions. There are 14 of these spewing hate, death to apostates and calls for Jihad, yet the television watchdog, OFCOM, does little more than issue nominal fines when breaches of its code comes to its attention.

Come on Britain! Do something! Those pea-brained propagandists do not represent mainstream Muslims and are not fit to be in the same room as our Holy Book. Indeed, they should be rounded up and tried for desecrating our faith. Do not listen to the ignorant rants of so-called human rights activists, more focused on preserving the rights of crazies than decent, devout people who work through their religion to better societies and further inter-faith understanding.

You have opened your doors with good intentions but now when you are being turned into a favoured extremist dustbin, it is time self-preservation kicks in. It is no accident of fate that over 500 Britons are known to be fighting alongside Daesh in Syria and Iraq, fuelled by the promise of an Islamist caliphate. That will not happen, because the West will not permit it, and then they will be back, battle-hardened and consumed with anger. Be warned that unless this type of indoctrination is nipped firmly in the bud in schools, mosques and on TV, the jihadists could decide to make the UK their next playground, spawning a rise of fascism and neo-Nazism in response.

Arabs helpless as the neighbourhood implodes

18 August 2014

FEELING PROUD TO BE ARAB is not easy nowadays. What is there to be proud of when bodies are piling high in Syria, Iraq, Gaza and Libya while the Arab World does little except to appeal for help from the US and its allies, who only intervene militarily when such intervention suits their geopolitical interests?

President Barack Obama is a maestro of finger-wagging and uttering condem-nations but when it comes to acting in dire emergencies his record is poor. His foreign policy is a maze of directionless confusion as his approval ratings evidence. He stepped in to relieve Libya of its dictator and subsequently abandoned the country to feuding militias while ignoring recent calls by the Libyan government for urgent assistance. He pledged to arm the Syrian opposition only to renege on that promise and, worse, he pulled back from military intervention there at the 11th hour, permitting the Assad regime to continue slaughtering its own citizens.

Likewise, he has displayed glaring double standards over Israel's massacre of almost 2,000 Palestinians in Gaza, handing out light criticisms of Israel's disproportionate assaults while re-supplying Benjamin Netanyahu with heavy weapons in equal measure. Moreover, the White House has chosen to bash Egypt, currently mediating sensitive negotiations between Israel and Palestine, over its jailing of three Al Jazeera journalists, which is laughable given the carnage throughout the region, not to mention that several journalists were arrested and others gassed during the recent riots in Ferguson, Missouri.

Just days ago, he gave a press conference announcing that he was sending the cavalry to rescue thousands of Yazidis trapped on an arid mountain top without shade, food or water, surrounded by Daesh terrorists, only to change his mind the very next day on the grounds there were *only*

2,000 left – a figure rejected by Yazidis who say there are still 10,000 in danger. The images of desperate women and children scrambling to get on aid helicopters and, in some cases, throwing their babies into the arms of someone inside, are heart-breaking. Dropping bombs just will not cut it.

Now Obama proposes to arm the Kurdish Peshmerga to take on an organization so bloodthirsty it hands its children severed heads to parade on social media, buries people alive or nails them to crosses. It is preposterous that 10,000–15,000 monstrous killers have been allowed to proliferate across northern Syria and Iraq terrorizing minorities, grabbing towns, villages, weapons depots, cash from banks, power stations and a crucial dam that could be used to flood entire areas of the country as far south as the capital.

One is left wondering on why he failed to support the Syrian opposition with sophisticated weapons, but has no hesitation in arming the Kurds. A sceptic would say that the oil-rich Kurdish region has been a US client state since Saddam's era, which is now supplying oil to Israel via a pipeline..

America's Commander-in-Chief seems to think that a mere change of face in Iraq's prime ministerial chair will do the trick in that Sunni tribes, sick of being oppressed and marginalized by Iraqi Prime Minister Nouri Al Maliki, will now rally around the government, even though his replacement Haider Al Abadi shares his predecessor's ideology. Obama is not being naive. His message is "We are punishing Al-Maliki for refusing to sign our status of forces agreement but we will support Al-Abadi as long as he accepts that the US now owns him."

In all honesty, it feels as if the US owns all of us and it is beyond time the unhealthy dependency of Arab countries on Western protection is ended because, for one thing, we are not being protected and for another, when we have armies, "Made in America" airplanes, helicopters, missiles and tanks, why are not we defending ourselves? Are our hefty arms purchases that help fill US and European state coffers and bump up the share prices of weapons manufacturers simply décor?

With the Arab region in such political and security disarray, Gulf Cooperation Council (GCC) states should band together and take the lead. The first step would be to form a joint military under a single commander, which has been talked about, but never implemented. Together, we could wield substantial military strength that would not be ignored.

The GCC should also take a unified position on the diplomatic front. Enough issuing statements disregarded by the international community because they are not backed up with serious clout! We have so many tools at our disposal that could be used for influence if only we mustered the guts to use them. Why is it that when the US, the United Nations (UN), the European Union (EU) and Russia throw out sanctions like confetti, all we do is grumble? The Arabian Gulf countries invest hundreds of billions in the US and the EU and private GCC investors account for hundreds of billions more.

Obama says he wants to pivot the US away from the Middle East. Let us help him on his way by taking responsibility for our own security. We should start with wiping Daesh from the face of the earth before its evil contaminates our own soil. The UN Security Council has unanimously passed a resolution barring all funding to Daesh and insisting that all UN member countries stem recruitment. Too little, too late! It is currently the wealthiest terrorist group in the history of a world that is flush with captured US weapons. What I find particularly distressing is the way Daesh is being treated by the US and other countries as though it really does constitute a de facto legal state, instead of the murderous gang it is. You do not boycott terrorists, you eradicate them. That should be self-evident, but in this world gone mad, a world where black is often portrayed as white and vice versa, apparently not. When Western Daesh fighters return to their home countries with an ingrained thirst for blood, perhaps then the international community will come to its senses.

Once again, I would strongly urge GCC leaders to adopt a unified strategy designed to tackle these new threats and injustices. If we continue living in the past, expecting to be taken care of by outside powers, our children's future will be betrayed by our apathy and if something is not done, we risk witnessing our own borders being re-drawn.

Frankenstein's monster turns on its masters

28 August 2014

A BLOODTHIRSTY BUNCH of crazed head-hunters are on the rampage in Syria and Iraq and not only threaten to disperse their poisonous ideology throughout the Middle East region but also to Western capitals. Sounds like a bad fairytale does it not, except there is no fairy godmother in this story to banish this bloodthirsty horde. This is real and happening. And what are the self-appointed guardians of our world doing about it other than dropping bombs here and there to defend their own interests, issuing threats and distributing care packages?

Are we seriously to believe the explosive conflicts in Syria, Iraq, Yemen and what remains of the Libyan state are mere happenstance? Or could it be that a grand plan to destabilize the region using extremists is underway so as to slice up Arab countries into easily manipulated weak entities whose natural resources will be ripe for plunder?

I believe "scientists" in suits bore a creature that was nurtured and assisted to develop its murderous skills in the same way that Al Qaeda was born and is now known as Daesh. But the creature grew so militarily, financially and ideologically powerful that it now threatens its creators' existence; a monster that is terrorizing the world with inhuman atrocities under the banner of Islam, the religion of tolerance and peace.

The reptilian creature that has announced a caliphate across northern Syria and Iraq with its sights set towards Jordan, Saudi Arabia and Kuwait, has shed its skin and is now spewing its venom against its masters. It was manufactured in Syria as a Western tool to jeopardize the Free Syrian Army's (FSA) growing popularity throughout the Arab World and its honourable cause with the result Assad's initially fictitious argument that he is battling terrorists has been bolstered.

The slaughter paraded on our screens, perpetrated by masked men driving around in identical brand new Humvees, are not the work of amateurs. And neither is the serpent's propaganda machine that uses sophisticated messages on social media to reach out to vulnerable, gullible or disaffected young Muslims in the US and Europe who view the establishment of a caliphate as an affirmation of their identity, whereas a caliphate built on rivers of blood, mountains of severed heads and girls sold as slaves is nothing but an evil abomination.

There is evidence to suggest Daesh was covertly trained by the regional and Western powers, who abandoned the legitimate opposition, the brave men of the FSA. Had the Leader of the Free World, President Barack Obama, done the right thing several years ago by heeding the just demands of the FSA, tens of thousands of Syrian and Iraqi lives would have been saved, the American journalist would have been spared and the region and beyond would not be facing this menace. The FSA did not ask Obama for boots on the ground or to engage in a full-scale war against the regime. He was merely requested to provide the FSA with air cover, heavy weapons and ammunition to assist its fight. But no, Western weapons mysteriously found their way into the hands of extremists like Jabhat Al Nusra and Daesh, who turned their guns on the FSA.

The US President should be thoroughly probed by a Congressional committee for his role in worsening the carnage in Syria and for fomenting the sectarian conflicts and lawlessness plaguing the Middle East. His intervention in Libya has brought division and destruction; his failure to respond to appeals for assistance from the Iraqi government last year has resulted in black flags fluttering over one third of the country. Moreover, his support of the Muslim Brotherhood in Egypt, over the will of the Egyptian people, would have ignited a bloody civil war if the people and the army were not united. Congress should investigate whether or not his actions or non-actions were in keeping with US interests and explore the real reasons behind his seeming support for religious extremists over moderates.

Furthermore, how can one explain the sudden flirtation between Iran and the West when for decades the United Nations (UN), the US and Europe have applied anti-Iranian sanctions to no real effect. If Iran had been an Arab country, I have no doubt in my mind that it would have been invaded long ago to remove the threat, even without concrete proof that it was, indeed, developing a nuclear weapons capability, as we witnessed when "shock and awe" was delivered to Iraq.

The governments of the UK and France should also be placed under a microscope for acting as America's mini-mes on foreign policy. They have spectacularly failed at tamping down on the monster's recruiting drives. The British press, in particular, is packed with news about jihadists openly touting their ideology on high streets, in universities and via UK-based media outlets; they have even been handing out leaflets on London's Oxford Street, but rather than face arrest, the police announced they needed to check on what laws may have been broken!

The BBC regularly interviews young British Muslims praising the so-called caliphate. At least 500 – some say the figure is near 2,000 – British citizens, including would-be jihadist brides, have travelled to Syria to take up arms targeting Sunnis, who reject ideological slavery, as well as Christians and other minorities. Hundreds more have flocked there from the US, Canada and Australia. Daesh welcomed over 6,000 new recruits in July alone, including 1,100 foreigners. The idea is catching on. Boko Haram has announced its own caliphate in an area of Nigeria. Where next?

Anyone with even half a brain cannot fail to wonder why no firm action has been taken to prevent this tide, which will sooner or later return to hit Western shores with a violent tsunami of cataclysmic proportions, under the pretence of free expression and respect for individual freedoms. Former UK Foreign Minister Kim Howells believes that home-grown terrorists may be planning a spectacular attack on the North Atlantic Treaty Organization summit to be held in Cardiff next month.

Why are terrorists, boasting of their exploits or encouraging their children to proudly display severed heads on the internet, being given a free pass when purveyors of child pornography are so easily be rounded up, not to mention celebrities accused of crimes committed more than thirty years ago?

A question that demands urgent answering is this. Are the implosions and explosions throughout the Arab World caused by internal circumstances or random acts of fate – or have they been deliberately orchestrated by unseen hands? I have come to my own conclusions; I will leave you to ponder on yours.

The West's flirtation with terrorists is a poor joke

22 November 2014

THE US AND ITS EUROPEAN allies allegedly out to destroy Daesh and topple the Assad regime are losing credibility. It appears their sophisticated surveillance apparatus is unable to track long columns of military Humvees and tanks decked out in black flags moving through Syria at will. And they are making no effort to free the long-suffering Syrian people from a dictator who has killed close to 200,000 of his own people.

It is unbelievable that US airpower has failed to put an end to the war of attrition still raging in the Syrian town of Kobani between Kurdish fighters attempting to wrest the town from the most vicious terrorist organization on the planet. One is forced to ask why the US, which waged a war and occupied an entire country for 13 years to get Osama bin Laden, has taken such half-hearted action to eradicate monsters proudly cutting off the heads of US and British citizens.

Evidence is piling up to suggest America's official policy towards both cruel entities is nothing but a façade to attempt to appease its Middle East allies and a sop to naive sectors of global public opinion that still have faith in so-called American values. I hope this is not a cover-up for back-door deals between the US, Iran and the Syrian regime to rearrange the region's geopolitical deckchairs to the detriment of Sunni states.

For instance, the US Department of State is about to quit funding the Commission for International Justice and Accountability (CIJA) employing human intelligence to gather material evidence of the regime's crimes against humanity. At the same time, it is spending more on ferreting out evidence on war crimes committed by Daesh, a move that leads some to suspect that Bashar Al Assad and his Iranian-controlled cohorts will ultimately be handed a get-out-of-jail pass.

In any event, anyone who imagines that either regime officials or the Mickey Mouse Caliph will ever see the inside of the International Criminal Court (ICC) in The Hague is either dreaming or easily fooled. In the case of Assad, Syria is not a member of the ICC, which leaves only one option – a United Nations (UN) Security Council resolution. That is dead in the water because Moscow will certainly use its veto to block any such attempt. But let us suppose for the sake of argument that President Vladimir Putin dumps his Syrian ally, thus paving the way. Even then, does anyone suppose that those indicted would be packing their suitcases and booking their flights to the Netherlands to face justice?

Lest we forget, Hezbollah still refuses to surrender four suspects wanted by the ICC in connection with the assassination of former Lebanese Prime Minister Rafic Hariri in 2005. If an armed militia is able to ignore the court with impunity, there is no doubt that a sitting president would do the same. And as for the "Caliph" and his henchmen, they must be chuckling at the very idea. Creatures that bury children alive, bartering women in a slave market for weapons and blowing themselves up to murder innocents are hardly likely to quake with terror at the thought of a panel of judges thousands of miles away.

And, let us face it, what is the point of tasking organizations to accumulate proof of their crimes when video evidence is all over the news and there is no shortage of witnesses lucky enough to escape the terrorists' clutches? In the days prior to the proliferation of the internet and citizen journalists armed with mobiles capable of taking videos and photographs, this type of con on the part of Western powers might have succeeded but fortunately the truth can no longer be hidden.

Worse, the US and other North Atlantic Treaty Organization (NATO) member states are seemingly turning a blind eye to Turkey's role in permitting Daesh to gain a foothold in Syria. It is no secret that Ankara is permitting its soil to be used as a secure re-supply and medical hub for Daesh whose fighters are being treated in Turkish hospitals, ostensibly for humanitarian reasons. Is President Recep Tayyip Erdoğan's heart so mushy that it welcomes killers, rapists, bombers, crucifiers and decapitators to enjoy his hospitality? What kind of humanitarian gives succour to murdering scum while doing nothing to save innocent Syrians being slaughtered a stone's throw away from his country's border?

Moreover, despite appeals from the US-led coalition, Erdoğan still refuses to join their campaign in Syria and Iraq because the coalition has yet to fulfil his conditions, he says. He has barred the US and its allies from using Turkey's Incirlik Air Base, and in fact the only concession he has made is permission for Kurdish Peshmerga fighters to access Kobani via Turkey.

The Turkish President criticizes US-led operations in Syria almost weekly with an unrestrained tongue. No surprise there! But I am mystified as to why the West is treating this renegade, supporting terrorism by default with kid gloves. Why are Washington, London, Paris and NATO not holding Turkey to account for providing facilities to crazed extremists threatening the entire region when it is supposed to be on the same side? They did not hesitate to slap Russia with sanctions over its stance towards Ukraine, yet Turkey that openly collaborates with the Muslim Brotherhood and its *takfiri* affiliates gets away with being belligerently obstructive.

Arab leaders must surely be aware of what is going on. Western powers are no longer sincere in cleansing our region from terrorists. Sure they tickle them with a few bombs and threaten to haul them off to the ICC and that is about it. The UK has even asked the Emirates to explain why the names of certain UK-based Islamist organizations and "charities" have appeared on the United Arab Emirates' (UAE) recently published terrorist blacklist, as though the British government is their advocate. For years, they have been urging Muslim countries to come out strongly against terrorism and when they do, they are being questioned!

Enough is enough! It is time that Arab armies acted independently without waiting for a green light from the West whose goals are far from transparent. This is our neighbourhood. This is our fight and we must take matters into our own hands. GCC states and their allies, in particular Jordan and Egypt, have well-equipped, well-trained military forces, and together they can destroy these threats to our existence once and for all. Once again, I must make a strong appeal to these leaders to recognize the dangers and the need for driving our own chariots into a battle that *must* be won at all costs.

It is our disease and we must cure it

11 June 2015

ENOUGH SITTING AROUND hoping for miracles! Enough waiting for the United States or its Western allies to cleanse the Arab World from the growing cancer of terrorism! Are Arab countries waiting until Daesh fighters are knocking down its citizens' doors in what still remains of Arab-controlled territories before acting in a meaningful fashion?

Almost every Arab country is under threat and those who have succeeded in preventing Daesh from penetrating their borders are being surrounded and infiltrated. The latest assessments suggest that Daesh is now based in 12 countries and is affiliated with extremist groups in others.

Whereas the international community, including much of the Arab World, has adopted a laid-back attitude to this menace, Gulf Cooperation Council (GCC) countries are the only ones treating the threat with the gravity it requires. GCC states are investing their armies, their weaponry and billions of dollars in the fight. And it is beyond time that other Arab countries showed solidarity with their Gulf allies and participated in the battle against this danger to the entire Arab nation with full force.

I am appalled that so far foreign powers have done little to amputate Daesh's fast-growing limbs or prevent its recruiters from polluting young minds, not only in the Middle East and North Africa (MENA) region but also in European democracies where they use laws guaranteeing freedom of expression to distribute their propaganda leaflets. The US Department of State estimates that 22,000 foreign fighters from 100 countries have joined Daesh; that fact alone should ring emergency bells loud when many battle-hardened radicals will return home one day consumed with hatred for all things Western.

Looking at a map of the Middle East nowadays one sees a horror story of bloody conflict, consuming Libya, the Sinai Peninsula, Yemen, Syria and Iraq. When viewed as a whole, the scenario appears so unreal that it is difficult for our minds to take it in. How is it possible that in the 21st century heads are being sliced off, women are being enslaved and swapped for weapons and thousands are being executed, face down on the ground! People are being beheaded for the "crime" of swearing!

It stretches belief to be told that half of Syria and over a third of Iraq has been taken over by crazies who have disgraced the noble word "caliphate" that speaks of a Golden Age of pure Islam when scholars flocked to Baghdad's "House of Wisdom" to share their knowledge and Arabs led the world in the fields of science, mathematics, medicine, architecture, law and philosophy. The four Rightly Guided Caliphs, who followed in the footsteps of the Prophet (PBUH) must be turning in their graves.

And now Daesh is gaining ground in Libya and controls the cities of Misurata, Sirte and Harawah along the Mediterranean coast between the capital, Tripoli, and Benghazi. Its aim is to control the country's oil facilities and related ports to feed its treasury that is already flush with profits from energy sales. While we are dissuaded against confronting the terrorists militarily by the US and the United Nations (UN) in favour of talks, Daesh is intent on grabbing Libyan oilfields to increase their wealth and influence.

For most of us those images are so divorced from our own experience that there is a tendency to think it cannot happen to us. It is like a scary movie that once we turn off our televisions is over. But this is no movie, even though, if no action is taken, a real-life version will be coming to theatres – and squares and streets – near to you soon.

What has our reliance on the US-led coalition brought us? President Barack Obama trumpets its successes in Iraq, but any gains it has made on the battlefield have been reversed. Air strikes just will not cut it because the terrorists secrete themselves within terrified civilian populations and, for some mysterious reason, even when they are out in the open, driving around in convoys, they have rarely been targeted.

Pleas from the Kurdish Peshmerga and Sunni tribes for weapons to take on Daesh have been ignored. Iraq's Prime Minister, Haider Al Abadi, blames the Obama administration for not doing enough in terms of air cover and intelligence sharing. It is no wonder conspiracy theories abound – ranging from the feasible to the absurd – speculating upon the reasons behind the US President's lack of commitment.

I had hopes that the Global Coalition to counter Daesh, which held a conference on 2 June in Paris, attended by the foreign ministers of 22 countries, would come up with a joint solution, a new strategy. But there was no dramatic announcement. Unbelievably, those nations have chosen to tackle the problem in the same old way, despite the fact their efforts so far have been dismal failures. In other words: "It is not working, but let us carry on as usual and hope for the best."

In essence, the US and the UK expect the useless, partisan Iraqi Army partnered with ragtag Shi'ite militias to finish the job. I suspect those militias have been busier killing Sunnis and torching their homes than defeating Daesh and this is exactly why many of the Sunni tribes in Anbar, some of which worked with the Iraqi government to drive out Al Qaeda, have reached the conclusion that Daesh is the better of two evils.

Syria was hardly discussed during the Coalition conference. There is no international resolve to defend the long-suffering Syrian people from the regime or from the Daesh, which is well dug in. What kind of policy is that when they are aware that even if the coalition could succeed in driving Daesh out of Iraq, it would cross the border to regroup and rearm?

This madness has gone on long enough. Maybe Western leaderships can bury their heads to the danger; there are many miles and oceans separating their respective countries from Daesh. But we who live in the Arab World cannot afford to be lax because the enemy is on our doorstep, biding its time to get a foot in the door.

I am forced to conclude that Arab lands have been targeted by a conspiracy in which multiple foreign countries are aligned against us, cynically using religious fervour as a tool to wage war against us. Unless we face up to this fact, we are lost. But it is not too late to block such plots delivering their end goal, which is to carve up our countries into weak defenceless entities.

I salute the leaders of the GCC for their efforts to guard their countries, as well as neighbouring Arab states, but this fight should not be on our shoulders alone, it requires Arab partners as well as non-Arab nations to join hands with us. The GCC is doing everything it can to keep its people safe and all credit must go to our GCC leaders.

The immediate short-term solution is for Egypt, Morocco, Jordan and GCC states to speed up the creation of a sizeable joint army, composed largely of well-equipped land forces, supported by air power and artillery and tasked with eradicating Daesh and various pro-Iranian Shi'ite militias.

If there is any hesitation in implementing a timely intervention on the advice of the very world powers seeking our devastation, we will be contributors to the sealing of our own fate. The second stage would be to seal all borders with Iran to thwart its hegemonic ambitions.

A parallel short-to-medium-term objective should be to reform educational systems so as to produce knowledgeable and enlightened populations able to think for themselves rather than falling for self-interested propaganda disseminated by unscrupulous individuals and groups. Poor quality education equals ignorance and those who capitalize on ignorance find fertile soil in which extremism flourishes and terrorists are bred. We must pull out all stops to battle false messages that radicalize our youth and discredit our faith in the eyes of the world.

Both Muslim and non-Muslim states should stand with the GCC to fight this alien sickness that is not only tearing our region apart. He who hesitates is lost and as long as the world chooses debates over decisive action, we will all be lost in a region where brain-diseased barbarians call the shots.

Their pain is our shame

7 September 2015

WHAT DOES IT SAY about our part of the world that our Syrian brothers and sisters feel the need to flee to a place where they are not wanted? To a place where they are being humiliated and insulted! What does it say about our wealthy Arab World blessed with vast empty tracts of land, that our doors are closed to our own?

The scenes dominating our screens are almost unbearable to watch. Tiny children washed up on the shore like flotsam. Hundreds lost under the waves of the sea of the dead or suffocating in the holds of boats. Pregnant women, children and the disabled in wheelchairs, determined to get to the lands of promise only to find the way is barred with barbed wire, teargas and the batons of riot police.

But on they go thirsty and hungry, their feet sore with blisters, catching a few hours of sleep in open fields, unable to wash themselves. On they go with babes in arms and toddlers astride their fathers' shoulders fuelled by hope that tomorrow will be a better day because every weary footstep takes them closer to Europe – and sanctuary.

It is there that their dreams turn to nightmares. They have survived barrel bombs. They have lived through chemical attacks and escaped the clutches of terrorists. They have seen their homes turned into dust and their cities reduced to pockmarked moonscapes. They have witnessed atrocities that most of us cannot even imagine. They have buried fathers, brothers, and sons.

And when the last leg of their marathon journey to the European Union (EU) is finally over with just a few hours' train journey to their final destination, Germany, they see their future slipping away, so near and yet so far. They have been told: "Halt". But fatigue and hunger does not make them waver. They refuse to be herded into wretched camps like criminals fearing they might languish there for months or even years.

Hot and thirsty, packed into a train for 24 hours, they reject the bottled water offered by the police. They will not be humiliated or treated like lesser humans. "No trains, fine! We will walk the 130km to the Austrian border" – and so an exodus of refugees not seen in Europe since World War II begins. They make me so proud. From the toddlers seen putting one foot in front of the other and still managing to smile to the elderly trying to keep up, their courage and sheer grit is an inspiration to us all.

God bless countries like Germany, Sweden and Iceland that have put out a welcome mat, but this tragic situation is not Europe's responsibility. Those poor people are Arabs, both Muslim and Christian. The inaction of Arab leaderships has forced not only Syrians but also Iraqis to seek safety wherever they can find it.

Why should we expect the EU to pick up the pieces of our neglect? Our Arab nation has collectively done nothing to rid Syria of the criminal Assad regime, whose viciousness turned this once beautiful historic land into a cesspool of violence and destruction. It will take generations to return Syria to any semblance of its former glory; lost forever are ancient mosques, temples, monasteries and churches, blown up by mad creatures who dare to call themselves Muslims. More importantly, lost forever are 300,000 human beings – and counting.

How many of those souls trudging along a Hungarian highway will ever see their homeland again I wonder? I was deeply touched by the message of a young boy standing outside the Budapest train station, who said he did not want to be in Europe. What he wants is for the world to stop the war in his country so he can go home. I have heard so many others say the same thing. But no one is listening. No one is doing anything.

Those people are not economic migrants. They are not freeloaders out to live on state handouts. They are fleeing war and persecution with rights under the United Nations Convention Relating to the Status of Refugees, which stipulates that no refugee must be discriminated against in terms of race or religion.

The Arab states have failed the Syrians and unless the leaderships do the right thing, Syrians will never be able to forgive the Arabs for abandoning them in their hour of need. The day will come when our grandchildren will ask what we did to save them. What shall we tell them, other than we sent some money and dropped a few bombs?

Just about everyone I know is upset about a photograph of two-year-old Aylan Kurdi lying face down on the sand of a Turkish beach. The terrible fate of this angelic child has put a human face to the Syrian conflict, galvanizing European public opinion in the refugees' favour.

Banners reading "Welcome Syrian Refugees" are appearing among the crowds in football stadiums. Thousands gathered in Vienna chanting their welcome. Some 10,000 Icelanders offered homes to Syrians. More than 260,000 Britons signed a petition demanding Prime Minister David Cameron agree to accept more. There are good people in Europe who care, so why cannot we?

It is no good saying, "It is not our problem." God is watching. I can only plead with Arab leaderships – especially leaders of Gulf states – to immediately respond to this emergency by firstly doing all in their power to host as many refugees as possible.

More importantly, I would urge Gulf Cooperation Council (GCC) states and their Arab allies to tackle this problem at its root. Just as we are fighting to free Yemen from Iranian proxy militias, so we must use all our resources to save Syria from its brutal pro-Iranian puppet and the other blood-thirsty mobs.

What has happened to the Arab DNA since the days of caliphs who looked after their people's wellbeing and fought for their dignity? Not only lives are at stake. So is what we once valued above all – our Arab honour.

Arab League's inaction is shameful

21 September 2015

EVERYONE IS TALKING about the refugee crisis overwhelming Europe; everyone apart from the League of Arab States that is. To date it has had little to say on the topic and, as far as I can tell, has no plan to help alleviate the problem. Why have there not been any emergency summits announced? Where are the voices from Arab capitals offering solutions? Perhaps there is a notice pinned to the League's front door with the words "Gone fishing".

Why is the League's Secretary General Dr Nabil Elaraby not holding crisis meetings with foreign ministers and jetting around the region to find ways of preventing Syrians and Iraqis from being treated worse than street dogs, expected to be grateful when they are handed a bottle of water every now and again?

Surely he sees their plight. The lucky ones have tents or blankets. Most are sleeping on pavements, unable to wash for days or weeks. Women are giving birth in the street. Mothers run out of baby milk. Diabetics have nowhere to keep their insulin refrigerated. Many report that the little money they had was stolen along with their mobile phones.

The very least the League of Arab States should be doing is finding temporary refuge to allow these unfortunate people to live in dignity, while pres-sing hard on the international community to solve the root causes of this exodus.

We Arabs are always stressing our honour, but just how honourably is the Arab League behaving watching as our Arab brothers are being shuttled from pillar to post like pawns on a chessboard?

Our countries have wealth, we have lands and, so it is little wonder that Europeans are increasingly asking "Where are the Arabs?" The League is made up of 22 countries, yet two of the poorest – Jordan and Lebanon – are bearing the brunt of the refugee influx.

The majority of the refugees are Syrians fleeing war and terrorism in their hundreds of thousands. Scared and tired, they trudge on hoping there is somewhere on this planet where they can live in peace. Instead, thousands have been met with barbed wire fences, riot police wielding batons, teargas and water cannons. You would have to have a heart of stone not to be moved by the hardships and indignities these people are being made to suffer.

The images of a well-known Syrian football coach holding his young son being deliberately tripped by a callous camerawoman or that of an anguished man seen carrying his child with blood streaming down his head or those of children choking from gas or lying comatose on the ground in the no-man's-land between Serbia and Hungary do not belong to Europe in the 21st century. Were we not given to believe that we would never again witness such examples of man's inhumanity to man, let alone to women and children, on European soil?

That said there are European states, notably Germany, Austria and Sweden, who are opening their doors and doing what they can to handle this enormous influx of humanity as best as they can even as others refuse to call terrorized people from Syria, Iraq and Afghanistan "refugees".

Instead they are being referred to by countries that do not want them as "illegal migrants", "gangs" or "mobs", their arrival characterized as "an invasion" with those who manage to break through prosecuted like criminals.

United Nations (UN) Secretary General Ban Ki-moon said he was shocked at the way refugees are being treated. "It's not acceptable," he said. Pope Francis has demanded that every Catholic parish or institution accept a minimum of one refugee family but he is facing a rebellion in some quarters with the words "Today's refugee could be tomorrow's terrorist."

The German Chancellor Angela Merkel has shown exemplary leadership. Together with the European Commission President Jean-Claude Juncker, she is calling for an European Union (EU)-wide quota system that would oblige member states to absorb refugees according to their capacity in terms of GDP and unemployment statistics, against strong objections from Hungary, the Czech Republic, Poland and Slovakia, threatened with losing their EU funding.

This situation now threatens to destroy the Schengen Agreement allowing for free movement between EU states and all the accusations flying between neighbouring countries with very different views could cause severe diplomatic rifts.

Bashar Al Assad says the refugee crisis is all the fault of the West for arming opposition forces. Naturally, he will say anything to lift the blame from his own shoulders. If he had heeded his own people by stepping down in 2011 instead of slaughtering them, none of this mess would have happened.

No one emerges from this with a halo and certainly not Barack Obama whose lack of leadership has allowed the Syrian conflict to fester into a terrorist swamp. Out of the so-called moderate fighters trained by the US only five remain in theatre. Not five thousand or five hundred. Just five guys wandering around with guns.

European leaders have done nothing other than make speeches and attend summits. Turkey's playing a duplicitous game, using Daesh as a pretext to kill its Kurdish enemies. And as for the Arab World ... well, what can I say. I am not sure what is going on behind the scenes, but on the surface it appears that Arab leaderships, except those of the Gulf Cooperation Council (GCC), Jordan and Lebanon, have a blind spot on Syria.

It has taken a flood of refugees into Europe and a Russian weapons build-up in Syria that could portend Moscow's full-scale military intervention to galvanize the UN into sending its envoy to Damascus to discuss peace proposals. Plus, John Kerry appears open to discussions with his Russian counterpart on military solutions.

Until when will we continue relying on foreign powers to save us? We did the right thing by intervening in Yemen and now the Houthi rebels are on the back foot. It is about time the Arab coalition turned its attention to Syria. The Arab World needs a union that is strong and resourceful with a mandate from all member countries to take action whenever the peace and security of our region is threatened otherwise what is it other than an expensive mega majlis administrated by clerks.

We will shortly be celebrating Eid Al Adha with family and friends, enjoying good meals and good company, while tens of thousands of Syrians at the mercy of European states go without food and shelter, their future uncertain. Enough! It is the time for the Arab League to resume its duties and try to salvage our Arab honour.

Assad must not get away with his crimes

6 November 2015

ANCIENT CITIES and World Heritage sites across Syria have been turned into wastelands of blood-soaked rubble littered with infants' shoes and toys. Almost 300,000 Syrians have been killed and 11 million displaced. If there is one person to blame for the four-year-long tragedy it is Bashar Al Assad, who instructed his army to slaughter his own citizens rather than heed his people's call to step down. He put his chair before his country and he is responsible for the influx of terrorists.

Assad is the greatest war criminal of our time, and as long as he is in Russia's embrace he can sleep soundly. He is assured of immunity because, firstly, Syria is not a member of the International Criminal Court (ICC) and, secondly, he is confident that the United Nations (UN) Security Council cannot refer him to The Hague thanks to Russia's power of veto. Russia makes a mockery of international laws and institutions set up to hold leaders to account for crimes against humanity.

What concerns me most is how impotent the international community has become, both diplomatically and militarily. Assad's future is being used as a bargaining chip in this disgraceful geopolitical power play in which Syrian lives are considered collateral damage.

Russian President Vladimir Putin's defence of Assad has nothing to do with warm personal chemistry between the two leaders. His longevity is dependent purely on his usefulness to Moscow's interests:

- Preservation of Russia's naval base in the port of Tatus – its only deep water base on the Mediterranean.

- Compliance with the demands of Russia's prime regional ally, Iran, seeking to maintain Syrian state control over the capital, the Mediterranean coast and areas of central Syria serving as a conduit for Iranian weapons destined for its Lebanese proxy Hezbollah.

- The necessity of proving to Moscow's allies that they will not be abandoned when the chips are down and also to encourage regional partners allied with the West to shift into Russia's sphere of influence.

- Projection of Russian power in the Middle East through the agency of an informal Russian-Syrian-Iranian (and a potential Iraqi) bloc.

Unfortunately, President Barack Obama's hesitancy to stop the bloodshed some years ago following the regime's used of chemical weapons, the ineffectiveness of year-long US-led coalition airstrikes against Daesh and his unwillingness to put boots on the ground left a vacuum for Russia to fill. Obama's "Syria strategy" has been marked by failure.

America's programmes to train and arm "moderate" rebels have had to be binned because without heavy weapons they were no match for the better-armed terrorist groups. Since Russia seized the initiative, the US is trying to play catch-up with ramped-up airstrikes and the insertion of a 50-strong contingent of Special Forces set to work alongside Kurdish and Arab fighters battling Daesh.

The White House has no plans to assist opposition forces fighting to bring down the Assad regime, as deduced by an irate Senator Lindsey Graham recently while grilling Secretary of Defence Ash Carter and the Chairman of the Joint Chiefs General Joseph Dunford on the administration's objectives during a Senate Armed Services Committee hearing recently.

Under the veteran lawmaker's relentless battering, Carter was forced to admit that US strategy is solely to assist rebels fighting Daesh. In his testimony Graham promptly lost his cool. "Russia, Iran and Hezbollah are gonna fight for their guy, and we're not gonna do a damn thing to help the people who want to change Syria for the better by getting rid of the dictator in Damascus," he ranted.

"So what you've done gentlemen, along with the President, is you've turned Syria over to Russia and Iran. You've told the people in Syria, who've died by the hundreds of thousands, 'we're more worried about a political settlement than we are about what follows ... '."

Western leaders, including President Obama, have at one time or another affirmed that Assad is the problem and insisted he must step down. But in light of Russia's military intervention, they are softening their stance, suggesting the Syrian President can take part in a transition leading to a transitional government in which top regime figures will be free to participate.

They have dumped their principles in favour of politics. In other words, they have folded out of expediency, which makes them look weak. In any case, what gives foreign powers the right to make deals that have not been sanctioned by representatives of all Syrian parties and factions?

Syrians have given their blood and sacrificed their parents and children to be free from a tyrannical regime. They have a right to a say in their future, but they have been shut out of negotiations. Not a single Syrian was invited to participate in the recent talks in Vienna, not even as an observer. The foreign ministers of 16 countries, including the enemy of Arab states – Iran – sat around the table to discuss Syria's destiny. It was a complete waste of time as some attendees were only there to block any progress.

Iran, the biggest threat to regional stability, was dignified with an invitation. That should have been a warning. It had no intention of compromising evidenced by its verbal attacks on Saudi Arabia, who the Iranian Deputy Foreign Minister Hossein Amir-Abdollahian accused of playing "a negative role", while threatening Iran's withdrawal from the peace efforts should they be found to be unconstructive. Good riddance!

Syrians will be able to choose their next government at the ballot box, according to US Secretary of State John Kerry and Russian Foreign Minister Sergei Lavrov, who told reporters after their bilateral meeting that all Syrians both inside and outside the country, including refugees, will get a vote. Is this a joke? How can they propose something so ludicrous? It is likely to be years before free and fair elections can be held. Let us not forget that regime barrel bombs still fall and over 40 terrorist and militant groups control large swathes of Syrian territory.

I am distressed that the world cannot get its act together to bring peace to Syria. Enough conferences and meetings! Enough talking! What is needed is decisive action so that Syrian families trudging through a freezing Europe with their babies can go home. Does the US or Russia or Iran truly have those poor people at heart or are they more concerned with their own hegemonic or economic stake in the issue? Russia is the kingpin, for without its backing the regime could not have survived until now – and Putin must be persuaded to desist from working to give Assad a free pass.

Syrians need closure before they can move forward with a process of forgiveness and reconciliation. The idea that Assad will be permitted to walk scot-free and enjoy a life of luxury in Tehran is unacceptable for those who have lost everything at his hands.

Too much time has been wasted and worryingly we now know that the idea of an "international community" is just a meaningless concept.

Self-serving countries trumpeting their values while juggling for influence and gain without real concern for humanity translates to our world having evolved into a dog-eat-dog planet where those with the biggest bombs rule.

The world must act to destroy this disease

16 November 2015

PARIS IS IN MOURNING. We are all in mourning for those who thronged the glorious French capital on Friday evening little knowing it would be their last. All except the terrorists and their brain-diseased following who have taken to social media to gleefully celebrate the deaths of 129 innocent people and 300 who have been injured, many critically.

My heart goes out to all Parisians and foreign visitors whose lives will for ever be impacted by the actions of evil creatures who have forfeited the right to be called humans let alone Muslims.

The stories of survivors are pure horror. An eyewitness who managed to escape from the Bataclan concert venue where over 100 were held hostage by four gunmen wielding Kalashnikovs said: "They were shooting at us like if we were birds."

Predictions based on volleys of threats have come true. Terror nurtured in the war-torn Middle East has infected European soil causing France to declare lockdown, a move unprecedented since the end of World War II.

Still reeling from the Charlie Hebdo attacks in January, French authorities were well prepared for a repeat performance. The country was placed on the highest alert.

French intelligence has already thwarted five similar plots but, as we have seen, even a state with a highly efficient security apparatus is helpless to prevent extremists wearing suicide belts from striking "soft targets" selected for maximum kill. Experts say it is only a matter of time before other European countries share France's fate. The US is tightening up its own security in its major cities.

Many thousands of European nationals have joined Daesh and other terror organizations in Iraq and Syria. Thousands are believed to have returned home battle-hardened and eager to continue their killing spree in their own countries.

Another concern is that Daesh fighters have infiltrated the floods of refugees fleeing bombs and barbarians and the fear is that those desperate people will be penalized as countries that once welcomed them are now pulling down the shutters on their own borders. Who can blame them when they are duty-bound to put their own citizens first!

The international community is rallying around the French President François Hollande. President Barack Obama earlier that same day had praised the demise of "Jihadi John" while announcing that Daesh was now contained. He was one of the first world leaders to go on camera to express his condolences. "This is an attack on all of humanity and the universal values we share. We stand prepared and ready to provide whatever assistance the people of France need to respond," he said.

But even as I heard the American President utter those comforting words, I could not help but contrast his willingness to help protect France with his negligent approach to Iraq and Syria where hundreds of thousands have been slaughtered.

Firstly, although the US broke Iraq in 2003 pitting Shi'ites against Sunnis, Obama has made no effort to fix it. Instead of negotiating with the Iraqi government to leave a residual US force in country in a serious fashion, he was out to beat a hasty retreat.

When just 10,000 or so Daesh terrorists took Mosul, the then Iraqi leader, Nouri Al Maliki practically begged the West to come to his country's aid and was rebuffed. Kurdish Peshmerga forces pleaded for weapons, which were refused. By the time an air campaign was launched, Daesh had grown into a ruthless unstoppable force. And despite coalition bombs and a contingent of US military advisors, this devil's spawn, hiding under the banner of Islam, controls almost a third of Iraq to this day.

Libya has turned out to be yet another fiasco. Thanks to the US, France and Britain, Muammar Gaddafi was removed but nothing was done to assist the Libyan people to rid the country of feuding militias or Daesh terrorists posing a direct threat to Egypt, Tunisia and Algeria. Worse, the Egyptian government was rapped on the knuckles for bombing Daesh in Libya in retaliation for its beheading of Coptic Christians and the US still bars the recognized government from importing heavy weapons.

Adding insult to injury, not only have the US and its European allies done nothing to free Lebanon from the boot of Iran's terrorist proxy Hezbollah, earlier this year it, along with its Iranian masters, was removed from America's terrorist threat list!

The US administration's approach to the carnage in Syria, where the regime has turned cities into rivers of blood and its country into a haven for terrorists, has been hopeless in the extreme. Obama erased his own "red line" on Syrian President Bashar Al Assad's use of chemical weapons, going back on his pledge to bomb regime targets at the nth minute, sending opposition plans to gain an advantage up in smoke.

Since then, efforts by the Central Intelligence Agency (CIA) and the Pentagon to train and arm "moderate" opposition elements was an embarrassing failure. Almost all either joined terrorist groups or handed over their American-made weapons in return for safe passage.

For over a year, the US and its coalition partners have supposedly been bombing Daesh strongholds with little result; that is until Russia joined the fray on the side of Assad. I am strongly against the Russian involvement to prop up Assad, but there is no getting away from the truth. Russia has wrought more damage on Daesh in just a few months than the US-led coalition achieved during a far longer period.

And now it appears that the US and its Western partners have done a deal with Moscow to leave the Syrian Butcher temporarily in place with the promise of eventual safe passage out, which the majority of Syrians view as a betrayal of everything they have fought so valiantly to achieve over the past four-and-a-half years.

President Obama could have and should have cut this disease at its roots while in its infancy but he blinked over and over again allowing the cancer to spread all over the Middle East and North Africa until it reached Europe's shores.

European Union (EU) states are now paying a very heavy price for his hesitancy in terms of refugees straining their finances and infrastructure as well as their increased vulnerability to terror attacks. Russia has accused the US of knowing exactly where the terrorists are but not bombing them. We must take that with a pinch of salt, but it is possible.

Europe is on edge. Britain worries its cities will be next. I am sad to say that the UK has made itself open to such attacks with its embrace of extremists free to march in the streets shouting threats and handing out recruitment leaflets. To this day, Prime Minister David Cameron has declined to label "terrorist" the mother ship of just about all *takfiris*, the Muslim Brotherhood, under the pretext that as long as they remain law-abiding there is no problem.

He is tempting fate and I strongly believe his words will come back to bite him sooner rather than later. They have been biding time, reluctant to dirty on their own doorstep, but if and when their fellows start turning British towns into rivers of blood, they will be at the forefront.

Will Paris be a game changer? Will major Western powers be galvanized to erase this menace from the face of the earth? Will Arab leaderships show their mettle as they are now doing to save Yemen? If not, as much as I hate to say this, the world, as we have always known it, is staring at its doom.

Syria is bleeding. Where are the Arabs?

1 May 2016

THERE ARE NO WORDS to express my fury and distress at the horrendous scenes shown on our screens. What kind of world is this that does nothing apart from hold conferences when hospitals are being pounded, the bodies of small children are being pulled from bombed-out buildings while wounded toddlers scream for their dead mothers! The words of a small boy forced to bury his baby brother because there is no one left still ring in my ears. "Why was I not taken instead?" he said through his sobs.

In recent days both a hospital run under the auspices of Doctors Without Borders and a clinic in Aleppo have been destroyed. The sick and the injured have nowhere to go for treatment when even medical facilities have become targets. These are serious war crimes and it is my fervent hope that those responsible will be made to pay a heavy price, even though no price can ever compensate for so much pain and suffering caused by man's inhumanity to man.

What kind of "President" sends his fighter jets to bomb his own people lying in their hospital beds? He does not even have the guts to admit it. He is nothing but a monster ultimately responsible for robbing the lives of over 400,000, displacing over half the population and reducing four-and-a-half million to refugee status, fleeing to countries where they are treated little better than criminals.

Five long years have passed since this nightmare began. All efforts to quell the bloodshed have turned to dust. Countries and coalitions have no other solutions than bombs and more bombs, talks and more talks.

Shame on President Vladimir Putin for protecting this barbaric regime! Shame on President Barack Obama, the great champion of human rights, so-called, for not intervening in any meaningful fashion! Shame on the United Nations (UN) for failing in its peace mission – and, yes, shame on us Arabs!

Syrians are our brothers and sisters; their children are our children. Have you seen the terror in their eyes? Have you heard their despairing cries? They have done nothing to deserve this hell on earth. They are crying out to be saved but it seems the decision-makers who can make a difference, those who can call upon airpower, ground troops and sophisticated weapons to bring to bear against the regime and the terrorists, are not really listening for if they were they would send in their armies without delay.

The Saudi-led 34 nation Islamic Military Counter Terrorism Coalition should unite against the greatest terrorist of all, Bashar Al Assad, before cleansing this ancient land of Daesh, Al Qaeda and its affiliate Al Nusra, so that Syrians can return to their homes, their children can return to school instead of having to beg in the streets of Lebanon, Turkey and Jordan, and the dignity of Syrian womanhood can be preserved.

News that large numbers of our Syrian sisters are sacrificing them-selves by becoming old men's temporary brides, or worse, just to survive and take care of their families is heart wrenching. For me this is a case of déjà vu. I was similarly disturbed by the crippling US sanctions on Iraq during Bill Clinton's watch believed to have caused the death of up to half a million Iraqi children.

Two UN officials resigned calling the sanctions "genocidal". The then-US Ambassador to the United Nations Madeleine Albright, when asked whether the death of so many children was worth it, answered: "I think that is a very hard choice, but the price, we think, the price is worth it."

Bill Clinton told Amy Goodman: "If they are hungry or if they're not getting medicine it's his [Saddam's] fault." I was furious. I railed at them for taking the bread from the mouths of Iraqis and for putting decent Iraqi women in positions where some chose to sacrifice their honour to keep their kids alive. Clinton drove nails into Iraq's coffin and George W. Bush hammered them in. The invasion of Iraq was a crime whitewashed by false pretexts.

Yet when faced with a righteous cause, a humanitarian cause, Barack Obama turned his back on the Syrian people and abandoned the Free Syrian Army (FSA) not to mention ordinary Syrians who left their jobs and their fields to defend their homes, encouraged by US pledges of support.

Syria remains one of the greatest man-made tragedies of our time. If we wait for the United States or Russia or the UN to find a cure, there will be little left of Syria fit for people to go home to. Assad is the stumbling block. He has to go one way or the other before any semblance of peace can reign. I appeal to the leaderships of the Gulf Cooperation Council (GCC) and their Arab allies to make every endeavour to ensure that he does.

In a recent column, I saluted the new independent spirit of predominately Sunni states to stand up to their enemies. Now I am pleading with them to hold out a lifeline to our Syrian brothers and sisters who have been left alone and adrift without hope. The world may consider Syrian lives cheap but what is our excuse? We like to trumpet our Arab honour. Well, here is the greatest test of all and it is one that we must not fail. God in his mercy may forgive us for not even trying, but the Syrian people, their children and grandchildren certainly will not.

6

Yemen: conflict and poverty

Introduction

How my heart breaks for Yemen. Who would have thought that the threat of civil war could come so close to our doorstep? The country is grappling with a multitude of problems. Separatist unrest dominates much of the south; there are frequent terrorist attacks as well as ongoing power struggles between tribal and military factions, and the Houthis have taken hold of the north. The United Nations (UN) says that the country is now teetering on the edge of civil war. (See Reuters, "U.N. says Yemen collapsing, on brink of civil war", 12 February 2015.)

I have warned many times of the consequences of the rising power of the Houthis. Sadly, the day has come when all my fears came true. So many innocent lives have been lost since fighting intensified between rival groups in 2015. The civilian death toll alone is already well into the thousands and, according to The Office of the High Commissioner for Human Rights (OHCHR), reached 2,300 by 30 September 2015.

The rebels achieved their long-sought-after goal of wresting power from the government while the Arab World was in a deep slumber. In March 2015, rebel forces closed in on President Abdrabbuh Mansour Hadi's southern stronghold of Aden – the de facto capital. They announced the dissolution of the Yemeni parliament and the creation of the Revolutionary Committee, led by several Houthi members, to rule over the country.

The Houthis, who are understood to be supported by military units loyal to the former President Ali Abdullah Saleh, formally seized power and placed Hadi under house arrest. He managed to escape and was forced to flee abroad, spending six months in exile. Hadi has since returned to the country, setting up a temporary base while the capital Sana'a remains in the hand of the rebels. Saleh meanwhile denies he has any ties with the Houthis – and maintains he has nothing to do with the war.

Thankfully, the people of Yemen did not have to wait for the West to "save" them from the rebels wreaking havoc within their country. A coalition led by their Arab neighbours – Saudi Arabia and the United

Arab Emirates (UAE) – came to their rescue militarily in a campaign known as Operation Decisive Storm , in a bid to rein in the chaos. This came at a high price. Many of our UAE soldiers were killed in the conflict. In September 2015 one single rocket attack claimed the lives of 45 of our finest soldiers, along with 10 Saudi soldiers and 5 Bahrainis. What a terrible loss for our countries. I am so proud of the sacrifice that our noble soldiers made for their homeland. May their souls, through the mercy of God, rest in peace.

Following the attack, rebel forces said it was revenge for the war of extermination being carried out by the Saudi-led coalition.

However, Abu Dhabi Crown Prince Sheikh Mohammed bin Zayed Al Nahyan, Deputy Supreme Commander of the UAE Armed Forces, remained defiant. He tweeted: "Clearing Yemen from the aggressive, rebellious militias which ran amok is a target that we will not be distracted from."

I was shocked beyond belief when the United Nations Secretary General Ban Ki-moon slammed the Saudi-led coalition for its campaign in Yemen. In its annual report the UN blacklisted the coalition for Operation Decisive Storm branding it alongside terrorist groups and rogue states who engage "in the recruitment and use of children, sexual violence against children, the killing and maiming of children, attacks on schools and/or hospitals and attacks or threats against protected personnel and the abduction of children".

How the UN could think that Saudi Arabia and its Arab allies would deliberately harm children is beyond me. The report reeks of double standards and unsubstantiated claims. (See "Tough response needed to counter UN slander", 5 June 2016, later in this chapter.)

As we go to print, I am waiting to see what the coalitions' reaction will be to the degrading UN report. I strongly urge the Arab states involved in Decisive Storm to respond to this injustice.

This proxy war has drawn in many nations – including the US and Iran. On one side, America is providing logistical support and intelligence to the countries conducting airstrikes. In April 2015, US officials confirmed that Washington was expanding intelligence-sharing with Saudi Arabia to provide more details about potential targets. Meanwhile, Iran is providing support to the Houthis – although it continues to deny the accusation.

The conflict between the Houthis and the government is part of a regional power struggle between Iran and the Kingdom of Saudi Arabia, which shares a border with Yemen. There is no doubt in my mind that Iran is not only backing the Houthis militarily but also financially. President Hadi concurs. He told the UN General Assembly that Tehran "would like to see the destruction of the country".

Kudos to the Gulf Cooperation Council (GCC) leaders who put their words into action to defend Yemen's sovereignty and our own borders with the implementation of Decisive Storm. The decisive action showed the strength of our collective nations, and proved we will not permit terrorists to invade our land.

I do not condone war, and I believe it should be a final option. Unfortunately there can be no meaningful dialogue with the Islamic Republic of Iran, a country that is striving for regional dominance at any cost, and cannot be trusted to keep its promises. There should be no stopping until Yemen is cleansed of its pro-Iranian traitors and the legitimate government has been reinstated.

I pray that Yemen does not go the way of Lebanon and Syria, and become another Arab country lost under Iranian domination.

To make matters worse, a Yemeni affiliate of Daesh emerged in late 2014 to rival the Al Qaeda in the Arabian Peninsula (AQAP), considered by Western intellence agencies as Al Qaeda's most dangerous branch because of its technical expertise, and global reach. The Daesh unit, which aspires to eclipse AQAP, carried out a number of terror attacks from its strongholds mainly in the south of the country. (See BBC, "Yemen in crisis: Who is fighing whom?", 26 March 2015.)

Two suicide attacks by extremists targeted mosques in the capital Sana'a killing more than 120 people and wounding scores of others. What is the world coming to when innocent people who are at prayer are killed so mercilessly?

No one is safe, and no matter how much protection senior officials receive, it seems safety is drastically compromised. In December 2015 Daesh assassinated a top regional governor in Aden in a suicide bomb attack. Jaafar Mohammed Saad died along with six of his bodyguards when a suicide bomber rammed a car into the Governor's convoy. All his security measures were not enough. If officials cannot be protected then how can the residents of Yemen feel safe in their beds at night?

It is not just the GCC that should be wary of the regional implications of the escalating crisis in Yemen, but also the West should be concerned about the impact on its security. There are financial implications too: Yemen is located on the Bab Al Mandab Strait, which links the Gulf of Aden with the Red Sea and where much of the world's oil shipments pass. If the Houthis take over it could threaten free passage through the Strait.

Let us not forget Yemen is one of the poorest countries in the Middle East, and the current "war" is further devastating the economy. Just think that in 2013 Yemen's economy was ticking along nicely, with growth of 4.8 per cent from the previous year and worth more than $35bn. The economy slumped to about 0.3 per cent in 2014. The World Bank says: "The difficult political and security situation in Yemen continues to weigh heavily on economic activity and Yemen's economic recovery is highly vulnerable." It estimates a 25–35 per cent contraction in real GDP in 2015 due to deteriorating stability, high employment, weak governance and failing institutional structures.

Unemployment is climbing by the day, infrastructure is weak and food sources are being depleted. The UN and other aid organizations are warning of "an impending famine in Yemen".

The conflict is having a devastating impact on civilian men, women and children who are living in the firing line every day. The United Nations Children's Emergency Fund (UNICEF) estimates that nearly 10,000 children under five years old may have died in the past year from preventable diseases. "The destruction of the health service has also left millions of children and their families without adequate nutrition, drinking water or sanitation and poses serious risks to the country's future beyond the end of the conflict," stated the report. (UNICEF report, "Unicef UK warns Yemen conflict is 'shattering' the lives and future of millions of children", 4 May 2016.)

Have people not suffered enough? Yemen is grappling with its most severe crisis in years, and unless stability is restored soon, the many competing forces who are fighting for control of the country will emerge victorious and pose an even graver threat – not only to Yemen but to the region and beyond.

It is not just Yemeni sovereignty that is at stake, the escalating tension has much broader repercussions. If Iran gets its way and undermines Yemen's statehood, it will strengthen the presence of radical terror groups in the region and spill over into neighbouring countries. This poses a grave risk to the countries bordering the Kingdom of Saudi Arabia – and to all of the Gulf states. We cannot afford to sit idle with this growing threat to regional security and stability. Let us stop it before it is too late.

Yemen needs help not criticism

1 April 2010

I AM DEEPLY CONCERNED about Yemen, whose government is in dire need of assistance. Southern separatists are attempting to thrust the country into civil war and Iranian-backed Houthi rebels are waging an insurgency in the north. The government is also battling extreme poverty affecting 45.2 per cent of its population, many of whom lack clean water, electricity and job opportunities.

Unfortunately, the future looks far from rosy on the economic front because Yemen's oil resources that currently fund 80 per cent of government revenue are fast running out and, according to some analysts, may be entirely depleted by 2017.

Exploiting unrest are Al Qaeda franchises said to have trained and equipped the Nigerian national, who, on 25 December, tried to blow up a US airplane. This failed attempt has hurtled Yemen into the international spotlight, prompting the US and Britain to close their embassies and issue no-fly advisories.

Amid Western fears that Yemen is in danger of becoming a failed state, the British Prime Minister Gordon Brown hosted a two-hour-long international conference in London, last week, attended by the Yemeni Prime Minister Ali Mohammed Majawar and 20 foreign ministers, including those from the six Gulf Cooperation Council (GCC) countries.

Delegates from the United Nations (UN), the European Union (EU) and the World Bank were also in attendance but an invitation to the League of Arab States had not been extended. Arab League Secretary General Amr Moussa referred to this omission as "a strange" and "very unusual sign". I beg to differ. Western powers usually keep Arabs out of the loop when it comes to making decisions concerning their own neighbourhood.

Yemen's Prime Minister and its Foreign Minister Abu Bakr Al Qirbi have been open about their nation's problems and have requested the support of the international community "to build infrastructure, combat poverty, create jobs" and assist in "combating terrorism".

Rather than lending support to the Yemeni government's efforts, during the summit, the US Secretary of State Hillary Clinton – who earlier referred to Yemen as "an incubator of extremism" – chose to undermine it. Indeed, she reminded me of Shakespeare's Anthony in *Julius Caesar*, who famously said: "I come to bury Caesar, not to praise him."

"Yemen must take ownership of the challenges it faces, and of its internal affairs," Clinton said. She warned the Yemeni government that international aid will not be forthcoming unless it can demonstrate improved security, a clampdown on corruption and show that foreign aid will be "used effectively". She even made excuses for donor countries that had failed to make good on $5.2bn pledges made during a 2006 donor conference saying their reluctance to pay up was due to worries their cash would be misspent.

Her disparaging tone must have been music to the ears of opposition leaders, insurgents, extremists and would-be secessionists not to mention those of her own all-important constituents; 53 per cent of whom have admitted to some level of anti-Muslim bias according to a recently-released *Religious Perceptions in America* report. Clinton recently told PBS that she would not serve as Secretary of State in a second Obama administration, fuelling suspicions that she plans to stand against her boss in 2012.

Whether her tough stance against the Yemeni authorities is exclusively her own or reflects a White House agenda is impossible to tell. There is no doubt, however, that Yemen is concerned about America's long-term policy. Yemen's Prime Minister and Foreign Minister have both stressed that the idea of US bases on Yemeni soil "is inconceivable".

That may be so, in principle, but as reported by *The Washington Post*, it is an open secret that US intelligence and military personnel from US Joint Special Operations Command have been in Yemen for more than six weeks where they are working with Yemeni troops to eliminate Al Qaeda affiliates. This is a sensitive issue, and as Saudi Arabia has warned, if US boots become visible on Yemeni soil their presence will be viewed as a propaganda gift to extremists and insurgents.

Rather than watch passively, allowing Yemen to go the way of occupied Iraq or an ungovernable pirates' paradise like Somalia, the Arab World must stand with the Yemeni leadership before it is too late. We must ask ourselves why we have allowed the Land of Sheba – some say the historic homeland of our ancestors – to descend into such poverty and why the American military is working alongside Yemen's instead of our own.

Saudi Arabia should be commended for successfully battling Houthi tribesmen who crossed its borders but, instead of declaring victory, it should offer military support to Yemen to prevent this Iranian-spawned infection from contaminating the entire region. Likewise, every GCC army should be at Yemen's disposal together with allocated funds to bring Yemen to prosperity.

It is well known that the US and its Western allies have no friends, only interests. This is why they must not be allowed to decide Yemen's fate. During the GCC hosted donor conference set to take place in Riyadh on 22–23 February, we should do much more than talk. If we believe that the Yemeni people are our brothers, we must prove it with much-needed military assistance and hard cash. Anything less is tantamount to an open invitation to Tehran, Washington and Al Qaeda to turn Yemen into a blood-stained and ideological battlefield for the foreseeable future.

Beware unintended consequences of Yemeni uprising!

29 November 2011

WHEN THE WORLD'S EYE is focused on the uprisings in Egypt, Syria and the President of Yemen's agreement to step aside in favour of his deputy, the spotlight has been diverted from the threat posed by Yemeni Houthi Zaidi Shi'ite, pro-Iranian rebels.

The Houthi anti-government rebellion has been waged to one degree or another since 2004 from their base in the north on the Saudi border. With over 100,000 armed fighters, by some estimates, they harbour not only an expansionist agenda but the will to topple the government and impose their own brand of Shi'ite religious law on the entire country and beyond – a type of Shi'ite caliphate presided over by their spiritual head Abdul Malik Al Houthi. They have made territorial claims to a number of Saudi villages and in 2009 they battled with Saudi forces.

For the Houthis, the Yemeni armed forces' preoccupation with maintaining security on the street has been a gift. Over the past 10 months they have succeeded in expanding their territorial control of their home base of Sa'ada into four Yemeni provinces and hold sway over the main crossing points into Saudi. Their success is mainly because opposing tribes in the region, backed by the besieged outgoing President Ali Abdullah Saleh, have been deprived of material support during the turmoil.

Until now a landlocked people, the Houthis are currently concentrating their attacks on the Hajjah governorate, which crucially offers access to the Midi Seaport. Some Yemeni officials believe securing the port is the first step in the Houthis' wider strategy; that of opening up a Red Sea route to import heavy weapons and supplies with which to attack the Yemeni capital Sana'a as well as the Saudi border to enable infiltration of Saudi Arabia. It is worth remembering that in 2009 Saudi Arabia accused Iran of supplying arms to the Houthis and instituted a naval blockade of the northern Yemeni coastline. At a time when Yemen is vulnerable to malign interior and exterior influences, this threat must be taken very seriously.

The Houthis' hatred of Saudi Arabia is well known and it is my belief that they have hatched a plan with the Iranian ayatollahs to sneak weapons and terrorists over the border into Saudi to launch terrorist acts aimed at destabilizing the Kingdom as soon as they get the green light from Tehran to attempt the destruction of our peaceful Gulf Cooperation Council (GCC) societies.

Like Hezbollah aided by Tehran and the Alawite rulers in Damascus, the Houthis are being used as Iran's proxies to infect the region with a regressive and repressive ideology at the point of a sword. Simultaneously, Iran is inciting Shi'ite minorities in Saudi Arabia and other GCC countries to cause trouble.

In recent days, Shi'ites have been demonstrating against the Saudi government in the city of Qatif in the oil-rich eastern region, where anti-royalist slogans have been scrawled on walls. The Kingdom's Mufti has pointed his finger firmly at Iran for the unrest and the hostility against the royal family, which is credible when Iranian clerics are calling for an end to the Al Saud ruling dynasty. The Kingdom's Interior Ministry has in the past blamed a foreign power for stirring up "seditious residents" – a couched reference to Iran's interference. Unfortunately, a section of Shi'ite minorities is allowing itself to be used as an Iranian pawn. The most glaring example of this trend is, of course, the violent events in Bahrain.

Bahrain's Shi'ite community was an inherent and respected part of Bahraini society until a segment saluted marching orders from Tehran and tried to overthrow the King. Many just went along with the herd but, to my mind, their ringleaders who have been whipped up by Iranian spies are traitors to their homeland. They had to be stopped in their tracks and I am grateful for the intervention of the Saudi military.

Bahrain's government had to act decisively to keep the country free from irreparable harm but it has been blasted by human rights groups for so doing. Gulf peoples and rulers respect everyone's freedom and dignity; that is until our own rights are breached by planted traitors out to create divisions. Those foreign-bought traitors who betrayed Bahrain got away easily in my opinion. They deserved to be tried and hanged as a lesson to others seeking to rob a nation of its security and peace.

I was surprised and disappointed at the "findings" of the Bahrain Independent Commission of Investigation into the uprising and the government crackdown, headed by Mahmoud Cherif Bassiouni – an Egyptian national UN war crimes expert, appointed by the King. It was so heavily biased in favour of demonstrators' claims and so critical of the government's human rights record that it is not worth the paper it is written on. Bassiouni has unwittingly or purposefully failed to see the big picture; he has blinded himself to the virulent and orchestrated Iranian infection creeping all over the Gulf and parts of the Middle East.

We are being surrounded and infiltrated from all sides, which is why the GCC, currently caught up with the problem of Syria, must be vigilant. With Iranian proxies gaining strength in Lebanon, Syria, Bahrain and Iraq, I recommend the GCC to take the following urgent steps:

- If Yemen's military is unable to protect the Red Sea, the GCC's Rapid Reaction Force should assist the Yemeni government to secure its coastline and ports.

- The GCC should support the Iraqi opposition, Iraqis who are true Arab patriots, not pro-Iranian figures whose loyalties lie elsewhere.

- GCC states should close their countries' borders to suspect groups working on Iran's behalf and make use of cutting-edge technologies to monitor their movements.

- Gulf intelligence services and security forces should go all out to eradicate traitors from our midst even if this requires turning a deaf ear to complaints from foreign capitals.

In the meantime, the Houthis are congratulating themselves on having a free hand. Their resurgence can easily turn into another nail in the coffin for the Gulf's stability and security unless our leaders decide to cut off this arm of Iran before it can get a grip.

The GCC woke up late to the Yemen threat

9 February 2015

IRANIAN-BACKED SHI'ITE HOUTHI rebels successfully achieved their long-held goal while the Arab World was sleeping. Under the pretence of seeking a more inclusive government, they have taken control of the country, including its capital Sana'a. After pressurizing President Abdrabbuh Mansour Hadi to resign on 22 January following armed Houthi protests, sit-ins and the takeover of government buildings, the militia has dissolved parliament and replaced it with a five-member revolutionary council.

The move has been condemned by all Yemeni political parties and is likely to result in either an all-out civil war or the splitting up of the country. There exists a very real risk that political and sectarian volatility will open a wide window for Al Qaeda, Ansar Al Sharia and other terrorist groups to gain an even greater foothold than they have enjoyed to date and, certainly, a Shi'ite minority takeover will ramp up recruitment.

Not only is Yemen's future as a unified sovereign state in peril, there are wider implications for the entire region. For one thing, the regional geopolitical map has been re-drawn to further empower Iranian ambitions to the detriment of Sunni Gulf states and, moreover, a Houthi-led "government" poses a grave threat to Saudi national security.

The Gulf Cooperation Council's (GCC) member states are clearly rattled. Warning that the "coup" would plunge the country into a "dark tunnel" the GCC has announced that it will take all necessary steps to protect its interests without going into specifics. The Council has also appealed to the international community and the United Nations (UN) Security Council to assist in resolving the crisis, which, sad to say, is like closing the gate after the horse has bolted.

I am shocked that the GCC's Secretary General waited until the nth minute to publicly react to this menace, and if he seriously believes that the Security Council or our so-called Western allies will heed his call in any meaningful fashion, he is in for a disappointment – especially during a moment in time when the West is more interested in forming a rapprochement with Iran than cleansing the area of terrorist militias.

To say that I am personally frustrated that no action was taken much earlier to prevent this easily predictable state of affairs is an understatement. For years I have been discussing my worries with prominent decision-makers and writing columns outlining my fears that a Houthi power grab was on the cards while strongly urging Gulf states to treat the matter with the seriousness it deserves.

Unfortunately, my warnings were not heeded. If a businessman like me could decipher the writing on the wall, why did our governments' political advisors and intelligence analysts fail to do so? Why do we always wait until the sword is poised to cut our necks before we think about taking preemptive measures?

As long ago as 1 April 2010, I had published a column headed "Yemen needs help not criticism", arguing that poverty-stricken Yemen was in danger of becoming a failed state. I criticized then US Secretary of State Hillary Clinton for depriving the country of international aid, suggesting that "Her disparaging tone must have been music to the ears of opposition leaders, insurgents, extremists and would-be secessionists." "Rather than watch passively, allowing Yemen to go the way of Iraq or an ungovernable pirates' paradise like Somalia, the Arab World must stand with the Yemeni leadership before it is too late," I wrote.

I followed up the above analysis on 29 November 2011 with an article titled "Beware unintended consequences of Yemeni uprising". In that, I warned that Houthis harbour an "expansionist agenda" and are endeavouring to open up a Red Sea route to import heavy weapons with which to attack the Yemeni capital and infiltrate Saudi Arabia.

I wrote that the "Houthis' hatred of Saudi Arabia is well known and it is my belief that they have hatched a plan with the Iranian ayatollahs to sneak weapons and terrorists over the border into Saudi Arabia to launch terrorist acts aimed at destabilizing the Kingdom as soon as they get the green light from Tehran to attempt the destruction of our peaceful GCC societies."

Then on 25 September, last year, my op-ed "Iran's agenda consolidates while the Arabs are distracted" showcased the boast of Iranian lawmaker Alireza Zakani to the effect that three Arab capitals (Baghdad, Damascus and Beirut) were now in Iran's hands and affiliated to the Iranian Islamic Revolution, with Sana'a well on its way to becoming the fourth. "Yemen – a country considered the birthplace of the Arab nation – has fallen into the hands of Shi'ite Houthis, former separatists turned terrorists no longer content with striving for part of the cake, they now seek to consume all of it," I penned, adding, "Due to the hesitance of our government to stand alongside the Yemeni government against these terrorist Iranian puppets, we have enabled their aspirations."

The last paragraph of that column illustrates my increasing despondence. "I can only cling to the hope that now some of our countries have been galvanized to act against Daesh and our armies and air forces will extend their operations to take back Syria, Iraq, Lebanon and Yemen before the Sunni Arab World is reduced to a shadow in a darkening Persian night."

My last-ditch attempt to convince major world powers to take decisive action was my column dated 29 December 2014 published under the headline "Global leadership lacking in 2014". Among those I called to account was President Obama, who failed to thwart Yemen becoming an Iranian hub following the storming of the capital by Houthi rebels "just as he earlier failed to rescue the Syrian people from the missiles, the chemical attacks and the prisons of one of the most brutal dictators the world has ever known".

The damage may already be done, but even so, we must not throw up our hands in despair allowing things to go from bad to worse or sit around drinking tea in the hope that a US cavalry will appear out of nowhere to save the day. America and its friends are engaged in their own missions, which may well contradict our interests. We have the intelligence, the forces, the weapons, the airpower and the maturity to cut the heads of the snakes in Yemen, Iraq and Syria – whether Assad's gangs or Daesh terrorists – ourselves. The only element lacking is a decision; a joint decision by all GCC member states to do whatever it takes before those same multi-striped serpents begin hissing in our direction.

A salute to our heroes liberating Yemen

26 March 2015

"And prepare against them whatever you are able of power and of steeds of war by which you may terrify the enemy of Allah and your enemy and others besides them whom you do not know [but] whom Allah knows."
Surah Al-Anfal [8:60]

ON THURSDAY, I AWOKE to news that brought peace of mind and filled my heart with pride, feelings I am certain are shared by my Emirati compatriots and nationals of Gulf Cooperation Council (GCC) states, and all dignified Arabs. Finally, we have taken command of own destiny and control of our own security. For many decades, I have been longing for this very moment. Just when Yemen was going the way of Lebanon, Syria and Iraq – all Arab countries under Iranian domination via proxies – the tide is turning in our favour as I write.

It goes without saying that conflict should always be a last option, but there can be no meaningful dialogue with the Islamic Republic of Iran, a nation with ambitions of reinstating the Persian Empire and quashing Arabs under its boot, just as it has stamped upon Sunnis and ethnic/religious minorities in Lebanon, Syria, Iraq as well as the long-suffering Ahwazi Arabs.

Perhaps Iran can succeed in pulling the wool over the eyes of the P5+1 whose representatives are negotiating over Tehran's uranium enrichment programme, but it cannot con its Gulf neighbours, who have fallen foul of Iran's tricks time and time again.

There should be no stopping until Yemen is cleansed of pro-Iranian traitors and the legitimate government is reinstated in the capital, Sana'a. There should be no concessions made to the Shi'ite Houthi militias; those Iranian operatives have forfeited the right to call themselves "Arab". They are betrayers deserving of the severest of punishments.

Fighters who choose to surrender do not merit trials; they should be shipped to their ideological motherland, Iran. Their actions – dissolving parliament, ejecting the democratically-elected president, taking over government buildings and terrorizing Yemenis from north to south – constitute the ultimate betrayal.

I have observed Iran's ideological and geopolitical expansion with great sorrow – and have long feared that without strong actions to thwart Iran's aims, Gulf states risk being targeted next. But now that Saudi Arabia has launched Operation Decisive Storm, together with its Gulf allies, in Yemen's defence at the request of the internationally-recognized government led by President Abdrabbuh Mansour Hadi, I feel that a positive new page has been turned. This is what we have been hoping for; this is what our people want.

Militias who paid obeisance to the ayatollahs and have made armed incursions into Saudi Arabia cannot be permitted control over Yemen's airplanes, missiles, tanks and other military equipment. And neither can they be trusted not to hold siege to the Bab El Mandeb Strait that not only connects the Red Sea with the Indian Ocean but is also a link to the Suez Canal.

Kudos to those GCC leaders who were courageous enough to take the right decisions! History will record this brave stance you have taken to defend Yemen's sovereignty and our region's security. Today we have leaders willing to lead rather than follow diktats from big powers. Your names will be engraved on monuments and will remain in the hearts of our children and grandchildren. Bravo! May God help you always to do what is best for our Arab nation!

"Decisive Storm" is the perfect name for this defensive military intervention taken by the descendants of some of the greatest Arab leaders beginning with the Prophet Mohammed (PBUH), whose victorious mantel was adopted by the second Muslim Caliph Omar ibn Al Khattab, commander of the Muslim armies who defeated Khosrau, King of Persia and Heraclius, the Byzantine Emperor.

We are showing Iran and the world that we will no longer bury our heads in the sand while keeping up the pretence that all is well. We are displaying our strength with a massive show of military might thanks also to staunch backing from our allies – Egypt, Sudan, Jordan, Morocco and Pakistan, who have all pledged to contribute to this righteous battle. Thank you to all our friends who did not hesitate to stand with their Yemeni brothers in their hour of need.

It is my hope that the League of Arab States Summit to be held in Sharm El Sheikh on 28–29 March will be just as decisive in its backing of a Joint Arab Force able to tackle any emergency in our part of the world. We can no longer rely on our Western allies to do the job for us, especially when their foreign policies are muddled and incoherent. The US is courting Iran in Switzerland and sharing intelligence with the Iranian military supposedly "advising" the Iraqi Army in its campaign against Daesh, even as it supports the Syrian opposition battling Iranian Revolutionary Guards and Hezbollah defending the criminal Assad regime.

I must admit that I have been irritated watching Western and Arab analysts discuss Yemen on various television networks. Invariably, presenters all ask the same question: was Decisive Storm launched with approval from the Obama administration? What kind of question is that?

We do not require a green light from anyone to defend our land, the safety of our peoples or our collective dignity. As a nation of 367 million, acknowledged as the birthplace of civilization, we resent being treated like underage children. We neither need nor should seek permission from anyone.

It is my fervent hope that once Yemen is delivered from the Houthi epidemic, this Saudi-led coalition made-up of 10 like-minded countries will be preserved and will turn its attention to freeing Iraq from Persian occupation. Iraq must be ruled by loyal Arabs, whether Sunni or Shi'ite, not those on bended knee to a foreign state working against Arab interests.

And, God willing, the day will come when our beloved Lebanon and Syria will no more be enslaved to Iran's bullying proxies, provided our leaders keep up this historic patriotic impetus. If we do not free our Arab territories from the silent diseases tearing them apart, the peoples of the Gulf and those of our allies will remain in constant danger.

Lastly, I must congratulate our GCC leaders. You have made us proud. Your firm action permits us to hold our heads high; I pray that you will continue to defend our nation, our independence and our dignity. And to our armed forces, especially our pilots that risk their lives during every mission, I wish you every success. Keep safe and may God strengthen you in your task of protecting our Arab soil, our Yemeni brothers and sisters and our honour!

No compromise with Houthi criminals

10 June 2015

THE DAY I LEARNED that Saudi Arabia took the initiative to rescue the people of Yemen from a belligerent pro-Iranian minority in partnership with Gulf Cooperation Council (GCC) countries, I experienced a great sense of relief. At last, Gulf states and their allies proved they were capable of solidarity, independence and commitment to rid Yemen of this malevolent Iranian proxy threatening not only Yemen but also the Kingdom and beyond.

Opertaion Decisive Storm was a source of pride for all nationals of GCC countries and their friends in the Arab World, considered as a first step in ridding our Arab lands of Iranian influence.

Sadly, however, the operation was not as decisive as its title promised. Rather than a short, sharp campaign, using our combined air and naval power to back up ground forces, it has mirrored the half-measures that have marked the ineffective efforts of the US-led coalition in Iraq. Airstrikes are just one tool in our extensive armoury, yet for some reason – probably due to unrelenting international pressure – it is the only one that been utilized.

But my disappointment with the campaign has been greatly compounded by the news that the United Nations (UN) has launched an initiative "to restore momentum towards a Yemeni-led political transition process" to bring together the legitimate government and all other parties, including the Houthi devils responsible for igniting the bloodshed.

When the Houthis have broken all previous agreements made with the government and rejected the terms of a UN resolution adopted last month as unjustly supporting "murderers and vampires", they cannot be trusted to keep their word, and moreover they deserve punishment not appeasement.

This wrong-footed peace initiative is scheduled to be discussed at a conference later this month, due to be attended by government officials, and rival Yemeni parties as well as representatives of the Houthis and that traitor former President Ali Abdullah Saleh.

At the time of writing, the legitimate president in exile, President President Abdrabbuh Mansour Hadi, insists he has no intention of negotiating with Iranian-backed rebels "more dangerous than Al Qaeda". He maintains that the only reason for government participation is to discuss the implementation of UN Security Council Resolution 2216, which demands that the Houthis withdraw from seized territory. Frankly I will believe it when I see it.

UN Secretary General Ban Ki-moon has made it clear that talks must be held without preconditions, a stipulation the Houthis have agreed to abide with. Why wouldn't they, when they have never stuck to any of their pledges! Does anyone seriously imagine that they will merely shrug their shoulders and bury their ambitions to rule the country on Tehran's behalf? Is it even within the realm of possibility, let alone probability, that they will simply throw their weapons into the sea and become models of respectability?

No, of course not! They are cleverly playing along with the UN game and the international community's unrealistic peacemaking goals. They will say anything expected of them to get the bombing to stop; then they will bide their time for a while before repeating their land-grab when I fear that Saudi Arabia will hesitate to get involved on the grounds "once bitten, twice shy".

Ban Ki-moon must be terminally naive if he seriously thinks other-wise; he is not a politician, he is not a political strategist and he does not represent the interests of leaderships within our region; rather one could be forgiven for believing that he is more interested in representing Iran's bands of terrorists.

President Hadi is being ambushed; he will find himself in a very lonely corner and may be pressurized to go with the flow aimed at resurrecting the Houthis as a respectable partner in the political arena. That would be a grave mistake on his part and to keep him resolutely fixed on his position of no compromise, Saudi Arabia and Gulf states must strongly reinforce his stance.

Firstly, GCC leaders should reject outright any participation in the Geneva talks or acceptance of any outcome that leaves both Yemen and surrounding Gulf countries vulnerable to Houthi aggression.

Secondly, they must not agree to any communiqué that empowers or legitimizes Houthis or allows them any participation in the political process going forward.

Thirdly, they must state in advance that they will not consider any agreement signed in Geneva as binding and they will continue with Decisive Storm as long as it takes to ensure the safety of the Yemeni people and the security of our own borders.

If GCC states cave in, they will be perceived as weak and their military intervention will be seen as a failure. The whole world will note that we threw our hands up, waving a white flag, handing victory over to our enemies – and, more crucially, to Iran. We will look like weaklings and losers still taking orders from Western powers, which have kept us under their thumb for as long as I can remember.

The US and its European allies want to keep us controlled and feeble, our sophisticated airplanes and missiles just for show to be paraded during national holidays. They have long had a plan to carve up the Middle East into easily manageable slices, and given the Obama administration's rapprochement with America's sworn enemy, Iran, we must be alert for any whiff of bargains or plots.

Our leaders or their representatives attended Barack Obama's calculated charm offensive in Camp David, orchestrated to woo them into accepting the Iran nuclear deal, which I believe was a mistake. And I can only urge them not to be conned into giving up their right to self-defence again.

If they go along with this UN attempt to appease Iran and its band of Houthis, they might as well invite "Caliph Baghdadi", Hassan Nasrallah, Naim Qassem and the head of the Badr Brigades along for the ride. Let us all have a jolly party with those people who all share the same aim – to weaken the Arab nation so as to empower Iran and its Persian agenda!

Giving up the fight; giving in to groups whose mission in life is to harm us would result in disaster and if that is the road we are going to take, we will find a dead end – in more ways than one – without any return.

I can only urge GCC leaders to reconsider and take note of the messages underlying many of my columns, warning of the dangers of leaving the Houthis unpunished and unrestrained in Yemen as a stepping stone to Iranian regional domination.

We must say a loud "No" to the Geneva talks and give President Hadi every support, whether morally, militarily or financially. And finally, we must send the message to Mr Ban and the White House that going behind our backs to cook up schemes running contrary to our interests, is not only grossly insulting but dangerous.

Farewell to our heroes

6 September 2015

OUR COUNTRY IS in mourning. Last Friday was one of the blackest days in the United Arab Emirates' (UAE) history, since its foundation in 1971. That was the day 45 of our finest were lost to us while unselfishly defending their Yemeni brothers and sisters from pro-Iranian Houthi killers.

The news that a missile had hit a weapons depot close to their camp shocked all Emiratis; everyone I know felt a sense of deep hurt. All I could do was sit for a while in silence feeling helpless. The unthinkable had finally happened and for all of us this war began to feel close up and very personal.

We are a population tied together by tribal roots and family connections. Every single Emirati life is more precious than all the pearls our forefathers once harvested from the seabed, and our tears more numerous. Their sacrifice, the greatest of all, must never be forgotten. A monument should be erected, inscribed with every name to keep their memory alive always.

My heart goes out to the families who have lost fathers, brothers and sons. And I pray for the swift recovery of our wounded young men in intensive care fighting for their lives. The bodies of those who died have come home now; they were treated with the utmost reverence. Their souls are with God. No one can ever harm them again. My condolences also go to the parents of the five Bahraini and 10 Saudi soldiers whose lives were so cruelly cut short; they are our sons too.

It fills me with pride to know that so many of my compatriots have rushed to hospitals all over the country in answer to calls for donations of blood. Our shared grief has welded us together as never before. Everything humanly possible must be done to care for the survivors, as I know it will because we Emiratis not only take care of our own but also of others, regardless of their nationality or religious beliefs.

We are very proud of the martyrs, they are defenders of the oppressed. We pray that they reach Paradise, their sacrifices a source of pride. Tributes are pouring in from our friends all over the region and the world to tell us that we are not alone.

I am proud of our great country, our rulers and my fellow citizens. The UAE never shirks its duty and has proved its courage time and time again.

We stood shoulder-to-shoulder with the Kuwaiti people during the 1991 Gulf War, welcoming them as brethren through the conflict. Lest we forget, our army was at the forefront of the fight to free Kuwait from Iraqi occupation.

Our pilots have taken to the skies to bomb Daesh in northern Iraq, and the Emirates did not hesitate in joining the Saudi-led coalition against

Houthi rebels to protect Yemen's sovereignty and ensure the return of the legitimate democratically elected government.

Our country is committed to this region's security and our hand is always open to help our friends and neighbours with financial support or assistance with preserving their freedom.

Our resolve to fight on the side of right will never falter and, if anything, our efforts to defeat Iran's proxy ragtag army in Yemen, our Arab heartland, are redoubled. We will never permit Iranian plots to be victorious when the future of our children and grandchildren are at stake. Whereas we extend our arms to embrace the future and provide the best life possible for our people, sadly the area around us has become a magnet for losers seeking nothing but death and destruction.

Yes, we are grieving. Our hearts are heavy remembering our faithful young heroes who did not flinch from putting their lives in danger. But their deaths will not be allowed to be lost for nothing. Our sadness will be replaced by anger and with it a determination to prevail over the Iranian-paid and armed thugs threatening to take Yemen into the dark ages and aggressing Saudi Arabia.

My message to you is that you will not get away with robbing Yemenis of their dignity or depriving the UAE of its beloved children. You *will* receive our answer. Do not doubt it! We Emiratis will never forget or forgive your crimes.

The funerals have taken place. Our fallen have been laid to rest; their coffins draped in the UAE flag. However, I and my fellow patriots will never rest until our country's sacred mission in Yemen is completed.

And it is my fervent hope that the Emirates will also contribute to the liberation of Syria, Iraq and Lebanon so our region can be returned to its pure Arab roots, unpolluted by the dishonourable bought-and-paid-for hordes that desecrate our faith and traditions.

Rest in peace our fallen heroes! Heaven was waiting for righteous warriors like you.

Transformational times for Saudi Arabia and Gulf states

28 April 2016

POSITIVE CHANGE IS taking place in my part of the world and for that I am grateful to the leaderships of all Gulf Cooperation Council (GCC) member countries, and especially to the governments of Saudi Arabia and the United Arab Emirates (UAE), for their decisive and foresighted geopolitical and economic policies. A new era of unity, self-reliance and self-defence is fast unfolding.

I have been alerting the leadership of Gulf states to impending threats, both internal and external, for many years. I warned about the possibility of a "Grand Bargain" between the United States and Iran designed to weaken predominately Sunni countries at a time when the idea was thought to be outside the realm of possibility.

I have long urged Gulf heads of state to adopt a more independent stance towards regional affairs, which involves being less reliant upon the "advice" of foreign powers that ultimately serves their own interests. I have outlined in detail my concerns over a shift in the regional balance of power while stressing that in a tumultuous neighbourhood plagued by conflicts, sectarianism and terrorism, there is an urgent need to shore up our defences and do all that we can to preserve our economic standing amid falling oil prices.

I did so because I care deeply about the security and stability of my own homeland, the UAE, as well as the safety of all our brotherly neighbours with whom we share tribal bloodlines, religion and culture. I have always longed for the day that we would be united, strong and well positioned to independently react to dangers moving in our direction.

We have been too comfortable for too long. But that was then and this is now. Saudi Arabia and its allies around the Gulf are taking a more assertive role in various fields. The message is loud and clear: "Anyone who believes we can be pushed around is in for a shock." President Barack Obama wrongly accused us of being "free riders" along with other uncomplimentary accusations. He did us a favour. His opinions related by Jeffrey Goldberg in *The Atlantic*, partnered with the resolve of various presidential candidates to bar Muslims as well as Congressional efforts to pass a law allowing individuals to sue Saudi Arabia for its fictitious role in the 11 September 2001 attacks, have rung alarm bells.

I have always been a proud Emirati and citizen of the Gulf but rarely as proud as I am today. Saudi Arabia asked no permission from foreign capitals to aid Bahrain in its efforts to quell an Iranian-backed insurgency. And neither did the Kingdom or its partner the UAE seek approval from Western leaders before they launched a military intervention to free Yemen from an unlawful takeover by Iranian proxies and to defend Saudi borders from enemy infiltration. We proved our ability to defend our lands, our people and our brothers.

Our men and women, who did not hesitate to respond to the call, showed exemplary bravery and commitment to the task of rescuing the Yemeni people and it is a certainty they will do the same if the day comes when they need to defend our homes and territories. I salute these fine young people and congratulate our leaders for decisively rising to the occasion. Thanks to them we can hold our heads up higher than ever and know deep in our hearts they will keep our families safe from predator foes.

When the chips are down, GCC states always stand shoulder to shoulder. I was gratified to learn that almost all predominately Sunni countries are with us as evidenced by their willingness to join a Saudi-conceived Islamic Military Counter Terrorism Coalition and to know that the formation of a Joint Arab Force is proceeding as planned.

In the short time since King Salman bin Abdulaziz became the Kingdom's reigning monarch, he has displayed rare leadership skills and is fearless in his pursuit of a powerful Arab World no matter how many toes he has to tread on to achieve his aim. He has proven his ability to coalesce Sunni states into a mighty defence bloc and is putting his progressive ideas concerning the Kingdom's economic trajectory into effect with his unveiling of a 15-year economic blueprint titled "Saudi Vision 2030".

"Saudi Vision 2030" includes three core themes – a vibrant society, a thriving economy and an ambitious nation – and is premised upon reducing the country's reliance on oil revenues through the expansion of its investment portfolio and the capitalization of opportunities in hitherto untapped sectors, such as tourism, industry, mining, trade, commerce and business.

During a rare interview on Al Arabiya aired on 25 April, Saudi Arabia's Deputy Crown Prince and Minister of Defence Prince Mohammed bin Salman revealed his nation's core aim. "We seek to develop our economy and create an attractive and perfect environment in our homeland," he said. To this end there will be job creation, improved health care and the provision of recreational and cultural opportunities.

People sometimes assume that GCC governments are captive to a fluctuating oil market. Saudi Arabia has put pay to that false assumption. Those oil producing countries that have flooded the market, driving prices to new lows, while piling pressure on Riyadh to cut production in the hope of bringing Saudi to heel, will be disappointed with this announcement.

This brilliantly-conceived plan will prove Saudi Arabia's capability of competing on a global level. No one should underestimate the Kingdom's economic know-how or determination to succeed and anyone who was rubbing his hands together in glee predicting the country's economic collapse should beware because it will not be long before Saudi Arabia and its Gulf allies are economic world leaders.

We Gulf Arabs are not empty boasters. Our actions speak louder than words and it is indisputable that we are now on the right economic, security and geopolitical paths. The Saudi Sovereign Wealth Fund is set to be the biggest in the world worth $1.9tn by 2030. At the same time, we are also leaders in philanthropy. The UAE was one of the largest donors in the world in 2014 and 2016, and the Kingdom has historically come to the rescue of its Arab allies in need and has shown unstinting generosity towards countries facing economic woes.

Our eyes are fixated on the target. We will show the international community that we are not dependent on anyone or anything, and prove that we can be successful, surpassing all expectations. Watch out world! We are very close.

Tough response needed to counter UN slander

5 June 2016

I HAVE LOST ALL RESPECT for the United Nations (UN). It has evolved into a largely impotent entity dominated by a handful of veto-holding nuclear powers, which wield undue influence over its decision-making. Not only has its lofty status been undermined with accusations of corruption, UN peacekeepers are alleged to have sexually exploited vulnerable women and children in Haiti and the Central African Republic.

Most significantly, it has been proven not to be fit for the purpose for which it was founded: "To maintain international peace and security" and, if necessary by "taking preventive or enforcement action". A glaring example of the organization's failure to live up to its responsibilities was the genocide that took place in Rwanda.

A report written in 1994 and released in 1999 accused senior UN officials of ignoring evidence that a slaughter of mega proportions was under way and of failing to protect the Rwandan people. Kofi Annan issued an apology. Its record since has been no better.

It was just as useless in Srebrenica as the mass graves of Muslim men attest and it has done practically nothing to end the bloodshed in Syria where over 150,000 have been killed and millions have been displaced. Conflicts blaze and all the UN does is hold high-profile meetings that more often than not achieve nothing other than give delegates the excuse to rub shoulders at cocktail parties.

It is one thing for the UN's New York headquarters to exist as an expensive and fairly useless white elephant, but quite another for its Secretary General to hurl unsubstantiated accusations at Saudi Arabia and nine of its Arab coalition partners invited by the internationally-recognized Yemeni president to help free his country from Houthi rebels funded and armed by Iran.

Saudi Arabia and its prime partner the United Arab Emirates (UAE) have sacrificed blood and treasure to this legitimate cause that has been supported by the America and Britain. Almost 1,000 coalition officers and soldiers have been killed and hundreds have been wounded. And now that the conflict is winding down, UN Secretary General Ban Ki-moon chooses to slap Yemen's rescuers in the face with the announcement that the Saudi coalition is to be equated with terrorists, militias and Houthi devils in the pay of expansionist Tehran.

For the first time ever, an international coalition, in this case the Saudi-led Arab coalition, has been included in the UN's annual blacklist, designed to shame factions that have engaged "in the recruitment and use of children, sexual violence against children, the killing and maiming of children, attacks on schools and/or hospitals and attacks or threats against protected personnel and the abduction of children".

Ban Ki-moon has arbitrarily attributed 60 per cent of almost 2,000 child casualties of the conflict to the Kingdom's air campaign while accusing the coalition of striking a hospital run by Doctors without Borders, which Saudi Arabia has vehemently denied. Here it is worth noting that while the US has admitted bombing a hospital in Afghanistan, also managed by Doctors without Borders, the report disingenuously blames that tragedy on "international forces", which are not being blacklisted.

Worse, the Israeli government is persistently let off the hook when over 1,000 Palestinian children have been victims of Israel's aggression on Gaza alone. Rights groups have condemned Israel for using Palestinian children as human shields and Defence for Children International – Palestine (DCIP) maintains 440 are currently illegally held in military detention, three-quarters of whom claim they have been physically abused. It seems the plight of the sons of Palestine are not worthy of Mr Ban's concern or alternatively he is too scared of his masters to open his mouth.

To be frank, I was shocked and angered to read this dreadful news. I am still struggling against disbelief that the powers that be within the UN could stoop so low as to infer that 10 Arab countries would deliberately target Yemeni children! Our Arab children we love and wish to protect just like the young ones we cherish at home.

While admittedly airstrikes are not always 100 per cent precise, in any theatre of war there are civilian casualties and all of us wish that were not so. Wars are sometimes necessary, but always ugly. Just ask Iraqis who lost up to a million of their compatriots as a result of the 2003 US-led intervention to deprive Saddam Hussein of mythical weapons of destruction or Afghans and Pakistanis who have lost hundreds of their innocent brethren to US drone attacks.

This damning UN report reeks of bias, double standards, insult and unsubstantiated claims. What is the game here? What is the agenda? What is the reason behind this unjust offensive classification? I have dismissed various claims that the UN acts as the political tool of certain nations. But now I am persuaded there might be something in those assertions, especially in light of the fact that there is a bill going through US Congress, supported by all presidential candidates, that would embroil Saudi Arabia in court cases related to the 11 September attacks, even though the 9/11 Commission report completely exonerates the Kingdom from playing any part in the 2001 terrorist attacks.

Whatever the truth may be, I would strongly urge the coalition's member states, the League of Arab States and the Gulf Cooperation Council (GCC) to issue firm statements in response to the UN's slurs. What is needed is for the Kingdom and its allies to take a firm stand. We need to be strong and unyielding. Diplomacy is a two-way street and since there is nothing diplomatic about the coalition's shameful inclusion in this disgusting list, we are not bound by diplomatic protocol to pull punches.

It needs to be made clear to Ban Ki-moon that either the coalition is immediately removed from this blacklist of rogues or we will cancel our memberships of this suspect body that is supposed to be a unifying force, not one that alienates and divides. Either that or we must insist upon his resignation forthwith.

He will not be missed. His grasp of crucial issues is negligible and when he speaks he is barely coherent. And for that matter what has he ever done to save the children of the Middle East or anywhere else apart from throwing food parcels in their direction and erecting tents?

I never imagined I would agree with anything from the lips of former US Ambassador to the UN John Bolton, who was instrumental in pushing for the invasion of Iraq, but his suggestion that the UN secretariat could do just as well without its top ten floors rings true. The UN needs to shape up and behave in a responsible fashion or the Arab nation should ship out.

7

Lebanon: the burdens of a tolerant society

Introduction

L EBANON HAS LONG been close to my heart. I have visited the country many times, over the past 40 years. In the early 1970s my frequent visits to a place where people were friendly and always welcoming were always special. It breaks my heart to say that today I would not set foot in the country, despite having hundreds of millions of dollars' worth of investments there.

Lebanon has to take a lot of the blame for its demise. However, Iran has played a pivotal role in the deconstruction of the country – once considered the Switzerland of the Middle East. Those days are unfortunately long gone, and there is little chance of them ever returning.

Iran's support of its Lebanese proxy Hezbollah has destroyed the country beyond repair, and turned it into a regional hub for terrorism. Lebanon will never be able to be freed from the clutches of Tehran. Iran is a regional hegemony and continues to strengthen its position in the region. My fear is that due to inaction of world leaders – both Western and Arab – other parts of the Middle East will follow, and succumb to Iran's ever-increasing influence.

Let us not forget that the Shi'ite group was created, nurtured and remains funded by Iran under the cover of Lebanese resistance against Israel's occupation of South Lebanon. And no matter what anyone says, Hezbollah is a terrorist organization, whether it be the military or political wing. How it can get away with acting under the guise of its so-called status as a legitimate political party I cannot comprehend.

Never mind how both Iran and the military wing of Hezbollah managed to worm their way off the global terror list in February 2015! The US cited Iran's efforts to fight Sunni extremists, including Daesh, in the unclassified version of the Worldwide Threat Assessment of the US Intelligence Community. The report praised Tehran's push to keep "ISIL from gaining large swaths of additional territory" in Iraq. Fortunately though, the US Department of State was not stupid enough to remove Iran from its list of State Sponsors of Terrorism and Hezbollah remains on its official terror list as a Foreign Terrorist Organization.

Nonetheless, you cannot separate the military wing of Hezbollah from the political wing. They are one and the same in my view. The group may label itself as a "resistance movement", but the fact of the matter is, it is a terrorist organization.

Hezbollah has also been recognized by the US for fighting Daesh militants in Iraq and Syria, even though they are not part of the US-led coalition that used airstrikes to counter Daesh. Both Iran and Hezbollah were in the 2014 version of the threat assessment report, which said then that both "continue to directly threaten the interests of US allies. Hezbollah has increased its global terrorist activity in recent years to a level that we have not seen since the 1990s."

So what changed in a matter of 12 months? What deal was made? And does one perceived good wipe out the atrocities of the past and give them a clean slate?

As if things are not bad enough, Lebanon is in the grip of a protracted political crisis. The presidency has remained vacant since May 2014 to date, and there is a lack of unity between the two main blocs, both being stubborn and digging their heels firmly in the ground, which is of major detriment to the country, hindering the passage of key legislation. The political bloc led by former Prime Minister Rafic Hariri's son, Saad, stands in opposition against the Iranian-backed Hezbollah block. The numerous self-proclaimed political leaders in Lebanon are hindering its progress.

The country is lacking a strong leader, and this has been the case for a number of years. What other country in the world takes months – or even years – to elect a president? The deadlock has paralysed the government. Political stalemate and childish bickering is not only costing the country vast amounts of money, but preventing it from flourishing again, not to mention the country's crumbling infrastructure that needs urgent attention.

The cabinet is so divided that it has barely met since President Michel Suleiman's mandate expired. It is time to elect a successor, someone who can stand on their own two feet and get on with the job.

To make matters worse, while struggling to rebuild its own nation 15 years after the civil war, Lebanon is bearing the brunt of the fallout from the ongoing war in neighbouring Syria. It is multi-pronged: the Lebanese army is doing little to protect its borders from insurgent Islamic groups like the extremist Daesh and Al Qaeda, while the country is under intense pressure from the influx of refugees spilling over the border.

The International Monetary Fund (IMF) has warned that the five-year-long crisis in Syria is taking its toll on Lebanon and threatening its outlook.

It states that refugees account for one quarter of the country's population, adding to poverty and unemployment and putting a further strain on the Lebanese economy with its already weak public finances. The unprecedented humanitarian crisis from the ongoing conflict in Syria is placing a huge burden on the country's infrastructure and its social fabric.

The IMF said: "The Syrian crisis and associated inflow of refugees continue to dominate Lebanon's short-term outlook, compounding long-standing policy weakness and vulnerabilities. Political paralysis has set in, with virtually no progress on the structural front." The crisis has also affected what the IMF calls Lebanon's "growth drivers", namely its tourism, real estate and construction industries, which in turn influence the way banks operate within the country.

Fortunately, for now, its strong banking sector is its saving grace, courtesy of technological and regulatory changes. The sector has proved its resilience to domestic and external shocks.

Further complicating matters is the fact that Lebanon is the most religiously diverse society in the Middle East. There are 18 officially recognized religious sects, many of whom still bear the scars of the 16-year-long civil war, when they were pitted against one other.

The country's "exceptional hospitality" as the United Nations High Commissioner for Refugees (UNHCR) puts it, is already stretched. Lebanon, with a population of four million people, has taken in well over one million Syrian refugees on top of the nearly half-a-million Palestinian refugees already living in tented settlements.

I can say one thing of the Lebanese people. They are resilient. They have bounced back so many times from one crisis after another – whether it is from civil war, invasion, conflict, terrorism or having to deal with the influx of refugees from nearby countries. They deserve better.

Open letter to the people of Lebanon

1 May 2005

I WOULD LIKE TO BEGIN by stressing the fact that my love and affection for this small country stands behind this letter. I am taking the liberty of sending out this public plea based on my known relationship with Lebanon and its people, a relationship founded over the years on warmth and a true partnership. My relationship with this nation is one of respect and an act of faith in the Lebanese people whose belief in their homeland is absolute.

For some of you, my Lebanese brothers and sisters, love of your country drove you to generosity in its service and sacrifice in its defence, sacrifice that is forever inscribed on the country's plains and its majestic mountains. From your beautiful shores, civilization spread to all corners of the world and the alphabet that you invented was the catalyst that illuminated the darkness that prevailed on all continents.

You represented, for Arabs everywhere, a free press, respected academics and excellent universities. You were the lungs through which many Arabs breathed the air of freedom and the printing press that recorded their history. Dear people, you have achieved a lot, which would take many pages for me to list.

Today, I am asking with apprehension: what are you doing? I have never doubted your love for your country and have never feared for the democratic way for which the Lebanese people have proven their commitment. Democracy was, and shall remain, one of the cornerstones of Lebanese society. I have also never doubted, even in the difficult years of war, Lebanese society's high concern for the national security of Lebanon.

The Lebanese have always shown great affection for their Arab brothers who share the same language, destiny and geography. I am confident that the people of Lebanon can do without any tutelage in the governance of their country.

However, my care and my love for this precious corner of the Arab World made me write this open letter from the heart, a letter that I address to the consciousness of the people of Lebanon. Many of you are aware of my deep attachment to your country, which I hold in the same esteem as my own country, the United Arab Emirates (UAE).

I hesitated for a long time before starting this letter because I strongly believed that by the time it reached you, the succession of events in Lebanon would have made it redundant, because the people of Lebanon know how to overcome their adversities, tolerate their pain and then to make the crossing from despair to hope and optimism.

I wanted to reveal to some of my Lebanese friends my fears and apprehensions regarding developments in their country. This fear is not for the unity of the Lebanese, nor for Lebanon, because I trust that the bond that holds the Lebanese together is much stronger than the forces that are trying to tear them apart. This bond is as strong as the one that holds the mountains of Lebanon firmly attached to its plains. God willing, the unity of the people and their country shall remain firm. It is my belief that the recent events in Lebanon are but a manifestation of the democratic process that crowns the political environment there; and that despite the apparent chaotic and troubled nature of the process, it is governed by the unity of the people under a common ceiling that is the unity of the country. That process is clear and probably irreversible unless these differences fester and make way for certain forms of foreign intervention that aim to destabilize the unity of the people and their economic and social potential.

Allow me to add that the high-pitched arguments and slogans, in addition to the agitation in your media, shall reflect negatively on the productivity and recovery of the country, when what is needed is cooperation with your Arab environment to increase employment opportunities and improve the performance of the economy.

Economic stagnation will increase corruption, unemployment, crime and even terrorism, which has relegated whole societies to pariah status on the international scene. I do not think that any sane person would knowingly and wilfully aim to cause such a catastrophe to his country and relegate it to the lowest rung in the hierarchy of nations.

Now is the moment of honesty when I have to say what I hesitated so much about out of my love for Lebanon. I have to say it now, in the middle of this storm of declarations and counter-declarations, demonstrations and counter-demonstrations, gatherings and counter-gatherings.

My fear is justified by this political crisis that demonstrates everything except your hidden love for your country, as if you are ashamed to declare it amidst the smoke and dust roused by the impact of these political events.

Who would, for the sake of political profit or a vote here or there or even for the sake of a position of power, sacrifice the economic and social fundamentals of his country? I am sure that there is no person or party in Lebanon that wishes that to happen. But watching the events from a distance points to an increasing possibility that some major calamity is about to happen to that dear country. That might not be the right conclusion but it is one that is justified by the ongoing agitation in the media.

It would be naive to expect that society in Lebanon would metamorphose one day into a homogenous entity with one political, social and cultural vision. That would also be an oversimplification of the issue. I just want to call my Lebanese brothers and sisters, the generous and good people that I have known, to put the good of their country above every other consideration. I call on them to become a mature political entity similar to the people of the Western world, in particular people in France, the US and Britain. In those countries, political campaigns are sometimes nasty and very hostile, but in the end all differences are set aside and the people unite behind their country when threatened by a foreign danger or when the national security of their respective countries is jeopardized

Have mercy on Lebanon

1 June 2005

A NEUTRAL MONITORING of political and parliamentary activities over the world proves that such activities would be bustling with life except for differences in outlook, opinions and analyses among the many trends that forms the nerve centre of the political scene in any nation. Such differences must be created if they do not exist, so as to reform performance. Furthermore, governmental change is a very important matter in rectifying the efforts of the civic, political and economical lives of all countries.

All countries realize this fact, and submit to its natural rules that focus on political pluralism, contradicting ideological currents. Every civic, political or ideological community throughout history abounds with diversified currents that sometimes contradict one another. However, differences in opinions in the civilized democratic world have never before led to serious structural and economic cracks as is the case presently in Lebanon. Let us take the UK for example – a country that is the mother of democracy; it experienced discord among its parties and political entities. But these differences were always solved via the institutions, and the final judgment came from the Parliament, which is binding. There is nothing in UK history that shows any reference to such discord that may be obvious to the man on the street, although the public, with their inflammatory nature, could be easily fooled.

Should we not learn a lesson from that?

Several years ago, Britain's capital, London, suffered from the bombings and subversive acts of the IRA (Irish Republican Army). Did those terrorist operations affect life in general in the UK? The answer is a definite "yes". The British press took a united stand despite their differences, and – without coordinating amongst themselves – carried front page headlines that continuously promoted security and stability, and stressed the importance of continued production and work. This helped the national economy to continue to grow despite those bad days. The media did not resort to scarring residents, whether British or expatriates, nor did they try to frighten the tourists and investors.

I have no intention of hinting, or making you guess what I am talking about. I am talking directly about the Lebanese media that was for a long period the eyes, the press and the TV of the Arabs. I want to say to the Lebanese media, which I respect and have a good relationship with: "Stop the incitement, focus on the cultural face of Lebanon far from the flames of politics." Months ago, out of fear for Lebanon, I made an appeal stating that the continuation of this state of factionalism would lead to something that is similar to a revolution of the hungry, as a result of the increase in unemployment. Would such a state not lead to an impasse? Now the gap between the leaders and the people is widening, and the wound is becoming deeper and could become even wider, or God forbid, incurable in the near future. Many employees have lost their jobs in the past six weeks, and more are expected to join them, which means that a lot of Lebanese families will enter the world of poverty and instability.

Who is responsible for this? Let any entity in Lebanon take the trouble to investigate the losses inflicted on the Lebanese economy in the recent past.

Do they know that Lebanon's losses stand at billions, and that those losses are expected to increase even further due to the paralysis of the companies?

Do they know how many investors were planning to invest or expand their investments in Lebanon, and cancelled their plans?

Who is the loser? Definitely there is a big loser, and there is no winner.

The loser is the Lebanese citizen, the Lebanese economy and treasury. And who is responsible, is not it the Lebanese political class?

When I talk about this, I am not neutral but biased towards Lebanon, in favour of its development, growth, security and economic stability. Hunger makes a good background for terrorism, and it is the gate to chaos, it is the right environment for the absence of law... so please, have mercy on Lebanon.

A big part of the Lebanese community is absent or forced to be absent. And I do not know why it does not play a stronger role. They are responsible before history and before the people.

Responsibility is not limited to the officials, for it is a patriotic act that should be carried out spontaneously by:

- The intellectuals.
- The businessmen.
- The economists.

They are the ones who should take the initiative to stand by their companies, so as to stop this continuous breakdown.

It is no secret that nobody will help Lebanon, if it does not help itself.

Are the Lebanese aware that the world is split in the way they see the Lebanese events? Some gloat, some just watch and some rejoice; but few are sad or even frightened and want to help Lebanon.

This is a painful situation, but it is true, and it can be changed only by the Lebanese. Nobody in the world would give a country what its own people refuse to give.

One final time I say: "Have mercy on Lebanon."

I do not regret writing this message and I do not consider it an intervention in your affairs, because I am not neutral towards what happens in your country.

I am with you. When you bleed, I bleed too. The end of the tunnel is within reach and clear, but it needs a brave decision that is unselfish.

I am sure that Lebanon abounds with high-quality leaders and people; but when will they rule?

Lebanon must unify against foreign influence

1 January 2007

WITNESSING THE PREVAILING political paralysis of Lebanon is a painful experience for someone like me who has a heartfelt love of the country and its cultured, entrepreneurial people. However, I cannot imagine how devastating it must be for the Lebanese, who for decades have suffered on a rollercoaster of serial crises, conflicts and sectarian rifts that have split communities and sometimes even families.

The crucial questions are these: why is Lebanon seemingly in a permanent state of turmoil and what can be done to address the situation?

There are several factors at the problem's root, not least the archaic and divisive constitution inherited from the French, which demands a Maronite president, a Sunni prime minister and a Shi'ite parliamentary speaker.

Such division of responsibilities based on a candidate's religious beliefs not only means the best person for the job is often excluded but also incites most Lebanese to identify themselves in terms of faith rather than as one people.

In my experience, Lebanese expatriates around the world do not view themselves in the same way as those in the country. Rather than Christian, Sunni or Shi'ite they are simply "Lebanese" who will tell you proudly that theirs is the most beautiful country on the planet and whose eyes often cloud over when listening to the patriotic strains of Fairouz.

In short, Lebanon urgently needs a new constitution to replace the badly thought-out, anachronistic document that has caused so much harm.

Moreover, such sectarian self-identification has opened the door to foreign powers, which over the years have ruthlessly used Lebanon as a surrogate battleground to take on their foes and have manipulated its politicians to further their own regional agendas. As long as foreigners are allowed to carelessly treat Lebanon as a playground and exploit divisions there will never be peace and prosperity.

When the Israelis quit Lebanon in 2000 followed by the Syrians in 2005, the country joyously celebrated. The Lebanese believed they were now masters of their own destiny, free to make their own decisions without outside interference.

Sadly, the euphoria was short-lived. It quickly became apparent that although Lebanon was free of a physical foreign presence it was still open to insidious and often malign foreign influences via a minority of its own politicians and militia leaders, who some maintain are robotically controlled from outside.

Such influences are apparent now that the tenure of President Emile Lahoud is constitutionally at an end, which requires the parliament to choose someone to replace him. The differences are so great that agreement on a suitable candidate was – and perhaps still is – in danger of ending in stalemate, triggering such scaremongering newspaper headlines as "A powder keg in Lebanon".

Indeed, some Western pundits are luridly warning that a new civil war could be in the offing, which could have repercussions throughout the region.

The stand off is between the 8 March opposition coalition, which is backing the leader of the Free Patriotic Movement, former General Michel Aoun, for president and the 14 March parliamentary bloc.

No surprises there. But what I find particularly disturbing is the way Lebanese politicians from all sides of the spectrum are actively seeking a green light from foreign powers and neighbours – including the US,

Russia, Iran and Syria – when it comes to selecting their next president. Is there any other sovereign country in the world that does this?

As long as Lebanon hangs onto a constitution that is based on sectarianism and encourages foreign influence, there will be a continued absence of cohesive national pride, which I believe is the main crux of the issue.

A tiny sliver of a country, covering only 10,452 sq km and with a population of less than four million, Lebanon must have a strong unified government with a powerful and fully-equipped army at its disposal if any kind of stability is to be achieved.

As long as there is government in-fighting, beset by divided loyalties, the country will remain at the mercy of foreign-funded militias, whose leaders often cite the inability of the army to protect the country as an excuse to retain their own weapons.

The international community, through such institutions as the United Nations or the League of Arab States, should help equip, fund and train the Lebanese military so that the nation has only one army that reports to a government of unity, which, in turn, must be answerable to its people ... all of its people.

"United we stand and divided we fall" should be Lebanon's motto. Sectarianism has no place in our modern world and with an economy in freefall, the sooner the Lebanese consign this antiquated concept to the dustbin of history and rally behind their one cedar flag the better.

A message to my loved ones in Lebanon

1 May 2007

IT WAS TIME to go back to Dubai after a week in London, for rest and some business.

Our jet had to stop at a Mediterranean airport to refuel.

There were five of us passengers: two United Arab Emirates (UAE) compatriots, two friends from Lebanon, and me. We discussed available options to stop and refuel. So, where would we land?

Well, it was Beirut that came to my mind first. That was not without reason. The famous city had always captured my imagination. It had played a remarkable role in shaping my conscience. My suitcases still breathe the city's pine scent. Images of its neighbourhoods have remained in my memory ever since like sweet dreams.

It was Beirut then and the question was open to discussion among my companions on the trip.

The date: 6 February 2007.

Beirut was undergoing heavy internal struggles. Confrontations between regional and international powers covered the city with smoke and black clouds. Different fronts filled the scene with demonstrations, counter-demonstrations, protests from both sides, and threatening political statements that were sufficient to start up an intra-state war, not only a civil war.

The place: a space for discussion between love and adoration, sorrow and pain, hope and despair, fear and awe.

We decided not to land in Beirut. And it no longer mattered where to land. The question became an insignificant detail.

Avoiding communicating our feelings through eye contact, our eyes were looking anywhere but at each other. No one wanted to betray his adoration of the city that had a suicidal harshness against itself. No other city had showed such self-destructing tendencies like Beirut.

So we could not land in Beirut, everyone agreed. But in the sky, my memory went back to the morning haze of Bhamdoon, the snow-crowned cedars of Marya, Tripoli, the history in Baalbak, the sea of civilizations of Sidon and the tobacco farms of the South.

Can a human being be afraid of his history and childhood memories? Can he or she be reluctant to recall the experiences of past years? Or can he or she sever from their past neighbours, friends and playmates?

Can a country be as harsh against its lovers as Lebanon is? Can a people be so unfair to their country like the Lebanese are?

What are you doing? I am asking you all without taking the side of any party, only your country.

What are you doing to this Oriental gem, this Mediterranean pearl, this Arab jewel?

What are you doing with the mermaid, the spring's breaths, water flows, the snow lanterns, your warm emotions, the spontaneous Lebanese generosity, your Arab traditions and hospitality and your eyes' joy?

What have you been doing? Once, you were our pride, our joy, you showed us elegance, you wrote our books and our newspapers, you worked in our hospitals and our universities, your country was our travel destination, our oasis, our resting place and where we found peace.

We, the Gulf people, were proud of your savvy people, with their sophisticated culture, their metropolitan environment, their lovely habits, their logic, their openness, their love for both one another and their homeland and their overwhelming attachment to their country's history and honour.

We need to retain this feeling towards you.

We want you to be entrusted again with our pride, confidence and love. And we will not spare any effort to support you. Your pains are ours. Will you wake up, regain control over your destiny and give the utmost priority to the interests of your country?

How far are you now from your past? I am asking as a partner, your lover and your country.

I tried to figure out why on earth the Lebanese are doing such harm to their country. Well, I confess that I could not. I failed to have any justification for this havoc; this blighting of a place described by a prominent poet as the gate of paradise.

However, I will not contend that this has been done by the Lebanese themselves.

God has entrusted the Lebanese with this heavenly gift, human heritage and natural miracle. There is no reason to do what you are doing now.

The Lebanese have reached the lowest point in their history. Unemployment is rampant, Arab and international investors are leaving, factories and even restaurants are closing, maybe permanently, causing crowds of unemployed, victimized by poverty.

Migration has become the buzzword among hundreds of thousands of Lebanese who bring their pains and despair with them to anywhere in the world.

Do you not deserve some time to think about the current situation? Do you not deserve to recall your deep-rooted national feelings, to regain your honourable past? You were among the first who demonstrated that homeland is the synonym of integrity, honour and pride.

Give Lebanon the opportunity to live, to be an oasis for our world. Go back and amicably and open-mindedly discuss your differences inside your constitutional establishments, your inclusive parliament, your multilateral government, which is meant to serve people, not the other way around.

Go back to constructive dialogue, a unified stand and logical resonance. There is no alternative to one Lebanon, one Lebanese people.

Differences, no matter how deep they are, should be minor issues when your homeland is under threat. Politics usually become insignificant when national sovereignty is at stake.

All losses are neglected when the loss of your nation is looming.

You are required to have some mercy for Lebanon, your sons and daughters, your seniors, and your youth.

Deny your enemies the opportunity to celebrate your blight. Try to mitigate your friends' fears.

No one needs to assure me about your love for your country. But what is going on now endangers even the national survival of your Lebanon. Everyone should stop for a moment and reconsider his stand, even make concessions if necessary. No one needs to be ashamed of concession in favour of the nation.

No one should be victorious or a loser vis-à-vis his or her nation. The real longed-for victory is Lebanon's unity and integrity.

Leave your assumed ditches to the daylight. Go beyond the walls of disengagement and hostility.

We need to extend our hands to each other, not on each other. Think of your country's blights. This is your only possible solution.

Public feuding harms Lebanon's growth

21 July 2010

I NEVER CEASE to be amazed at the ability of the Lebanese to bounce back swiftly from crises that would hamper the progress of most other countries for decades. Civil war, invasions, conflicts and political in-fighting have blighted the country for decades and although Lebanon has paid a terrible toll in human life and infrastructure, the people's spirit remains indestructible.

In theory, this relatively small mountainous country, hugging the Mediterranean, should be the envy of all. Blessed with a diverse and spectacularly beautiful landscape and an educated, entrepreneurial people who live life to the full, Lebanon's potential to be the most admired country in the Middle East in terms of lifestyle is boundless. But, sadly, there are certain factors that hamper the realization of that God-given potential.

My deep and abiding affection for Lebanon is well-known. Almost from the moment I first stepped on Lebanese soil during the 1970s, I felt a special connection with its warm and hospitable sons and daughters who have contributed so much to civilization and proved their solidarity with the struggles of their Arab brethren time and again. Nowadays, when my airplane touches down at Rafic Hariri International Airport I experience a sense of "coming home" just as I do each time I return to my homeland, the United Arab Emirates (UAE).

It was my belief in this wonderful country that fuelled my desire to invest heavily in its future rather than projected profit margins. I may be a businessman but this does not mean that I am not sometimes led by emotion. And so, as someone who genuinely loves Lebanon, I consider it my duty as a friend to point out the flaws that stand in the path of its true destiny.

Firstly, Lebanon's system of government known as "confessionalism", meant to distribute political power proportionately between religious communities, needs to be overhauled. Far from bringing diverse groups together under one flag it perpetuates sectarianism and often blocks the most suitable candidate from securing high office. The Lebanese are a proudly patriotic people but a system that serves to unite them under various banners of religious belief dilutes not only national unity but also purist democratic principles.

Secondly, as a small country with a population of little more than four million, Lebanon should adopt a policy of neutrality similar to that of Switzerland, which remained intact even as two world wars raged. The Lebanese have sacrificed too much already. It is high time that other nations stopped turning their soil into killing fields on which to wage proxy wars that devastate the Lebanese people, leaving their own nationals virtually immune from negative consequences.

Thirdly, all Lebanese politicians, without exception, must put their country's interests first without reference to competing foreign powers that should have no say in the country's internal or external policies. As long as ministers and politicians allow themselves to be guided by outside influences, Lebanon will remain vulnerable to decisions taken in faraway capitals.

Fourthly, while it is natural for politicians to hold differences of opinions – this happens everywhere in the world – in Lebanon such differences become the subject of hostile argument rather than meaningful debate. Such aggressive exchanges are often televised when political proponents launch personal attacks on one another and feel free to use crude language. Heated disputes like these destroy the credibility of those involved and should be held behind closed doors or during closed parliamentary sessions.

I cannot understand why Lebanese politicians are unable to resist the urge to publicly broadcast their opinions; no matter that those views could be detrimental to the country's security or economy. It intrigues me, too, just how many "experts" there are who are invariably rolled out on TV to opine on events like the recent crash of an Ethiopian Airlines airplane when they have no technical expertise whatsoever.

The Lebanese media happily give a platform to know-nothing charlatans and politicians out to gain prominence by fuelling incitement. Free speech is one thing but commentators who wilfully ruin the country with damaging predictions about a possible upcoming war, based on rumour, should be kept on a tight leash. If the media cannot or will not behave responsibly then the government should step in.

Confidence and stability are the commodities that Lebanon must nurture to attract foreign investment and tourists that are so essential to its economy. Their lack has resulted in half-empty hotels this summer. Yes, Lebanese nationals are flocking in from overseas, which is great, but where are the big-spending tourists and visitors from the Arab countries and all over the world? Where are the foreign investors with ideas for new projects or an interest in investment opportunities and acquiring property?

Sad to say, the Lebanese are their own worst enemy. Lebanon is like "a camel abandoned with its rein still on its back", to use an Arabic expression. It is up to the government to monitor and, when necessary, exercise control over harmful elements.

Lebanon could be and should be "heaven on earth". I wish with all my heart that the Lebanese government would unite to join hands with the people with the common purpose to make it so.

The Lebanese should back their besieged Syrian brothers

3 February 2012

ATTEMPTS BY THE Syrian opposition to unseat President Bashar Al Assad and his cronies have divided Lebanon. Those who support the 14 March coalition broadly sympathize with anti-regime demonstrators. The 8 March alliance is strongly backing the Syrian government while others, fearful that violence will spill across the border, are closing their eyes hoping the danger will simply fade away. The Lebanese government is out of step with the majority of League of Arab States member countries, officially disassociating itself from United Nations (UN) Security Council condemnations of the Syrian regime's crackdown that has robbed thousands of innocent lives.

Within the political sector, tempers are fraying. Mustapha Alloush of the Future Movement and the Lebanese Baath Party's Fayez Shukr physically attacked one another during a debate on Syria, broadcast on a Lebanese network. And, last Thursday, Muhieddine Ladkani, a Syrian opposition activist, was assaulted by a Lebanese supporter of Assad during a discussion on Al Jazeera.

It is surely about time that the Lebanese realized that what is happening in Syria is now beyond personal political affiliations. In December, the UN announced that the death toll had reached 5,400 and since then the murder of civilians by government forces has been ongoing with 210 killed in just four days last week. Refugees from Syria have taken refuge in Turkey and Libya; untold numbers have fled to the mountainous region of northern Lebanon where they are being hosted by local families. Many dissenting regime officials have also left while some are hiding amid civilian populations. Others are under house arrest. They have read the writing on the wall and fear repercussions when the government finally falls.

The extent of the Syrian government's barbarity against its own people, whom it has a duty to protect and serve, not only means that the President and his cohorts are unfit for purpose but also that what was initially an internal political dispute has erupted into an humanitarian crises that the international community is morally-bound to resolve. The Arab League has now rightly withdrawn its monitors, convinced that Assad has no intention of complying with its plan to end the violence and embark on a Syrian transition process. A video on the internet of an Arab League observer entering a mosque in city of Homs to witness the bullet-ridden body of a tiny five-year-old "martyr" speaks volumes.

It seems to me to be entirely wrong for Lebanon to obstruct the will of the Arab League and the United Nations in their efforts to bring peace to its neighbour teetering on the brink of civil war. If anything, the Lebanese should be leading the charge against Assad instead of behaving like unaligned Switzerland during World War II. Lebanon cannot remain neutral because Syrians and Lebanese share history, culture and familial blood lines. The Lebanese and the Syrians are like one family; certainly, there have been some low points between the two as there are in every family but in times of dire need families should come together as, indeed, occurred when Israel launched airstrikes against Lebanon in 2006, when Syrians opened their homes and their hearts to Lebanese fleeing the conflict. Those same Syrians who provided hospitality to Lebanese families are facing unbearable suffering now.

Aside from the compelling humanitarian argument for Lebanon to put all its weight behind the Syrian people, it is wrong-thinking on the part of the Lebanese government to back a losing horse. Once the Syrian opposition takes power, as I am sure it will sooner or later, the fact that Lebanon assisted their oppressor will not bode well for the future of Syrian-Lebanese relations. Syrian opposition parties and the fledging Free Syrian Army (FSA) will have long memories. They will remember those in Lebanon who rallied against them, including those factions of the Lebanese Army that shamefully surrendered fleeing Syrians to the Syrian military.

It is a little late but it is not too late for the Lebanese to correct their position not only for the sake of their Syrian brothers and sisters but also their own. I would appeal to the people of Lebanon to put politics and sectarian interests to one side long enough to stand with Syrians desperate to throw off the yoke of authoritarianism in the way Tunisians, Egyptians, Libyans and Yemenis have done. They should denounce public figures who announce their support of the Syrian regime at the cost of the freedom-seekers.

Time is running out for the Lebanese government and people to materially aid and protect Syrian refugees suffering from a lack of essential facilities in the mountains of the north and the Beka'a valley, where night-time temperatures are currently plunging as low as minus two degrees centigrade. The government should support the Syrian people in their quest for liberty, a human right, and should apologize for standing next to those who are killing and torturing them.

Ordinary Lebanese people should ignore self-serving sectarian leaders and open their hearts and their homes to Syrian refugees. The Lebanese have been slaves to political parties, politicians and tribal leaders for more than century. When will they decide to claim their own thoughts, their own Lebanese identity for the greater good? No leader should be followed blindly and unquestioningly. The people should demand true and honest leaders who love Lebanon enough not to impose foreign agendas.

Moreover, should the Lebanese choose to do the right thing, Russia and China would be isolated and embarrassed over their stance against people who refuse to be controlled by a tyrant. Those powers are actively harming

Arabs to suit their own ends and I, for one, would support a Muslim/Arab boycott of Chinese and Russian imports until they quit endorsing dictators.

Bravo to Turkey for slamming the actions of its Syrian ally from the get-go. I just wish Ankara would "stop the talk and walk the walk". Bravo, too, to Qatar for its unequivocal moral standpoint. If Qatar can show such admirable leadership on the world stage, there is no reason why Lebanon that will always be inseparable from its northern neighbour should not do the same.

Lebanon will sink without a competent captain

18 April 2012

THE ONLY CONTINUITY in one of God's most beautiful creations, Lebanon, is its protected cedar trees. For me, personally, the fact that the Lebanese seem unwilling or unable to put their house in order is an endless source of frustration because this country, blessed with nature's finest bounty, has potential that other countries would die for.

I lost my heart to Lebanon as a young man in the 1970s and have been a frequent visitor since. While looking-up some of my old friends in Beirut during the 1990s, they encouraged me to take in the country's amazing diversity with a tour from north to south, east to west. It was then that I decided to inject the hospitality industry with substantial financial investment.

Given Lebanon's instability that was hardly a sound business decision; I was rather driven by emotion. I sincerely wanted to help the Lebanese prosper and live in a dignified fashion by providing business opportunities and jobs. I truly believed they would purge themselves of sectarian divisions, demand a democratic political system that would allow effective governance, bolt the door to damaging foreign influences – and show the door to any leader willing to sacrifice Lebanon, whether for ideological reasons, personal benefit or foreign affiliations. How wrong I was!

It took me years to fully understand the complexities of the Lebanese people's national character that on the one hand is courageous and dynamic and on the other complacent and accepting. Their ingrained loyalties to political and religious figures who have failed to lead them in the right direction and to out-of-date political systems are imprisoning them as spectators in a static time capsule.

I cannot even count the number of people I have spoken with on this topic or how many times I have attempted to reason with them that it is in their interest to free themselves from the diktats of sectarian heads with less-than-patriotic agendas. It was usually the same story. No matter their faith, background or social status, they would often just shrug their shoulders before telling me that they have lived this way all their lives and are used to it. Oddly, most settle for surviving from day to day in an atmosphere of insecurity; some proudly portray themselves as invincible and put on a show of bravado when the majority of people around the world without a stable future for themselves and their children would be eager for change.

To be fair, the Lebanese have suffered more than most from a series of foreign occupations and internal/external conflicts. Nobody can criticize their resilience and endurance; they have a way of swiftly bouncing back from misfortune. But is it not time that they moved away from their crisis-mode way of thinking to one that will be more productive in the long term?

As I have written before, the nub of Lebanon's problems is its confessional system of governance bequeathed by the French. It is inherently undemocratic and promotes disunity. Its mandatory Maronite president, Sunni prime minister and Shi'ite parliamentary speaker often have competing agendas, loyalties, attachments and programmes that undermine the overall personality of the government. Each time the president or prime minister tries to implement a solution to the nation's economic or security woes, he is blocked by his colleagues' political parties.

It does not help that there is a disparity between parties in terms of strength and influence. Some are out to dictate Lebanon's destiny by moving the government in any direction they choose; others are genuinely trying to make things better but are virtually impotent. Then there are those who unhesitatingly sell out their country to foreign powers to be used as a proxy battlefield.

Such continual inter-party differences of opinion do not attract investor confidence that leads to job creation – and they are no recipe for the harmonious existence that most Lebanese crave but have no idea how to achieve. These never-ending political stalemates make me nostalgic for the 1970s when President Suleiman Franjieh was at the helm. That was a time when the country was ruled by law-and-order and when this ship called Lebanon had a single, experienced captain.

At this moment in time, Lebanon's economy is on the brink according to the head of the Lebanese Industrialists Association, Nemat Frem. "We are on the verge of collapse," he announced. "Our public debt has reached US\$ 60 billion while the Gross Domestic Produce remains at US\$ 41 billion. ...The budget deficit will grow more than 10 per cent this year but growth will not exceed 2.5 per cent." Grim news indeed!

The head of Beirut's Chamber of Commerce Mohammad Choukeir blames politicians for having "turned a deaf ear" to the economy's deterioration and the drying-up of foreign investment. He warns of a worsening situation ahead if the government does not quit its "endless bickering" and take concrete action. But even as the Lebanese reel from rising unemployment, soaring fuel prices, power cuts, a scarcity of drinking water and neglected infrastructure, the powers that be do little other than squabble.

I can only conclude that since the Lebanese are unable to rescue themselves, they need rescuing. They like to portray themselves as sophisticated and intelligent but if the proof is in the pudding, collective intelligence is sadly lacking. Lebanon is the pulse of the Arab World. It is not expendable. If the Lebanese will not rally behind a wise captain, regardless of his faith or personal allegiances – in other words the best man for the job – then perhaps this is the moment for its sincere Arab friends to send in the lifeboats to save a people who clearly are not politically mature enough to save themselves; a people beloved by Arabs everywhere. Since the League of Arab States has have failed to save Syrians, then that leaves the Gulf Cooperation Council (GCC) countries to, once more, step in to save the day.

Put simply, the GCC – or one of its member states – should be tasked by the Lebanese to supervize the country's transition from a confessional system to a real democracy led by a robust decision-maker; a system that can empower the people of Lebanon to lead free and fruitful lives within secure, solid parameters rather than be blown around like straws on the wind by the whims of politicians and their masters in foreign capitals.

Lebanon's problems could be resolved in an instant, if only the Lebanese would agree to admit they need help and request the help of the GCC long enough for our wise, elder statesmen to use their proven powers of alchemy that fuelled the transformation of Gulf states so that this fragrant land on the shores of the Mediterranean, Lebanon, may bloom in splendour once again. But let us be clear. I am not advocating interference in Lebanese sovereignty. I am talking about friendship and the obligation of friends to help each other out in the way that Saudi Arabia has recently stood with Bahrain.

As someone who cares, I would appeal to the Lebanese to allow our GCC leaderships to offer their help, as they are always here to give it.

It is time the Lebanese removed their shackles

30 October 2012

WHEN THE NEWS BROKE that Lebanon's head of internal intelligence, Wissam Al Hassan, and eight others had been killed by a car bomb in a residential area of Beirut on Friday morning, I was angry and saddened but not surprised. Al Hassan is yet another prominent Lebanese assassinated because murderous lowlifes objected to something he said or did. I remembered with a shudder that terrible day, 14 February 2005, when I learned that my dear friend former Lebanese Prime Minister Rafic Hariri had suffered a similar fate and rushed to Beirut to offer my personal condolences to his widow and children. Al Hassan was Mr Hariri's Chief of Protocol and a leading figure in the 14 March movement.

When will the Lebanese band together to put an end to this nightmarish plague that has begun to be inextricably associated with their beautiful Mediterranean country even in the minds of those who love Lebanon as I do. When we think of Lebanon nowadays, our thoughts no longer dwell on spectacular God-given landscapes or the wonderful times we enjoyed in what was once our prime vacation destination. Now, the first thing that springs to mind is murder and mayhem. Is Lebanese life so cheap that killing has become a run-of-the-mill solution to resolve political disputes?

Lebanon is supposed to be a democracy with a parliament made up of sophisticated, often glamorous, politicians who put on a good show. Yet all their carefully-crafted speeches and promises of reform are not backed with action. Each time a good man is cut down in his prime for trying to make a difference, they make another plea for "national unity". Unfortunately, unity does not feature in the Lebanese collective psyche. They are privileged to live in a small gem of a country. They are dynamic and well-educated. But rather than put those gifts that many people of other nationalities would die for to good use, they remain glued to a self-destructive path, strewn with vengeance and vitriol, which has brought them nothing but violence, civil war and damaging outside interference. As if they do not have enough problems already, they are fighting each other over Syria!

Government and politicians must accept the lion's share of blame for this tragic state of affairs. They are doing a disservice to the people they are duty-bound to protect. They should take time out from arguing with one another to keep their citizens safe. That is easier said than done you might think. However, in reality, many of the divisions and consequent bloodshed within Lebanon stems from the country's vulnerability to outside influences. It does not need to be that way. It is surely beyond time that the Lebanese, whether Christians, Sunni Muslims, Shi'ite Muslims or Druze, refuse to permit their land to be used as a proxy battlefield, and reject leaders who are little more than marionettes manipulated by foreign powers.

I struggle to understand why the Lebanese never seem to learn from past mistakes. Clearly history has taught them nothing. It is no cruel accident of fate that Lebanon has been invaded, bombed, brought to an economic standstill and carved up into sectarian ghettoes so many times in recent memory.

Firstly, the system of governance requires urgent overhauling. Lebanon's citizens should quit labelling themselves according to their religious beliefs and become one people. Whether they worship in a church or a mosque should be nobody's business but their own and should not preclude anyone from sharing an allegiance to one flag. As it stands, the confessional system is detrimental to achieving unity among the population because it forces voters to think in terms of Sunni, Shi'ite and Christian when they should be free to choose the most suitable candidates regardless of his or her faith. Lebanon's finest minds know this and for decades there have been discussions about dispensing with this outdated formula born in the summer of 1943 when Lebanon gained its independence from France. Thus far, nothing has been done for fear of upsetting powerful individuals and groups that might lose out were real change to be effected.

Secondly, a nation smaller than Switzerland, consisting of just over 10,452 sq km with a population of well under five million, is not in a position to act as a surrogate regional player for other, far larger countries. Instead, it should declare neutrality. The Lebanese should focus on prosperity, not others' hostility.

Thirdly, Lebanon should be cleansed of all weapons and explosive materials except those in the hands of the Lebanese military and state security forces. Militias and guerilla groups should be outlawed as they are in every other state that calls itself a democracy. The army should be reinforced and empowered to protect Lebanon's land and borders instead of the badly trained, poorly armed shell of a force it currently is.

It is evident that the government is neither courageous enough nor sufficiently motivated to do what requires to be done to make Lebanon safe and bring its citizens together. The job, therefore, falls to the people themselves. Indeed, the Lebanese were the first to ignite the Arab Spring in 2005 when their demonstrations helped oust the Syrian occupiers, heralding a new era of independence. Now they must grab the bull by the horns once more to rid their country from politician wannabe"religious leaders" and false guardians, purporting to be Lebanon's "friends". Only a popular storm can topple the current cabal that is leading the nation into darkness. Those pontificating posers should be replaced by a strong leader wise enough to see the light; someone with enough guts to find it no matter how many toes he has to tread on along the way.

Lastly I would appeal to the Lebanese people: do not be slaves to the will of self-interested, agenda-led politicians and religious leaders from all religions. They have misled you and manipulated you long enough. Now is the time to control your own lives and choose your future.

Only when you the people decide to unchain yourselves can you breathe the sweet air of freedom when, believe me, Lebanon will blossom like never before.

Lebanon's Sunnis must refuse marginalization

4 July 2013

LEBANESE POLITICIANS INVARIABLY cite "Sunni moderation" when they characterize Sunnis, who make up 28 per cent of the country's population, in terms of their political stances, societal behaviour and their responsible approach to their own self-defence. Attaching the word "moderation" to a community is generally viewed as complimentary elsewhere on the planet but, in this case, "moderation" is a couched indictment of Sunnis being pliable, easy to push around; people unwilling to stand up for their rights. Is it moderation never to react with unity and strength to opponent's libels and physical attacks?

One Lebanese politician insists that all religious groups in Lebanon are moderate. Unfortunately, he is dreaming. If that were the case, Lebanon would be one of the most peaceful, stable and secure places on earth. Instead, the atmosphere is one of dog eat dog; every man for himself. There is an Arabic saying that Lebanese Sunnis would do well to heed – "If you are not a strong, Alpha wolf, then even the foxes will attack you." In other words, if you give the impression that you are weak or afraid, there will be those who will take advantage of you.

My relationship with Lebanon stretches back to the early 1970s before the country became enmeshed in sectarian violence and foreign occupation. I was bowled over by the sheer natural beauty of this part of the Levant, hugging the Mediterranean, as well as the warmth and hospitality of its people, without distinction between Sunnis, Shi'ites, Christians or Druze. Although I am not a citizen, I am both emotionally and financially invested, which is why it deeply pains me to witness its takeover by a foreign power via its proxy Hezbollah that is out to alter its moderate character and drag it into conflicts.

For as long as I can remember, Sunnis in Lebanon have never taken a meaningful stand against those disguised as patriots willing to turn it into rubble for the sake of their ideological masters. Mahatma Gandhi may have succeeded in ousting the British from India by asking his followers to abide by the adage: "If someone strikes you on the cheek, offer him the other one as well." But that does not work in our part of the world as the Palestinians and minorities all over the region can attest. If Yasser Arafat had emulated Gandhi or Nelson Mandela, Palestinians would have been ethnically cleansed from Jerusalem and the West Bank decades ago. When the late Lebanese Prime Minister Rafic Hariri was in charge, at least Sunnis had a powerful and influential voice who spoke not only on their behalf but also championed Lebanon and all its nationals, but since his life was brutally stolen, none of his successors have been able to match up.

I understand that the Lebanese are saddled with a divisive confessional system of governance and I respect the authorities and the military for their past efforts to cement the country in the face of almost impossible obstacles. But in recent times, Sunnis have complained that the army is biased in favour of certain factions and has invited Hezbollah fighters into its camp, which it denies. In reaction to thousands of Sunnis protesting the army's storming the headquarters of a Sunni cleric, who is an outspoken critic of Hezbollah and its ally the Bashar Al Assad regime in Syria, the military faced off against people it termed as "Sunni militants".

Eyewitness reports from Sidon indicate Hezbollah's military wing was engaged alongside Lebanese soldiers. If true, Sunnis will feel deprived of their national military's protection that will only add to their sense of insecurity during an era when Hezbollah imposes its will on the political arena and the Sunni voice is being drowned out. Moreover, any covert marriage between the army and Hezbollah will ignite an already simmering sectarian tinderbox and increase polarization in a country fractured over Syria whose civil war threatens to spillover the border and consume its neighbour.

Sunnis must not forget that they represent one of the largest sects and so deserve to be treated as equal partners by state institutions as well as security forces and the military that have sworn to defend all Lebanon's sons and daughters. They must stop burying their heads in the sand else wake up one day to discover they are second-class citizens like Sunni populations in Iraq, Iran and Syria. They must refuse to be intimidated by men in turbans who pay allegiance to the mullahs in Tehran. They must forcefully and loudly answer attempts to trample over their rights or insult their personal dignity and honour. Sunnis should also petition government bodies to be firm and fair with every individual and party without discrimination or bias and without favouring one religious community or sect over another.

This summer's visitors to Beirut may have returned wide-eyed and enthused about a capital that is superficially picture perfect and high energy but underneath the gloss, are seething sectarian tensions that could erupt at any moment. The authorities should go all out to dampen those embers before they turn into flames incinerating the hopes of a generation. When almost a third of Lebanon's people are being made to feel their opinion and well-being do not count with the powers that be, the chances of a flare-up increase to the detriment of all.

I can only urge Lebanon's Sunni communities to hold their heads high in an open field where only the strongest will survive. This should not be interpreted as an encouragement to Sunni Muslims to carry weapons or engage in violence on the street. My message is clear and simple: be brave enough to defend your principles. Be persistent enough to achieve your demands. Reject unequal status and show that you are once again a force to be reckoned with. Many throughout the Arab World are with you, support you – including myself – but if you cannot or will not hold your honour high, then neither will anyone else.

Saudi Arabia's generosity to Lebanon repaid with insults

9 April 2015

NOW I REALLY *do* despair of Lebanon's golden era ever returning; at least not during my lifetime. In the early 1970s, my frequent visits to a place where people were friendly and always welcoming were always special, which is one of the reasons I was driven to invest in Beirut, so beautiful and so blessed. Sadly, whereas Gulf nationals appreciate everything Lebanon has to offer, a Lebanese minority is willing to sacrifice the country's future on the altar of sectarianism and hatred.

Gulf states have always stood by Lebanon in good times and bad. Saudi Arabia, in particular has been a good friend to the Lebanese people; last year alone, Riyadh pledged to provide the Lebanese government with a $3bn grant to upgrade its military that was followed up with a further $1bn in military aid to assist the army to fend off Daesh fighters.

Lebanon has traditionally been the go-to holiday destination for Saudis and Gulf Arabs and by some estimates there are hundreds of thousands of Lebanese expatriates in Saudi Arabia, the United Arab Emirates (UAE) and Qatar alone, many of whom send regular remittances to their families at home. So when the Lebanese economy is depressed – weighed down by the needs of 1.5 million Syrian refugees – and its tourism industry has taken a severe knock due to Lebanon's unstable security environment, Hezbollah's Secretary General Hassan Nasrallah decides this is the time to be as offensive as he possibly can to the Saudi leadership and its coalition partners.

Not only are Saudis upset over his vicious diatribe, re-broadcast on Lebanon's State TV, so are their Gulf neighbours. I do not want to repeat Nasrallah's exact words. I will paraphrase. In essence, he behaved like the obedient Iranian puppet he is by announcing his hope that the Saudi-led Arab coalition battling Houthi militias in Yemen would be defeated, which, he said, would impact the Kingdom's internal stability and its ruling monarchy. He is no savvy politician. If he thinks insulting Saudi Arabia will resurrect Hezbollah's dwindling popularity, he is mistaken.

Lebanon's Minister of Information subsequently apologized to the Saudi ambassador for the broadcast and even politicians from the 14 March bloc have issued statements criticizing Nasrallah – Lebanon's actual leader – for over-stepping. But no amount of apologizing can erase the hurt, and I would imagine that many Saudis will think twice about investing or vacationing there for the foreseeable future. Nowhere else in the world does state television provide a platform to militias to spew their propaganda, let alone those under the wing of foreign governments!

However, Nasrallah is not the only Lebanese going after the Kingdom's jugular. There are frequent attacks on Gulf Cooperation Council (GCC) states, especially targeting Saudi Arabia, by certain Lebanese politicians and so-called analysts on television and in newspapers. This trend is self-defeating and dismaying and if it continues, the consequences will backfire on the Lebanese people.

I quit being shocked years ago at anything Hezbollah does, especially since its triggering of a war with Israel in 2006 and its decision to join hands with the Assad regime, one of the most ruthless our planet has ever known. Those are brands of shame it can never shake off. But I do admit feeling disappointment with prominent politicians allied to 14 March who have neglected to take strong measures to ensure respect and appreciation for Saudi Arabia and the other GCC member states, the 14 March coalition's biggest allies and material backers.

How would they feel if Saudi channels had championed an Israeli victory in 2006? 14 March is duty-bound to hold accountable any politician or anyone else who trashes Lebanon's closest regional friends. I am sure they would love to hide behind the arguments that Hezbollah is too powerful to cross or Lebanon believes in the democratic principle of free speech.

The country is just a sham democracy as long as Hezbollah's hand rocks the cradle and those proponents of free speech merely use that argument to cover their own cowardice. In any case, anything that threatens Lebanon's economic health or national security should trump the free expression of traitors with Persian loyalties.

The 14 March bloc has the resources to act but lacks the courage or the will; the Ministry of Defence, the Ministry of Interior, the Ministry of Justice and the media are all under its control – or that is what its leaders would have us believe. It is about time they stopped burying their heads and stood up for what is right. If their positions are nothing more than honorary to keep up a façade, then they should let us know, so that our heads of state do not waste their time holding discussions with them.

Lebanese ministers and politicians must stop playing Hezbollah's game. They were elected and funded to defend the people's interests and those of the Lebanese diaspora in the Gulf, which should include deterring agenda-led thugs to hurl insults at Saudi Arabia or any other GCC country. Instead, they stand and watch while those thugs throw boulders in the well that they drink from. If they are not very careful, they will end up having to find jobs for returning Lebanese expatriates because if hostile sentiments keep coming our way, our leaders may be forced to conclude that Lebanese nationals doing business or working in their countries pose a risk to national security.

How long is this sad state of affairs going to continue? How long will it be until the Lebanese people – whether Muslim Christian, Druze or Armenian – refuse to allow their strings to be pulled by ayatollahs threatening not only their safety and livelihoods but their very Lebanese identity. I can only hope they will find their voices to speak up against this dark cloak stifling any chance of a new Lebanese dawn. And in the meantime, I am watching intently for signs that they reject absolutely any insult to brotherly nations that have always sheltered them with open arms.

Nasrallah opens his Iranian playbook

23 April 2015

DURING HIS RECENT VISIT to Lebanon to hold talks with government officials, the US Deputy Secretary of State Antony Blinken found Hezbollah's policies perplexing. "If I am Lebanese and I want my country to be peaceful and stable, it is hard to understand their actions," he said. His criticism was levelled at Hezbollah's military support for the Assad regime, which Blinken asserts is contributing to the refugee crisis in Lebanon and serves as a recruiting tool for Daesh in neighbouring Syria.

In reality, there is nothing perplexing about Hezbollah's behaviour when, although its members hold Lebanese nationality, their loyalty is firmly with the ayatollahs in Iran – and always has been since its foundation in the 1980s. Hezbollah's Secretary General Hassan Nasrallah receives his directives from Iran's Supreme Leader, so it stands to reason that he would agree to join the fight, irrespective of whether that decision harmed his own country's security or economy.

Similarly Nasrallah's remarks pertaining to the Saudi-led Arab intervention in Yemen could have just as well emerged from the mouth of the Ayatollah Ali Khamenei's ventriloquist's dummy. Just like his master in Qom, he launched a vicious attack on Saudi Arabia. "Yemenis do not need to prove their Arab or Islamic identity," he said. "It's those invading Yemen who must prove they are real Arabs ..."

He should be challenged to prove he is a real Lebanese when a true son of the soil would feel gratitude for last Monday's delivery of French-made weapons and anti-tank missiles, paid for by Saudi Arabia as part of a $3bn Saudi initiative to upgrade the Lebanese army.

Adding insult to injury, he threatened the Kingdom, saying: "The revolutionary leadership of Ansar Allah, this great leader Badr Al Din Al Houthi, now has the chance to attack and infiltrate into Saudi Arabia; however, he does not because he is performing what is called 'strategic patience'." At last, a glimmer of truth from his lips!

Saudi Arabia, that is Iran's end game, not the Arab World's poorest country Yemen that is fast running out of natural resources, including clean water.

Nasrallah is acting true to form. But I was shocked to see a "Breaking News" strap line on Future TV that read: "Nasrallah's speech against Saudi Arabia is just one of big mistakes added to [his] many mistakes." I was further surprised to read the Future Movement's uncharacteristically vehement response to his anti-Saudi rhetoric, which cut to the core of the problem. Its leader, Saad Hariri did not mince words. He accused Hezbollah's chief of importing his rhetoric from Iran and of using "falsification and deception" detrimental to Lebanon's interests on Twitter.

In a statement, Hariri slammed Hezbollah for luring Tele Liban into airing Nasrallah's rant against the Saudi leadership, originally broadcast on Syrian state TV. Government-controlled media should not be used as a platform "to offend an Arab country and insult Saudi Arabia, its officials and its role ... for the sake of Iran and its regional policies," he said.

Hariri did not say anything that anyone who knows anything at all about Lebanon already knows. But now that he has admitted in unmistakable terms that Hezbollah works for Iran, the real question is: "What does the 14 March bloc, more particularly the Future Movement, plan to do about it? Lebanon is an Arab country. Lebanon is a member of the League of Arab States. In this case, how can any Lebanese patriot tolerate the continued presence of an armed militia in the knowledge it pays obeisance to a foreign leadership that is hostile to the Arab World?

However, I do not derive any sense of hope from Hariri's straight talking or his party's clear statement, because talk is cheap unless backed up with action. The 14 March alliance is ostensibly in control of the Ministry of Justice and the Ministry of Interior, which should have issued an arrest warrant for Nasrallah and his associates by now.

Unfortunately, the Minister of Interior Nouhad El Machnouk – formerly the late Prime Minister Rafic Hariri's political and media advisor and one of Hezbollah's most hawkish critics – is now a proponent of dialogue with Hezbollah. When asked by the Lebanese paper *The Daily Star* why he softened, he replied "What other choice do I have?" Should we understand from that response that, in reality, he is not in control of his own ministry?

Nevertheless, I am prepared to give him and the other 14 March ministers the benefit of the doubt. I must assume that even if they had the will, until recently they lacked the means. But now that they control the Ministry of Justice and the Ministry of Interior, they have no excuse for shirking their duty to their country and its people.

Convictions without courage are worthless. It is their responsibility to ensure "Iranian" traitors face justice in a court of law. How long will they continue appeasing betrayers who stab Lebanon in the back time and time again?

When they have no problem getting together with Hezbollah officials socially I cannot help but wonder whether their harsh rhetoric against Nasrallah is little more than an attempt to appease their own constituents. If that is the case, they will lose their following. The Lebanese are not stupid; they will eventually see through this facade, this sham, if they have not already.

As long as 14 March politicians manoeuvre this way and that like skilled chess players without ever actually shouting "checkmate", Hezbollah will strengthen its grip – especially when it stands to benefit from increased Iranian funding when sanctions are lifted on Iran if and when the P5+1-Iran nuclear deal is sealed. I can only urge the GCC states to be wary of these masters of manipulation whose prime goal is to safeguard their own political futures without taking necessary risks.

One of the few open and transparent major political players is the Free Patriotic Movement head, Michel Aoun, who says whatever he feels – for which he has my respect – even though he is in Hezbollah's camp, which he entered not out of a shared ideology but rather through political expediency. If this presidential candidate decided to position himself at the heart of Lebanon's camp and distance himself from the Iranian proxy, he could prove to be a game-changer. I would challenge Aoun to do the right thing ... to reject those who would crush his homeland underfoot if so ordered by the leaders of Iran and stand with those who want nothing more than their country strong and independent.

Lebanon should restore presidential power

27 May 2015

TOO MANY COOKS spoil the broth and that is exactly why Lebanon is in a state of paralysis. It has been more than a year since President Michel Suleiman left office and, because there is no agreement on a successor, politicians engage in endless horse-trading.

This is not the way a country should be run. This is not democracy or a system benefitting the people; it is a grand power souk permitting politicians to hold on to their chairs in what has become a virtual old boys' club; a place where fresh ideas are not welcome because they are all terrified of rocking a boat so rickety it is a miracle it has not sunk.

Moreover, while most are aware that the confessional system inherited from the French is antiquated, failing to deliver the best man for the job, there is no will to change it out of fear they will lose their own jobs.

There is no comparison between Lebanon today and its golden era when President Fouad Chehab, a man with principles and integrity, held a tight rein on his country. He is remembered with fondness to this day as working to bring harmony between different sects and security for all. He not only steered Lebanon's transformation into a modern state that was the envy of the region, he improved the economy, forged close relationships with Arab states – and he strengthened the country's security apparatus to keep foreign interference at bay.

Chehab never played the sectarian game; he was truly a president for Muslims and Christians. Unlike those clinging on to their chairs like leeches, President Chehab declined to run for re-election in 1964. His inclusive policies were continued by his successor, Charles Helou, until 1970 when he lost the election to Suleiman Franjieh.

In the early 1970s, Lebanon was a heaven on earth in every respect. Visitors flocked there from all over the world, awed by its atmosphere of prosperity, culture and sophistication. Hotels and restaurants were full. Businesses expanded. In short, the Lebanese people were united, proud and happy in "The Paris of the Middle East" infused with a spirit of gaiety and entrepreneurship.

In 1970, Lebanon's literacy rate was the highest of all Arab countries. Today it has fallen below that of Jordan, Libya, Bahrain, Kuwait, the United Arab Emirates (UAE) and Qatar. The Lebanese pound exchange rate then hovered around LBP 2 to the dollar as opposed to the current average of LBP 1,500. Then its GDP ranked 73rd in the world; in 2014 it had descended to 138th.

Those were the days when Lebanon boasted the region's most dynamic economy fuelled by a strong banking system and a balance of payment surpluses, low inflation and stability enticing foreign corporations, international businesses and banks. In 1975, public debt was a mere 3 per cent of GDP but by 1990 that percentage had soared to 99.8 per cent.

261

Last year, the government recorded a public debt accounting for 146 per cent of GDP.

Lebanon flowered when Christian presidents and leaders who were not afraid to administer tough love, had absolute control, as evidenced by the above statistics. But no statistic can reflect those glory days as effectively as anecdotes from those old enough to remember just how wonderful it was.

The civil war, sparked when violent clashes broke out between Maronite Christian and Palestinian groups in 1975, thrust the country into bloodshed and a downward spiral from which it still has not fully recovered. Franjieh's greatest mistake was to invite Syrian troops to bring calm. The forces sent to save Lebanon soon morphed into occupiers.

Scratch the surface and you will see an impotent government that is little more than an elaborate show hiding a maelstrom of competing sectarian interests. Not a single politician is courageous enough to put his country first. No one speaks the truth, except behind closed doors. And almost all make obeisance to the hand that rocks the Lebanese cradle – Iran's proxy, Hezbollah, whose marching orders come directly from Qom. Lebanon's politicians, out of cowardice and selfishness, have collaborated with Hezbollah in turning their homeland over to Iran.

The restructuring of Lebanon's political system subsequent to "the National Reconciliation Accord" negotiated in the city of Taif, Saudi Arabia and signed in October 1989 brought with it devastating unintended consequences. Authority was partially stripped from the president so as to empower the prime minister and the Speaker of the parliament. Instead of answering to the president, the prime minister came under the direction of squabbling lawmakers, which is why the country is gridlocked.

The Taif Agreement did not bring about national reconciliation, other than on paper. It heralded rule by committee, whose members hold wildly divergent world views. Each bloc drags the country in a different direction and neither the president nor the prime minister has any real authority.

Unfortunately, the only part of the Taif Agreement that was implemented was political restructuring. One of its most important components, the disarmament of militias, was ignored by Hezbollah that falsely branded itself as "the Lebanese resistance". If that were so, then what is it doing defending the Assad regime in Syria and fighting alongside Shi'ite militias in Iraq and the Houthis in Yemen?

Lebanon's future, whether politically, economically or socially, looks bleak without a strongman, a charismatic figure able to take needed tough decisions; someone with the ability to coalesce the nation behind him. Lebanon must be taken in hand by a patriotic leader able to unite all citizens under the cedar flag rather than religious standards or the flags of other nations.

As we age, we like to talk nostalgically about "the good old days" when in most cases, we enjoyed superior lifestyles. For instance, when I compare the conditions of my home country, the UAE, during my youth and now, there is no contest. But it is a different story for the Lebanese. Life really was genuinely much better in the '50s, '60s and early '70s, when the presidency was not as restricted as it is today.

Chehab, Helou and Franjieh were empowered to respond to all contingencies. They could think on their feet and act fast, without having to plead for parliament's permission to do the right thing in any given circumstance. I was one of the lucky ones who knew Lebanon in its heyday. I know first hand how amazing it was and, therefore, what it could become again, provided there was sufficient political will to reform the system.

Because I know what could be, my wonderful memories are now tainted by annoyance at the status quo, in the same way a parent feels when he sees his beloved child going down a wrong path. I have no words to evoke "my Lebanon" which exists only in poetry, song and old movies.

As long as there is nobody in charge, the country will remain in a state of flux without direction, jogging along on a wing and a prayer. The antidote is the return of power to a president untainted by corruption scandals and with a reputation of operating in accordance with his personal ethics, not a man willing to switch sides for a handful of carrots.

Most importantly, he should be someone with proven patriotic credentials; a person whose love of his country's soil is beyond dispute. He should be chosen to lead because of his character attributes, not just because he happens to be a Maronite from a well-known family or because he served in the army or because his father once held a prominent position in government. The Lebanese thirst for a leader with a successful track record, capable of satisfying their craving for security, stability and economic health; someone they can trust.

In recent decades, career politicians and relics from the military have consistently let down the Lebanese people, so I would argue that now is the time to look over their shoulders for candidates at the top of their respective fields, be they captains of industry, business moguls or technocrats either resident in the country or drawn from the diaspora.

Beirut may have undergone a glitzy transformation, clawing back some of its fabled glamour, but without firm political foundations, a solid economy, and leadership that is not reliant upon consensus, the country is a house of cards vulnerable to being collapsed by a gust of wind in a region fraught with tornadoes of threats. Rescuing Lebanon is bigger than a mere figurehead president or a prime minister engaged with currying parliament's favour. It needs a man with muscle and the wisdom to know when to flex it.

Lebanese Shi'ites could save the day

29 May 2015

SECTARIAN DIVISIONS ARE the prime cause of Lebanon's instability and political deadlock. And, tragically, those splits have been cynically used by different groups and parties, under the sway of foreign powers, for their own ends. As long as Lebanese loyalties are not directed towards the motherland, the country's very survival as a unified state is at risk.

It is beyond time that the Lebanese people understood that they are being played. Power-hungry elements are using religion to manipulate them in a certain direction mirroring the scenario in Iraq where Sunnis, Shi'ites, Christians and other minorities that once lived in harmony are at each other's throats. Those who manufacture hatred are the enemies of peace and tolerance that are the cornerstones of Islam and Christianity.

One could fill a book with Lebanon's structural problems. But they would not be insurmountable provided the country could count on a united population, one that was not being pulled this way and that by unscrupulous clerics and politicians, whose allegiances are not to the state, but to their own power bases – or even worse, to foreign capitals.

Let us say it like it is. Any country that puts up with the existence of an armed mini state within its borders is destined for ruin. Hezbollah runs the country and takes the decisions that matter. Government officials are little more than administrators. The president (when there is one) has no power and the prime minister answers to a parliament dominated by Hezbollah partnered with the Amal Movement and their Christian allies.

Hezbollah's obligation to disarm under the Taif Accord has been trumped by Lebanese Sunni, Shi'ite and Christian leaders, who, whether by choice or under coercion, back Hezbollah as a Lebanese resistance organization, independent of the army, with the right to bear arms to defend Lebanese territory.

Those blessings are bordering on traitorous because as Michael Young, the veteran *Daily Star* columnist correctly wrote: Hezbollah's militia "has been shown to be no better than an auxiliary force regionally for both the Iranian and Syrian regimes".

When Hezbollah and Amal militants have turned their guns on the Sunni population, and when Hezbollah has dragged the country into ruinous wars and is now defending both the Iraqi and Syrian regimes, it can hardly be characterized as patriotic. No responsible leader anywhere on the planet would sign up to such an agreement unless he had a gun to his head, and if he succumbed, in many parts of the world he would be prosecuted or lynched.

Shi'ites should put aside the notion that their allegiance should automatically go to a pro-Iranian Shi'ite paramilitary. During World War II, British Catholics did not rush over to Italy to fight alongside Mussolini's battalions merely because they shared the same faith. British Protestants were not given to join up with their co-religionists, the Nazis. People put the country that bore them first, which is how it should be.

Moreover, Iran is not the spiritual home of Shi'ism, although the less informed might be forgiven for thinking so. Apart from Mecca and Medina, the most holy Shi'ite sites are to be found in the Iraqi towns of Najaf and Karbala where Shi'ite pilgrims flock to worship at the Imam Ali Mosque and at the Imam Hussein Shrine, respectively.

Until comparatively recently, Arab peoples made little distinction between Sunnis and Shi'ites; people's beliefs simply were not an issue. I have had Lebanese Shi'ite friends since the late 1960s. The majority of my closest friends are the sons of the Wazni, Abbas, Khalifa, Murad, Aashi, Moussawi, Dalloul, Baydoun, Fayad, Hoteit, Fawaz and Koteich Shi'ite families, who were – and still are – some of the most patriotic Lebanese I have ever encountered. Several of my employees in Lebanon were Shi'ite. I trusted them implicitly and it never occurred to me that their loyalties did not lie with Lebanon.

I am proud to have known those fine people who have enriched my life with good conversation and warm hospitality. But, quite honestly, I am forced to wonder why they and others have permitted an Iranian armed gang in all but name to create a chasm between them and their fellow Lebanese? Why are they allowing a militia to tar them with the same brush and to lead them by the nose into a dark future? Hezbollah is not "the Party of God" but rather "the Party of the Iranian Ayatollahs".

I would strongly urge Lebanese Shi'ites to come together to reclaim their Lebanese identity. They should stand courageous and tall as proud Lebanese and persuade their friends, families and colleagues to reject destructive Iranian influence.

Were Shi'ites to rise up en masse against the pro-Iranian policies of Hezbollah – thus proving to the nation that those who heed the call of Iran's mullahs are not representative of their sect – that would be an important first step towards bringing the nation together under the cedar flag. A wave of anti-Hezbollah public opinion would likely persuade the Free Patriotic Movement leader, Michel Aoun, to shred his incomprehensible pact with Hezbollah and quit defending its legitimacy.

If Christians, Sunnis and Shi'ites were committed to joining hands in common cause, a bright new dawn awaits. Hezbollah would be sidelined; its authority diminished. The international community, including Gulf Cooperation Council (GCC) states, would be encouraged to help the country get on its feet with financial aid, and investments as well as further assistance in strengthening the Lebanese army.

Politicians, currently burying their heads in the sand out of sheer impotence, would be empowered to claw back Lebanon from de facto Iranian control by enforcing a clause within the Taif Accord that demands the disarming of militias. No more would a Maronite presidential candidate have to seek Hezbollah's approval based on his commitment to Iranian interests. And, hopefully, good people with strong hearts and true Lebanese blood flowing through their veins would be free to restore this tarnished jewel to the glittering gem it once was.

Lebanon exposed as an Iranian satellite

13 January 2016

HOW MUCH LONGER will we fool ourselves that Lebanon's loyalties rest with the Arab World? During a recent League of Arab States emergency meeting of foreign ministers, called by the Kingdom of Saudi Arabia to discuss measures to be taken in answer to Iran's "terrorist acts" and its aggression against Saudi Arabia, it was clear that Beirut stands with the enemy.

Ignoring the urging of the League's Secretary General Nabil Elaraby for all "to adopt a strong and clear position calling on Iran to stop all forms of interference in the affairs of Arab nations", Lebanon abstained from voting on a resolution denouncing Iran's threatening actions, supported by all other member states.

Lebanon's failure to stand shoulder-to-shoulder with its Arab brothers proves its independence has been quashed under the Iranian boot. This sorry state of affairs is well known but now that Beirut has taken sides there is no room for doubt; it has been rubber-stamped

The statement is to be followed up with the formation of a committee to include representatives from Saudi Arabia, the United Arab Emirates (UAE), Bahrain and Egypt – countries that have either severed or downgraded relations with Iran – tasked with monitoring the crisis and proposing further measures against Tehran, if necessary. Saudi Arabia will also hold talks with its Arab allies on future steps.

I was shocked and disappointed to learn of the Lebanese stance, apparently prompted by the statement's admonition of Iran's Lebanese proxy Hezbollah over its blatant interference in Bahrain's domestic affairs. "The statement that was made with regard to Bahrain does not reflect the position and the policy of the Lebanese government nor that of the political party [the Aounist Free Patriotic Movement] I represent," Lebanon's Foreign Minister Gibran Bassil is quoted as saying. Why some Maronite Christians are hand-in-glove with Iran's puppet is beyond my understanding unless their motive is to feather their own nests.

"Lebanon's implicit position does not differ from that of the Arab states in their statement regarding non-interference in the affairs of Bahrain. However, the statement that was made was against Lebanon or a certain Lebanese party, which I certainly rejected ..." said this individual, who had previously held ministerial posts in the cabinets of 14 March leaders Fouad Siniora and Saad Hariri.

Bassil poured salt in the treacherous wound adding: "It is worth noting that the statement was issued in contradiction with the principles of the Arab League and its charter, but we did not want to raise this point since we do not want to cause problems with any Arab state." How considerate of him! The truth is that any suggestion of impropriety from him would have been shot down by all other Arab League members, and he knows that.

He went on to grumble that promised Arab aid has yet to manifest itself. In other words, he slaps Lebanon's traditional Arab benefactors while expecting those states to prop up a paralysed government unable to cleanse the country from mountains of rotting garbage, a parliament that has failed to agree upon a new president in over 18 months and an ineffective army dominated by Shi'ite militias backed with billions of dollars.

The fact is that in 2014 the Kingdom gifted the Lebanese army $1bn and, in April last year, marked the first delivery of French-made weapons and military equipment to the Lebanese armed forces under a $3bn Saudi grant to re-establish "a Lebanese army capable of responding to new security realities".

In my view Lebanon's army is in greater need of patriotism than weapons. Just as the political arena has stopped functioning due to Hezbollah's blackmail, the infiltrated military machine has Hezbollah's cog in its wheel preventing it from doing its job. No amount of cash in the world can buy love of country from those with a mandate to defend it from hostile entities, whether outside the country or within.

It is true that Lebanon is financially burdened by a massive influx of Syrian refugees in addition to the hundreds of thousands of Palestinians. But it is also the case that if Hezbollah and its Iranian Master had not thrown their backing behind the criminal Assad regime, that regime might have collapsed years ago when there was a viable opposition waiting in the wings to form a caretaker government in Syria as a prelude to elections.

Hezbollah's military involvement in Syria had nothing to do with securing Lebanese interests but was carried on a command from Iran's ayatollahs. Hezbollah is responsible for contributing to the mass displacement of the Syrian people fleeing regime bombs and for making Lebanon a target of terrorist groups.

Gibran Bassil asserts that Lebanon has a policy of non-interference in the affairs of other countries. If so, it is not worth the paper it is written on when the militia he defends did not think twice about tearing it up to serve its masters.

Head of the Future Movement Saad Hariri expressed his regret over his country's abstention in a statement released by his press office, which read: "The abstention of Lebanon's Foreign Minister to vote on the Arab League's resolution does not reflect the opinion of the majority of the Lebanese who are suffering from the Iran interference in their internal affairs." I believe him.

I have many Lebanese friends and almost all would celebrate the day Hezbollah disappeared in puff of smoke. They variously refer to themselves as Arabs or Levantines; certainly not Persians. Most Lebanese I know are passionate about their country and its beautiful blessings from God but, sadly, the political and military establishment continue to thwart their ambitions of seeing Lebanon bloom as it did in its glory days during the 1950s, '60s and early '70s before civil war halted its progress.

Let the good Lebanese stand up with courage and fortitude to ask for help in chopping the Iranian hand that strangles their children's future. And in the meantime, I would call upon Saudi Arabia not to throw any more money Lebanon's way, which could so easily end up fattening the militia's pockets. Moreover, the Arab League should reconsider Lebanon's membership until it is ready to pledge on which side of the fence it is truly sitting.

Dear Lebanon, do not give up

17 February 2016

THE INTERNATIONAL COMMUNITY has turned a blind eye to Iran's domination of Lebanon. Pleas for help to rid this Arab country of an armed militia under Tehran's orders have gone unheard because world powers do not consider that this small Mediterranean country has sufficient strategic significance to warrant military involvement. Adding insult to injury, both Hezbollah and Iran, the world's biggest terrorist sponsor, have been removed from America's threat list.

And now that Iran is being courted by the US and Europe to the detriment of the Sunni Arab World and the regional balance of power, it is understandable that some political leaders within the 14 March bloc have opted for reconciliation with Hezbollah to end stagnation. Negotiations to nominate a new president that have been underway for 19 months resulted in stalemate because Hezbollah would not accept any candidate that was not sympathetic to its camp.

Last month I was disappointed to learn that Hezbollah's long-time foe Samir Geagea, the Executive Chairman of the Lebanese Forces has capitulated by backing Michel Aoun, who is an ally of Hezbollah and the Syrian butcher Bashar Al Assad, for the presidency, while former Lebanese Prime Minister Saad Hariri is now lending his support to another pro-Assad figure – Suleiman Franjieh.

This is a mistake! The day the Lebanese choose slavery and lose their will to take their country back would be a knife in the hearts of all those who love Lebanon, including my own. I do not wish to judge them unfairly. Both Geagea and Hariri are Lebanese patriots who would like nothing more than to see their country proud and free, but without tangible heavyweight assistance, they have been fighting windmills.

In recent days, Mr Hariri has made a rare visit to Lebanon where he held a rally to mark the anniversary of his father's assassination. "We will not allow anyone to pull Lebanon to the camp of hostility towards Saudi Arabia and its Arab brothers," he told the crowd. "Lebanon will not be, under any circumstances, an Iranian province. We are Arabs, and Arabs we shall remain." A year ago, those fighting words would have been little more than inspirational rhetoric without any real substance. Not so, today.

Lebanon has been taken over by force and only force can smash the Iranian yoke. Aside from Hezbollah, the only other force is the Lebanese army but unfortunately it has been infiltrated and is not up to the task. However, the situation is no longer hopeless in light of an Arab reawakening in the face of threats to our very existence.

My message to the good Lebanese people who resent being treated as Iran's vassals is this. Do not give up. Be optimistic and stay strong. You, the great Lebanese people who hold fast to your Arab roots and your culture, once a beacon of light for all of us, get ready to take your country back! You, the noble people of northern Lebanon who have proved your worth and shown courage, should be an inspiration to all others. And you, the people of Beirut, you must stand tall against the followers of paid Iranian lackeys and those cowardly self-appointed leaders who have exchanged their principles for their comfortable chairs and the luxurious trappings that go with them.

A new reality is on the horizon. Predominately Sunni Arab states led by Saudi Arabia have woken up to the danger Iran presents to the region and are taking matters into their own hands as we have witnessed in Bahrain, stabilized thanks to Saudi/United Arab Emirates (UAE) intervention, and in Yemen where Decisive Storm was waged to cleanse this Arab heartland of pro-Iranian traitors and terrorists. Liberty is within reach and when it knocks on your door be ready to grasp it.

The Kingdom is seizing its rightful leadership role – backed by Gulf states, Turkey, Egypt and many others – not only as defender of the faith but also as the defender of brotherly countries. I am grateful to King Salman bin Abdulaziz for his courage and guidance and would salute this exceptional monarch who has given us a reason to once again hold our heads up high – and I could not be prouder that my own country, the United Arab Emirates (UAE), stands with him hand-to-hand, heart-to-heart.

A newly-assertive Riyadh is now calling the shots. The Obama administration may have dropped its demand for Assad to go, under pressure from Moscow, but the Saudi Minister of Foreign Affairs Adel Al Jubeir is adamant that if peace talks fail, Assad will have to be removed "by force".

Again, that statement might have been viewed as wishful thinking some months ago, but with reports that Saudi Arabia has stationed troops and warplanes at Turkey's Incirlik air base in preparation for a ground invasion potentially involving 150,000 soldiers, Saudi resolve is crystal clear. Syria will be cured from its multiple cancers of the regime's war crimes, terrorist atrocities and armed Iranian interlopers so that the millions of displaced persons and refugees can return home to live in peace.

I strongly believe the Lebanese people should ready themselves for a better future, free of Iranian influence. The chains dragging Lebanon down will be broken. Release from the yoke of Hezbollah or any other occupying or terrorizing force – whether internal or external – will happen sooner rather than later. Mark my words, soon we will see Lebanon's so-called leaders fleeing the country to escape the people's anger at being sold out to a foreign would-be power.

It is my fervent hope to see Lebanon unfettered from Hezbollah's strangulation blossom as it did in the 1960s and early 1970s when it was truly independent. I long for the day the true Lebanese identity that has been robbed by outside forces can reveal itself in an atmosphere of free expression. I want to stroll along Hamra Street soaking up the gaiety there once was in a country where whispers are no longer needed, before driving north to Damascus to visit the resting place Salahuddin Al Ayyoubi and onward to Homs to pray at the tomb of Khalid ibn Al Walid – two of the most fearless warriors in Arab history.

This is no idle daydream but a soon-to-be reality, provided the Lebanese people choose well between serfdom under a gang of Iranian puppets or an opportunity to reclaim their heritage with the help of their friends.

Hezbollah's accomplices deserve terrorist branding

5 March 2016

ANY ARMED GROUP holding a country hostage on behalf of a foreign state is a traitorous terrorist militia not a resistance and certainly not a legitimate political party as Hezbollah has always claimed. Its tentacles stretching from Tehran have rendered Lebanon a failed state posing a threat to the region.

With diminishing hope that the honourable Lebanese would reclaim their country, this sad truth has been acknowledged by Gulf Cooperation Council (GCC) member states with an official declaration branding Hezbollah a terrorist organization together with "its leaders factions and affiliated organizations" for "hostile acts" in Syria, Yemen and Iraq, inciting sedition, smuggling weapons and recruiting terrorists.

The majority of Arab states were supportive of the move but it was no surprise to learn that Syria and Iraq were disapproving when they, like Lebanon, are under the Iranian boot. The Tunisian president's rejection was, however, mystifying as was Algeria's distancing stance. Saud Arabia has rightly declared that it will no longer engage in the myth of Arab solidarity on the grounds that it does not exist.

The move comes on the heels of Saudi Arabia's decision to freeze $4bn in military/security aid to the Lebanese government and advice from GCC governments warning their nationals not to travel to Lebanon for their own security. At the same time, Gulf states are cracking down on known Hezbollah sympathizers and funders within their borders. These actions could not come soon enough!

Ironically, while Lebanon's Minister of Interior Nouhad El Machnouk was quick to reject the GCC's labelling during a recent Arab Interior Ministers Conference held in Tunisia, last month he declared on the Lebanese channel LBC that terrorist cells were trained in Lebanon under the supervision of Iran's Revolutionary Guard.

In reality, members of those cells were trained by Iranians jointly with Hezbollah as we know from intelligence gleaned from the group's spies and agitators arrested in the United Arab Emirates (UAE) and Saudi Arabia. To imagine the Interior Minister does not know this is preposterous; either his intelligence-gathering capabilities are sorely lacking or more likely he is afraid to say what every Lebanese politician knows.

They are all fearful of being added to Hezbollah's list of assassination targets. The Special Tribunal for Lebanon formed to investigate and try the killers of the former Lebanese President Rafic Hariri is still waiting for Hezbollah to hand over four of its accused members for trial.

El Machnouk also revealed that as of 2015 there were sleeping and active Revolutionary Guard cells in Saudi Arabia, the UAE, Kuwait, Bahrain, Kenya, Nigeria, Cyprus and Bulgaria.

Now that Hezbollah's terrorist status is etched in stone, GCC leaderships would be wise to focus on its collaborators and appeasers within Lebanon's political arena. For instance, pro-Syrian Lebanese hopeful Suleiman Franjieh has strongly denounced Hezbollah's terrorist blacklisting. Moreover, he tweeted "Hezbollah as a resistance movement makes Lebanon and the Arabs proud."

The only proud Arabs are those who share Iran's ideology and others who have betrayed their Arab roots by selling their souls to Persian mullahs. In this case, should Franjieh not be classed as a terrorist supporter?

And should Parliamentary Speaker Nabih Berri, who heads the Amal Movement allied with Hezbollah, not be treated as a collaborator? Amal's political bureau rushed to Hezbollah's defence with a statement blasting the GCC announcement and emphasizing Hezbollah's "credentials" as a resistance movement when the only thing it is currently resisting is the dislodging of the barbaric Syrian regime under direct orders from Tehran. In my view, Amal deserves the same fate as Hezbollah – a place on the GCC's terrorist listing.

Likewise, the Free Patriotic Movement and its founder General Michel Aoun, who is Hezbollah's pick to fill a presidential vacuum that has endured for almost two years, has strange loyalties. Ten years ago, Aoun, a Maronite, signed a political Memorandum of Understanding with Iran's proxy in Lebanon following 15 years in exile.

At the same time, he described the new partnership as cemented, to build a consensual Lebanese democracy on the basis of transparency, justice and equality, knowing that Hezbollah's manifesto calls for Lebanon to become a *Wilayat al-Faqih* – following the Iranian example. He has since blinded his eyes to Hezbollah's crimes.

Druze leader Walid Jumblatt, who characterized Hezbollah as part of an Iranian system in Lebanon just weeks ago, has also rejected Hezbollah's terrorist tagging. Jumblatt is a fierce critic of Hezbollah's involvement in Syria and has warned its Secretary General Hassan Nasrallah that his anti-Saudi statements could negatively impact Lebanese expatriates in the Gulf. Yet when push comes to shove, he has declined to back the GCC's decision.

The real disappointment is the figurehead of the 14 March bloc and the leader of the Future Party Saad Hariri who until recently was considered the GCC's most trusted Lebanese politician. We believed he was a lion capable of taking back his homeland. Throughout his self-imposed exile, his anti-Iranian, anti-Hezbollah rhetoric rarely faltered.

On 14 February, marking the anniversary of his father's death, he told his followers that under no circumstance would Lebanon become a province of Iran. His recent behaviour, however, belies that pledge. Just weeks prior he made the shocking announcement that he was prepared to share power with Hezbollah before throwing his weight behind Suleiman Franjieh for president. When asked why he would cooperate with a group deemed responsible for his father's assassination, he replied he was committed to the principle "innocent until proven guilty".

Unlike most other politicians, Hariri did admonish Lebanon for not standing with Saudi Arabia in the League of Arab States over the torching of the Kingdom's diplomatic missions in Iran. Asked why he was now supporting Franjieh for president, he said he was backing a candidate from the 8 March bloc to fill a void."For me, better to have a president that I will maybe have some problems with than a total void in the presidency." he said. In other words he has gift-wrapped Lebanon to be awarded to the other side. It is not better to have a president hand-in-glove with Hezbollah/Iran/Syria than no president at all! The question is whether he will continue negotiations with Hezbollah or withdraw based on its terrorist designation?

If the Lebanese government does not give its green light to the GCC's ruling and proceed to issue arrest warrants for its commanders and funders, then it should be classed as a terrorist abetter. I understand that it is not within their power to make arrests but at the very least its position would be clarified. Gulf heads of state and their allies should consider governments and individuals standing against Hezbollah's branding as partners within the same counter-terrorism framework.

There is no room for playing both sides or holding to a middle ground. The same demand should be made to the Lebanese army. Either it is against the terrorist organization, in which case it should make a public announcement to that effect or it must declare its alliance with Hezbollah.

Chief of the Lebanese Armed Forces Brigadier-General Jean Kahwaji and his top generals should affirm their allegiance to the state over the militia and for once rise to the task of protecting the country from falling. If not, then we are forced to assume that suspicions that the military is serving Hezbollah's goals are correct, in which case commanders must be considered terrorist colluders. Any army proven to be hand-in-glove with servants of a foreign entity deserves to be at the very least dismantled.

It is crunch-time for Lebanon's political and military decision-makers who have reached a fork in the road. Are you with us or against us? Do you stand with Saudi Arabia and its Gulf allies or with Hezbollah and Iran? Those are questions the GCC should ask and demand answers to before reacting accordingly. Which path Lebanon takes will decide its destiny, not only for the foreseeable future but for generations to come.

Open letter to Lebanon's Arab Shi'ite communities

5 May 2016

PEOPLE OFTEN QUESTION why the Arab World in particular is in such a mess. The fact is that so many of our problems have been triggered by the interference of foreign powers eager to dominate this strategically-located and resource-rich area. The Ottomans, the British and the French carved up the region, separating tribes and families with borders. The international community rubber-stamped the theft of Palestinian land, igniting a series of Arab-Israeli wars.

As for Lebanon, it inherited a "confessional" system of governance, which in itself is separating rather than unifying, encouraging sectarianism. More recently, US military interventions in Iraq and Libya have fomented sectarian tensions while opening the door to terrorists of all ugly stripes. Worse, the Obama administration has enriched, empowered and emboldened Iran, that has boasted of its control of Arab capitals with a stroke of a pen, thus making our region a more dangerous place than ever.

Arabs have been used as pawns of foreign powers who have only one goal which is self interest. If we Arabs had stood tall and together instead of submitting to or, in some cases, shaking hands with foreign states, our neighbourhood would look very different today. Admittedly, in the past we lacked the financial and military wherewithal to resist outside interference. But that is changing fast thanks to the leadership of Saudi Arabia that is consolidating its allies into a powerful military, economic and diplomatic bloc.

The question is this. Where do the Lebanese stand; with Persians vying to become a regional hegemonic power or with their fellow Arabs? Are you with us or against us? The choice should be no contest when Iran's Arab populations are severely oppressed and excluded from the mainstream; denied being taught Arabic in schools, excluded from top jobs and even forbidden from giving their newborns Arabic names.

Make no mistake, Hezbollah owes its creation and pays it allegiance to the ayatollahs. Its 1985 Manifesto clearly states the Ayatollah Ruhollah Khomeini – the former Supreme Leader of Iran – is the leader whose "orders we obey", it calls on Christians to "embrace Islam" and supports Lebanon becoming an Shi'ite state. The Manifesto may have been revised and softened by Hassan Nasrallah in 2009 to have a broader appeal but who is he kidding? His organization is bought, paid for and armed by Tehran.

Hezbollah is Lebanese in name only. It is nothing short of a tool wielded by a foreign state clothed as Lebanese resistance. It is a resistance alright; it resists the rights of the Lebanese people whether Sunni, Shi'ite, Christian or Druze, to live in an open, free, secure and prosperous society. It alienates Lebanon's natural Arab allies, has infiltrated the country's army and insists on its pick for president. Moreover, it dragged Lebanon into war with Israel in 2006 and into supporting the Assad regime responsible for the death of over 400,000 Syrian people.

I understand the reaction of some of my Lebanese friends to Saudi Arabia's freeze on $4bn aid to the military and security services. They complain they have been abandoned to Iran whereas, in truth, as long as Hezbollah keeps its grip, instilling fear in the hearts of political and military leaders, Lebanon will remain a toy in the Iranian pocket.

The Kingdom could no longer buy into the pretence that Lebanese decision-makers have tied hands, or that the patriotic Lebanese are the ones in charge. If they were, the country would have a president, a budget and there would be no rivers of garbage threatening the health of citizens. Anyone who believes anything different has been duped by a prettied-up façade.

The bottom line is that no amount of aid pumped into Lebanon will make a difference. Lebanon's economy would boom without the insecurity and instability Hezbollah delivers. This entity must be defeated by all means. Without another civil war, which no Lebanese citizen wants to even contemplate, saving Lebanon and bringing it back to the Arab fold lies in the hands of our Lebanese Shi'ite brothers and sisters, who I know from personal experience are generous, hospitable and proud to call themselves Lebanese.

You, my friends, are your country's salvation. Without support from sections of your community, Hezbollah would wither and fade away. I have known you since the late 1960s when I visited Lebanon with no penny in my pocket. I was welcomed by the Wazni family and other kind Lebanese Shi'ites. The Shi'ites I have known were passionate in their love of country and they count as some of my closest friends. They are proud Lebanese and proud Arabs. I do not want to see the day my grandchildren are forced to speak Farsi and neither do they.

There is no escaping from our blood lines, our DNA or our history. We are a different race from the Persians. We do not share the same traditions or culture. I wish all Lebanese Shi'ites thought the same way and hope with all my heart that those connected to or in support of Nasrallah or his second-in-command Naim Qassem will see the light before Lebanon is viewed as an Iranian satellite, a foe of the Arab World.

I have so many wonderful memories bound up with my stays in Lebanon and I have always felt a strong emotional tie to this land of amazing natural beauty and its beautiful-hearted people. I know that I am not alone. Many Arab nationals of Gulf Cooperation Council states feel exactly the same. Believe me, were Hezbollah to collapse, the country would be flooded with new investment, businesses, banks and, of course, tourists! Lebanon would open its petals to flower again just as it did in the '50s, '60s and early '70s.

Reject Hezbollah's propaganda and lies. Its Iranian roots will never change. Its leaders may have been born in Lebanon but they have forfeited the right to call themselves Arabs. And as known drug dealers, money launderers, diamond smugglers and terrorists, both within Lebanon and without, they have forfeited their honour and are undeserving of any respect.

I am asking Lebanese Shi'ites to do what is right. Lebanon is badly injured and is bleeding politically, geopolitically and economically. Our arms are open to you. Come back to us and reclaim your Arab identity; not behind closed doors or in whispers. Have the courage to shout your rejection of what the Iranian Hezbollah stands for from the hilltops, in the squares and in the streets – and, rest assured, that in no time, we will be by your side to lift you out of this downward spiral before Lebanon, like several of its neighbours, are in need of intensive care.

8

Palestine: finding a path to peace with Israel

Introduction

WHY HAS NO DECISION been made over the Israeli-Palestinian conflict, particularly by the US, the so-called Leader of the Free World? Since 1970 world leaders have come and gone, promising to prioritize the Middle East Peace Process. No one can deny there is no quick fix to lasting peace, but the lack of any progress over the decades is shameful to say the least.

The nib of my pen has almost run dry from the numerous articles I have written on the subject. This is why, in 2014, I personally launched "Pathways to Peace" in Illinois, US, alongside former US President Jimmy Carter. It aims to work towards a more objective resolution by creating awareness in the American community to the real issues – and not those influenced by politics.

World leaders have tried and failed too many times to remedy the situation. We have seen Oslo Accords, Camp David summits and other high-level meetings where negotiations for a possible two-state solution have failed to make it off the table. We have seen handshakes and smiles as the meetings "successfully" draw to a close, but no sooner do the politicians walk away, so too does the hope.

In 2004, when then-US President George W. Bush denied the Palestinian people the right to return to their homeland during a meeting with Israeli Prime Minister Ariel Sharon, I wrote an open letter to Palestinian President Yasser Arafat urging him to cut ties with the US. (See "An open letter to President Yasser Arafat", 1 August 2004, later in this chapter.) Bush's sudden announcement not only denied Palestinians their legitimate right but also shattered hopes that had been held onto for decades. The move was obviously a desperate attempt by Bush to win over the Jewish voters in the subsequent presidential election. Sadly, the Palestinians paid the price.

Bush, like presidents before him, made little or no progress towards the two-state solution that he promised to bring about in 2003 when he announced his "Road Map". President Barack Obama – who visited

Israel and the Palestinian West Bank on his second term in office – admitted "It is a hard slog to work through all these issues." However, he boldly said that his administration would "actively and aggressively seek a lasting peace between Israel and the Palestinians". We should have known then that his unwillingness to challenge the Israel lobby would result in failure. Let us not forget the President had already secured a Nobel Peace Prize in his first year in office. What has he done to deserve it? It is shameful, and he should hand it back to someone more deserving.

I wonder too what the so-called Middle East Quartet made up of the United Nations (UN), the European Union (EU), Russia and the United States, has achieved. It is so far removed from the situation that it can achieve very little in my view. All it can do is talk and churn out ridiculous statements calling for "maximum restraint and avoidance of provocative rhetoric and actions" in an effort to quell violence. Nobody is going to listen to its official statements calling for calm to "restore confidence and hope in the viability of a negotiated two-state solution". Does it really think a drafted statement is going to reach the goal of ending the occupation that began in 1967? Or resolving the status of Jerusalem?

I personally endorse a one-state solution, even though Israel would never accept it. The Palestinian population is growing too fast for the Israelis' liking and soon there will come a day when the Palestinians outnumber the Israelis. I do not think a two-state solution will work, and I do not think the politicians do either, otherwise headway would have been made a long time ago. But no matter what the system, it is time that Israel is not considered "The Enemy". The world is growing tired of that age-old excuse. The Israelis need to be thought of as an ally instead. Both sides need to forgive and learn to respect one another.

I believe a federal government system is the most viable option. Jerusalem should be the capital where everyone could have the freedom to worship no matter what religion. But to get to that point – in theory – compromise has to be made on both sides – Israeli and Palestinian – to make any lasting deal work. However, it is an unfair competition in the first place. How can a midget compete with a giant? And as far as I can see no concessions have ever been made on Israel's part. As for the Palestinians, they have nothing to bargain with in the first place, and they do not have the support of the US that Israel has, nor the military or financial power.

The world has left Palestine to fend for itself, which has resulted in its falling under the influence of Iran. Hamas, the Palestinian faction that runs Gaza, keeps on rejecting any peace accords with Israel signed by the Western-backed Palestinian Authority (PA), while some Hamas leaders have suggested they would accept a Palestinian state on land Israel occupied in a 1967 war in return for a long-term truce. But they would continue to refuse to recognize Israel's right to exist.

Negotiations should be based on 1967 borders with occupied East Jerusalem as Palestine's capital. The right of return is set in stone within United Nations (UN) resolutions and should be non-negotiable. On those fundamentals there should be no compromise. Israel's apartheid wall should be dismantled. Jewish colonies on Palestinian land should be evacuated before being handed over to the PA to house a growing population. And to ensure prosperity, a "Marshall Plan" should be devised with those countries primarily responsible for the Palestinian catastrophe being the prime financial contributors.

Sadly, the Palestinians are lacking a strong leader since the days of Yasser Arafat. (See "Arabs must stand firmly for Palestinian statehood", 29 September 2011, later in this chapter.) Palestinian Authority President, Mahmoud Abbas, now in his eighties, is in the eleventh year of a four-year term, because the lack of Palestinian unity has prevented elections. His long reign is not down to his popularity as a leader. Most Palestinians do not want him, but their hands are tied.

Generations have suffered for far too long. Palestinians living in dire conditions in Gaza, the West Bank and Arab Jerusalem have no hope of a decent life. They are downtrodden and impoverished.

When the Palestinians were forced from their homes in 1948 the West came with promises they would return home "soon". They have repeatedly failed to come through with that promise. From 1948 until 1966 the Palestinians in Israel lived under military occupation, where they faced restrictions on freedom of movement and opinion. Land and property was taken from them. When military rule extended in 1966 there was a glimmer of hope. However, inequality remained – as it does still today. The Palestinians are discriminated against socially, politically and economically.

In 2007 I wrote a letter to the Palestinian President and Lebanese Prime Minister urging them to work together to help improve the living standards and job prospects for Palestinian men, women and children.

I have questioned numerous times why Middle Eastern issues are left to the West to sort out, only to make matters far worse than they were before. What gives America the moral legitimacy to meddle so deeply in affairs that are nearly 10,000km away from its capital?

Middle East issues should be left to Arab states to sort out. Over the past decade or so the Gulf states in particular have risen from the desert to become well-run countries that are flourishing thanks to the foresight of their leaders. They are politically strong, financially strong and have proven they are more than capable of competing and winning on the world stage. The West has tried so many times to find lasting answers for a two-state solution – and failed. Let Arab nations find the solution instead.

In my article, "Arabs must broker Israel–Palestine peace" (5 October 2010, later in this chapter), I wrote "... the Jerusalem site of Islam's third holiest shrine, the Haram Al Sharif, is not a Palestinian problem; it is an Arab problem, a Muslim problem. The Palestinian people are our brothers and sisters. Have they not been abandoned for long enough?" It is time for Arab leaders to step up to the plate.

In the meantime, Arab countries that host Palestinian refugees should treat them as human beings instead of political pawns. There are almost three million in Jordan, Syria and Lebanon, large numbers of whom are still consigned to squalid camps with the barest minimum of educational and medical facilities. Many do not have the right to work or own land; many more are stateless.

The Quartet on the Middle East has started waking up to the idea of getting talks between Israel and Palestine back on track with the help of key Arab states, involving Saudi Arabia, Jordan, Egypt and the League of Arab States. The French have also called for an international contact group that would include Arab states to help revive the process. Is it not worth a try?

We need to teach both parties to respect one another and believe that they are brothers and sisters. Imagine a country where Palestinians and Israelis work together to defend their land. If this were to happen – via a one-state solution – then it would be the new centre of the Mediterranean. The economic benefits for both parties would be plentiful. Investors would flood in. Mark my words, the country would prosper.

Palestine yesterday, Iraq today! Whose turn comes tomorrow?

1 February 2004

DURING A GATHERING with some Asian, European and American friends and colleagues, we talked about the grave and touching events in Palestine – events that are probably unprecedented politically and militarily.

Everyone expressed their displeasure and discomfort with the Arabs seeking the help of the US and Europe to solve their problems and heal their wounds. Some thought that the time had come for the Arabs to put their hands together, like any other nation, and solve their problems and disagreements themselves.

Because I believe that the opinions and comments expressed at that gathering were quite important, I wish to convey some of them to the readers.

One of those present said that the Israeli acts in the Palestinian occupied territories such as assassinations and the murdering of children, breaching of all beliefs, laws and religions, constituted an attempt to wipe out a whole nation, not only geographically, but probably from history too.

Another friend pointed to the horrible Israeli decision to execute a head of state under the guise and pretext of deporting him from his homeland.

A third friend interrupted to say that at the moment the Israeli decision was announced, it constituted a violation of a president's right to live in dignity and immunity in his country and amongst his people. Actually, it constitutes, as well, a flagrant call to exterminate the Palestinian president, following the ongoing annihilation of his people.

It was my turn to express my opinion. I pointed to the fact that the nature of the Zionist state, since its very early days, had produced nothing but such criminal acts. Consequently, its culture and attitude are restricted to a one-way path that leads only to more crimes.

Another friend, an Asian, said that what he could not comprehend, accept or justify, was the prevailing suspicious and disgraceful silence from the rest of the Arabs.

"What does not make sense", he added, "is that many Arab countries – people and rulers – can't even stand to denounce Sharon, who is attempting to crush the Palestinian people and their valiant resistance of the occupation".

We all agreed that the Israeli leadership is trying, in its devious way, to assassinate the Palestinian people through murdering their leaders one after the other; those leaders who are safeguarding Arab and Muslim honour, and who are protecting this nation from annihilation.

Another friend from Europe said that expelling Arafat, a leader elected legally by his people, who enjoys international legitimacy, is an insult, not only to the Arabs, but also to the whole world. He wondered how Israel dares to take such a decision and why the Arab states continue to turn a blind eye to this serious issue, satisfied by only issuing calls for help and statements of denunciation, or requesting European and US intervention to solve the problem.

Another friend pointed out that America is the supporter, ally and full partner of Israel. So, how could the jailer and executor be asked to be fair to his victim? He added that this applies to the American administration, and not to the American people, as many of them understand the seriousness of the Arab problems, especially the conflict concerning Palestine. He called on the Arabs to stop their escapism and their reliance on others and to stand as one man in support of the Palestinian people – a matter that they have the capability to do. He also stressed that the appeals made by presidents and officials, requesting Europe or America to interfere, were a waste of time. He stressed that neither America nor Europe would respond, and wondered why some Arabs do not even dare to criticize the US administration, adding how could they ask for help in resulting regional problems, knowing well the extent of the disregard for the Arabs and their cause?

I interrupted, to affirm that supporting the Palestinian cause required a firm resolution that could be taken only by people who strongly believed in the justice of our cause.

One of those present noted sadly: "Yesterday was Palestine, today is Iraq. Whose turn comes tomorrow?"

I believe that we should cease our appeals that lead us nowhere. Let us rely on ourselves for once, for a change, and not seek the help of the West. It is also time to stop relying on the US, which extends unlimited support to our enemy. We are the only party that knows what the solution is, because we know what the deep root of the problem is.

A letter to George W. Bush, President of the United States of America

1 August 2004

MR PRESIDENT, THE TIME HAS COME to admit and believe that miracles can happen. We know that you are a believer; some say that you are even a firm believer. This however is not the subject of this letter. The important thing is that you believe in one of the divine religions that is based on tolerance, sacrifice and love, a religion that tells you that miracles can happen at any time or place.

A miracle, if we may call it that, is occurring nowadays in occupied Palestine; a miracle planned, written and played out by the Palestinian people. It is not arrogance, but pride; nor violence, but strength of belief in God, in the Homeland and in the cause.

It is time to admit that the people of Palestine are determined not to surrender, either now or in the future. What would the F-16s, the Apaches and the latest Weapons of Mass Destruction (WMD) do to a nation that decided to take the road of martyrdom in order to live, and not the other way around?

Do you really believe that those children, the women and the elderly should be slain like sheep? Or that they do not possess human feelings? Is this really God's will? Do you not see that their perseverance is granted to them by God, to enable them to stand and face that huge arsenal, supplied and financed by the USA?

This legendary perseverance is even described by God in the Holy Quran, Surah Al-Ma'idah [5:21], when talking about Palestine in the era of Prophet Moses (PBUH): "Indeed within it is a people of tyrannical strength".

The people of Palestine will not give away its honour and dignity, the dignity of all Arabs; will not give away its holy places and the homeland of its ancestors. They are being annihilated, but they are standing firm, ready to die, but on their soil, to lie there forever.

These peoples have only their land and their belief; and they have had more than enough of deportations and taking refuge in other countries. They have had to endure much more than what most of the whole world could tolerate. Enough is enough.

We were told once that you are realistic; and that you appreciate democracy and support its growth around the world; and that you are a religious man. A true believer is one who respects the teachings of other religions. This must make you accept the irrevocable facts, concede God's instructions and admit the lawfulness of the Palestinian cause.

To admit one's faults is a virtue, correcting one's faults is yet a bigger virtue. A real man would not hesitate to correct his faults. I believe that this would be looked upon as a merit in his favour.

Mr President, One of our greatest leaders, Salad Eddin Al Ayoubi, who defeated the Crusaders and took Jerusalem back, set an example through his treatment of prisoners. He gave them freedom. They could choose to stay where they were living, as peaceful citizens, or leave in peace. He sent his personal physician to treat the captured enemy commander who was sick, with a message that read: "That is how our religion ordered us to treat our enemies".

History tells us also of an incident that Napoleon Bonaparte faced. His army encountered very stiff resistance in a certain area. And his soldiers could not overcome the resistance except by paying a very heavy price. Once they took position, he ordered his soldiers to salute the enemy soldiers who had been killed and to untie their commander who had been taken prisoner.

It is time for the US to take that brave stand and to force Sharon and his army to go, for the sake of peace. It is time to stop the annihilation of the Palestinians and to start the task of reaching a comprehensive and just solution for all parties. It is especially time to recognize the right of the Palestinian people to be able to survive.

Open letter to President Yasser Arafat

1 August 2004

PRESIDENT YASSER ARAFAT, I AM SURE that you have heard and read the recent declarations of the American President George Bush during his last meeting with Sharon. He was very open and removed the mask completely as he announced his personal and his government's beliefs:

- "No" to the right of the Palestinian People to return to their lands.
- "No" to the return of the 1949 borders.

This horrendous stand of the US requires, in my opinion, that we face it and encounter the seriousness of the current stage with whatever available means that we have.

Therefore, I would like, Mr President, to point out briefly some facts that I am sure you are aware of, so as not to lose our way in the middle of mirages and illusions.

Influential Arab forces have distanced themselves from the struggle over Palestine, neighbouring countries are living in cocoons, Iraq is suffering, some other countries are struggling to survive in a world subjected to US hegemony and the Arabs are subjected to unprecedented pressure.

You must from now on depend on the Almighty and on your persevering people and abandon all political deals adopted so far, which led us to this deteriorating situation.

What the American President and his government announced openly is in fact a decision to annihilate the new Palestinian generation that is not yet born. It requires a brave response from the Palestinians and the rest of the Arabs, that includes:

- Breaking all contacts and negotiations with the US administration.

- The League of Arab States must request all governments to stop their cooperation with the Bush administration and cease all exchange of information. They must also cease rejecting initiatives by Arab and Islamic countries. This is especially important for American and European countries.

- The immediate halting by some Arab countries, and by a part of the Palestinian authority, of their disgraceful cooperation with the US and Israel. This would lead to the loss of the cause, but it will not win immunity or priority from the superpower.

- All Arab countries must withdraw from international organizations, which are controlled by American-Israeli policies, including the UN.

- All Arab countries and the Palestinian authority must stop all forms of diplomatic or cultural relations with the Zionist entity and expel its representatives from all Arab territories.

- Using all means to recover occupied Arab territories by force and return them to their rightful owners, because what is taken by force can be recovered only by force.

The weakness of most Arab governments has led others to encroach upon Arabs and Muslims.

Abu Ammar, I would not try to be polite because this occasion does not need politeness. We must review all Arab policies, including yours, which brought us to the edge of disaster.

Wrong decisions by leaderships are not unheard of, but they are usually corrected after a thorough evaluation of the situation, and then a new path is selected.

Our Palestinian brothers are facing a declaration of annihilation, which is being executed. How should we respond if we do not change our policies? Do we know what we are doing?

You are requested to quit all policies adopted before and take the following resolutions immediately:

- Announce the cancellation of the road map, reject and revoke all agreements, particularly those of Oslo and Geneva, which contain the immediate policies and diplomacies that have led the Palestinian people to the present dilemma.

- Reaffirm the right of return as a basic right, as well as rejecting all settlements and the Zionist regime in Palestine.

- Proclaim a secular state for all people of all religions and ethnicities on the basis of democratic elections.

I am not calling on our people to commit suicide, but stressing a firm fact in our belief: never give up our rights nor our sovereignty and dignity, which is our land.

Brother Abu Ammar, the defeated Arab people are waiting for your decision, and this one is the most difficult one ever.

A Joint Letter to Mahmoud Abbas and Fouad Siniora

10 June 2007

PRESIDENT MAHMOUD ABBAS, Prime Minister Fouad Siniora, God All Mighty said in his Holy Book *"never hate anything and it is good for you, never love anything and it is bad for you"* True is God All Mighty

And our ancient wise men said "and many times harm is beneficial".

I say that in comment on the recent tragic bloody misfortunes that are happening in the Nahr Al Bared (cold river) camp and other camps as well. In consequence to that I write to you this letter, trying to conclude the significance of what is happening and hoping to find solutions to prevent its repetition forever, if God permits.

I promised myself, when I thought about the content of this letter, to steer away from politics and to concentrate on the human, social and economical aspects. But I find myself required to focus on two main rules that do not bare arguments, and that is before I begin my letter.

First; the total and utmost respect of the sovereignty of the Lebanese government on all Lebanese soil. And the nonexistence of any other force that can disturb or diminish in any case this dominance.

Second; the absolute faith in the sanctity of the "Right To Return" for our Palestinian brothers to their occupied land. This right was declared and acknowledged by a series of United Nations resolutions, and is proclaimed by all practices and international laws.

You both know very well that what is happening in the Nahr Al Bared camp is actually the result of compiled heritage, which unfortunately, both Lebanese and Palestinians have to bear without any misdeed of their own. Here and now, I would like to present a realistic solution that consists of four points;

First: to call for the creation of an "Arabic Construction Fund" that supplies buying decent housing and procures them to Palestinian refugees spread all over Lebanon, not just in camps. This Fund will be financed by Arabic countries, other nations, and businessmen. The contribution of the Arabic countries and others in this Fund should be publicized without periphrasis, that it is only temporary and will be requested at the time of the final solution of the Palestinian cause.

Second: to allow Palestinian refugees to hold decent jobs freely on Lebanese grounds. Economically flourished Lebanon will need all the workforce of its Lebanese citizens and their fellow Palestinians. The success of the Palestinians in the Gulf countries, who arrived in the 50's, is the biggest testimony to the high productivity and professionalism that they work with when allowed decent opportunities.

Third: to take swift action, in collaboration with the League of Arab States and its members, to facilitate the travel and passage to Palestinian refugees, for them to be treated with dignity and respect, and not to regard them as second class citizens constantly.

Fourth: the Lebanese government, with its army and all its military forces, must protect all the residents on Lebanese soil, including Lebanese citizens and Palestinians. And to apply strict control on unauthorized weapons possession.

My dear brothers, it pleases many to describe me as the biggest non-Lebanese investor in Lebanon, but it gratifies me more to be portrayed as Lebanon's biggest non-Lebanese enthusiast. As for the Palestinians and the Lebanese, I grew up in a home, a city and a country whose main obsession is to help and heel the pain of their brothers in Palestine.

Arabs need a proactive approach to Palestinian woes

1 July 2008

IF THERE WAS AN OLYMPIC MEDAL for talking politics, teams from this part of the world would take gold every time. If you browse the Arabic satellite networks you will find so-called experts endlessly discussing regional flashpoints and mulling over the exact same problem as their parents and grandparents did. The inescapable truth is that we are no nearer to witnessing a Palestinian state than we were 60 years ago when Israel was violently born.

Thousands of articles and books have been written on the subject. Untold numbers of documentaries have been produced and aired about it and there are annual conferences devoted to the subject. But what have these exposés and discussions yielded in terms of concrete results? Absolutely nothing.

It is not talkers we need but doers. When the region's leaders meet at League of Arab States summits we no longer anticipate earth-shattering conclusions. Instead, we are left with watered-down statements that everyone can grudgingly sign up to before they are filed away.

Where are the bold heroes, who will stand up for what they believe is right even in the face of adversity, and work towards cementing the Arab World instead of standing by and seeing it shredded apart? When will our leaders realize that only by standing shoulder to shoulder in a relationship of trust will we as a nation, the Arab nation, be heard and respected? It is time we had our own version of the North Atlantic Treaty Organization (NATO) with a commander-in-chief who has the authority to speak and act for all of us.

Sometimes when I read the morning papers I feel like I have entered a time warp. Across the front pages – or more often tucked away at the back – are the same regurgitated headlines about Gaza, the world's largest open-air prison, whose innocent civilian "inmates" struggle to find something to eat or medicines that can prolong someone's life.

An 18 April Reuters headline reads: "Carter calls Gaza blockade a crime and atrocity". The former US President says Palestinians in Gaza are being "starved to death". He called the ongoing situation "an abomination", which, of course, it is. Carter is outraged, but where is our outrage? How many of our leaders are prepared to get involved in a hands-on manner?

A few weeks ago, I watched one of the *Doha Debates*. The motion was "This house believes the Palestinians risk becoming their own enemy", which was carried by more than 70 per cent of the audience in Qatar.

It seems a large percentage of young Arabs now blame a people barely subsisting under decades of occupation for their own ills. Perhaps it is easier this way. They can return to their comfortable homes or go to meet friends in the café with their conscience intact. If the Palestinians are their own worst enemy, then everything is their fault and we get to sleep soundly at night.

Burying our heads in the sand may be comforting in the short run but as long as we shy away from taking charge of our own destiny we can expect to be disrespected and kicked around. We knew the Roadmap and Annapolis were based on empty promises that were unlikely to happen. We knew they were attempts to bluff us into thinking progress would be made, yet, between yawns, we went through the motions of believing.

And when are we going to quit pretending to ourselves that the US administration is our friend when we know in our hearts that it has only one real friend in the area; a friend that can massacre Palestinians, erect apartheid fences, expand illegal settlements and stockpile nuclear weapons with impunity. America is a great country and I am blessed with so many good American friends but I am under no illusion about its one-sided foreign policy, which is always angled in Israel's favour.

For how much longer are we willing to hand over our own decision-making to a foreign power, which we know full well is not acting in our interests but out of self-interest and is in cahoots with our enemies?

It is about time we came up with a plan and saw it through to its logical conclusion. We must decide whether Hamas is the real obstacle to peace or whether it merely supplies a pretext for Israel to ignore its obligations. We should mull over this question: if Hamas magically disappeared tomorrow would the Palestinians be closer to a final settlement with Israel?

Based on history, I do not think they would. After the death of Yasser Arafat in 2004, Israel announced a new turning point for peace. At the time Hamas did not feature in the equation. Fatah leader Mahmoud Abbas, a moderate, was in charge of the Palestinian Authority. But instead of working with Mr Abbas towards a settlement, Israel virtually ignored him.

His authority was further eroded when the US demanded free and fair elections, which brought Hamas to power. And as we know from leaked US Department of State memos, Washington, unhappy with the election result, pressured Abbas to sever ties with the Hamas leadership and work towards its physical ousting. American policy caused the split between Palestinians, whose cause has suffered accordingly.

How many more children in Gaza have to be slaughtered before our leaders say enough is enough? Many kids were killed recently and their crime was what? The killing is relentless. Israel will not stop it. The US sees no evil and speaks no evil when it comes to Israel. And all we in the Arab World are doing is holding televised debates that conclude that the Palestinians are their own worst enemy.

Unless we start calling the shots in our own neighbourhood and show that we mean business we will remain ineffective; destined to complain until our jaws ache, perhaps, for another 60 years when newspapers will run the same sad stories for our grandchildren to pour over. And how will our children excuse us when their own kids are asking why we talked so much and did so little?

Arab silence on Gaza is shameful

1 March 2009

THE TERRIBLE CARNAGE inflicted upon a starving people, caged in the dark, is too much to bear for anyone with eyes that see and a heart that beats. This unfolding crime against humanity must be stopped or else we should merely throw up our hands in despair and submit to the principle of "might is right".

As a human being, I am disgusted by the inaction of the so-called international community. For, indeed, our laws, conventions, treaties and international bodies are seemingly powerless in the face of Israel's inhumane aggression.

As an Arab, I am appalled at the deafening silence of the Arab leaders and governments. Have Arabs become so weak that our leaders cannot even express an opinion any longer? The angry sentiments on our streets are obvious but they are not being reflected by Arab governments.

When Israel's Foreign Minister Tzipi Livni was asked whether some Arab countries gave Israel the green light to launch its assault on Gaza, she hesitated before saying: "Moderate Arabs" share Israel's aim to destroy

Hamas. If there is a kernel of truth in her between-the-lines message then the entire Arab nation is being dishonoured.

Since when did "moderate" translate to "cowardly"? Does being a moderate mean we should relinquish our rights, abandon our families (brothers and sisters) and throw away our dignity?

Do we even deserve to equate ourselves with such heroes as Omar Bin Khattab, Khaled ibn Al Walid, Tariq ibn Ziyad, Al Moutassem Bellah, Salah El Din or those brave souls who lost their lives in 1948, 1967 and 1973 defending Arab lands and honour? They must be turning in their graves. We cannot hope to demand respect if we do not respect ourselves and our history.

Arab leaders have shied away from attending an Arab Summit Meeting as well as expelling Israeli ambassadors or cutting communications with the Jewish state – the very least they should do. I am no fan of Hamas or its ideology. I believe in one Palestinian authority, but this assault goes beyond politics. There is a far greater moral imperative that must be heeded. If you came across a burning house filled with women and children would you ask their political affiliation or dissect their worthiness before you tried to save them?

I cannot help wondering how the West is so tolerant and understanding of Iran when it comes to its nuclear file, while it is pretending to be deaf, dumb and blind to the Arab's central case. Iran, whose people are impoverished and whose economy is in shambles can dictate its terms to the international community, while our richer, more populated, more strategically located and historically rich Arab World is ineffectual.

Every hour the toll of death and misery rises. At this moment, over 550 Palestinians are dead and almost 3,000 are wounded. Gaza's parliament building, ministries, mosques, schools, a university and even ambulances have been targeted in Israel's quest to destroy "Hamas infrastructure", which is a reference to Israel's well-oiled propaganda machine.

In a cynical PR ploy, Israeli pilots drop leaflets warning householders to flee if they know there are rocket launchers hidden in nearby structures. But in such a tiny, densely populated enclave there is nowhere to run; no mountains or caves, no bomb shelters and only few basements.

Their long-depleted hospitals cannot cope with the influx of wounded bodies and soon they will have no fuel for generators, meaning premature babies will die. People are queuing for hours for a few loaves of bread; women have to gather sticks just to make tea, children are traumatized and unable to sleep, wondering if the next missile will bring their homes crashing around them. But no-one with the power to effect real change is listening.

Late on Saturday, the United Nations (UN) Security Council met in an emergency session but predictably the US blocked even a joint statement calling for an immediate ceasefire. George W. Bush has made his stance clear: the situation is entirely the fault of Hamas. President-elect Barack Obama who ran on the ticket for "change" remains mute. No matter who is commander-in-chief, US Middle East policies are likely to remain the same.

It is really disturbing to know that the European Union (EU) has contributed €3m in relief for people in Gaza. Would they have allocated such petty cash if the victim was a country other than Gaza? This help must be rejected and our Arab countries must provide the required assistance in full since they have the resources to do so.

Similarly, the EU has shown itself to be toothless. The Union's new Czech presidency actually described Israel's incursion as "defensive" rather than "offensive". When the region's most powerful army attacks cold and hungry innocents with the full force of its military might from land, sea and air this cannot be termed "self defence" by any stretch of the imagination.

Gaza's courageous people, who have somehow managed to survive an 18-month-long siege and who are now captive to the terrifying sounds of Israeli F-16s, helicopters, drones, bombs, missiles and tank shells, are calling out for help.

They do not want pretty words, fancy speeches or even well-meant protest marches. They want an end to their pain and imprisonment. Like every one of us, they simply want to live.

If Arabs turn their faces away from such desperate pleas then we might just as well fill our pockets with shekels, our hearts with stones and call ourselves Israelis for we will be just as culpable as they are for Gaza's destruction ... and ultimately our own.

Obama should choose right over self-interest

7 June 2010

WORDS FAIL ME when it comes to describing how I feel about Israel's murder of civilians in international waters. There were over 600 men, women, children and a one-year-old infant on the *Mavi Mamara* – one of six aid ships sailing to Gaza under the banner of the Free Gaza Movement in hopes of breaking the cruel, illegal blockade.

Their only weapons were their kind hearts. Their only intention was to cast a spotlight on the terrible plight of 1.5 million souls confined to the world's largest open-air prison. Yet Israel sent its naval vessels and zodiacs to surround them before its elite commandoes dropped out of helicopter gunships, when nine unarmed activists were killed and dozens injured. One female passenger described the scene a "river of blood".

The French Minister of Foreign Affairs, Michèle Alliot-Marie, said she was "shocked", but we have come to expect this barbaric behaviour from the Jewish state. Turkey's Prime Minister Recep Tayyip Erdoğan has expressed rage. His fury is understandable but what use is verbalizing anger if Israel is allowed to get away with such atrocities time and time again? It is just like shouting at the wind. What is needed is concerted international action.

Even before the captured flotilla had docked at the Israeli port of Ashdod, Israel's slick propaganda machine was put into gear. They were not peace activists but terrorists with links to Hamas and Al Qaeda, said one Israeli official, which is laughable when one considers they have all now been released without charge and sent back to their home countries. They were armed with guns and planned to attack our soldiers, said another, which proved to be blatant lie when all that was shown to the press were slingshots, marbles, scissors and metal bars; items that the besieged passengers used to defend themselves.

Perhaps the greatest insult to our intelligence is this: Israel claims that it was within its rights to infringe Turkish sovereignty in international waters by killing its citizens and seizing its vessels together with those sailing under the flags of other countries. This was not only a gross infringement of international law but also an act that could be interpreted as an act of war. Just imagine if the shoe had been on the other foot and Turkey had seized Israeli vessels and shot Israeli civilians.

Israel had not been attacked by any of the ships. Its territorial waters had not been penetrated. Besides, its ally Turkey had thoroughly checked the boats' cargo for weapons. Therefore, Israel's assertion that it was acting in self-defence does not ring true. In reality, Israel was not defending its citizens. It was defending its much condemned policy of stripping the people of Gaza of their God-given freedom.

Thankfully, on this occasion, the international community is not falling for Israel's spin. The backlash from European, Arab and Asian nations was instant. The European Union (EU) and the United Nations (UN) loudly condemned the incident. Several countries summoned Israeli ambassadors; others called for an end to Gaza's strangulation. An emergency session of the UN Security Council was held when Turkey, Lebanon and the Palestinian National Authority drafted a strong condemnation urging an independent probe into what took place.

But, as we might have anticipated, Israel's ally the US – a veto-holding permanent member of the UN Security Council – negotiated with Turkey to deprive the statement of its bite. How the Israeli Prime Minister Benjamin Netanyahu must have chuckled when he heard that the UN Security Council expects the perpetrator Israel to investigate itself. This is tantamount to asking an accused convict to be his own policeman, judge and jury.

Following President Barack Obama's speech in Cairo a year ago when he reached out to the Arab and Muslim World, this region dared to hope that, at last, here was an American leader who was prepared to be even-handed and fair-minded. In fact, all his grand promises have come to naught. The Israelis are still expanding illegal colonies on the West Bank, still constructing an illegal "apartheid wall" on Palestinian land and still show no real interest in discussing a Palestinian state.

The US President has shown only a certain coolness towards Netanyahu, who, during his last visit to the White House was deprived of the usual joint press conference and photo-ops. In response, Obama faced a barrage of criticism from the notoriously pro-Israel Congress as well as from members of his own Democratic Party. Netanyahu's scheduled visit to Washington this week was meant to repair the damage. With mid-term elections coming up in November, Obama is wary of upsetting the powerful pro-Israel lobby which can make or break political careers.

President Obama is fond of quoting the man who was arguably America's greatest leader, Abraham Lincoln. In fact, he is a long way from approaching that great man's stature. Lincoln stood up against slavery when it was not politically fashionable to do so. He was a person who put integrity and truth before personal benefit. On the other hand, President Obama refuses to condemn Israel's crimes on the high seas or on Palestinian territory for fear of risking his re-election chances.

If Obama stands firm and does right, he actually improves his chances to win re-election. When George W. Bush had a showdown with Israel over settlements, he had 90 per cent public approval. With an approval rating hovering at around a low of 46 per cent, Obama is unlikely to achieve a second term in office. He should summon the courage to stand up to the Israeli gangsters, who are leading his country and the rest of the world by the nose. He may be uncomfortably positioned between two feuding US allies but as Prime Minister Erdoğan has said, he is not expected to choose between Turkey and Israel but between right and wrong.

Obama is not doing the US any favours either. At least two of his top military commanders have said that America's perceived bias in favour of Israel is endangering US interests and the lives of American troops throughout the Middle East.

By contrast, the Turkish Prime Minister should be applauded for his humanitarian concerns for the residents of Gaza and his willingness to speak out against the Israeli pirates to the point of endangering Israeli-Turkish relations and alienating Washington. In recent times, Erdoğan has stood firmly against Israeli onslaughts on Gaza and has proved to be fearless when it comes to calling a spade a spade.

It is embarrassing that the only regional leader to staunchly defend the Palestinians is a Turk. Where are the Arabs? Yes, Egypt temporarily opened the border between Rafah and Gaza. Yes, the League of Arab States held an emergency meeting of Foreign Ministers on Wednesday, but to what end? Will they send ships to pierce the blockade? Will those countries which have signed peace treaties with Israel seek to end them? I think not.

Instead, they have decided to make Israel answerable to the International Court of Justice and have promised to break the siege by all means. Fine talk, but will it be translated into action? Let us see.

Arabs must broker Israel–Palestine peace

5 October 2010

PALESTINIAN PRESIDENT Mahmoud Abbas has been thrown to the wolves. No matter how sincere he may be in his efforts to bring a Palestinian state into being, all the cards are being held by Israel and its ally the United States. He is like a man trying to negotiate a bank loan without income or collateral assets hoping he will find the bank manager in a charitable mood. Unfortunately, there is nothing remotely charitable about the Israeli Prime Minister Benjamin Netanyahu. He rejected a two-state solution until he was pressured by US President Barack Obama into paying lip service to the notion.

To be brutally frank, the leader of a people who have been suffocated under occupation for more than six decades has very few bargaining chips. Gamal Abdel Nasser once said: "What was taken by force must be restored by force."

In principle, there is a grain of truth to that. For instance, if Egypt had not triumphed in the 1973 war, it would not have regained the Sinai Peninsula, captured by Israel in 1967. When President Anwar El Sadat negotiated the 1979 Egypt–Israel Peace Treaty, he sat down with his protagonists as an equal partner armed with his country's – Egypt's – battlefield victories.

The Palestinians have no such clout. Their fighters have fought bravely against the occupier since 1948. Much Palestinian blood was sacrificed during the First and Second Uprising but AK-47s and rockets forged by local blacksmiths are no match for tanks, drones, F-16s, Apache attack helicopters, missiles, cluster bombs and white phosphorus.

Moreover, despite the right of an occupied people to resistance and self-defence, due to the West's overwhelming pro-Israel bias, when Palestinians use violence they are designated "terrorists". Thousands of such Palestinians labelled as "terrorists" are children locked up in Israel's prisons for daring to throw stones at soldiers.

Indeed, as current peace discussions are stalled President Abbas has assured Israel that there will be no violent reaction in the case of a breakdown, which must have been music to Netanyahu's ears. "We tried the Intifada and it caused us a great deal of damage," Abbas said. That smacks of defeatism but it also happens to be true. Even the fiercest lion cannot prevail when faced with a hunter's rifle.

So, if the Palestinian leader has publicly acknowledged the futility of armed resistance and does not have any chips to bring to the table, what does he have to bargain with?

Not much. Not only is President Abbas not authorized to speak for all Palestinians – who are split between Fatah and Hamas – his presidential tenure expired over a year ago. Therefore, his signature on any peace agreement would not be worth the paper it was written on. Within no time, Hamas, Islamic Jihad and other militant organizations would be lobbing rockets at Israeli population centres in the Negev when any peace deal would be considered null and void.

Over the past weeks, one thing has become crystal clear. As far as the Israeli leadership is concerned the current push for peace is nothing more than a time-wasting chore to keep the international community off its back.

Netanyahu's refusal to extend the settlement freeze shows a complete absence of goodwill as does his insistence that President Abbas acknowledge Israel as a Jewish state. Israel's leader knows full well that however high the stakes, Mr Abbas cannot accept that precondition without compromising refugee rights of return and the rights of Israeli Arabs to continued citizenship.

If Abbas were foolish enough to acquiesce over this ideological hot potato, he would be branded a traitor by his own people. It saddens me to watch the Palestinian leader shaking hands with Netanyahu for camera-ops as though they were recently reunited best friends. He is genuinely open to compromise but Israel's crafty fox is an accomplished actor with a hidden agenda. He is doing everything he can to gum up the works.

With Israeli colonists already laying the foundations for new constructions on the occupied West Bank, and Israel's Minister of Foreign Affairs Avigdor Lieberman promoting an exchange of territory mostly populated by Israeli Arabs as part of a land swap, President Abbas has put the peace talks on hold until he meets with other Arab leaders. Lieberman may be a loose-lipped renegade but Netanyahu has not taken him to task or said anything to indicate his disapproval of that revolting plan.

President Abbas is shortly expected to consult with Arab heads of state at a League of Arab States summit to be held in Cairo. I can picture it now: lots of handshaking and hugs, plenty of heated discussion and condemnation of Israel, and a nice, neat joint statement to be filed away with hundreds of others. Sorry, but this simply is not good enough.

Israel's occupation of the Palestinian land, and, in particular, the Jerusalem site of Islam's third holiest shrine, the Haram Al Sharif, is not a Palestinian problem; it is an Arab problem, a Muslim problem. The Palestinian people are our brothers and sisters. Have they not been abandoned for long enough? What kind of family is it that stands by doing nothing while their siblings or cousins are humiliated, starved, displaced, imprisoned, assassinated and bombed?

Ideally, parties involved in a dispute should be the ones to solve it, but when those parties fail to resolve those differences time and again, they should take another tack. President Abbas cannot go it alone so he should step away from the negotiating table in favour of an Arab committee made up of, say, leaders from Egypt, Saudi Arabia, Syria and Turkey.

Once Mr Abbas has garnered a majority consent from his people in the form of a referendum, he should issue a written authority or a "power of attorney" empowering those countries to negotiate on his behalf. The US and Europe should also remove themselves from the arena as they can no longer pretend to be honest brokers. They inundate Israel with carrots sent without sticks.

Arab leaders must step up to the plate before Netanyahu and his expansionist ilk smash it to pieces. They are already blaming President Abbas for the failed talks and, no doubt, laughing up their sleeves. This giant con has gone on for far too long already. I appeal to every Arab king, president, prime minister, emir and sheikh. Don't let them get away with it! Do not just listen to President Abbas. For once, do something constructive to help him!

Middle East peace requires fresh thinking

18 June 2011

ISRAEL'S FIRST PRIME MINISTER David Ben Gurion tried to reassure Israelis that Palestinians would never return to their homes. "We must do everything to ensure they never do return … . The old will die and the young will forget," he said. He could not have been more wrong; the word "forget" is not in the Palestinians' lexicon. For 63 long years, they have borne terrible hardships, suffered unbearable humiliation and fought for freedom with nothing but stones and their bare hands. But, sadly, they not only face a cruel adversary, their own leaders have let them down.

The late Palestinian President Yasser Arafat had his faults, but he was a great patriot who genuinely loved his people. He did his utmost to forge the "Peace of the Brave" with Prime Minister Yitzhak Rabin. However, when George W. Bush came to power the man who was once the most frequent visitor to the Clinton White House was treated like a pariah by the Americans while the Israelis kept him prisoner in his bombed-out Ramallah compound.

Arafat was not able to achieve what he set out to do because he refused to compromise the future of Palestinian children. Nevertheless, he earned his people's loyalty and spoke for almost all of them. The same cannot be said of those who came after him. Mahmoud Abbas and Prime Minister Salem Fayyad lack charisma and because they have put too much faith in the US intermediary they have lost currency with the voting public.

And, judging by "The Palestinian Papers" leaked by Al Jazeera, they were willing to accept any crumbs that fell from Israel's table and sell out the refugees' right of return. Moreover, they were alerted about Israel's Operation Cast Lead in Gaza in advance and, under pressure from the Obama White House, they shamefully "stonewalled" a United Nations

Human Rights resolution supporting the Goldstone Report on war crimes committed during that offensive.

Likewise, Hamas has little credibility to negotiate peace, primarily because it is funded by Iran and has been classed as a terrorist organization by the US, the European Union (EU), the UK, Canada and Japan. In any case, the Israeli Prime Minister Benjamin Netanyahu has said there will be no peace negotiations with any Palestinian Authority that includes members of Hamas.

So where do the Palestinians go from here?

It seems to me that both Fatah and Hamas must put their people before their political ambitions and admit failure. There is no time to waste as long as Israel continues expanding Jewish colonies on the West Bank and ousting Palestinians from East Jerusalem. The 22 per cent of their homeland that Palestinians were due to receive under the Oslo Accords is shrinking year on year and it is probable that soon a two-state solution will no longer be viable.

I have thought hard about this impasse and would suggest a practical option: the current Palestinian government should agree to act as a caretaker authority charged with the day-to-day running of the territories. At the same time, it should work with prominent Palestinians around the world to appoint a committee solely responsible for negotiating peace.

This would be made up of respected Palestinian individuals chosen on the basis of their loyalty, reputations and resumés rather than on their bank accounts or crony connections; every potential member would be thoroughly security vetted and have a proven record of success.

Included in such committee with the irrevocable power to negotiate on behalf of all Palestinians could be a senior representative of the Gulf Cooperation Council (GCC). To kick-start the process the Palestinian Authority (PA) and other Palestinian bodies could organize a conference – under the GCC's umbrella if desired – to which eligible candidates would be invited. To give selected candidates legitimacy, a referendum should be held on the West Bank and Gaza as well as in the diaspora under the auspices of United Nations Relief and Works Agency for Palestine Refugees in the Near East (UNRWA) with which all Palestinian refugees are registered. With committed backing from Saudi Arabia and all Gulf states, the committee would have far more international clout than the PA has ever had.

All negotiations should be based on 1967 borders with East Jerusalem as the capital of the new Palestinian state. The right of return is set in stone within UN resolutions and should be non-negotiable. On those fundamentals there should be no compromise.

Israel's apartheid wall should be dismantled but ideally Jewish colonies constructed on Palestinian land should be evacuated before being handed over to the PA to house the growing Palestinian population. And to ensure the prosperity of the new state a "Marshall Plan" should be devised with those countries primarily responsible for the Palestinian catastrophe being the main financial contributors.

In the meantime, those Arab countries that host Palestinian refugees should begin treating them as human beings instead of political pawns. There are almost three million in Jordan, Syria and Lebanon, large numbers of whom are still consigned to squalid camps with the barest minimum of educational and medical facilities. Many have been abandoned without the right to work or own land; many more are stateless.

Governments have been promising them that one day they will go back to their homes for too long. For the elderly still holding keys to houses that no longer exist that would be ideal but for the sake of Palestinian babies born with a God-given right to a decent and prosperous future, reality must be faced.

Stateless persons living inside camps need urgent rescuing. They should be offered full citizenship and if they get the chance to go home one day, it will be up to them whether to stay or go. It is hypocritical for Arab leaders to complain at the way Israel treats Palestinians when so many have been condemned to a life of misery by their own Arab brothers. Which wealthy brother would allow a sibling or cousin to drink polluted water or rot in a rat-infested shanty town?

Fresh ideas as well as a strong commitment from the Arab World to get involved are needed before Palestinian hopes can be realized. The old guard has had its day; time for dynamic new faces willing to roll up their sleeves and think out of the box.

Arabs must stand firmly for Palestinian statehood

29 September 2011

EVER SINCE PRESIDENT Yasser Arafat passed away, the Palestinians have lacked a strong leader with the authority to speak on their behalf. His successor Mahmoud Abbas took an entirely different approach to the issue of statehood in the belief that Arafat's confrontational stance had failed and the road to peace ran through Washington. And to that end he has been unfailingly conciliatory and ready to compromise even on some of his people's basic demands. His statements were always designed to be non-inflammatory and whereas the Israelis and their American backers thought of him as a good guy – perhaps even a pushover – Palestinians themselves expected a lot more from him.

Last Friday, in the United Nations (UN) General Assembly, President Abbas was a different man. His appeal for Palestinian statehood was not couched in diplomatic jargon. He spoke calmly and truthfully about the crippling effects of occupation, the illegal Israeli blockade of Gaza and the need for Palestinian refugees to return to their homeland. He insisted that any future Palestinian state would be drawn on 1967 borders with Jerusalem as its capital and stressed that while he was keen to return to the peace table, he would not do so as long as Israel continued its policy of settlement expansion.

He told the world how Palestinian hopes and dreams have been dashed on the rock of hollow promises for decades, evoking Arafat's plea to the Assembly in 1974 "Don't let the olive branch fall from my hand". "Enough, enough, enough" was the main thrust of the Palestinian leader's message and judging by the rapturous applause and the lengthy standing ovation he received, for the first time in decades the world was truly listening.

Almost overnight, President Abbas has turned into a dignified statesman with gravitas. His courage in defying the US president's "order" not to go the UN route else risk damaging the peace process should be saluted. His tenaciousness to fast-track the UN Security Council vote in the face of outrageous threats from the Netanyahu government, the White House and the US Congress has proved that this time he means business.

The fact that Tel Aviv has threatened to withhold Palestinian taxes should the bid proceed while Foreign Minister Avigdor Lieberman warns of unspecified "tough repercussions" illustrates Israel's moral bankruptcy when the PLO (Palestine Liberation Organization) has long put down its guns to proceed down the highway of international legality.

While Congress mulls cutting US aid to Palestinians and punishing United Nations Relief and Works Agency for Palestine Refugees in the Near East (UNRWA) and the UN body with the cessation of US funding, President Obama says his country will veto Palestinian chances of statehood in the UN Security Council. It is a shameful reflection on a country that was once a beacon of justice and democracy that his diplomats are busy behind closed doors twisting the arms of diplomatically and economically weaker UN Security Council members to vote "no", as former PA negotiator Hanan Ashrawi has recently disclosed. Such behaviour is reminiscent of old Chicago mafia tactics in the days when godfathers would browbeat witnesses against them not to turn up in court while seeking to pay off jury members.

As someone who believed that President Barack Obama was a just man eager to be peacemaker, I was shocked and disappointed to hear his own address to the Assembly that contravened the message he delivered on the same podium last year. As many commentators have pointed out, this time he sounded more like Israel's lawyer than an honest broker, neglecting to mention either 1967 borders or Israeli settlements, which he had previously said are obstructing peace.

It is a bitter irony that while he praised Egyptians, Syrians, Yemenis and Libyans for pursuing freedom, he seeks to thwart the Palestinians from getting theirs. He said nothing about Palestinian suffering preferring to focus on America's "unshakeable" commitment to Israel's security. "Let's be honest with ourselves: Israel is surrounded by neighbors that have waged repeated wars against it," he said, neglecting to mention Israel's invasions of Lebanon and onslaughts on Gaza.

He spoke of Israeli citizens killed by rockets while ignoring the thousands of civilians murdered by the Israel Defense Forces (IDF). He brought up the six million Jews slaughtered during the Holocaust – a dark shadow on Europe's history that has nothing to do with Arabs who lived peacefully with Jewish populations prior to the 1948 Nakba. I wonder whether Mr Obama even believes his own words when he has been such a strong proponent of a Palestinian state based on 1967 borders until now. Cynics say that he has put his principles aside to garner Jewish and evangelical Christian votes in upcoming presidential elections; they might be right.

For us Arabs, the bottom line is this. We cannot and must not in all good conscience allow President Abbas to face the music from the US and Israel alone. We have allowed the Palestinian struggle to fall from our hands for far too long and now that we see that the international community overwhelmingly empathizes with their cause, we should not only embrace it but be prepared to put ourselves on the line in its defense. Our leaders should unite against any nation that prevents Palestinians from attaining statehood in the same way that the Israelis, Americans and their sycophants are united to thwart Palestinian rights. Because the role of the League of Arab States is not being properly met, as its host country remains unstable and various member countries need to take care of grave internal problems, I believe it should be temporarily moved to a Gulf Cooperation Council (GCC) state with a respected GCC figure as its Secretary General who can speak with authority on the Palestinian issue and will be taken seriously.

We must open our hearts and our pockets to the Palestinian Authority and sanction any country that stands in the way of right. This year, the Arab people have gained their voice and this is what they want. Ours is no longer a region where the wishes of citizens can be disregarded; our people are with the Palestinians and their leaders should reflect their will.

Winston Churchill once said: "The pessimist sees the difficulty in an opportunity, while the optimist sees the opportunity in difficulty." For the sake of the Palestinian people and the stability of our region we Arabs must grasp this opportunity to show our commitment to justice and regain our *karama* (dignity) on the world's stage whatever the cost. Our once proud Arab nation needs to prove its relevancy once and for all or it will splinter and become a mere historical afterthought. Now is the time to become brothers, real brothers, again and lift our own Palestinian people out of their misery.

Tell me! Who is with me? Are *you* with me? Or are people like me who care deeply about old-fashioned concepts of honour and truth simply crying to the wind?

Will Arabs ever regain their dignity?

7 October 2011

I HAVE ALWAYS THOUGHT of myself as a proud Arab but lately I have been seriously wondering whether there is anything to feel proud about. There was a time when our leaders spoke, and the world heard them loud and clear. But those days are, unfortunately, long gone. I cannot comprehend the present generation of Arab leaders. Where is their courage? What happened our Arab dignity? They behave like they do not have eyes to see, ears to hear or the ability to feel their people's anguish.

Nevertheless, until I turned on my television some mornings ago to catch the news, I still held on to the belief that there was hope for the Arab nation, perhaps because that was what I needed to believe. But what I witnessed on Al Jazeera was for me the last straw. I cannot continue wearing rose-coloured spectacles when there is an unpleasant reality staring me in the face.

What I saw was a live feed of a rather grand conference on Palestine. I was initially delighted to listen to a Kuwaiti official addressing the delegates on the topic; that was until I saw that Iran's revolutionary leader the Ayatollah Sayyid Ali Khamenei was presiding when I was shocked to realize it was being held in the Iranian capital Tehran.

It turns out that this was the fifth time that Iran has hosted a conference on the Palestinian Intifada attended by influential Arabs such as the parliamentary Speakers of Sudan, Iraq, Kuwait, Syria and Qatar as well as parliamentary delegations from Lebanon, Egypt and Jordan. My first thought was what are our Arab leaderships doing sending politicians to discuss Palestine on the soil of their greatest enemy, an enemy that is infiltrating Arab states so as to gain influence by indoctrinating our people with extremist Iranian ideology, funding militant groups and trumpeting territorial rights over Gulf states – and which is probably developing a nuclear capability that will alter the regional balance of power forever? As far as I am concerned this is an enemy that is just as dangerous to Arabs as Israel; perhaps even more so as Israel cannot cross certain red lines as long as Washington is there to rein it in.

I could not help questioning how those Arab delegates felt inside as they flew to Iran, whose people are being crushed by a tyrannical regime, to talk about a topic so dear to every Arab's heart – and especially when there are few such conferences being held in their own countries and none that I can think of on a similar scale. Surely any such international summit on Palestine should be hosted by an Arab country.

If I were in their place I would have been ashamed at the reticence of Arab leaders to get involved, allowing non-Arab countries like Iran and Turkey to step into the breach. It is sad to say but people like the Turkish Prime Minister Recep Tayyip Erdoğan and Iran's President Mahmoud

Ahmadinejad often use rhetoric that sounds more "Arab" than that of their Arab counterparts. In the case of Mr Erdoğan, however, I very much appreciate his efforts because I believe they are sincere, whereas Khamenei and Ahmadinejad use the Palestinian cause to further their own agenda.

It goes against the grain but, in all honesty, I have to admit that the Iranians are smarter than we are; they have a clear agenda and a carefully-designed master plan on how to implement it. Unlike us, Iranians are focused on their country's progress. Indeed, most successful nations on the planet put their own interests first, which we Arabs fail to do. Instead, we live from day to day hoping for the best. We do not formulate our future; we don't have a unified economic, diplomatic or military strategy. We sit back and react to situations as they happen rather than proactively shaping the region to suit our needs. We are like straws blowing in the wind, which is why we are thought of as weak and ineffectual nowadays.

This is the first time ever that I have experienced such negativity and doubt as to what tomorrow holds for us. It looks like this generation is lost; I can only pray that the next will show their mettle and regain the respect in which we were once held during the era of Gamal Abdel Nasser, Sheikh Zayed bin Sultan Al Nahyan, King Faisal bin Abdulaziz Al Saud and the one man able to hold all Palestinians together, Yasser Arafat. Those leaders had their faults but the one common thread that bound them together was the courage of their convictions. They did not bow their heads to foreign powers and were never fearful of speaking their mind.

I am at the end of my rope, constantly worrying about the fate of our Arab nation – or even whether it exists at all – and I know that there are still a few true Arabs who are as exhausted as I am trying to warn our leaders to change direction. With the League of Arab States in disarray due to the Arab Spring, I genuinely believed that Gulf Cooperation Council (GCC) heads of state would guide us and protect us. But now that I have seen their emissaries kowtowing to Iran, I think only God can help us now.

All I can do is leave those in power with some food for thought from the late Martin Luther King Jr who once said: "Not only will we have to repent for the sins of bad people; but we also will have to repent for the appalling silence of good people."

Prisoner swap pours cold water on peace

24 October 2011

I HAVE LIVED LONG ENOUGH to know that not everything is as it seems at first glance. I am sure that most Arabs view the prisoner exchange between Israel and Hamas as a good deal. After all, who can complain about exchanging one skinny youth weighing around 45 kilograms for 1,020 Palestinian prisoners, including many who were serving life sentences? Sounds great until one analyses the motivations and ramifications.

While I fully understand the joy of Palestinian families welcoming home their fathers, husbands, sons and brothers or happy in the knowledge they are free abroad, the bigger picture looks bleak.

Firstly, the swap represents an enormous public relations coup for the Israeli Prime Minister Benjamin Netanyahu whose popularity within Israel and without has waned over the past year. The Israeli newspapers have complained that the freed Israeli conscript Gilad Shalit was interviewed on Egyptian TV without commenting negatively about Netanyahu inviting Israel's television cameras to broadcast his warm reception of the once unknown boy turned international celebrity. The Israeli media has also hammered home that while Shalit was handed over looking pale and malnourished, the Arab prisoners appeared healthy.

Not only does Shalit's homecoming elevate Netanyahu's re-election chances, it has also quelled internal protests against rising prices. More importantly, it has illustrated the value Israel puts on one of its own while giving the impression that Arab lives are cheap. I would echo the points made by Faisal Al Qasim in his column "Israel's Shalit eclipses Arab Shalloots": "Why have the whole world including many Arab leaders been so busy trying to free Shalit when there are tens of thousands of Arab 'Shalloots' languishing in Israeli and other prisons unnoticed? Why are they so cheap and unimportant?" he writes.

Al Qasim is also right to characterize this as "humiliating". The fact that a number of the prisoners have been packed off to foreign countries rather than their homeland is yet a further humiliation – and at least two of the 27 female prisoners refused to cross from Egypt into Gaza saying they did not want to be imprisoned there.

Notable, too, is the high proportion of senior Hamas prisoners released compared to members of Fatah as well as the glaring absence of two politically influential Palestinians – presidential contender Marwan Barghouti – a man the Israeli writer Uri Avnery has called "Palestine's Mandela" – and Secretary General of the Popular Front for the Liberation of Palestine (PFLP) Ahmed Sa'adat, whose trial was blasted by Amnesty International as being unfair. Hamas has stated any insistence their release would have scotched the deal but there is little doubt that their continued imprisonment deprives Hamas of serious political competition.

Humiliation aside, the swap has undermined the Palestinian President Mahmoud Abbas who has been trying to secure a prisoner exchange for five years, mainly due to the stubborn attitudes of Netanyahu and Hamas leader Ismail Haniyah. Hamas is now showering itself with glory for succeeding where Abbas failed and is basking in the glow of a rocketing domestic approval-rating in Gaza and the West Bank.

Apparently, Netanyahu prefers to do business with his sworn Islamist enemies rather than the man he calls his peace partner. Of course, he knew full well that Hamas would be greatly bolstered by the deal and that by agreeing to it he was upping the potential for further abductions of Israeli soldiers to be used as pawns. Indeed, Gaza's militant groups have openly stated their eagerness to grab more "Shalits".

You might find Netanyahu's thinking hard to fathom. But there is method in his madness. At a time when Israel is under heavy international pressure to return to the peace table and quit colony expansion, the more Palestinian enemies in positions of power Netanyahu can cite, the more his hand is strengthened. And should Hamas win the next election, he can put peace on the backburner indefinitely on the basis that Hamas is a terrorist organization, without alienating the international community.

Just look at the timing. The Palestinian National Authority (PNA) lodged its application for statehood recognition in the United Nations when world opinion towards Israel was at an unprecedented low and the Palestinians were at last being seen as the victims of occupation they are. However, the sight of a traumatized Israeli resembling a concentration camp victim going home to his hilltop village when Hamas leaders are thumping their chests and lauding armed militancy may alter the equation.

Indeed, to imagine that Israel and Hamas have been in cahoots over this is not that much of a stretch of the imagination when one remembers that Hamas was partly a creation of the Israeli Mossad formed to split and thus weaken the Palestinian people. Zeev Sternhell, a historian with the Hebrew University of Jerusalem once said: "Israel thought it was a smart ploy to push the Islamists against the Palestinian Liberation Organization." Pitting the Palestine Liberation Organization (PLO) against Hamas was also a strategy of the Bush administration once they discovered their push for transparent and monitored elections boomeranged against Western interests.

Now Netanyahu is using the exact same tactic; except that as far as he is concerned his mild-mannered friend Abbas is, in fact, the worst enemy of Israeli expansionist plans. Israel cannot exist as an aggressive, militarized occupier without a visible enemy when officials can trumpet their worn out "poor little Israel" pretexts. Netanyahu must have shuddered when he saw the rousing welcome and standing ovation President Abbas received at the United Nations (UN) General Assembly, especially when his own speech elicited scant applause. One thing is for sure, if one of Hamas' political leaders, Ismail Haniyah or the organization's head Khaled Meshaal based in Syria – both in the pocket of Tehran – were to stand before the UN General Assembly, the chamber would empty.

And so the power play continues. Hamas, its backer Iran and Israel all have something in common; they do not want peace. In movies the good guys usually win; I can only hope that the Palestinian people are wise enough to see through the tricks and back the right side.

Realpolitik can alleviate Palestinian suffering

4 May 2012

THERE IS NO CAUSE dearer to my heart than that of the Palestinians and it saddens me greatly that international efforts towards a Palestinian state have been placed on the backburner. In the 1980s, I got together with Emirati friends to form associations committed to supporting the Palestinian people's right of return under international law, which is now a far less viable prospect than it was 40 years ago. Unfortunately, the idea of a Palestinian state is on the point of being shelved as a mythical Shangri-La unless we take advantage of a sliver of space in a rapidly closing window.

This tragic state of affairs is primarily due to Israel's unwillingness to compromise and its unending colony expansion and theft of Palestinian land in East Jerusalem and the West Bank. The international community is also guilty by default. Most United Nations (UN) member countries, including the US, affirm their backing for a Palestinian state, yet shy away from holding any Israeli government's feet to the fire. However, I do not intend to waste column inches apportioning blame. The blame game gets us nowhere. Each side has its own concerns, gripes and grudges that are set in stone.

So let us put aside the rights and wrongs of the argument and get real.

There is one point on which everyone with an ounce of compassion can agree. Palestinians, whether on the West Bank or Gaza or in the diaspora are condemned to live lives that most of us would not wish on our worst enemies. Arab governments can do little to help Palestinians struggling under occupation; it is not in their hands. But there is nothing to prevent them from improving the living conditions of Palestinian refugees herded into squalid camps within their own borders.

A visit to one of those camps in Lebanon and elsewhere is an emotionally painful experience, not recommended for the faint-hearted. As an Arab, I cannot help but feel ashamed that they have been abandoned to such needless misery and humiliation. In most of their host countries they are fated to remain stateless and jobless. In many cases they are deprived of the right to own land or open their own businesses and they are forced to put up with sub-standard education for their children and poor health care facilities. Why?

Are they not human beings with bodies, minds and souls crying out to be nourished? They have done nothing wrong. They are innocent victims. Most were born inside one of those ramshackle shanty towns. Babies take their first cries while their parents' joy is tempered with the knowledge that their offspring's future is bleak. When I see the happiness in the eyes of my own grandchildren, I cannot imagine how those mothers and fathers must feel.

Enough blinding our eyes to their pain! Enough using those poor people as poster-children for a political cause! It is incumbent on all Arab states to agree on a strategy and pool their resources for its implementation.

Every Palestinian refugee should be offered a home in an Arab country of their choosing. Once there, they should be afforded equal rights with citizens. They should be offered first-class education and training so that they can gain skills that can benefit both their families and their newly-adopted homelands. That should not take away from the fact that they will always consider Palestine as their motherland.

A less ideological approach should also be taken with respect to Israel, again for the sake of Palestinians hemmed in by walls and checkpoints. Like it or not, it is clear that nuclear-armed Israel under the patronage of its big brother the US is here to stay. So rather than incessantly battle over this sacred soil beloved by all Abrahamic prophets, Israelis and Arabs must find a way to peacefully coexist.

We should ignore those who care little about the Palestinian people, yet ruthlessly use their cause to further their own interests, whether Arabs, Iranians or Westerners. Palestine should be cherished not treated as a commodity to be traded inch by inch or turned into a PR tool to give credibility to liars and manipulators. It is time we called out those who have been ruthlessly playing on our emotions.

Let us also dispense with labels such as "Little Satan" or "enemy Zionist state" designed to incite and prevent us from sitting at one table. In truth, we have far more dangerous foes than Israel, disguised as friends. Insult only keeps the flame of enmity burning. It is time to begin negotiations with Israel in a spirit of goodwill – although, of course, one hand cannot clap.

Plan A, embodied in the Camp David Accords, may have sounded good at the time but, in practice, it has been an abject failure. It is time that we admit that and move to Plan B, which I believe should be based on the Arab Peace Initiative proposed by King Abdullah of Saudi Arabia during a 2002 League of Arab States summit. However, due to changing circumstances since then, I would suggest the following stipulations:

- Palestinian/Israeli negotiations brokered by the US have been fruitless time and time again. Instead, a committee should be appointed made up of respected Palestinians and representatives of Gulf Cooperation Council (GCC) states. Such a committee should be empowered to negotiate directly with the Israeli government without the presence of any third parties.
- Talks should take place without preconditions on both sides, with one exception: Israeli settlement expansion should come to a halt before their creep precludes any possibility of two states living side by side because Palestinians will never sign up to one that is hardly bigger than a postage stamp without sovereignty over their borders, shorelines and airspace.

If all fails, or an independent Palestinian state is no longer practical in light of realities on the ground, the Palestinians should be offered the choice to pursue either a "one-state solution" or an autonomous region within an Israeli/Palestinian federation.

Whatever works for them, whatever gives the Palestinians a life, the kind of existence most of us take for granted, Arabs should support. Likewise, Israelis should conclude that isolating high walls and militarization will not keep them nearly as safe as an olive branch extended to the Palestinian people and their Arab neighbours.

Ultimately everyone involved in this conflict or on its peripheries must make a choice: are they prepared to perpetuate pain and suffering indefinitely by dredging up the past and pointing fingers – or are they open to fresh ideas and new solutions? The choice is simple: love of life or morbid celebration of death. For people like me who care, there is no contest.

A big-hearted US president dedicated to peace

19 October 2014

EARLIER THIS MONTH I HAD the privilege of spending quality time exchanging ideas with President Carter and his wife Rosalynn at The Carter Center in Atlanta as well as at Illinois College, Jacksonville, where he came at my invitation to initiate "Pathways to Peace" – a proposal designed to find solutions for the Palestinian-Israeli conflict, an issue afflicting our region and the West.

Regularly-held seminars involving 12 Illinois College students and faculty members will be held in the spring of 2015 so that participants can study methods of resolving ethnic, cultural and religious conflicts with a view to nurturing fresh ideas on how to bring an end to the Israeli-Palestinian conflict. Students will travel to Jordan, Palestine and Israel to meet with other students and decision-makers and to garner their opinions. Final papers will be presented to me in Dubai for evaluation.

"I really think the problem is we don't see other people's points of views," was the insightful message from Illinois College President Barbara Farley. "We just try to push our own. So we need to get people over there to see what's going on and then say how can we change what's going on over there based on their beliefs not on our beliefs."

Having President Carter on board gives this initiative impetus and the gravitas it deserves. Thank you Mr President for answering the call without hesitation and for being an outstanding leadership role model at a time when true leadership is sorely lacking worldwide. While you are out there, working hard to assist the poor and disenfranchised, unafraid to speak the truth about the plight of the Palestinians, others make meaningless diplomatic noises. Presidents, prime ministers and human rights organizations are big on talk but do not do anything to back up their words. You make a difference.

Not for you a quiet retirement on the golf course. You fly from country to country, even those that are conflict-ridden or undergoing epidemics, risking your life for the betterment of mankind irrespective of race or colour. To quote my friend, Congressman Paul Findley, who has worked tirelessly for the Palestinian cause: "Jimmy Carter is the only president whose presidency didn't end after he left the White House."

Like Barack Obama, President Carter was the recipient of a Nobel Peace Prize. The difference is that whereas as Jimmy Carter earned his "for his decades of untiring effort to find peaceful solutions to international conflicts, to advance democracy and human rights and to promote economic and social development", Obama has done nothing but make hollow promises.

When Carter said: "I'll never tell a lie" and "I'll never avoid a controversial issue" during the run-up to his election, he meant ever word, but, unfortunately, the Iranian hostage crisis and America's failed attempt to release its citizens forcibly held by Iranian radicals in the US embassy, cast a shadow over his re-election prospects. He told the packed-to-capacity hall at Illinois College that when he is asked about how his life has been in the last few years he cites a cartoon depicting a small boy telling his daddy "When I grow up I want to be a former President."

President Carter's presidential achievements should not be glossed over. One of the most outstanding was his mediation at Camp David that helped to seal an Israeli-Egyptian peace deal and laid the foundations for future Israeli-Palestinian negotiations on two states. His reflections and insights on that era can be found in his book *The Blood of Abraham*. He aspired to make his government competent and compassionate; he produced eight million jobs and reduced the budget deficit. He expanded the national parks by millions of acres, improved the Social Security system and ensured that government jobs were available to women, African Americans and Hispanics. Moreover, he boldly established diplomatic relations with China and successfully negotiated a nuclear limitation treaty with the Soviet Union.

Determined to continue making a difference, Mr and Mrs Carter opened The Carter Center – a nongovernmental, non-profit organization to "advance human rights and alleviate human suffering" in 1982 in Atlanta partnered with Emory University. Besides being a respected, neutral election-observing body, it mediates conflicts, champions human rights, and works to eradicate diseases. President Carter has been a hands-on founder clearing the path for a US–North Korea nuclear pact; accompanying Colin Powell to Haiti to restore the country's democratically-elected president, negotiating a treaty between Sudan and Uganda and making an historic visit to Cuba aimed at improving US-Cuban relations.

However, elusive peace between Israel and the Palestinians remains close to this heart. His best-selling book *Palestine: Peace not Apartheid* was

307

praised for its honesty in a climate hostile to opponents of Israeli policies and condemned by the pro-Israel lobby for bordering on anti-Semitism, a label Israeli advocates throw around like confetti in an attempt to cast a slur on anyone who dares to challenge Israel's impunity.

Undeterred, President Carter said: "Many controversial issues concerning Palestine and the path to peace for Israel are intensely debated among Israelis and throughout other nations – but not in the United States. This reluctance to criticize any policies of the Israeli government is because of the extraordinary lobbying efforts of the American-Israeli Political Action Committee and the absence of any significant contrary voices."

Following Israel's recent onslaught on Gaza that robbed over 2,000 Palestinians of their lives and displaced 250,000 from their homes, President Carter condemned Israel for committing war crimes. He called for international judicial proceedings to hold Israel to account and for Israel to immediately lift the blockade on the Gaza Strip.

President Carter's career is indelibly associated with compassion for those less fortunate and his passion to further human rights. His humility is well known. At his inauguration he waved away a limousine in favour of strolling with his wife down Pennsylvania Avenue and he always carried his own bag when boarding Air Force One. I have met him three times, including twice in Dubai where I hosted him and members of his family at my farm. A former farmer, he was entranced by our farm animals and felt right at home.

I have always found him to be very humble, gracious, positive and energetic. In short, an impressive human being who takes his Christian values seriously. His wife, former First Lady Rosalynn Carter, has been his right hand since they wed in 1946. A forceful personality in her own right, she was present at Cabinet and Policy meetings during her years at the White House and was appointed US envoy to Latin America. I think President Carter would willingly endorse the saying: "Behind every great man is a great woman." One thing's for certain. If there were more people of influence with President Carter's courage and commitment our world would be a far better and more peaceful place.

Hezbollah uses the Palestinian cause as a pretext

22 February 2016

HEZBOLLAH'S SECRETARY GENERAL Hassan Nasrallah uses every trick in the book in an effort to cement his militia's credibility within the Sunni Arab world and to justify its existence. His speeches are deliberately crafted to con Arabs, specifically Palestinians, into thinking he is the hero who will defend Jerusalem and free the occupied territories.

Not content with turning Lebanon into an Iranian vassal state, using the pretence that he puts Lebanese interests first even though he has triggered war with Israel, turned his guns on his compatriots, and dragged his country into the Syrian conflict, Nasrallah has cynically ramped up his pro-Palestinian, anti-Israel rhetoric to lure Palestinians and their sympathizers into his camp.

As several Middle East commentators have noted, he is out to win a place in the Palestinian good books with anti-Israel threats at a time when he is viewed throughout the Sunni Arab world as a betrayer for propping up the brutal Bashar Al Assad regime.

Nasrallah's latest rant boasts that Hezbollah has the capacity "to cover the entirety of Israel with missiles" adding that the militia would be the victor in any coming war with nuclear-armed Israel. He is even more specific concerning his plans. An ammonia plant in Haifa would be targeted in order to cause a nuclear bomb-type explosion.

Those threats are mere flimflam, empty of substance, because, if carried out, Israel would adopt a scorched earth policy in retaliation while every Palestinian would have a target placed on his back. To prove how nonsensical they are, in the event Israel were in danger of being obliterated, no American president would sit on his hands witnessing its destruction. That is just a fact which this big-mouthed paper tiger knows only too well.

Until now, neither Iran nor Hezbollah have done anything tangible to aid the Palestinians other than throw them a few dollars and low-grade missiles. They merely hold out the freeing of Jerusalem as a recruitment carrot, one that offers hope to Muslims and, of course, Palestinians in areas where hope is becoming a rare commodity.

Nasrallah vows to support the Palestinians year upon year and so far he has done nothing tangible to that effect. Instead, he has ordered attacks against Saudi Arabia; one example is the attack on the Khobar Towers residential complex near Dhahran carried out by Hezbollah's branch in the Kingdom. Moreover, Cairo alleges that Hezbollah, together with other groups, murdered guards to release tens of thousands of prisoners during the 2011 revolution, many of them convicted terrorists.

I have advocated for a Palestinian state throughout my adult life. I feel deeply for the suffering of the Palestinians and their frustration in the absence of even a small chink of light. I understand why a small minority may be tempted to grasp at Nasrallah's straws, but have no doubt that they are being set up for disappointment.

I am sure President Mahmoud Abbas understands Hezbollah's ruthless game. I do not doubt his patriotism for a second, but I do wonder at his silence. He should dissuade his people from being fooled by Hezbollah with propagandist statements designed to attract recruits who will no doubt be farmed out to fight elsewhere.

Nasrallah's agenda is transparent. Last year, he called upon all Palestinians and their supporters to rally behind the Islamic Republic of Iran on such duplicitous reasoning as "Iran's enemies are the enemies of Jerusalem." He was later to claim Iran and its backing of "resistance movements" was "the only hope left for this region, after God".

When he is not thumping his chest against Israel, he is slamming Saudi Arabia for its "aggression" against Yemen, which is a legitimate, lawful intervention carried out to reinstate the democratically-elected government and to preserve the Kingdom's security.

On Sunday, Lebanon's Minister of Justice Ashraf Rifi resigned his post saying Nasrallah should be "ashamed" of his attacks on Saudi Arabia while describing Hezbollah as "a mere tool" of Iran, adding, "Hezbollah is turning Lebanon into an operations room to spread Iranian hegemony." Never a truer statement has been said. That is exactly what he wants Palestine to become – an Iranian puppet enclave.

Hezbollah has been bleeding popularity among Palestinians, many of whom were outraged when in December 2015 he spoke against the backdrop of a map of Palestine superimposed with the Iranian flag. That speaks volumes as to his hidden agenda. He does not care about the Palestinians; his interests lie with extending the so-called Shi'ite Crescent.

I would urge President Abbas to encourage our Palestinian brothers to reject Nasrallah's blatant lies designed to hijack their just cause and he should emphasize strongly that Hezbollah talks the talk but has never once walked the walk. The US may have scratched Hezbollah from its threat list while it was courting Iran to sign up to the nuclear deal, but history does not lie. It remains a terrorist organization with both Arab and Western blood staining its hands.

I would also counsel Lebanon's Palestinian residents to assist those of their Lebanese friends struggling to reclaim their country from Hezbollah's domination, which is alienating Saudi Arabia, the majority of Gulf states and other predominately Sunni countries. Hezbollah's control of the country both politically, diplomatically and militarily has resulted in Saudi Arabia freezing $4bn set to bolster the Lebanese army and domestic security services because it cannot continue indirectly funding its enemy's proxy militia.

Palestinians, wake up! You are being played. Disassociate yourselves from Hezbollah and its master. Reject false partners for those who have stood shoulder to shoulder with you rather than those with silvery tongues and anti-Sunni agendas. If you let him, Nasrallah's weasel words will lead you down a hellish path with no return.

Time for Palestinians to choose sides

26 March 2016

AT LAST THE LEAGUE OF ARAB STATES and the Gulf Cooperation Council (GCC) have officially branded Hezbollah a terrorist organization, a designation long overdue. Hezbollah is recognized as a mere tool in the Iranian expansionism box with no legitimate footing within the Arab World. Setting aside its bombings, killings and assassinations, it has suffocated Lebanon's free spirit and fought for the survival of the Syrian gangsters whose hands drip with the blood of their own people.

This is rare Arab unity in action, although admittedly countries under the sway of Tehran, Lebanon and Iraq expressed "reservations" while Algeria and Tunisia registered their objections. Arab-Israeli parties in the Knesset have loudly condemned the designation as one that serves Israel's interests.

Hamas has taken the line "silence is golden" on the issue but its political chief Khaled Meshaal told French television France 24 that Iran is no longer a main backer of Hamas due to differing stances on the Syrian conflict. Meshaal's main priority is mending strained ties with Egypt who accused Hamas of being involved in the assassination of its Prosecutor-General so as to get the Rafah Crossing re-opened.

Other Palestinian groups have been more forthright in slamming Hezbollah's branding. But where does the Palestinian President Mahmoud Abbas stand?

His position on Hezbollah is not at all clear. He is, however, more transparent on Iran. He recently revealed to Kuwait's Scoop TV that "there are no official relations between us and Iran", adding, there is an embassy and an ambassador "but they don't have direct contacts with us". He told the interviewer that the Palestinian Authority (PA) has "released a statement saying that we do not know anything about Iranian funds and we are not responsible for them".

"I say to Iranians, 'you want to engage in Palestine? Then you must do so in collaboration with the Palestinian Authority (PA). If we have an embassy in Iran, why does it operate indirectly, through the back door?" he said.

He recalled his visit to Iran to meet with former President Mahmoud Ahmadinejad who told him "I love the Palestinian people" and said he responded saying: "No, you don't love them. If you love them, love all Palestinians, not half or a quarter of them. Iran only loves Hamas and Islamic Jihad."

That message is ambiguous from a Palestinian leader who referred to Iran as "a sister country" just last year while announcing his plans to visit. Is he critical of Iran overall or is he angling for Iranian funding for the PA? In any event, he did not tell Tehran to stay out of Palestinian affairs.

It seems to me that President Abbas must acknowledge the new regional reality. Iran and its Lebanese satellite are inextricably linked and share the same hostility to Arabs, in particular towards Saudi Arabia and Gulf states.

In the current climate, fence-sitting is not an option as the Lebanese government discovered to its cost. We cannot be expected to continue giving our diplomatic and financial support to states or entities sympathetic to Hezbollah and Iran or hand-in-glove with either behind the curtain.

Throughout my adult life the Palestinian cause has been dear to my heart and in my youth I considered the Egyptian President Gamal Abdel Nasser a champion for his efforts to free the Palestinian people from occupation. Our pockets were always open to Palestinian President Yasser Arafat who despite his faults was a Palestinian patriot who devoted his life to liberating Palestinian lands. Unfortunately, he backed the wrong horse during the 1991 War with Iraq to oust Saddam Hussein's forces from Kuwait when the Palestinians paid a price in terms of reduced funding.

Over time that hurt receded, but GCC states threatened by Iran's push for regional hegemony may not be so forgiving if the Palestinian leadership plays both sides of the fence, willing to shake hands with the Devil in the hope of receiving handouts from our foes.

Moreover, Abbas was wrong when he told Ahmadinejad that Iran "only loves Hamas and Islamic Jihad". Love does not come into it. Despite their flowery rhetoric and threats targeting Israel, which never amount to anything, neither Iran nor Hezbollah care about the Palestinians and have done nothing tangible to help them all these years. They cynically use their affiliations with Palestinian resistance groups to bolster their credibility with Arabs.

In its early days Hezbollah wrote an open letter pledging allegiance to the Ayatollah Ruhollah Khomeini and vowed to turn Lebanon into a Shi'ite state. It has since re-jigged its manifesto to appear more benign. Its goals are Iran's goals. If it is so concerned about the welfare of Palestinians why did it refuse to allow Palestinian refugees in Lebanon the right to work and own their own homes? And if Iran was serious about promoting Arab causes why does it oppress its Sunni minorities, including the Ahwazi Arabs deprived of decent jobs, homes and basic utilities?

Author Trita Parsi, the founder and president of the National Iranian American Council rightly asserts in his book *Treacherous Alliance* that Iran pays mere lip service to the Palestinian struggle whereas its real motivation is the export of Shi'ite ideology.

With all my respect to President Abbas, who is obliged to walk a tightrope between the demands of his people, the Israeli occupier and militant groups, he cannot continue burying his head in the sand when it comes to the terrorist Hezbollah. He should publish a declaration disassociating Palestinians from Hezbollah and Iran and ideally close the Palestinian mission in Tehran.

My message to Abu Mazen is to stand with us and we will stand with you!

9

Revolution in Egypt and the long road to recovery

Introduction

EGYPT HAS BEEN through the mill in recent years. Since 2011 it has witnessed revolt, uprising and revolution and has undergone several changes at the top. Fortunately, stability is returning to the country even as it continues to tackle insurgency and cracks down on dissent. However, the 2011 calls for democracy crippled this ancient civilization. Egypt paid a heavy toll – socially, economically and politically.

When Egyptians took to the streets in their millions calling for the resignation of former Egyptian President Hosni Mubarak who had held on to power for 30 years, little did they know what the ramifications would be. All this in the name of democracy – or so they thought. There is a saying: "Be careful what you wish for. It may just happen."

Scenes of chaos splashed across our screens for far too long as young men and women demonstrated in the streets for a so-called "better future". Thousands lost their lives, the economy nearly collapsed and martial law sadly became the norm.

This was not the Egypt I knew and loved. I had foreseen that, tragically, there may be "much worse to come". As a consequence, Egypt fell into the hands of the Muslim Brotherhood who brought false promises of hope and prosperity.

The Egyptian people believed they had achieved the impossible. They had ousted their leader and held the country's first supposed democratic elections. But the ramifications were unsurmountable.

Egypt, one of the oldest – and one of the most advanced civilizations for about 3,000 years – was almost sent back into the dark ages following the fall of Mubarak, which resulted in his successor, Mohammed Morsi, being elected Egypt's fifth president on 30 June 2012, the first president outside of the military.

The election was a sham to say the least. The man elected to lead the country turned out to be a prominent figure in the Muslim Brotherhood. He hijacked the process under the pretence of "fair" elections.

The day the Muslim Brotherhood came to power was a nail in Egypt's coffin. The Egyptian youth, who had come out in their swathes in large cities across the country, had tasted success, or so they thought. In fact, the demise of the country had already been mapped out by the Muslim Brotherhood who had hijacked the process.

Egyptians became diametrically divided. The youth movement wanted a Western-style democracy run by a civilian government with no military oversight. Copts wanted greater political representation and modernists wanted an open, secular society. It was a lose–lose situation. Sadly, this resulted in a domino effect throughout the country and had far-reaching implications for the region.

Egypt paid a heavy price. The human loss was catastrophic and the economy went into freefall. "Egypt is still celebrating but I fear that not everyone understands the pitfalls ahead. The nation is beset by strikes. The economy is said to be losing $300mn daily and, according to some reports, capital flying out of the country is running into billions." (See "Our region is in grave danger", 17 February 2011, later in this chapter.)

Violence and instability are the death knell for foreign investment. No surprise then that Egypt's economy was hit hard, with the political situation putting a huge strain on the government coffers and further jeopardizing the lives of some 90 million Egyptian citizens who were already living in hardship.

The economy was ravaged and foreign currency reserves slumped to their lowest since 2007. Tourism, once the mainstay of the country's economy, was in tatters; it was virtually non-existent. Gone were the visitors typically drawn in by millennia-old monuments, the Pyramids and Great Sphinx in Giza. The famous Nile was no longer casting its spell on visitors.

In May 2011, the then ruling Supreme Council of the Armed Forces warned of the catastrophic consequences of the revolution, telling the nation that the country's economy was under threat of collapsing. "The poverty rate is approaching 70 per cent and domestic and foreign debt has reached 1,080 billion Egyptian pounds, which is 90 per cent of GDP," said the Assistant Defence Minister for Financial and Administrative Affairs, Mahmoud Nasr. (See "Egypt's economic recovery in the balance", 23 May 2011, later in this chapter.)

Meanwhile, foreign investors were fleeing for the exits. There was practically no foreign money coming in, largely because the global rating agencies downgraded Egypt to "risky".

It would have taken a miracle to return the largest Arab country to its former glory and reassert its role as a key regional player with a strong, stable and pluralistic political system. Unfortunately, some people's obsession with retribution and the promotion of sectarian interests were harming those goals.

With the failing economy, chaos on the streets and no proper leadership, there was a complete disregard for human life. Humanity went out of the window – even for the former President who was once revered as a hero in the 1973 war. I found scenes on our TV screens of an 83-year-old Hosni Mubarak lying ill on a stretcher in a courtroom cage as his son bent down to kiss him hard to watch. He had been overthrown, was later tried for corruption and ordered to stand trial for the killing of protesters undertaken before his downfall.

"I am sure that many Egyptians, even those who were glad to see him go, feel the same way," I wrote in 2011. (See "Only God's mercy can save Egypt", 6 August 2011, later in this chapter.) Strangely, the accused – Hosni Mubarak, his sons Ala'a and Gamal and former Minister of the Interior Habib Al Adly – seemed more dignified than the attorneys in the courtroom. "Verdicts should be passed by impartial judges based on hard evidence. My fear is that Mubarak's day in court will become a political show trial with judges either riding the revolutionary wave themselves or under pressure to please the crowds on the street. If that is the case, Mubarak and others should be tried by an international tribunal." It should never have been allowed to become the circus show that it was.

Meanwhile, the Muslim Brotherhood was doing its best to hide its true objectives during the revolution's aftermath promising not to field a presidential candidate or to target more than 30 per cent of all parliamentary seats, having launched a PR campaign to display its new moderate, all-encompassing face. However, the layers eventually peeled off to reveal its true identity. The Muslim Brotherhood formed a coalition with Islamist extremist groups and spawned new parties headed by former Brotherhood leaders who were going after the presidency. The veil dropped on Friday 29 July 2011 when its members, together with other Islamists, called for the creation of an Islamic state under Sharia law chanting "Islam, Islam, we do not want a liberal state," with a few holding up photographs of Osama bin Laden.

It is only right that Islamic principles are taken into consideration by a predominantly Muslim state, but not the kind these fanatics were wanting that mimic the Shia Islamic Republic of Iran.

Under the rule of the Muslim Brotherhood, as I feared, Egypt was very quickly beginning to imitate the Iranian style of rule. The country, considered the heart of the Arab land and known to Arabs as "Umm Al Donya", which translates into "Mother of the World", was en route to becoming an Iranian ally and proxy just like Iraq, Syria and Lebanon. When Iranian delegations started to visit Egypt for discussions with political and religious entities, it cemented the intent.

How I wish the authorities would have heeded the alarm bells and my repeated warnings: "... the Muslim Brotherhood has informal ties to the Iranian regime primarily through its strong links with Hamas. The group welcomed Iran's Islamic Revolution and in 2008 its former Supreme Guide Mohammed Mahdi Akef told an Iranian news agency that: 'the Muslim Brotherhood supports the ideas and thoughts of the founder of the Islamic Republic.'" (See "A worrying turn for Egypt's Revolution", 6 April 2011, later in this chapter.)

Mubarak himself had once warned: "If the Muslim Brotherhood succeeded in taking over the country, the world would isolate them, as they have done Hamas ... . Many will take their money and leave the country. Investments will stop. Unemployment will grow... ." Say what you will about the former leader, on this point he was right. And he was also right in keeping the Muslim Brotherhood under a tight leash during his rule.

A disgruntled minority had resorted to violence and was holding the majority hostage. Egypt witnessed an increase in bombings targeting the police, allegedly carried out by Ansar Bait El Maqdis, a terrorist group allied to the Brotherhood, believed to have been funded by its former Deputy Supreme Guide Khairat El Shater.

One catastrophic failure led to another, and the Egyptian people eventually woke up to the fact that Mohammed Morsi was the devil in disguise in the presidential palace. On the first anniversary of taking office, in July 2013, millions of people took to the streets demanding Morsi's resignation. Quite frankly, I am surprised it took so long. The violent demonstrations that led to the toppling of Morsi eventually resulted in the alienation of the Muslim Brotherhood, despite it being the country's oldest Islamist organization.

The fate of Morsi will be decided upon soon. For now he is languishing in jail – on death row – alongside other Muslim Brotherhood leaders. How ironic that the country's first democratically elected president almost destroyed the nation, and his actions resulted in his being on death row today. If, and I doubt it will happen, his conviction holds up, he will be the first former president to be executed since Saddam Hussein. What a dramatic fall from grace.

Fortunately, Egypt is restoring its tarnished image, and earning its rightful place again thanks to the election of the country's new President, Abdel Fatah El Sisi. While he is being harshly criticized in some circles for sharply curbing political and media freedoms, Sisi has firmly defended his controversial piece of legislation, enacted in November 2013, which allows for the detention of protestors for up to three years, unless they obtain permission from authorities first. Sisi said: "There are millions of people and families who can't earn their living because of the protests."

The new President, who is cracking down on protests, has already proved his economic prowess despite grappling with multiple internal threats and encountering some big economic hurdles. But Sisi has won the praise of foreign investors for implementing tough reforms, like cutting fuel and food subsidies, and he also has Western and Gulf allies on his side, who are pumping much-needed funds into the economy. Sisi is behind the creation of the second Suez Canal, a mega project promising significant revenue streams. But whether or not it will filter down to the masses remains to be seen. The world is watching to see if he too will deliver on his promises to create jobs and improve the living standards for the Egyptian people.

It is time to restore Egypt to its former glory and let it flourish once again.

Egypt's youth uprising has been hijacked

5 February 2011

NO ONE CAN FAIL to be moved by the sight of young, educated men and women demonstrating in Cairo's Freedom Square (Tahrir Square) for a better future. When so many Arab republics allow their presidents free rein to hold onto their positions indefinitely and groom their sons to take over as though they are monarchs, it is no wonder that people all over North Africa and the Middle East are demanding change.

That said, there is a fine line between freedom and anarchy and, frankly, the images on our television screens point to the latter.

Egypt has become a lawless land. Thugs are torching historic buildings, businesses and shopping centres. Thieves are on the prowl forcing Egyptian families to barricade themselves into their homes. Foreigners are leaving in droves. The once peaceful Egyptians are beating one another to death. The economy is being decimated by the day.

This is not the Egypt I know and love. Tragically, there may be much worse to come. There is a saying: "Be careful what you wish for. It may just happen."

It is true that the ageing President Hosni Mubarak has made mistakes in recent times and has been divorced from the aspirations of the street. Let us not forget, however, that that he was head of the Air Force that regained Egypt's dignity during its 1973 conflict with Israel.

As President, he has maintained Egypt's stability and cemented relations with the international community. He has improved infra-structure, cultivated a climate for foreign investment and presided over a growing economy. That is why I was disgusted to see Egyptians hanging effigies of their President and waving shoes at his image. Hosni Mubarak, for all his faults, is a patriot and wants to die on the soil of Egypt.

Moreover, he immediately responded to protestors' demands by sacking his cabinet and promising that neither he nor his son will stand during upcoming presidential elections.

For the first time, he has appointed a vice-president and instructed his new government to overhaul elements of the constitution, talk to opposition figures and ensure that university leavers can find employment.

At the same time, the former Minister of the Interior, responsible for police brutality, along with the Minister of Tourism and the Minister of Housing, believed to be corrupt, have been barred from travelling and their bank accounts frozen.

319

It is my belief that President Mubarak was not aware that people around him were abusing their power to line their pockets. I blame those closest to him for their cowardice in failing to inform him about corrupt practices and police brutality.

He must have been deeply hurt to suddenly find himself as an object of hate. I do not know whether the makers of the Egyptian movie *The President's Chef* had insider knowledge but the President's isolation from the real world orchestrated by his aides was portrayed in that film.

The initial demands of the core demonstrators have all been fulfilled but the Facebook/Twitter movement has been hijacked by agenda-led, self-interested individuals and parties – in some cases, sponsored by foreign powers.

The hijackers are nothing more than opportunists seeking power. They are out to humiliate President Mubarak. They want to see him flying around the world seeking a country prepared to take him in like the Shah of Iran and, more recently, Tunisia's former President Ben Ali. It is no wonder that Mubarak rejects such degrading banishment.

He has admitted to ABC News that he is "fed up" of being president but fears that his exit will hurl Egypt into chaos. He wants to complete his term so as to supervise free and fair elections and an orderly hand-over of power.

But the hijackers are refusing even these unprecedented concessions and many insist they will only engage in dialogue with the vice-president when Mubarak has gone. That condition is totally unreasonable when even a sacked employee usually gets one month to clear his desk.

More crucially, Egyptians need time to consider who comes next when people like Mohamed ElBaradei, who has lived abroad for 20 years, and the Ghad Party's Ayman Nour have little grassroots support. The only organized opposition party is the banned Muslim Brotherhood, which joined the tail end of the demonstrations, and has since played a clever game by announcing it will not field a presidential candidate and is content to coalesce being secularists. That is now, but what about down the road?

Those people fund Hamas, have admitted they want Sharia law and support an Islamic caliphate. They should not be allowed to participate in any election. I am also concerned that Egypt will fall victim to mob rule in the future now that the crowds have tasted success and I am worried that the entire region will suffer from the domino effect of this contagion.

I am particularly surprised at the duplicity of the Obama administration, which is now insisting on President Mubarak's swift departure when he has always been Washington's obliging friend. Mubarak is right to say President Barack Obama does not understand Egypt or the implications of his hasty removal. There is a cautionary lesson to be drawn from Saddam's ousting. True, he was a strongman, but he united all Iraqis under one flag and ensured strict law and order. Democracy is an admirable goal, but it cannot be instituted in one day and one night in a state that has never known it.

I admire President Obama but the US would be better served if he stayed out of internal Arab politics and concentrated on resolving the problems of those in his own country without homes and living on food stamps, as well as the fall-out from his predecessor's invasions of Afghanistan and Iraq.

We do not want Egypt to end up like fundamentalist Iran or Iraq, that was once the Cradle of Civilization and is now the Cradle of Terrorism. And we do not want Egypt to mirror Lebanon and end up in bloody civil war. And we certainly do not want every government in the region to be held to ransom by the mob.

Finally, I would say this to the Egyptians on the squares:

Please go home before you unwittingly destroy your country's economy, divide its people and tarnish its reputation forever. You have had your say, the state has responded and now you should exercise patience. Give your President a chance to restore Egypt's dignity and stability while it is still possible to do so. God bless you all!

Our region is in grave danger

17 February 2011

WHILE I HEARTILY congratulate the Egyptian people on achieving the impossible, I am also a realist. There are many aspects to this revolution that may have negative implications for the entire region. Looking beyond the current euphoria, following the ousting of an out-of-touch leader and his corrupt capitalist cronies, I fear a jagged road lies ahead.

Let us move beyond the romanticism. It is one thing for people to successfully overthrow a government, but often they are no better off. Fidel Castro's Cuba is one example where a dictator was overthrown only to be replaced by another. The 1979 Iranian revolution, that sent the Shah packing, began as a secular uprising but was later hijacked by an ayatollah in exile. I suspect that many Cubans and Iranians long to turn back the clock. I hope the day does not come when Egyptians do the same.

Egypt is still celebrating but I fear that not everyone understands the pitfalls ahead. The nation is beset by strikes. The economy is said to be losing $300m daily and, according to some reports, capital flying out of the country is running into billions. What happens when the bourse opens is anyone's guess. Egyptians may dream that the billions alleged to have been systematically milked from the country and deposited abroad will return, but that is easier said than done.

No country on earth can prosper when it is being run on people power; even a corner shop needs a manager. As of now, the revolutionaries are holding their military rulers hostage instead of allowing the Supreme Council time to fulfil its undertakings. They have warned that if their demands are not met within their own timetable they will bring Egypt to a standstill.

Those threats can go two ways. Either a loose coalition of inexperienced youth organizations holding a Sword of Damocles will become the de facto rulers or the military will lose patience and impose a strict crackdown that could result in a bloodbath. No group should hold a country's leadership to ransom. Now that the "people power" genie is out of the bottle can any future leader stuff it back?

Without effective authority, Egypt will become irrevocably destabilized. Weakening the mother of the Arab World could be part of a neo-conservative conspiracy to enable Israel to get back the oil and gas-rich Sinai. Iraq was destroyed by lies. Sudan has been split in two. Is Egypt next on the list, followed by the Arab heartlands of Yemen, Algeria, Morocco, Syria, Saudi Arabia and certain Gulf countries, such as Bahrain, where Shi'ites are attempting to ride on the back of Egypt's revolution?

The thinking is that oil-rich Saudi Arabia and Gulf Cooperation Council (GCC) countries, where citizens enjoy a good standard of living, are less vulnerable to the domino effect but they are not immune to troublemakers. I am a great admirer of the United Arab Emirates' (UAE) hybrid federal system of governance, allowing each of the seven emirates autonomy while respecting people's traditional allegiances to their respective ruler. It works seamlessly as it is. However, there are Arab states that do need to modernize, allow their people a greater say and listen to their just grievances. Dictatorial dinosaurs have no place in today's world.

It is generally believed that Egypt's revolution was spontaneous. But, as Wael Ghonim and his associates in the April 6 Youth Movement have confirmed, it was long planned using learned Eastern European tactics. Wael seems overwhelmed by his celebrity status. He says all he wants to do is return to his job. The clamouring agenda-driven satellite channels should let him do just that and quit whipping up emotions to attract viewers.

I believe the intentions of those youngsters were honest. But I cannot help suspecting that they have naively allowed themselves to be manipulated by foreign powers, keen to see the region in disarray. Tehran has strongly backed the revolution, which it has wrongly characterized as an "Islamic Revolution" and Washington is cheering it on even as three troop-filled US warships are moored off Alexandria and Israel has placed its military on high alert.

The biggest question is what happens now on Egypt's political front?

I am enthusiastic about democratic principles but it is unrealistic to expect a Western-style democracy to emerge overnight in a country that has never experienced it and where the military has been all powerful for almost 60 years. Egypt requires a firm hand at the rudder until such time as democratic values can be absorbed into its culture. Any democratic system hurriedly crafted now will be a sham.

Egypt should postpone parliamentary elections and concentrate on electing a secular progressive president with a mandate to form a government that should include charismatic popular figures, capable of beating back the Muslim Brotherhood, which has announced its intention to become a political party.

Worse, Iran is building up its strength to become the region's most powerful player. Tehran is already gloating over its success in certain areas. Should Arab nations implode like a house of cards due to the Tunisian/Egyptian contagion, the winners will be Tehran, Tel Aviv and Washington, whose Middle-Eastern influence derives from the principle of "divide and conquer".

If the Middle East was not a coveted location due to its natural resources or was not such a hotbed of competing sectarian interests, Iranian spies, Central Intelligence Agency (CIA) spooks and Mossad agents, I might be less troubled. Our leaders must coordinate to decisively act to stem this whirlwind before it consumes us. Unless we become masters of our own destiny soon the malevolent elements, burning to become our masters, will prevail. It is ironic that while people in city squares are calling for freedom, we have never been this close to being enslaved.

The fine line between freedom and anarchy

1 March 2011

THE YEAR 2011 will forever be known as the year of revolt; I just pray that it does not become the century's most revolting. There are so many revolutions and civil uprisings it is almost impossible to keep up with them all. And they are not confined to the Arab World either. The fashion has spread to Athens, where anti-austerity demonstrators have been throwing petrol bombs at riot police.

Even the US has not escaped the trend. Up to 100,000 people have rallied in Wisconsin over a bill to limit the unions' collective bargaining rights, supported by dozens of protests in other American cities. Former Texas Agriculture Commissioner, Jim Hightower, joined a demonstration outside the state Capitol, saying he was happier than "a flea at a dog show".

If you imagine that protests in the West are unrelated to the fever gripping the Middle East and North Africa (MENA) region you are wrong. The rallying cry of demonstrators carrying placards comparing their governor to Hosni Mubarak, in Madison, Wisconsin have come up with the rallying cry, "Fight like an Egyptian". Mr Hightower feels like a flea at a dog show and that is his privilege but should civil disobedience become uncontrollable around the world, I fear that our freedom will quickly turn into anarchy.

While I sympathize with the revolutions in Tunisia, Egypt and Libya, where people have suffered from corruption and oppression, I am appalled that sectors of the public in peaceful, prosperous countries, that look after their citizens, such as Bahrain and Oman, have chosen to take to the streets, instead of appointing representatives to put forward their demands to their governments.

God forbid this contagion should spread to the Gulf countries. What could they complain about in a place where the nationals enjoy a lifestyle that is the envy of the world? Could they say that the sea was not blue enough?

Freedom to peacefully demonstrate is one thing; setting fire to government buildings and lobbing petrol bombs at the police quite another. The idea that a state can run efficiently on people power alone might be utopian but it is nothing more than a pipe dream. Once the heady days of revolution, when everyone is united, are over, people revert to their own opinions, affiliations and divisions. This is the time to avoid a power vacuum. Any interim government has to assert its authority before chaos prevails. Law and order must be reinstituted. Citizens must return to their jobs. The economy must be kick-started again so that the state can fulfil its undertaking to provide a better future for all.

Take Egypt for example. As revolutions go, this one was a textbook success. A tyrant is now holed up in his Red Sea villa. His loot is being frozen. His corrupt cohorts are being arrested and investigations into their dealings are being carried out. World leaders are queuing up to heap praise upon the courageous youth who braved tear gas, live bullets and even tanks in pursuit of their dream. But let us be realistic. Without the support of the Egyptian military their story could have turned into a tragedy.

Egypt's Supreme Military Council has, thus far, behaved in an exemplary fashion. Its leaders are currently meeting with youth committees and opposition groups. They have also appointed a panel to revise certain articles of the Constitution, which were unveiled on Sunday, and they have promised to hold elections within six months.

Also promised is the lifting of the emergency law and an increase in salary for public sector employees. In return, they are asking for people to exercise patience and work together to bring some normality to the towns and cities. I think their requests are very reasonable. Tahrir Square is going nowhere. Yet a few of the hard core revolutionaries seem hell-bent on holding a knife to their throats.

When the military does not respond to their demands – such as a request to sack the Prime Minister Ahmed Shafik who was appointed by Mubarak during his last hours as President – as speedily as they might like, they shout "Everybody out". Ahmed Shafik is just an administrator until there is a ballot. Nobody with political ambition wants to replace him for fear of being tainted, and no one enjoying any popular standing is rushing to join his cabinet.

On Friday, protesters once again pitched their tents in the square and were forcibly moved on by soldiers. Their response was to call on the millions, provoking an apology from the Supreme Military Council, which denied issuing any such orders. Just who is in charge of the country – the military in its role as caretaker or the revolutionaries?

The youth are playing a dangerous game that could end up being counterproductive. What happens if the military gets fed up with being held over a barrel? Are they prepared to face off against the army? Cooperation is always more effective than continuous confrontation.

Even worse is the public's attitude towards the police force. The entire country is lawless, yet the police are being treated as pariahs. Few dare to wear their uniforms or drive police vehicles for fear of being insulted or attacked. A case in point was highlighted on Nile TV. A civilian brutally attacked a police officer who defended himself by firing a non-lethal shot. The result was shocking. A crowd rushed to the scene and beat the policeman unconscious.

My sources in Egypt tell me that this is far from being an isolated incident. Policemen have fallen victim to revenge attacks. Prison guards have been beaten, shot at and held hostage. And a rift between the security forces and the people is emboldening criminals and angering policemen. One-and-a-half million armed and angry police officers roaming the cities is a disturbing thought.

Egypt urgently needs leadership. The revolution is over. Authority must be respected. All Egyptians should roll up their sleeves. The real work must now begin.

A worrying turn for Egypt's revolution

6 April 2011

WHEN I PENNED my column "Egypt's youth uprising has been hijacked" in early February (5 February 2011), I experienced a deep sense of foreboding. I hesitated to dampen everyone's optimism because, of course, I wish the best for the people of that great Arab nation. I knew I was bucking the trend but I refused to see the situation through rose-tinted glasses. Two months on, everything I feared is, sadly, unfolding.

As I predicted, the country is still beset by protests, strikes, sit-ins and lawlessness. According to the Associated Press: "Crime has soared by 200 per cent since Hosni Mubarak's ouster from the presidency" with "murder, violent theft and kidnapping leading the surge". (See "A worrying turn for Egypt's Revolution", 6 April 2011, later in this chapter.)

The cancellation of an African Champions League football match between the Egyptian club Zamalek and Tunisia's Club Africain due to Egyptian fans attacking players and officials on the pitch was shameful. People's empowerment is one thing but ultimately law and order must prevail.

Equally disturbing is the ravaged economy. Foreign currency reserves are at their lowest since 2007 and growth projections have been downgraded. Tourism is almost non-existent. Hotels are empty. Adding to Egypt's economic woes is the mass influx of Egyptian workers escaping Libya.

I am most worried about the political front. Almost as soon as Mubarak made his retreat, prominent figures in the youth movement faded away. Moreover, whenever young protesters were asked why they did not appoint a leader they would invariably say that they did not have one.

When the former International Atomic Energy Agency (IAEA) chief Mohamed ElBaradei tried to vote during last month's constitutional referendum he was booed and shoved by opponents who believed he was an agent for the US. I am beginning to wonder whether some of revolution's instigators were being paid off by foreign powers all along.

It is no secret that Washington's relationship with Mubarak had cooled or that the 2005 presidential contender Ayman Nour was cosy with the White House. Likewise, Saad Eddin Ibrahim, an Egyptian pro-democracy activist and critic of Mubarak, has been financed by American non-governmental organizations (NGOs).

The fact is there are no credible applicants for the top job and not enough time for new ones to emerge. The Muslim Brotherhood has announced that they will not propose a candidate this time around but its leadership is waiting patiently in the wings, strategizing a plan to grab the attention of the electorate in four years' time. That does not mean that they will not support an "independent" candidate as their puppet in the meantime.

The Brotherhood is currently trying to model its soon-to-be-formed political party along the lines of Turkey's ruling Justice and Development (AK) Party, which was founded on moderate Islamic principles. Do not be fooled by its makeover.

This group is the parent of Hamas with offshoots throughout the Middle East and North Africa – and plans to turn Egypt into an Islamic state run on their own perception of the Sharia law. In a country with substantial Coptic and secular minorities, that would be a recipe for violent dissent.

President Mubarak once warned that "if the Muslim Brotherhood succeeded in taking over the country, the world would isolate them, as they have done Hamas … . Many will take their money and leave the country. Investments will stop. Unemployment will grow … ." Say what you will about the former leader, on this point he was right.

Worst of all, the Muslim Brotherhood has informal ties to the Iranian regime primarily through its strong links with Hamas. The group welcomed Iran's Islamic revolution and in 2008 its former Supreme Guide Mohammed Mahdi Akef told an Iranian news agency that "the Muslim Brotherhood supports the ideas and thoughts of the founder of the Islamic Republic".

It is, therefore, not illogical to assume that should the Brotherhood assume power, it could become a conduit for Iranian influence in the heart of the Arab World. That would be a coup for Tehran, which has already spread its tentacles to Lebanon, Syria and Yemen – and is trying to infiltrate Kuwait and Bahrain. Last week, a court in Kuwait City sentenced Iranian spies to death and expelled Iranian diplomats for their involvement in a spy ring.

Egyptian-Iranian relations have already warmed following the passage of Iran's warships through the Suez Canal and a meeting between the interim Foreign Minister of Egypt Nabil Elaraby with Mugtabi Amani, a top Iranian official. "Cairo is ready to re-establish diplomatic ties with Tehran after a break of more than 30 years," Elaraby said.

An appointed caretaker government has no mandate to take such important decisions on policy. Prime Minister Essam Sharaf and his cabinet are supposed to limit themselves to the day-to-day running of the country until elections have been held. Mr Sharaf should be focusing on the more pressing needs of the Egyptian people. It was a bad omen when last month he spoke on a podium in Tahrir Square with leading Muslim Brotherhood figure Mohammed El Beltagy at his side.

Egyptians must remain alert to destructive exterior forces that are being channelled through proxies within their borders. If Egypt, the Mother of the Arab World, is weakened from division and infighting, it would be like a knife through the heart of every Arab, as well as a gift to the strategic ambitions of Washington, Tel Aviv and Tehran. The writing is on the wall. I pray that the Egyptian people will see it before it is too late.

Revenge tarnishes post-revolution Egypt

15 April 2011

THERE IS A very real danger that mob rule is destroying Egypt's reputation, stability and economy. While Egypt's young revolutionaries are admired at home and abroad for the peaceful way they have conducted themselves, it would be a great shame if their efforts were stained by revenge masquerading as justice.

Egyptians are confronted with two choices. The first is a South African-style Truth and Reconciliation Commission enabling former regime members to admit mistakes and seek amnesty. Or, alternatively, they can take the "off with their heads" approach like post-revolutionary France and Russia. Sadly, it appears that Egyptians are choosing the latter course.

On Friday 8 April, hundreds of thousands took to Tahrir Square demanding the arrest of Hosni Mubarak and his sons. The next day, Egypt's Public Prosecutor Abdel Meguid Mahmoud called for their interrogation when Mr Mubarak made a defiant speech on Al Arabiya refuting allegations of corruption and offering to open his bank accounts to the public.

On Tuesday, the frail 82-year-old was hospitalized after suffering a heart attack while under interrogation. Thousands gathered calling for Mr Mubarak to receive the death penalty. Then, on Wednesday, Mubarak's two sons, Gamal and Ala'a, were incarcerated in a cell at the notorious Tora prison while his wife, Suzanne, was being questioned.

Prominent regime figures also behind bars at Tora include the former Minister of the Interior Habib Al Adly, the Presidential Chief of Staff Zakaria Azmi, Parliamentary Speaker Fathi Sorour, ex-Prime Minister Ahmed Nazif, businessman Ahmad El Moghrabi and steel tycoon Ahmed Ezz. Their court appearances were turned into a fiasco by infiltrators to the youth movement haranguing the judge and yelling "you will die", "you dogs". Personally, I find it repulsive that people are calling for blood and chaos. It is no wonder the judge walked out of the courtroom.

Those foul-mouthed accusers would do well to contemplate the Holy Quran, in particular Surat Al-Hujurat [49.6] "O you who have believed, if there comes to you a disobedient one with information, investigate, lest you harm a people out of ignorance and become, over what you have done, regretful."

Also to blame are the Egyptian newspapers that are whipping up sentiment with gloating banner headlines. Mr Ezz's daughter Afaf said: "The foundation of a democracy is the rule of law. This is not the rule of law, it's a vendetta." She is right. It is a vendetta fuelled by one of the basest human instincts, envy.

As many as 150 businessmen are currently under investigation and at least 23 have been banned from travelling. It is as if Egyptians are saying to the world: "Beware of investing in Egypt. Your investment is not safe."

I am not suggesting that suspects should not be brought to justice when there is a hard-and-fast case against them. But the enthusiasm with which Egypt's Public Prosecutor is rounding up these people looks like a witch hunt. When the country is beset by a crime wave, the Public Prosecutor's teams would be better employed reversing the trend instead of targeting public figures.

The question is why did Abdel Meguid Mahmoud not crack down on corruption when Mubarak was in power? Was he unaware it was going on? If that is so, then the speed of his evidence-gathering is either miraculous or was hastily done to satisfy the new "top men" ready to heap insult on Egypt's businessmen and foreign investors. How did he complete his investigations in weeks when his French counterparts took years to compile a case against former President Jacques Chirac, and Britain has taken eight years to decide whether the Iraq War was legal?

Furthermore, the Public Prosecutor is being selective. His investigations do not stretch to those close to Mubarak in the military, such as Chairman of the Supreme Council of the Armed Forces of Egypt, Mohamed Hussein Tantawi and others of Mubarak's staunchest supporters. If Mubarak is deemed to be corrupt, then they should also be scrutinized on the grounds of association. He could begin by talking with Mr Azmi who would likely be a font of information on this score.

In its role as guardian of the state, the Supreme Council of the Armed Forces must get a firm grip on the country as it heads towards political and economic insecurity and counter-revolution. I would say this to the armed forces: you are the heroes of Egypt's freedom. Do not abandon your people when they are vulnerable, when they risk falling victim to a plot to demolish the historic columns on which your country proudly stands. Only you can stop these demonstrations that have become a regular blight on Fridays, only you can prevent the crowd-pleasing humiliation of Egypt's former leadership.

This is not the Egypt that I know. When a military coup deposed King Farouk in 1952, Gamal Abdel Nasser and the other Free Officers gave the monarch a 21-gun royal salute before politely escorting him to a ship sailing for Italy.

Lastly, my message to our brothers and sisters in Egypt is this: keep your heads high; maintain the moral high ground and work positively towards a bright future in which revenge should have no part. Resist playing into your enemies' hands; they will always cheer wrong-doing. Listen instead to your true friends whose duty it is to pinpoint errors and give good advice even when the truth hurts.

Egypt's economic recovery is in the balance

23 May 2011

UNLIKE THOSE WHO cheered the collapse of Egypt's former government, I had serious doubts about the country's future. It was uplifting to witness young people ready to sacrifice their lives for their convictions. However, while I hoped for a happy ending for the sake of this nation close to the heart of every Arab, I am also a realist. Idealism alone cannot solve Egypt's fundamental problems, which have worsened since President Mubarak's downfall.

On Monday, the ruling Supreme Council of the Armed Forces warned the Egyptian economy could collapse. "The poverty rate is approaching 70 per cent and domestic and foreign debt has reached 1,080 billion Egyptian pounds, which is 90 per cent of GDP," said the Assistant Defence Minister for Financial and Administrative Affairs, Mahmoud Nasr. Moreover, there is zero foreign investment largely because the country has been downgraded to "risky".

Mr Nasr said tourism is down 80 per cent causing losses of $40m a day. The foreign currency reserve has been reduced by $8bn, there is a burgeoning budget deficit – and growth will not exceed two per cent.

The reasons he gives for this grave downturn are mixed. They include corruption, declining social values, poor education and worsened relations between the public and law enforcement. But, all is not lost, he says, as the economy's infrastructure remains. His panacea for improvement rests on "true democracy", eradicating corruption and creating of a stable investment climate. Those are fine aspirations but how can they be fulfilled while 70 per cent of Egyptians worry where their next meal is coming from?

The extent of the emergency has not hit home yet, but I predict that when it does there will a revolution of the hungry – at this rate within three months – along the lines of the 1977 "Bread Riots" when millions took to the streets shouting "The people are starving." Last month saw rising food and beverage prices (up 21.7 per cent on last year) due to the high cost of fuel and a weakening of the Egyptian currency making imports more expensive.

It seems to me that the caretaker government needs to get its priorities in order. It is one thing to be open to the concerns of the street and quite another to be its slave. When people do not have jobs and cannot afford to educate their kids, "democracy" rings hollow.

The first thing that should be done is the interim government should get a grip on internal security. My friends in Egypt tell me people are afraid to go out late at night for fear of being robbed or kidnapped for ransom, which was not the case before the uprising. Young men on previously banned motorbikes are snatching handbags and thugs are extorting cash from motorists by threatening to damage their cars.

Then there is the growing rift between Muslims and Copts that spiralled out of control last month in Upper Egypt and again earlier this month when sectarian violence left 12 dead and over 200 injured in one of Cairo's poorest areas where, until recently, Copts and Muslims lived together peacefully.

Instead of pandering to the people's lust for revenge by jailing politicians and businessmen, the military should institute a South African-style Truth and Reconciliation commission and then, once they have admitted their mistakes, draw upon their experience and expertise to put the country to rights.

Those currently in charge may be worthy individuals but they are mostly political novices. Furthermore, locking up high profile business people representing the country's economic backbone is destroying confidence. Their wealth will disappear abroad, their companies will falter and what message does their incarceration send to potential investors?

I admire the efforts of Egypt's former leader Gamal Abdel Nasser to unify the Arab World but his greatest error was to persecute the rich, expropriate their lands and factories and drive them from the country; a mistake that Egypt has never completely recovered from.

Watching Egypt's economy freefalling amid strikes, protests and lawlessness I cannot help wondering whether the uprising was truly grassroots and spontaneous. Or whether some of the young leaders of the April 6th and January 25th movements were, indeed, funded and trained by big powers eager to see Egypt brought to its knees to suit their own geopolitical agendas, as certain US newspapers have suggested.

If the Mother of the Arab World is reduced to a shell by poverty, sectarian violence or civil war or carved up like Sudan to allow for a separate Christian mini-state, the entire Arab World will be traumatized – and the powers that be in Israel and Iran will be rubbing their hands with glee.

There must be wise people in Egypt who see disaster on the horizon if action is not taken now to get things under control. Those people must be courageous enough to dampen unrealistic revolutionary fervour with a dose of tough love. They must not allow chants of "the people want ... " to drown out hard reality. There is still time. I can only pray that influential Egyptians will make good use of it before it is too late.

An impatient minority holds Egypt hostage

24 July 2011

EGYPTIANS HAD THEIR UPRISING that brought about the ousting of their president plus most of the old guard closest to him and they should be looking forward to free and fair, multi-party elections in November. Their revolution has the potential to be hailed as a success story; the people have a voice for the first time and, although the economy remains shaky, offers of economic aid/debt relief have been flooding in from Gulf Cooperation Council (GCC) states as well as Western powers. But instead of capitalizing on interior and external goodwill, disparate elements of the population with the taste of people power still on their lips appear bent on fracturing the country.

Many ordinary Egyptians, who threw their weight behind the young revolutionaries earlier this year, are fed up. They are the ones looking forward to a brighter tomorrow and are willing to exercise patience in order to achieve their common goals. They have had enough "Days of Rage", "Second Revolutions" and "Million Men Marches". They are tired of negotiating traffic jams each Friday because the squares are clogged with activist sit-ins and youths with nothing better to do taking advantage of the party atmosphere.

But people craving security, stability and prosperity are in danger of having their hopes shattered by anarchists, power-seeking activists, parties with self-interested agendas and elitist intellectuals eschewing realpolitik for unrealistic ideologies. Their demands are diverse. Some are more interested in taking revenge on former regime figures and members of security forces than anything else. Not content with the arrest of Hosni Mubarak and his sons or the sentencing of various former ministers and corrupt regime cronies, they demand swift trials and severe punishments for police officers suspected of killing protestors under orders. Others demand an end to military detentions and tribunals.

Yet others, dissatisfied with changes made earlier to the constitution demand a new constitution prior to the November ballot for the purpose of precluding a possible takeover by the Muslim Brotherhood in tandem with other Islamist parties. In response, the Supreme Council of the Armed Forces has appointed a committee to draft a new constitution giving the military overall responsibility for ensuring national unity and maintaining the secular state. However, committee members have rejected giving the military powers of intervention in policies made by any future elected government.

Most dangerous of all are those calling for the resignation of Egypt's military chief Field Marshall Mohamed Hussein Tantawi, accusing him and his colleagues of having betrayed the revolution's principles. Until now, the military has gone out of its way to show solidarity with the people and has allowed them to demonstrate unimpeded. On 8 July when protestors erected tent cities in the squares of Cairo, Alexandria, Port Said, Tanta and Aswan, soldiers distributed bottles of water and shouted "The people and the army are one hand" amid chants of "Down, down with military rule".

When I saw an officer being thoroughly disrespected when he tried to talk to protest leaders in Tahrir Square during last Friday's televised demonstration, I was appalled. Egypt's armed forces used to be the pride of Egypt and the entire Arab World but since the revolution, like the interim governments, they have done nothing but pander to the protesters' every whim. Its willingness to roll over not only makes the military seem weak and ineffectual it leaves decent people without any real protection.

While I understand that military chiefs want to avoid violent clashes with the people that could result in a bloody schism, they should not allow their authority to be undermined at every turn by all and sundry claiming to speak on behalf of the Egyptian people.

The fact is that until elections take place, nobody has any right to represent the will of the people. However, I keep seeing various unknowns introduced as leaders of this or that group being interviewed on Arabic networks, who talk as though they have been given a mandate. They do nothing but moan and groan and rarely have any sort of vision. For them, the revolution has become a video game. In all honesty, watching "Great Egypt" being treated in such a frivolous manner by jumped-up, unqualified nonentities fills me with anger and disgust. Whoever those guys are, if the country's future rests on their shoulders, Egypt's "liberation" will be a mockery as well as a stamp of shame for all proud Arabs.

The only constant within Egypt is the military, which its detractors either fail to understand or are being manipulated by foreign puppeteers eager to see the country weakened, divided or even split in two like Sudan. Egypt's enemies are many and they will do anything to ensure the largest Arab country does not emerge strong to readopt its role as Arab World leader, permitting Israel and Iran free reign throughout the region and allowing the intervention of nations greedy for oil, as is occurring now in Libya due to Muammar Gaddafi's stubborn selfishness. Should Egypt fall the Arab nation will topple along with it and the Gulf will be more vulnerable to outside forces than ever.

Instead of watching from the sidelines, Arab leaders should work with prominent and responsible Egyptian leadership figures, whether military or civilian, in order to preserve the country's integrity. GCC states, in particular, should help Egyptian authorities to straighten the mess and should delay massive sums of economic aid until they know who is in charge to make sure the money will not end up in corrupt pockets.

I am convinced that ordinary hardworking Egyptians will be relieved once they know who is in charge of their country; I can only hope they choose wisely. Only a strong and experienced leadership, prepared to take the reins and unafraid to step on troublemakers' toes, can give them the stability, security and economic growth they crave.

Only God's mercy can save Egypt

6 August 2011

FOR ME, THE SIGHT OF an 83-year-old, former Egyptian president and hero of the October 1973 War lying ill on a stretcher in a courtroom cage as one of his sons bent down to kiss him was hard to watch. And I am sure that many Egyptians, even those who were glad to see him go, feel the same way. On the other hand, provided this historic trial brings closure it is a necessary part of the transformational process.

Strangely, the accused – Hosni Mubarak, his sons Ala'a and Gamal and former Interior Minister Habib Al Adly – appeared more dignified than the attorneys milling around the courtroom most of whom were there to register civilian cases on behalf of their clients.

Such undisciplined and noisy scenes did not reflect well on Egyptian justice in the eyes of billions of viewers and, unfortunately, were grist to the mill of Arab critics such as Israeli military leader and politician Moshe Dayan who has been quoted as saying: "If the Arabs cannot organize their shoes in front of the mosques when they go for prayer, which is the bare minimum, then there is no hope for them … ."

More importantly, the trial should be fair unlike the kangaroo court in Iraq that sent sent former Iraqi President Saddam Hussein to the gallows; it should set the standard for justice in post-revolutionary Egypt.

Verdicts should be passed by impartial judges based on hard evidence. My fear is that Mubarak's day in court will become a political show trial with judges either riding the revolutionary wave themselves or under pressure to please the crowds on the street. If that is the case, Mubarak and others should be tried by an international tribunal.

I want to see Egypt strong, stable and united under a pluralistic political system – and, as the largest Arab country, able to reassert its role as a regional key player. But I fear that the people's current obsession with retribution and promotion of sectarian interests may be harming those goals.

If some interpret my valid concerns as sympathy for the old regime they are wrong. For instance, my column titled "An impatient minority holds Egypt hostage" earlier in this chapter was one of the articles discussed last week on the BBC's 7 Days programme; in particular my assertion that unknown know-it-alls are appearing on Arabic networks falsely claiming a mandate to speak on behalf of the Egyptian people. It is my view that until parliamentary and presidential elections are held in the late autumn, nobody has that right.

One of the BBC's guests was Abdullah Hamouda, an Egyptian journalist based in London, who reacted to the excerpt from my column saying: "Everyone sees what is happening through their own eyes, from their point of view and through their own interests." The host sought to clarify his statement by asking: "You mean that the papers have interest? The Gulf papers you mean and the attitudes in them?"

"Yes, I mean what Al Habtoor, the businessman, said reflects the attitude and position of businessmen in the Gulf who came to Egypt in the time of the old regime and who received all the privileges and all the special treatments at the time and their ability to deal with the corrupted people who were controlling everything at that time," he replied.

"Unfortunately, many of them accomplished a lot this way. I wish that a man like Khalaf Al Habtoor, who is a businessman with a lot of interests in a lot of countries, wouldn't speak in this way. Everyone should see what is happening from the Egyptian people's point of view and what the Egyptian people want, not what these people [outsiders] want," he continued.

To set the record straight, I have never met former President Mubarak, his family or any others accused. I have never been the beneficiary of special treatment or privilege from officialdom during my visits to the country and I have no business interests in Egypt.

It seems to me that Mr Hamouda has fallen into the category of so-called experts believing they know what the Egyptian people want and who are unwilling even to listen to the advice of Egypt's friends who are away from the fire and might, therefore, possess greater objectivity.

Actually, it is not so much what Egyptians want as what they need, which are basically the same needs as people everywhere, especially the ability to hold their heads high, The fact is that Egyptians are diametrically divided. The youth movement wants a Western-style democracy run by a civilian government with no military oversight. Copts want greater political representation and the right to construct churches. Secularists and modernists want an open society and a government in which religion plays no part.

Then there are the Islamist organizations such as the Muslim Brotherhood, which did its best to hide its true objectives during the revolution's aftermath promising not to field a presidential candidate or to target more than 30 per cent of all parliamentary seats while having launched a PR campaign to display its new moderate, all-encompassing face. Since, the layers have peeled off. The Muslim Brotherhood has formed a coalition with Islamist extremist groups and spawned new parties headed by staunch "former" Muslim Brotherhood leaders who *are* going after the presidency.

The veil dropped off the Muslim Brotherhood on Friday 29 July when its members together with other Islamists called for the creation of an Islamic state under Sharia law, chanting "Islam, Islam, we do not want a liberal state" with a few holding up photographs of Osama bin Laden.

As Egypt is predominantly Muslim it is only right that Islamic principles are taken into account by the state, but these fanatics want a kind of Sunni Islamic Republic of Iran that would result in Egypt's international isolation, economic disaster and an end to personal freedoms. If this happens, the Egyptian leadership could look to Tehran for political and economic support, and fall under the ayatollahs' sway in the same way as Iraq, Syria and Lebanon have done.

Now they have finally shown their true colours, I hope the Egyptian people will understand just how dangerous the Muslim Brotherhood are. Iranian delegations have already begun regularly visiting Egypt for discussions with political and religious entities.

Egypt urgently needs a firm, principled captain but until then the military must stop kowtowing to demonstrators without real vision hanging about on the streets and give the Islamists a red line that cannot be crossed.

Just as it was the military that ousted King Farouk in 1952 and bravely defended Egypt against foreign aggression it must step up now to prevent its own ship sinking, taking the rest of us down with it. Egyptians are in the fight of their lives and if they are unable to see that then it is the duty of people like me, a proud Arab who has always loved Egypt, to help open their eyes.

Egyptians require saving from themselves

14 October 2011

ONE OF THE THINGS I despise is wasted potential. It is bad enough witnessing a friend possessed of God-given personal attributes and opportunities self-destruct, but it is much worse to watch helplessly as a country I love disintegrates when, in reality, it has everything going for it.

I am especially disturbed at the direction Egypt is taking when with the proper guidance and utilization of its natural resources, it could undergo a life-changing economic and social transformation that would benefit

335

all levels of society. Egyptians have had their revolution and in a perfect world should be looking forward to a new era of prosperity, political self-determination and personal freedom. Everything in the garden should be rosy, but it is not.

On the contrary, a grave situation has developed because the country is virtually leaderless. There is no one in either the Supreme Council of the Armed Forces or the interim government strong enough or courageous enough to quell the chaos on the street and put the country on a right path. Prime Minister Essam Sharaf and his cabinet take orders from the Egypt's real rulers, the military, while the military goes out of its way to appease protesters.

As each day passes Egypt's future is being suffocated by groups with competing interests, striking workers, anti-government protestors and interfaith violence. People who before the popular uprising were fatalistic when it came to their lot in life and were happy just to find their piece of bread each day not only want more, they want it now. Egypt has long been a pressure cooker and now that the lid is off it may be about to boil over.

Those who were once powerless have tasted what people power can do and are using this newfound tool as a weapon with which to beat the interim government and the Supreme Council of the Armed Forces to get what they want. They have no idea that freedom does not give people the right to torch places of worship, damage foreign embassies, deface state property and battle state security forces; they may believe they are exercising their democratic freedoms whereas, in fact, they are engaging in criminal acts.

The irony is that the thuggish behaviour of the few could so easily rob all Egyptians of their hard-won freedoms and poison the growing bud of democracy for decades to come. With the population increasingly split between those who trust the military's leadership and those who accuse the Supreme Council of wanting to retain power for itself, there exists the danger that some foolhardy suicidal types will try to take on the army, eliciting civil war.

To avoid blood in the streets, it is crucial for the Supreme Council to get a handle on things before they escalate out of control. Now is the time for Field Marshal Mohamed Hussein Tantawi to get tough, to give people red lines that cannot be crossed – and especially to make them aware that all Egyptians must be respected no matter their religious affiliations. The international community and, in particular, the United States will not stand by if the Coptic minority that makes up around 10 per cent of the population is discriminated against or has justifiable fears for its community's safety.

There were news reports that the US Secretary of State Hillary Clinton had told CNN that Washington would intervene to protect the Copts, which the US Department of State has denied. However, when the US has invaded Iraq and led a military intervention in

Libya, both oil-rich Arab countries, this is not as far-fetched as it might sound. Egypt has oil and gas and its Suez Canal makes it a unique strategic asset that could tempt the US to go in under the pretext of a humanitarian intervention.

Moreover, it is up to the military in partnership with the interim civilian government to stabilize the economy, which according to the *Financial Times* "is in the mire". Egypt's foreign currency reserves have dropped by one third since 25 January and both its share index and tourism industry are negatively impacted following each violent incident.

Allowing a minority of troublemakers to dictate terms is ludicrous. Most Egyptians are fed up with the disturbances; they want to get on with their lives in peace. If there is no one in Egypt ready, able and willing to firmly take the people by the hand then the best solution would be for a trusted strong and stable friendly nation to temporarily intervene to establish stability and security – and institute a fair judicial system based on just laws applicable to all.

I would have loved to have been able to share everyone's revolutionary zeal; I would have been delighted to join in Egypt's celebrations with an open heart. But deep inside I knew there might not be a happy ending, which is why I have written several newspaper columns warning of the dangers and obstacles ahead – and urging those in charge to gain control over the Arab World's largest country, which my generation of Arabs regarded as highly as our own mother countries.

I will say it one more time. Democracy can wait. The army must take charge to save Egyptians from themselves else once-mighty Egypt will turn into an impoverished and lawless banana republic.

Al Arabiya should vet its guests for brains

27 May 2012

WITH TENS OF PROFESSIONAL Arabic TV channels to choose from, over the years I have narrowed my viewing down to just two – Al Jazeera and Al Arabiya. Why? Because in my opinion those have evolved into our Arab World's trusted flagship networks, providing viewers with comprehensive reporting and balanced viewpoints. So when a few of my friends called me the other morning suggesting I watch a re-run on of one of Hassan Moawad's "Noqtat Nitham" (A Point of Order) on Alarabiya.net I did not hesitate. They should have warned me that I was in for a shock.

On this occasion, Moawad's guest was the Egyptian-American founder and president of "Arabs for Israel" Nonie Darwish (born Nahed Mustafa Hafez Darwish) who is believed to have written two books with the controversial titles *Now They Call Me an Infidel: Why I Renounced Jihad for America, Israel and the War on Terror and Cruel* and *Usual Punishment: the Terrifying Global Implications of Islamic Law.*

337

I use the phrase "believed to have written" purposefully because, in all honesty, after seeing her shambolic performance on the show, it is hard to imagine that she has authored anything, with the possible exception of brainless hate-screeds designed to incite die-hard Islamophobes with even less grey matter than her own.

Her latest effort is called *The Devil We Don't Know: the Dark Side of Revolutions in the Middle East* penned around the thesis that all Middle East revolutions have been failures since the disintegration of the Ottoman Empire. She likens the Arab Spring to what she calls Egypt's failed 1952 revolution, even though that was a popularly-backed military coup that unseated King Farouk – and she erroneously characterizes Gamal Abdel Nasser, Hafez Al Assad and Muammar Gaddafi as Islamists while warning that if Egypt's new president fails to live up to the Muslim Brotherhood's expectations he will be assassinated like President Anwar Sadat.

I certainly did not expect to agree with Ms Darwish's opinions and anticipated they might be slightly off the wall. Nevertheless, I was looking forward to a lively discussion between two knowledgeable individuals holding opposing viewpoints. I was, in fact, impressed by the level of professionalism involving meticulous preparation and research displayed by Mr Moawad but was astonished at Ms Darwish's sheer ignorance about both Islam and Middle East politics.

The disparity between the mindsets and debating skills of the host and his guest was embarrassing, almost akin to Einstein attempting to discuss his Theory of Relativity with Bugs Bunny. As she jiggled her hands about, squirmed in her seat, flicked through her notes in desperation or gazed up in the air clutching for answers I might have felt sorry for her if it were not for the baseless anti-Islamic propaganda and traitorous anti-Arab sentiments she was spouting.

Okay, she may have converted to Christianity after marrying and moving to the US, but whatever the colour of her passport her blood will always be Egyptian and Arab whether she likes it or not. Her father Mustafa Hafez, an officer in the Egyptian army, was the victim of a targeted killing by Israeli soldiers in 1956 – and was referred to by the former Egyptian President Gamal Abdel Nasser as a *shahid* (martyr) whose death would be avenged. That poor man who gave his life for his country would be turning in his grave if he knew that his own flesh-and-blood was going around exonerating his murderers because "the *fedayeen* were killing Israelis".

"Your father was one of those *fedayeen*, does that mean your father was a terrorist?" asked Moawad. She fumbled for a reply before announcing her feeble definition of a terrorist – a person who straps something around their body!

Darwish did express her love for the Egyptian people while blasting the youth in Tahrir Square for not carrying placards demanding separation of religion and state or insisting upon the removal of Article 2 of the constitution whereby legislation should conform to the principles of Sharia law. But when she was questioned why she neglects to criticize the Jewish state on similar grounds, she was stumped. Criticism of Israel does not feature in this lady's manual. On the contrary, she displays little sympathy for the Palestinians and in a 2009 interview she regretted that "acts of goodwill and decency by Israel are never mentioned in the media", adding "I felt that this is not giving justice to Israel."

When she was asked what she thought of Terry Jones, the Texas preacher who burned the Quran, her answer illuminated her absence of any moral compass. She actually equated that heinous act with the burning of the US flag, which is the way some Muslims (among others) have vented their political frustrations. She was equally confused about the people behind the ousting of President Mubarak for which she credited the Muslim Brotherhood, forgetting that just a few minutes earlier she had acknowledged that the youth were responsible for the uprising.

She clearly has a bee in her bonnet against Sharia claiming that if Egyptians demand Sharia they cannot ask for democracy and freedom in the same breath. There was one entertaining moment of levity. She said she has visited two mosques in the US that advocated an Islamic White House and said British Muslims are out to convert the monarchy to Islam which, according to Ms Darwish, explains why Islamophobia is rampant in the West.

Illogical people just out for self-publicity should not be promoted or given a platform; they merely damage themselves, waste the viewers' time and, ultimately, undermine the credibility of the network. Salman Rushdie's book *The Satanic Verses* received little critical acclaim but became a best-seller following the Ayatollah Ruhollah Khomeini's death sentence fatwa, fattening the author's pocket.

Nonie Darwish is a self-hating nonentity who enjoys stomping on her roots. She could be a Mormon, a Scientologist or even a Moonie as far as I am concerned. There is an Arabic saying that says it all. When a man called Hanoun, who had a reputation for being useless, converted to Islam, people around said "Hanoun didn't enhance Islam and neither did he damage Christianity". I could say the same about Ms Darwish who is no loss to Islam and no credit to Christianity. She is no asset to Al Arabiya either. I hope that Mr Moawad has the sense to grab a large black marker with which to cross her name forever off his guest list.

Egypt needs "tough love" to reject Iran's overtures

7 April 2013

THE VISIT OF IRAN'S ENVOY to the Egyptian capital, coinciding with the first direct flight from Cairo to Tehran in 34 years, was ostensibly to deepen his country's ties with Egypt and discuss solutions to the Syrian crisis. But rather than a goodwill visit, it was shamelessly used as a platform to castigate Arab leaderships for giving Syria's seat at the League of Arab States to a representative of the opposition coalition.

Iran's Deputy Minister of Foreign Affairs Hossein Amir-Abdollahian blasted the Arab League's decision in the presence of its Secretary General Nabil Elaraby and accused member countries of serving the goals of Western governments in the Middle East. "It would be better if the Arab leaders drew attention to defending oppressed people," he said.

Talk about the pot calling the kettle black when Iranians are among the most downtrodden people on earth! I too wish that Arab heads of state would defend the oppressed, in particular, the Arabs of Ahwaz and Iranian Sunnis who have been persecuted and treated like second-class citizens for decades. Iran's treatment of its Arab and Sunni communities is a disgrace and its "concern" for Syrians nothing but a sham.

Tehran's core interest in Syria is the retention of its stranglehold over that geo-strategically important Arab country, serving as a conduit for the funding of and supply of weapons to terrorist organizations in neighbouring countries. That aside, we are still waiting to hear Elaraby's riposte to that diatribe expounded on Arab soil – I guess we will have a long wait. If he had any kind of backbone, he would have told Amir-Abdollahian on the spot to keep his nose out of Arab affairs. By contrast, Sheikh Al Azhar Ahmed Al Tayyeb told the visiting Iranian President Mahmoud Ahmadinejad not to interfere in Bahrain or attempt to influence Egypt's Sunni majority. We are used to Iranian aggression but the fact that this violation of our sovereignty occurred in Egypt, which used to be considered "the heart of the Arab World" when Gamal Abdel Nasser, Anwar Sadat and Hosni Mubarak were at the helm, makes my blood boil.

Amir-Abdollahian went on to tell the press that he had held a "constructive discussion" with Elaraby with whom he "exchanged views especially on Bahrain, Syria and Palestine". How dare this Iranian official equate the issues of Bahrain and Palestine with the tragedy unfolding in Syria! Bahrain's problem arises from an Iranian fifth column on the island, inciting traitors to rise up against the monarch. And no one with even a scant knowledge of the true state of affairs should label it differently. Then to sweeten the pill, he audaciously expressed "Iran's approval of the efforts of the Arab League in regard to the Syrian crisis". I was not aware that we need Iran's rubber-stamping of our internal decisions.

The extent of Tehran's meddling in Arab matters has reached an intolerable level. Why have Elaraby and Egypt's Minister of Foreign Affairs Kamel Amr provided Tehran with a free pass to express its dissatisfaction with Arab League positions? Where are the voices of Arab and Gulf Cooperation Council (GCC) leaders, especially those directly threatened by Iran's belligerence? Are they content to be bystanders permitting Iran to manipulate our region's future?

This disrespectful ticking-off on the part of a top Iranian official and Egypt's failure to appropriately respond should be considered a deafening wake-up call. It is time we mulled some hard questions as to the loyalties of the Egyptian government; questions that would have been unthinkable a few years ago. When the Muslim Brotherhood's man President Mohamed Morsi first moved into the Al Ittihadiya Palace offices last year, I adopted a wait-and-see attitude. *Let us give him a chance*, I thought based on his speeches and statements pledging that Egypt would remain the Arab World's heartland and the guardian of Arab interests.

Initially, he talked a good talk and promised to be a president for all Egyptians regardless of their religious or political affiliations. Yet, not only has he let down the Egyptian people, driving the country towards bankruptcy and internal conflicts, he has laid out a red carpet for Iran's ayatollahs, ministers and the secretive Revolutionary Guard Al Quds Force, which, by the way is grossly misnamed. Iran has no right to name a terrorist organization, currently murdering Syrians, after one of Islam's holiest places, Jerusalem, site of the Haram Al Sharif, and it is a mystery to me why the Organisation of Islamic Cooperation (OIC), the Arab League and Muslim leaders have not voiced their objections.

GCC leaders and the few remaining true Arab leaders must take a firm stand against Egypt, which is sinking under the Muslim Brotherhood's regime before our very eyes. Constructive intervention is urgently needed before it is too late. Today, Tehran's representatives are strutting around Cairo presiding over press conferences and there are numerous flights arriving from Iran packed with "tourists" eager to visit Egypt's tourist sites. Iran estimates as many as 2 million Iranian "tourists" will head to Egypt annually. Tomorrow, we will see the nation's Sunni mosques flying Shi'ite flags and Khomeini's portrait on billboards like in Lebanon. Think that is far-fetched?

Egypt's Minister of Tourism Hesham Zaazou is clearly concerned about the ramifications of this potential influx. He wants to impose restrictions permitting only "entertainment trips", allowing Iranian visitors free access to tourist sites and resorts while barring them from mosques. That policy been challenged by the acting Iranian ambassador in Cairo. "Iranian tourists have the right to visit whatever places they want in Egypt ..." he said.

Some Egyptians have been so rattled at the new cozy Iranian-Egyptian relations that include a tourism agreement that they are organizing protests against Iranian Shi'ite proselytizers. Egyptian cleric Safwat Hijazi told Al Arabiya that Iranian tourists will not come simply to enjoy what the country has to offer, but will actively spread religious doctrine. Iran tends to "stir problems wherever it exists" like in Iran and Syria, he rightly noted.

In conclusion, there are two pressing issues that need addressing:

The GCC should inform the Egyptian government where it stands.

The time for coddling Cairo with billions in financial aid/loans should end as long as it embraces Iran, which, by its actions in Iraq, Syria, Lebanon and Bahrain, has proved an enemy of Arab states. Any pledges of financial aid should be withdrawn on the grounds it will be used against us by Iran's seeming new proxy in Egypt – the Muslim Brotherhood – that is doing its utmost to infiltrate and poison Gulf states. Any GCC member country that refuses to quit propping up the Brothers should be condemned. An iron hand must be used to push Cairo in the right direction; they must choose – them or us?

All Arab leaderships, including Egypt, Iraq and Lebanon, should prevent Iranians treating our lands as though they were the owners, else call themselves Persian and be done with it. If Iranians wish to make demeaning statements on wholly Arab issues, they can be as offensive as they like on their own ground. Arab territories are precious and should not be open for Iranians to pour vitriol on our dignity, ignite dissent or proselytize Shi'ite ideology.

"The Arab world is writing a new future; the pen is in our own hands," said Jordan's King Abdullah II. True, but without the courage and conviction to draw a secure tomorrow a pen is just a hollow stick filled with ink!

Erdoğan an pours oil on troubled Nile waters

20 July 2013

THE ARMY'S OVERTHROW of the failed former Egyptian president Mohammed Morsi, in order to rescue Egypt from the spectre of civil war, has stripped the Turkish Prime Minister of his moderate mask. In September 2011, Recep Tayyip Erdoğan used Dream TV's platform to urge Egyptians to adopt a secular constitution that would put Egyptians of all faiths on an equal footing, adding: "Secularism does not mean atheism". In the event, that advice was ignored.

Morsi issued power-grabbing presidential edicts, appointed Islamists to parliament's Upper House and pushed through a constitution that ignored the rights of minorities and women. And instead of listening to warnings from the EU as well as his own advisors that his non-inclusive stance was polarizing the country, he proceeded to insert governors from the Muslim Brotherhood and the Jamaa Islamiya in nine Egyptian governorates. Hours-long queues for petrol, winding bread queues and regular electricity cuts marked the final seal on his political demise.

Over 30 million Egyptians, representing a third of the population, said he had to go. Whether one views the military's intervention as a coup or democracy's correction by popular demand is purely academic. Egypt's future track is for Egyptians to decide – and the majority have made the decision to put right mistakes made following their 2011 revolution. As far as they are concerned, Morsi was impeached by the street for leading the nation down a dark and dangerous tunnel. To give their sentiments context, if the general manager of a multinational corporation broke his contractual obligations by setting that corporation on the road to bankruptcy, he can hardly complain when shareholders demand the termination of his contract.

However, instead of respecting the Egyptian people's will, Prime Minister Erdoğan has been surprisingly antagonistic, going as far as to announce that he would not recognize Egypt's new interim government while insisting: "My president in Egypt is Morsi because he was elected by the people." Emphasizing his stance was his refusal of an invitation to meet with Egypt's interim Vice President Mohamed ElBaradei. Erdoğan told a Turkish daily "If we don't judge the situation like that it is tantamount to ignoring the Egyptian people." Ah, this is telling. Just about the only sector of Egyptians refusing to accept the transition are members of the Muslim Brotherhood, which indicates that Erdoğan is siding with his ideological brethren against the Egyptian people. Turkey's Minister for European Affairs asked the United Nations (UN) Security Council to "take action" in response to "the coup". A spokesman for the interim president has accused the Turkish premier of meddling in his nation's affairs.

At a time when Turkey has its own problems with anti-government protestors, dispersed by riot police using teargas and water cannon and arrested in their hundreds, its government seems unduly concerned by events in Egypt. Arab leaders have wisely taken a back seat on Turkey's problems whereas Erdoğan is behaving as though the Ottoman Empire is still up and running. His own country in crisis, Erdoğan was driven to cut short his vacation on the Aegean coast to summon senior cabinet ministers for an emergency meeting to discuss events in Egypt! Following that cabinet session, representatives of the Global Muslim Brotherhood and other Islamist organizations were secretly hosted in a hotel close to Istanbul's Ataturk Airport, according to Al Watan News, to discuss developments.

The message is crystal clear. Prime Minister Erdoğan perceives Egypt's rejection of the Brotherhood as a threat to his own Islamist AK Party, which until now held up as a successful model of political Islam in the region. With the domino theory at the forefront of his mind, he rightly worries that anti-government demonstrators who flocked to Taksim Square and Gezi Park may feel empowered by Egypt's example – or, worse, that they, too, will look to the powerful Turkish military, with which the Erdoğan government has had fraught relations, to come to their aid. Like his friend Morsi, Erdoğan is shoring up his party's interests and has abandoned fair judgment in so doing. If Egypt's caretaking cabinet succeed in stabilizing the country and achieving a pluralistic democracy, his dream of exporting the AK party's brand of Islamic democracy throughout the Middle East will be dashed.

It is obvious that Erdoğan could not care less about Egyptians, which prompts one to wonder about his other stated commitments. For instance, he talks a good talk against the brutal Syrian regime – and, to be fair, he has done a lot for Syrian refugees – but so far his aggressive posture against Assad has not been translated into action. The same can be said for his support of Palestinians. Following an attack by Israeli commandos on a Turkish-led aid flotilla attempting to break Israel's siege on Gaza, causing the death of nine Turkish citizens, Erdoğan, who has provided material support to Hamas, described the raid "as a cause for war". The attack elicited icy relations between long-term close allies, Ankara and Tel Aviv, diplomats were withdrawn, but that is as far as it went. Today, Israel and Turkey are almost as cosy as ever.

While the Obama administration and the EU were initially cautious following Morsi's sudden downfall, they now accept this fait accompli provided the country forges ahead quickly with a new constitution followed by parliamentary and presidential elections. Erdoğan is increasingly out on a limb and if he fails to treat his paranoia and take the hand of friendship that Egypt's new leadership still extends, the future for Turkish-Egyptian relations looks grim.

From my personal viewpoint, I heartily welcome the changes taking place in Egypt. The Muslim Brotherhood was not satisfied with getting their man in Al Ittihadiya Palace, it was out to spread its poisonous world view throughout Gulf states. We do not want glassy-eyed fanatics causing trouble in our countries – and neither do our brothers and sisters in Egypt, hoping for a prosperous new dawn. I wish them luck.

Obama's true colours shrouded in mystery

2 January 2014

WHAT AN INSPIRATIONAL FIGURE US President Barack Obama once was! He rode on a wave of positive change. His hope-filled rhetoric was spell-binding. I was convinced that he was the genuine article, a compassionate human being resolved to win hearts and minds within and outside of his nation's borders – the opposite of his predecessor, George W. Bush, whose aggressive foreign policies soiled America's reputation as a force for good.

Many of those who rooted for Obama in 2008 forgave him his failure to fulfil most of his pre-election promises – his pledge to close Guantanamo, to bring about a Palestinian state, withdraw troops from Afghanistan by mid-2011 and reach out to the Arab World – as US presidents tend to towards caution during their first terms with an eye on re-election.

Once the shackles were loosened during Obama's second term, we counted upon him to do what is right. We were wrong. Drone attacks on Afghanistan and Pakistan that sever the lives of civilians are ongoing. The Palestinian-Israeli peace process is nothing but a behind-closed-doors PR farce to cover expanding Jewish colonies on the West Bank. And, rather than guide his nation closer to America's allies in the Middle East and the

Gulf, Obama's decisions have pushed Saudi Arabia, Egypt and even its Middle East proxy, Israel, to seek greater self-reliance.

The American people are disappointed too for reasons of their own. Today, Obama's domestic approval rating, according to a Gallup poll, stands at just 39 per cent, several points lower than that of President Bush at the same stage of his presidency.

It seems Obama lacks the courage of his convictions and has been dubbed by newspapers as "Ditherer-in-Chief". But does he really suffer from hesitancy or confused thinking? Or, are those "personality traits" deliberately contrived as a façade to hide a murky foreign policy agenda – or even a personal ideology – from the American people and US allies?

I have no interest in conspiracy theories and I am not inclined to point a finger without being sure of my facts. However, I am flabbergasted by some of Obama's twists and turns in recent months that have shocked and dismayed America's long-time regional partners.

For instance, why does the White House regularly criticize the Egyptian government when it was virtually silent over Morsi's litany of authoritarian edicts and crackdowns on protestors last winter? When Representatives Michelle Bachman, Steve King and Louie Gohmert visited Cairo in September, they addressed the Egyptian people, saying: "We are here as members of Congress to say we are with you, we encourage you because together we are going through the same suffering – the United States and Egypt have the same enemy – terrorism."

Americans shudder at the very word terrorism, yet although Egypt has been plagued by terrorist attacks since Morsi's toppling on 3 July by public demand, the US, which says it supports "the will of the people", has seen fit to punish and condemn the largest Arab nation for its attempts to rein in violence. In this connection, there are important questions that require answering:

Firstly, is there any truth to the allegations that the President's half-brother Malik Hussein Obama, who manages the Barack H. Obama Foundation, is the Executive Secretary of Sudan's Islamic Da'wa Organization linked to the Muslim Brotherhood and headed by the Deputy Head of a Hamas fundraising organization? More to the point, why has the mainstream media shied away from investigating this?

Secondly, did the Obama administration secretly fund the Muslim Brotherhood's political campaigning in Egypt as announced on various Egyptian television networks – and if so, why? Saad El Shater, the son of Khairat El Shater, a senior Muslim Brotherhood leader, told a news agency in Anatolia that his family "has evidence" tying Obama directly to the Brotherhood, warning that such evidence would become public knowledge unless Egyptian authorities released his father from prison; shortly afterwards he was also detained.

Thirdly, is former member of the United States House of Repre-sentatives Allen West right in claiming that the Muslim Brotherhood has infiltrated the Obama administration? In June 2012, West urged the President to repudiate the Brotherhood and later wrote on Facebook: "We do have Muslim Brotherhood-affiliated groups and individuals infiltrated into this current Obama administration." If, indeed, the White House is occupied or influenced by the Muslim Brotherhood, it is no wonder Iran is suddenly America's new best friend, never mind that in the process the US is seriously jeopardizing its relationship with Israel, previously believed to be off-limits. Never before has a US leader U-turned so dramatically while snubbing Israel's security concerns in the process.

Questions of crucial importance to Saudi Arabia and Gulf states are:

- Why did Obama step back from military action to destroy Syria's chemical weapons capabilities at the last minute, thus abandoning the Syrian people to their fate and leaving the Free Syrian Army (FSA) he claimed to support high and dry?

- Why is Obama prepared to alienate trusted American allies, such as Saudi Arabia and Israel, in order to leave the Assad regime in place and fortify US relations with its backers – the Islamic Republic of Iran? What act of good faith has Iran displayed to grant it entry into the community of nations when nothing has changed in-country apart from a fresh face in the number two slot?

- What drove Obama to threaten use of his veto to halt a bi-partisan Senate bill aimed at imposing more sanctions on Iran on 19 December, especially when great swathes of Congress oppose any cosy détente with Tehran?

Unfortunately, we may never be privy to the realities behind the scenes. Is it even conceivable that the US President's sympathies could lie with the Muslim Brotherhood and its Shi'ite ally Iran that is provided safe haven for Al Qaeda terrorists? That is almost beyond belief, which is probably why those allegations have not hit the headlines.

However, given our region's vulnerabilities and the chameleon nature of this White House, we must be alert to all possibilities. I trust our intelligence agencies are working behind the scenes to find clarity within the fog of suspicion for the benefit of Arabs and Westerners alike.

Are foreign and regional hands plotting Egypt's downfall?

4 February 2014

IT IS COMMONLY SAID that one only discovers his true friends during times of trouble and that goes for countries too. Today, the Egyptian government is battling a Muslim Brotherhood-led insurgency that, if permitted to succeed, could hurtle the nation into civil war. A disgruntled minority has resorted to violence to hold the majority hostage. This past month has witnessed an increase in bombings targeting the police, allegedly carried out by Ansar Bait Al Maqdis, a terrorist group allied to the Brotherhood, believed to have been funded by its former Deputy Supreme Guide Khairat El Shater.

When Saudi Arabia's King Abdullah met with US Secretary of State John Kerry in November, he stressed that Egypt is too important to fail, which is one reason why the Kingdom, together with the United Arab Emirates (UAE) and Kuwait, have lent diplomatic and financial backing to the transitional authority. Needless to say I was extremely disturbed to read a report in *Al Khaleej* published on 30 January, about a recent meeting between Qatari, Turkish and Israeli intelligence services that allegedly met to discuss how those countries can best support the outlawed Brotherhood.

The report further highlights the stance of the Turkish Prime Minister Recep Tayyip Erdoğan, who is apparently keen to ensure that the Muslim Brotherhood continues to be funded via sacrosanct diplomatic pouches, given that the assets and bank accounts of at least 702 of its leaders and over 1,000 Brotherhood-affiliated non-governmental organizations (NGOs) have been frozen. The supply of weapons and artillery enabling the Brotherhood to foment even greater chaos and bloodshed was also discussed.

If proven to be factual, this news is serious cause for alarm. The idea that a cabal of foreign intelligence agents have come together to cook up plots against an Arab nation struggling to regain its footing, is beyond belief. The only actor missing from this axis is Iran, whose involvement would automatically render the grouping a lethal enemy to all moderate Arab nations. Such solidarity with the Muslim Brotherhood, that spawned Hamas, the Egyptian Islamic Jihad and served as inspiration to leaders of Al Qaeda, on the part of Qatar and Turkey in collaboration with Israel, is impossible to analyse accurately.

Al Watan News has reported Erdoğan's hosting of global Muslim Brotherhood conferences on Turkish soil, designed to undermine the Egyptian government. The beleaguered Turkish leader, whose own grip on power is now shaky, has unashamedly embraced the Brotherhood, going as far as to flash the *Rabaa* hand sign. Clearly he is personally invested on an ideological level and is uncaring that his anti-Egypt tongue-lashings have been detrimental to Turkish-Egyptian trade and investment – and have resulted in the downgrading of diplomatic relations.

Israel is no fan of Islamists and is known to be cooperating closely with the Egyptian military to rid the Sinai Peninsula of armed radicals. It is known, too, that the Israeli government petitioned the US President against instituting punitive measures against Egypt. Does Israel fear a resurgence of Arab nationalism if and when an adored military man, who is being likened to Gamal Abdel Nasser, becomes president? Or is Israel merely playing both sides in an endeavour to keep Egypt on its knees?

Qatar's hostile position towards Egypt is even harder to fathom. It is no secret that once warm relations between Cairo and Doha descended to freezing point over the toppling of Mohamed Morsi, whose government was the recipient of a $7.5bn Qatari aid package, now in the process of being returned. Last month, Egypt's Foreign Office summoned the Qatari ambassador following a statement from Doha describing the decision to label the Muslim Brotherhood terrorist as "a prelude to a shoot-to-kill policy".

I know of Qatar's former ruler Sheikh Hamad bin Khalifa Al Thani, and I know the former Prime Minister Sheikh Hamad bin Jassim Al Thani, on a personal level and would love to know whether they and the current Emir Sheikh Tamim bin Hamad Al Thani are truly aware of what is happening.

For instance, do they know that Yusuf Al Qaradawi, Doha's revered guest, has launched verbal attacks against the UAE, which has always backed its sister nation Qatar, and more recently against Saudi? Are they aware that Al Jazeera is feting Muslim Brotherhood leaders holed up in five-star hotels at the network's expense? If they are not aware, then that is a problem. If they are, that is an even bigger problem. Why is Al Jazeera being permitted to destroy its journalistic integrity with its relentless bashing of the Egyptian government and interviews with Muslim Brotherhood spokespersons masquerading as academics? And why is Qatar refusing to comply with Egypt's legitimate request to extradite Qaradawi, wanted for inciting the killing of Egyptian security forces?

To say that I am disappointed at Qatar's pro-Brotherhood position would be an understatement. The Gulf Cooperation Council (GCC) should require the Qatari government to reverse course because one member country's actions negatively impact the entire body. Qatar should clarify whether or not reports that it is colluding with Turkey and Israel against Egypt are true. And if Qatar cares about the unity of Gulf states, it should show good faith by putting Qaradawi and his cohorts on a plane to Cairo and bring an immediate halt to the vicious broadcasts from Al Jazeera against our beloved Egypt, the cradle of Arabism, whose sons have unstintingly given their blood during wars to preserve the dignity of our Arab Ummah.

Lastly, I would urge the Qatari leadership not to sacrifice its good relations with neighbours in favour of a failed organization that is gasping its dying breaths within Egypt and will soon wither away globally. I pray that our Qatari brothers will realize that supporting the Brotherhood is a lost cause. Instead, they would do well to remember that we who are privileged to live around the Arabian Gulf are interwoven as one family, one body – and, God willing, we will always remain so.

Egypt must crush its enemies and ignore critics

19 April 2014

D ESPITE SEVERE ECONOMIC problems and sporadic Muslim
Brotherhood protests that frequently turn violent, most Egyptians
are optimistic that next month's presidential elections will bring stability.
But, tragically, there are those determined to crush 90 million hopes and
will readily shed blood to achieve their goals; terrorists who pose a threat
to the most populated Arab nation and even to the security of Arabian
Gulf states.

While it is known that the Egyptian military is working to purge the
Sinai Peninsula from armed jihadist groups, such as Ansar Beit Al Maqdis
(founded by the Brotherhood's Deputy Supreme Guide in coordination
with Hamas), a recent article titled "Free Egyptian Army being formed
in Libya" published in the state-owned Egyptian daily *Al Akhbar* quotes
the following warning from security sources: "Attempts to create a Free
Egyptian Army in Libya [led by Al Qaeda commander Abu Ubaida
who's been active in Syria] have been identified with the participation of
the Muslim Brotherhood and Al-Qaeda under Qatari-Turkish-Iranian
patronage, in addition to plans to target vital installations, including
Cairo International Airport, the storming of prisons to free Muslim
Brotherhood detainees – and spreading chaos to sabotage the presidential
elections." The report goes on to reveal that Libyan factories are making
army uniforms in preparation for "zero hour" to be decided by foreign
intelligence agencies.

There is no time to waste! The Egyptian government is aware that
several foreign countries are conspiring to bring Egypt to its knees,
supported by certain Western powers, and must act with urgency. There
should be no negotiations or compromises with bloodthirsty traitors and
foreign scoundrels. The generals should open their eyes and move with
all power to eradicate the threat before the presidential ballot, else with
a heavy heart I predict that Egypt as we know it will cease to be and the
Arab World will lose its pulse. I would, therefore, urge Cairo to execute the
following steps without delay:

- Ensure that Egypt's border with Libya is 100 per cent sealed using
  all necessary force.
- Insert state security and military intelligence operatives within
  Libyan territory to assess the threat and, if necessary, authorize
  targeted short sharp military operations to annihilate militias hostile
  to Egypt – a defensive/pre-emptive strategy drawn from the US
  military playbook.
- Destroy all smuggling tunnels between Gaza and Egypt and close
  the Rafah crossing indefinitely.

- Use all possible means to cleanse Sinai of jihadist bases and militias before this disease multiplies.

- Closely monitor visitors from countries known to be unfriendly and investigate non-governmental organizations (NGOs) suspected of being a cover for foreign intelligence services.

Egypt has already withdrawn its ambassadors from Turkey and Qatar and should now focus on its diplomatic relations with Iran. Just days ago, the Ministry of Foreign Affairs summoned the Iranian chargé d'affaires to protest the fact that his mission has been engaged in meetings with individuals affiliated with the banned Brotherhood. Iran cannot be trusted. It is a puppetmaster in Lebanon; it is behind the civil unrest in Bahrain and its emissaries are fighting alongside the Syrian dictator. In January, Egypt objected to an announcement by the Iranian Foreign Ministry to the effect Tehran is concerned about the escalation in violence between Egypt's army and Brotherhood protestors. Such hypocrisy when Iranians, many living under the poverty line, are not permitted to demonstrate against economic deprivation, human rights or freedom of speech! Iranian diplomats in Egypt should be sent packing along with their wooden spoons.

Egypt is on the brink and cannot afford the luxury of pandering to human rights concerns at this juncture. Plotters hiding under the cover of human rights pretending they want the best for Egypt deserve to be silenced. The Western world righteously demanding Egypt adheres to its own standards in human rights should back off. When the West was attacked by Al Qaeda it was quick to trash the Geneva Conventions as well as conventions against torture; nowadays they wield words like "freedom", "democracy" and "human rights" like battering rams with which to attack Arab countries defending their security and sovereignty. In 2012, on the heel of riots in Britain, Prime Minister David Cameron, who is constantly criticizing Egypt's authorities, announced that he was working to scrap the Human Rights Act, saying "We cannot go on with a situation where people who are a threat to our national security ... are able to cite their human rights when they are clearly wholly unconcerned about the human rights of others." Enough worrying what the world thinks! Egypt is at war.

Almost all Gulf Cooperation Council (GCC) member countries are ready to stand by Egypt in its effort to eradicate terrorism at its roots because our leaders know that our own homes are similarly threatened. The GCC in coordination with the League of Arab States should unite against the Brotherhood and eliminate subversives, fanatics and criminals from our region, such as Al Qaeda, Jabhat Al Nusra, Daesh as well as uniformed thugs in the pay of Tehran and its ally Baghdad carrying out a well-planned agenda to undermine Gulf states.

Frankly I am amazed that with all the advanced surveillance technologies available to Gulf states and our Washington ally, it is apparently difficult to track down armed extremists when we regularly watch gun-toting fanatics being interviewed on TV against a background of black flags or training for battle. Why are they being filmed and promoted rather than being captured? If brutal killers proud to sever heads are considered honourable freedom fighters nowadays then perhaps I should throw away my pen in a world where morality counts for nothing.

For centuries we Arabs have been too trusting. The world is arguably a far more dangerous place than ever before and so we should not trust anyone other than ourselves. We must no longer count on others to fight our fights. We should not believe promises made by foreign powers claiming they have our interests at heart. Now, more than ever, is not the time to let down our guard. Instead, we should shelve diplomatic-speak in favour of forthrightness and transparency to show that we care for our people and will put their protection before all else. GCC states are not known for harbouring hidden agendas like so many other countries, but we can no longer continue battling adversaries with our hands tied behind our backs. We must come up with our own effective strategies instead of counting on the benevolence of big powers, which history shows are not benevolent at all. The US and its European allies will not help us. They will side with the winner, whether it is Daesh or some Shi'ite militia; they will applaud whoever has the upper hand.

Finally, my message to Egypt and the heads of Gulf states is this: the difference between a leader and a great leader is the ability to take decisions. And this is a moment in time that calls for fearless decision-making. Our leaders need to think out of the box during these critical times and should choose straight-talking advisors who cherish their nation's security, not yes-men. Protect your countries and your peoples; start now, not next week or next month. The road ahead may be strewn with boulders and some of our traditional "friends" may voice their disapproval but, as the old saying goes "He who hesitates is lost". This is one fight where losing is not an option.

Message to Egypt: no mercy for terrorists!

5 February 2015

IN RECENT WEEKS, terrorists linked to the Muslim Brotherhood have gone on the rampage throughout Egypt murdering security forces, placing explosive devices that have killed passers-by, torching trains, trams and businesses. Coincidentally – or so I must suppose – this heightened terrorist activity was perceived just days after, the US Department of State held meetings in Washington with members of a Muslim Brotherhood delegation that were said to be "fruitful". Just two days after that visit, the Brotherhood called upon its followers to launch a Jihad against the Egyptian authorities and to embrace martyrdom.

As widely reported by the US media, including Fox News, the US Department of State spokeswoman, Jen Psaki told reporters the visit was organized by Georgetown University, a claim the university later refuted. And now, the Muslim Brotherhood's Raba'a channel, airing from Turkey, has warned foreigners to quit the country by 11 February or face the consequences.

Shockingly, at a time when Egypt is under attack from within, the United Nations (UN), the European Union (EU) and Britain's Foreign Office, together with a slew of human rights agencies, have issued statements condemning the country's human rights record. The UK's Secretary of State for Foreign Affairs, Philip Hammond, just days ago called upon Egypt to release "political prisoners" knowing full well that all those detained are either awaiting trial for crimes committed or have been sentenced. Whether in response to his nation's critics or otherwise, President Abdel Fatah El Sisi has advised the commander of the police force and the military "to be mindful of human rights", which may result in their hands being tied.

Murderers masquerading as Muslims are no better than the flesh-eating zombies in a grotesque horror movie such as *The Walking Dead*. They are subhuman beings without a shred of humanity and, as such, are undeserving of human rights. While the world is still reeling from the stomach-churning sight of the young Jordanian pilot and devout Muslim, Moaz Al Kasasbeh being incinerated by a gang of monsters while trapped in a metal cage, I applaud Jordan's fast retaliatory response.

Within hours of the video appearing on social media, the Jordanian government executed two Iraqi terrorists – Sajida Al Rishawi and Zaid Al Karbouly – who had been sentenced to death in 2005 and 2008 respectively. It is unfortunate that those two were permitted the privilege of breathing, eating and talking at the expense of taxpayers for so long. Jordan had placed a moratorium on executions for years, but there is a very different mood within this grieving Arab country now. No doubt human rights activists will soon be popping up on Twitter and Facebook weeping over the fate of that despicable pair.

What will it take for Egypt to wake up to the fact that enemies of the state, who think nothing of shooting, bombing and burning to achieve their goals, must be treated with an iron fist? The international community condemns its judiciary for issuing mass death sentences, but few of those sentences are being carried out.

In the first place, their implementation, by custom, requires the approval of the Grand Mufti, currently Dr Shawki Abdulkarim Allam, who, in many cases, has displayed his reluctance to do so, and, secondly, appeals courts are regularly reducing such sentences to life imprisonment. Life imprisonment, in Egypt, is rarely longer than 20 years, and history tells us that many sentenced to life in the past have either had their sentences commuted or have been the recipients of presidential pardons.

I find it incomprehensible that the process requires rubber-stamping from the Grand Imam. The law should be changed to bar convicted terrorists, or those working to bring down the state, from appeals courts. Better still, they should be tried, convicted and summarily sentenced by military tribunals like inmates of Guantanamo. If that system is good enough for the US, then it is good enough for all Arab states afflicted by this evil scourge.

The combined result is this. The death penalty is no longer acting as a deterrent to the Muslim Brotherhood and their affiliates in northern Sinai, and Egypt is beginning to look soft on terrorism. If that impression is permitted to take root, the government's efforts to improve the economy so as to better the lives of 90 million citizens, 40 per cent subsisting below the poverty line, will go for naught.

Violence and instability is the death knell for foreign investment, which Egypt so badly needs. It is time that the powers that be show that they mean business; they must prove to their people who went to the streets in their millions to give then-Field Marshall El Sisi a mandate to do whatever is necessary to eliminate traitorous terrorist scum, that their safety, security and prosperity is the government's number one goal.

While I understand that the President and his team are eager to have good relations with other countries and are keen to show the world that Egypt is on the path to democracy with parliamentary elections scheduled for March, they need to get their priorities right. The eradication of terrorism by any means should trump diplomatic pandering to Western states that have actively impeded the country's transition since Mohamed Morsi's ousting in July 2013. The US and its allies have been cuddling the Muslim Brotherhood ever since, while dismissing the will of the Egyptian people along with their hopes and aspirations.

Those countries have consistently wielded the human rights card over the heads of the Egyptian government like a weapon; never mind that they trashed their own human rights records with illegal wars, illegal renditions, illegal spying on citizens ... the list is long. It is almost laughable that those same countries, directly or indirectly, responsible for the death of up to a million of Iraqis have been hammering Cairo for arresting three Al Jazeera journalists, while staying silent on journalists languishing in Turkish prisons. Propaganda at its finest!

In a nutshell, my message to the Egyptian authorities is this: do what it takes! Put so called human rights and civil liberties on the backburner. The only ones that count are the rights of the 90 million that count on you to keep the streets safe, improve services and provide jobs. You should hold dear the rights of decent citizens over bombers and arsonists. Close your ears to the twittering of hypocritical outsiders who, if their own countries were under attack, would launch fierce crackdowns in the name of national security. The Arab World needs a strong, united Egypt. Please do not let us down!

Egypt revs up for the fast lane

21 March 2015

AS SOMEONE WHO is seriously looking at investment possibilities in Egypt, I took a close interest in the country's three-day-long Economic Development Conference, recently held in the resort town of Sharm El Sheikh. Such events tend to be dull, dry, and flavourless, but this one was anything but on so many different levels. In fact, it kept me riveted, on the edge of my seat.

"With 22 heads of state and 3,500 delegates, it's the largest summit of CEOs and world leaders I've ever seen," said the summit's organizer, Richard Attias, whose company has organized tens of major conferences worldwide. I have never come across anything like it before either; it was more results-oriented than most United Nations or G8 summits – which are all talk and little action – and vastly more good-natured.

Permeated with positivity, often from unexpected quarters, and punctuated with genuine emotion, standing ovations and hearty laughter, it was a phenomenal triumph, resulting in $32.6bn contracts signed, $90bn in Memoranda of Understanding (MOUs) as well as $12.5bn in grants and investments from Gulf states.

I am so proud that our leaders have once again joined hands to support the Arab World's backbone, Egypt, now under the leadership of President Abdel Fatah El Sisi – a true Arab patriot who has not only gained the respect of his people during some of the most challenging times the nation has ever endured, but also their love. The young ushers he invited to join him on stage at the start of his inspirational closing speech could hardly contain their exuberance at being up-close and personal with their hero, a spontaneous and somewhat boisterous display of affection for the President, delighting all in attendance.

Just as iconic was an emotive address delivered by Prime Minister Ibrahim Mehleb, who was so overflowing with happiness and gratitude, particularly towards the leaders of Saudi Arabia, the United Arab Emirates (UAE), Kuwait and Oman, that he fought back tears throughout and was later mobbed with hugs from his own cabinet ministers. Both he and President El Sisi expressed their gratitude to the late King Abdullah of Saudi Arabia for coming up with the idea of a summit in the first place.

Another factor that made the conference exceptional in our part of the world was that there was no attempt on the part of the organizers to kowtow to Western powers. Indeed, the order of speakers exemplified the Egyptian government's independent outlook with priority given to heads of state and representatives of countries that Cairo considers to be true friends and partners in the Middle East and Africa.

And nobody was left in any doubt as to the strength of not only their economic support but also their political backing, beginning with Saudi's Crown Prince Muqrin bin Abdulaziz, who called upon the world to recognize Egypt's historical and cultural importance, while urging the international community to abandon its double standards vis-à-vis the Egyptian government.

Likewise, the speech of HH Sheikh Mohammed bin Rashid Al Maktoum, Vice-President and Prime Minister of the UAE and Ruler of Dubai, emphasized the ironclad relationship between the Emirates and Egypt: "Egypt is the home of peace, the heart of Arabism," adding that the UAE's stand with Egypt "is simply out of our affection towards the people of Egypt .... Our stand is not a favour to anyone but a duty in its own right and not for a quick return, it is an investment in the future of our nation. What we are doing in Egypt today is an investment towards the stability of the region that we shall see in the near future, God willing."

Kuwait's Emir Sabah Al Ahmad Al Sabah praised Egypt's new economic reforms and investment legislation as being positive. Passed just one day before the start of the conference, on the President's executive authority, the overhauled investment laws cut burdensome red tape, grant rights to non-Egyptians to own land and buildings, allow for foreign labour, offer taxation incentives – and most of all provide security to foreign investors. The cutting of fuel subsidies and increased taxation was applauded by the International Monetary Fund (IMF) and galvanized ratings agencies to upgrade their outlooks for Egypt to "stable".

Following years of upheaval, Egypt is not only open for business, the government has its eye firmly on the future. Its new Suez Canal project and associated industrial zones furthers ambitions to turn the waterway into a major logistical, commercial and industrial hub between Europe and the Arab region, attracting revenues anticipated to make up a third of the economy.

Even more ambitious is a mega project unveiled at the conference – a new administrative and financial capital city, approximately the size of Singapore, to be sited 45km east of Cairo on over 7,000 sq km, with the first phase slated to emerge from the desert sands within five to seven years. It will have an airport bigger than London's Heathrow and a theme park four times larger than Disneyland.

Also on offer to investors are various projects in the fields of oil, gas, petrochemical and mineral wealth. There are great opportunities in the IT and telecommunications sectors. Moreover, the Tourism Ministry has announced projects, including hotels and entertainment venues, in areas on the Red Sea. Tourism is expected to be boosted with Chinese, Russian and Algerian tourists; around 1.5 million Algerians are expected to visit Egypt annually beginning this year.

With growth expected to reach or surpass 4 per cent by the end of the fiscal year ending in June, a bourse recording record highs and a stable currency, kudos must be given to the government. But I would also salute our Gulf Cooperation Council (GCC) heads of state, notably the UAE's President Sheikh Khalifa bin Zayed Al Nahyan, King Salman bin

Abdulaziz of Saudi Arabia, the Emir of Kuwait Sheikh Sabah Al Ahmad Al Sabah as well as Oman's Sultan Qaboos. I am proud of you for standing strongly with Egypt and President El Sisi and for energizing the GCC's investment and business communities in Egypt's direction.

Egypt's Economic Development Conference is now scheduled to be an annual event. I cannot wait to see the country's progress and what the government has in store for investors this time next year!

A strong, stable and secure Egypt capable of reassuming its traditional leadership role in partnership with GCC states will quicken the pulse of the entire Arab Ummah, whose heart has been in intensive care for many years. Now, at last, there is real hope that we can come together to overcome those who threaten us. Welcome back, Egypt! You have been truly missed.

10

Getting an Arab voice heard

Keynote speeches delivered by
Khalaf Ahmad Al Habtoor

Introduction

I AM OFTEN ASKED to give keynote speeches at high profile events
all over the world. I pick my platforms carefully. The majority of the
speeches featured in this chapter were given in the United States;
New York, Washington DC and Illinois.

I believe it is important to get the Arab voice heard on key issues
impacting our world today, especially given the dramatic rise of
Islamophobia, due in part to a growing epidemic of radicalization.
The world is at risk of segregation based on a person's religion. I believe
there is a disturbing silence from Muslim and Arab leaders. I know I do
not speak for the entire Arab World, and my views are my personal views,
but with xenophobia – or the fear of "the other" – dramatically on the rise, it
is more important now than ever before to prevent a further escalation in
anti-Muslim rhetoric.

My speeches address key issues impacting the Middle East. They give
a candid view from an Arab perspective.

Righting the wrongs (democracy and human rights)

6 October 2014

C3 US Arab Business Summit, New York

The C3 Summit is an exclusive event dedicated to exchanging best practices
and knowledge transfer between the United States and the Arab region in
healthcare, business and corporate social responsibility.

I AM HAPPY TO BE at the C3 Summit today and to be recognized to
receive the first Lifetime Achievement Award. The C3 Summit and its
focus aspects are commendable and I wish you all the success this year and
in the coming years.

I pride myself on being an ambassador of my country to the world.
I have always been conscious about the importance of bridging the East
and the West, finding the similarities instead of the differences between
different cultures.

I founded the Al Habtoor Group in 1970 and am proud to see it grow into what it is today, and for it to be recognized on international levels.

As I wrote in my autobiography; *Khalaf Ahmad Al Habtoor – The Autobiography*, I was not born into a rich family, I did not hold sand in my hand and turn it into gold. I have had many successes for which I am grateful, but those came after many failures.

I look back now at my life and my adventures and laugh. You will laugh with me as well if you read my autobiography. I am grateful for God's blessings and for being born in the United Arab Emirates (UAE).

The UAE was blessed with visionary leaders; the late Sheikh Zayed bin Sultan Al Nahyan and the late Sheikh Rashid bin Saeed Al Maktoum – the founders of my country.

At the Al Habtoor Group, my company's motto is "Growing with the UAE", and we have always worked vigorously to grow in parallel with my country. My country's stellar growth is my responsibility and my privilege. No one should stand back and wait for things to be handed over to them.

In the words of John F. Kennedy, "Ask not what your country can do for you, ask what you can do for your country." I am a firm believer in that. In the United Arab Emirates, we are partners in our country's success and we do our best to protect the safety of our nation and its growth. Thank God, the UAE was the first country to recover from the economic crisis in 2008, and it is still growing stronger and stronger by the day.

However, despite this phenomenal growth story, the United Arab Emirates, in particular Dubai, has been the target of the Western media for a long time; being criticized for its firm laws and low tolerance of corruption, and our handling of people who threaten our safety and national security. But the criticism is not justified. Who can blame us? Yes, we are firm with criminals and we are proud of it! Some might object to or frown upon our laws, but people from all over the world have decided to make the UAE their home because of what this nation has to offer.

This brings me to two topics that appear to be preferred by the Western media and the fault-finders when discussing the UAE: democracy and human rights.

Human rights is one topic in particular that seems to be a favourite among my country's strongest opponents. What is the definition of human rights? The Universal Declaration of Human Rights in 1948 referred to human rights as the basic civil, political, economic, social and cultural rights that all human beings should enjoy. Human rights issues include adequate housing, democracy, rights for children, education, economic rights, food, health, freedom of religion and belief etc.

If we compare what the Western nations provide for their citizens and what the UAE offers, the difference is huge. All UAE citizens have homes. Young couples who cannot afford to buy homes receive financial support. And I am not talking about community housing, this is a decent home where a couple can raise a family. Young people who want to get married are provided with money to have a ceremony and start their married life debt free.

Education is available in the UAE at the highest standards. We have some of the top schools and universities in the world and they are available for all. We provide people with free medical care inside and outside the UAE.

My country is stable, our economy is strong and striving. We have the best infrastructure in the world; world-class banks, hospitals, two major airlines (Emirates and Etihad), and everyone wants to come to work, live and even retire in the UAE.

We have virtually no unemployment while the streets of the richest cities in the world are full of homeless people living under bridges, tunnels and train stations. Safety and security are the number one priority for us. And we do not compromise on them. We have used an iron fist with anyone who jeopardizes our security, but this is our right and our duty – and we will not apologize for it!

Some might say that this is against human rights and democracy. I say: a parent or a head of family needs to know that their loved ones are safe, and that they will have jobs to provide for them. I need to know my employees will have jobs tomorrow to care for their families. My country's stability, safety and security allows them that.

There is nothing wrong with democracy as a theory, where everybody gets equal opportunity, enjoys the same rights, has a safe and comfortable lifestyle and has a voice. Do you really think we, in the UAE, are missing on democracy? Think again!

Leaders in the democratic countries are locked away in their ivory towers, with thousands of guards keeping them from the people they are supposed to listen to. In my country, I can meet the rulers any time I have a need, and they will listen. I can call them and they will pick up the phone. The leaders in the UAE are reachable and approachable, and they are interested in what their people have to say. Our rulers care about their people and the residents of the country. The leaders of the UAE care about all humanity, and not just in words, but also in actions.

What have the democratic leaders of the world achieved for the Syrian men, women and children being butchered daily except talk and make empty promises? What have they done for the Palestinians who are constantly denied their basic rights such as food, safety and education? Never mind the Arab World, what is the West doing for its veterans who end up homeless on the streets?

I wish the human rights organizations and the Western media would stop trying to fit us into Western moulds. We do not want to be influenced by foreign concepts of democracy and human rights. We know what works for us! Everyone is invited to come and see with their own eyes how we are living in my country and the blessings that we have.

In the United Arab Emirates we do not differentiate between human beings whatever their nationality, colour, religion, sex, or any other status. We believe that all human beings are equally entitled to a decent life without discrimination. These beliefs have been inherited from our fathers and forefathers.

I am currently working on a proposal that I hope one day will materialise because its benefits will have a worldwide effect. For now, it is known as the "Poverty Alleviation Proposal". The name is debateable, but for now, my focus is on the concept.

What I am proposing is a global system of revenue-raising or a global poverty tax. The idea is not novel; but the attempts before have not succeeded. My proposal is more ambitious. It requires governments to pledge an agreed percentage annually to a new independent body tasked solely with poverty-reduction.

All the world's greatest faiths teach us to take care of the poor. Giving to the less fortunate is required by Islam and Judaism.

I invite everyone to read my proposal and give me their input. Copies of the proposal are available today and online on my personal website www.khalafalhabtoor.net.

Ladies and gentlemen, allow me to address another subject of equal importance in my speech. Palestine has always been at the forefront of my thinking. We may be diverted from the Palestinian issue with other current matters only temporarily, but Palestine and the peace process are always in my mind and my heart.

I am a realistic man and I set my goals with a real view. I will not dream and stick to the romantic idea that the Palestinians will return to Palestine, because there are different facts that have made this impossible and we have to live with them.

I have shared my passion and concern for the Palestinian-Israeli conflict resolution with two great men that I admire: former US President Jimmy Carter and former US congressman the Honourable Paul Findley. I am proud to call Paul Findley my friend. Because of him, I have come to learn more about the great Abraham Lincoln and his history.

Through my foundation, the Khalaf Ahmad Al Habtoor Foundation, I have supported The Carter Center for several years now and will continue to do so in their efforts towards the Palestinian-Israeli conflict resolution. President Carter and his team have worked tirelessly to find solutions, and many like him and Paul are loyal to the cause and will not hesitate to do what it takes.

But I was thinking about it and decided to try a different approach. The idea came to my mind, and after careful consideration I discussed it with my team and we proposed it to Illinois College. With the assistance of my great friend Paul Findley and the faculty, we have drafted a proposal that we call "Pathways to Peace". I will have the honour to launch it personally with President Jimmy Carter next week at Illinois College.

Everyone hopes this issue is resolved sooner rather than later, but most probably it will fall on the shoulders of our children. Their minds and way of thinking are different from ours. So they should be asked to find scenarios and solutions to the conflict. They understand what their generation thinks and how they need to address this issue.

"Pathways to Peace" is a seminar focused on historical examples of different religious, ethnic and cultural conflicts and steps taken to resolve these problems. These examples of methods used to resolve those conflicts can be applied as potential "Pathways to Peace".

The faculty and students involved will travel to Jordan and, if the security situation allows, to Palestine and Israel. They will meet with Palestinian and Israeli students and try to understand them and their needs first hand. My hope is that they can achieve a realistic solution that could help the peace process move forward.

I realise that the project might not be successful the first time around, but we will try again and again. This is too important an issue for us not to try every possible way to see it happen.

I would like to end my speech this morning by saying; the world is very small, and we all have to share it. This is why we need to find the best way to co-exist, to work together to make it a better place for everyone. From the C3 Summit in New York, I will use this platform to ask the US and the first-world countries to look at us at eye-level. We are grateful for everything you have done for us, and we have learned a lot from you. We have benefitted from your technology and your knowledge, but sometimes we have succeeded where you have failed!

It is time you started looking at us as equals and listen to our advice and recognize our achievements. It is time the West realizes we do not need to be picked on for not following Western-style policies that quite frankly do not seem to be working for the West that well either.

You have always had our respect and our acceptance, but it is time you accepted us, respected our choices, and looked at us on the same level. We want to help, and we can help – and given the chance this world will be a much better place for every one of us.

Pathways to peace

14 October 2014

Launch of "Pathways to Peace" Initiative, Brunel Center, Illinois College

Official launch in the presence of President Jimmy Carter; former US Congressman, the Honourable Paul Findley; faculty and students of Illinois College; and members of the Phi Alpha Literary Society.

IT IS WONDERFUL TO BE back at Illinois College. Illinois College is a very dear place to my heart. And the credit in introducing me to this place goes to my good friend the former US congressman – the Honourable Paul Findley. Thank you Paul.

I am honoured that President Jimmy Carter has accepted my invitation to visit Illinois College. And I look forward to the launch of the "Pathways to Peace" initiative with him. Thank you President Carter.

As you all know, President Carter tirelessly calls for a solution to the Palestinian-Israeli conflict.

Through my Foundation, the Khalaf Ahmad Al Habtoor Foundation, I have worked with and supported The Carter Center for several years now and will continue to do so in their efforts towards the Palestinian-Israeli conflict resolution.

I have big hopes that my idea, the idea we are launching today, can help bring about a realistic solution to the problem and in time bring lasting peace.

I am a realistic man and I set my goals with a real view.

I will not dream and stick to the romantic idea that the Palestinians will return to Palestine, because there are different facts that have made this impossible and we have to live with them.

President Carter and his team have worked very hard to find solutions. Many like him and Paul are loyal to the cause and will not hesitate to do what it takes.

The Palestinian-Israeli struggle is always at the forefront of my thinking. And while exhausting all the current solutions, I thought, why not try a different approach?

The idea of this initiative came to my mind. And after careful consideration, I discussed it with my team and we suggested it to Illinois College.

With the assistance of Professor Andrew Findley and the faculty, we have drafted this proposal that we call "Pathways to Peace".

Everyone hopes the Palestinian-Israeli conflict is resolved sooner rather than later, but most probably, it will fall on the shoulders of our children.

Their minds and way of thinking is different from ours. And for that reason, they should take part in finding the solution.

They should be asked to find scenarios and solutions to the conflict. They understand what their generation thinks and how they need to address this issue.

"Pathways to Peace" is a seminar focused on historical examples of different religious, ethnic and cultural conflicts and steps taken to resolve these problems.

The examples of methods used to resolves those conflicts can be applied as potential "Pathways to Peace".

The faculty and students involved will travel to Jordan and, if the security situation allows, to Palestine and Israel.

They will meet with Palestinian and Israeli students. They will try to understand them and their needs first hand.

My hope is that they can reach a realistic solution that could help the peace process move forward.

I realize that the project might not be successful the first time, but we will try again and again. This is too important an issue for us not to try every possible way to see it happen.

Thank you very much.

Call for action

15 October 2015

> **24th Annual Arab-US Policymakers Conference, Ronald Reagan Building and International Trade Center, Washington DC**
>
> US–Arab Relations at a Crossroads: What Paths Forward?
> Organized by the National Council on US–Arab Relations

I WOULD LIKE TO START by thanking the National Council on US–Arab Relations, led by Dr John Duke Anthony – Founding President and CEO, for inviting me to speak at the 24th Annual Arab–US Policymakers Conference. I thank you for having me!

In the face of what is happening in our world, there could not have been a more relevant topic to discuss than the topic selected for this year's conference: "The future of the US–Arab relations."

The relationship between the United States of America and the Arab countries is at a turning point.

For decades, the alliance between the US and the Arab countries, mainly the GCC states, has proven to be paramount for regional and global stability, prosperity and peace.

We recognize with gratitude, and cannot deny that we have greatly benefitted from your knowledge for decades.

As per the Office of the United States Trade Representative, the volume of trade between the US and GCC countries is worth hundreds of billions of US dollars every year.

Americans in the United Arab Emirates form one of the largest Western communities in the UAE; around 50,000 US nationals reside in my country.

However, what the previous administrations have done to the Arab World in the last decade, particularly to the Sunni populations, leaves a dark stain on this great nation's history.

America has nurtured Ayatollah Ruhollah Khomeini to replace the Shah of Iran, its former best friend.

Under false pretences, the George W. Bush administration invaded Iraq.

When American troops pulled out, they handed Iraq to Iran on a silver platter, and this former great Arab nation, the Cradle of Civilization, was turned into a cradle for terrorism.

I cannot understand why the Obama administration is championing our common enemies and their expansionist agenda in our region.

Right now, we are witnessing the US' lack of decisive action against one of the most ruthless criminals of our century – Syrian President Bashar Al Assad – and the empowerment of Iran, the patron of terrorism in our world ... and most importantly, turning a blind eye to the continuous Palestinian tragedy.

The daily suffering of our Palestinian brothers and sisters is marginalized; it rarely makes the daily news.

But the US Department of State was fast to make a statement on Monday "condemning in strong terms the terrorist attacks against Israeli civilians which resulted in the murder of three Israelis".

I never take the death of a human being lightly, any human being, whether Palestinian or Israeli.

But the fact of the matter is that Israeli forces are murdering Palestinian families in bulk on a daily basis, even burning them in their homes, and the American authorities have not once condemned those criminal acts.

I will not comment further on the Palestinian issue today. I leave this issue to you, ladies and gentleman, to consider what differentiates one man from another man? It is the decision-making! It is the ability to make difficult choices when no one else can. That is what leadership is! And that is what is lacking right now!

We are currently facing one of the biggest challenges of our time, and that is the issue of refugees around the world.

According to the United Nations High Commission for Refugees (UNHCR), the number of refugees and the internally displaced has reached its highest point since World War II.

The annual cost of this displacement, according to the Internal Displacement Monitoring Centre, has reached almost $100bn.

It is no surprise that many of these people are concentrated in the Middle East and in particular in Iraq and Syria. A third of the world's refugees come from those two nations alone. Twenty-one per cent of the world's refugees are Syrians. More than 9.5 million have been displaced. That amounts to nearly half of the Syrian population – men, women and children. This is a human tragedy!

Hundreds of thousands of desperate Syrians have flooded to Europe, risking their lives for a chance of a better life. This tsunami of desperate people is unlikely to ease anytime soon. Do you think they want to leave their country? Their homes? Their family members? No! These people have no choice. This is a last resort, and they have given up hope completely.

Unfortunately, the reception the refugees are met with, in some parts of Europe, is not much better than the conditions they are running away from. And some of the European leaders are refusing to host Syrian refugees for fear of jeopardizing Christian history.

It is a real disappointment to hear such statements from leaders in Europe in the 21st century. The fact that Syrians are being turned away based on their religious belief is totally unacceptable! The discrimination is blatant and unforgiving!

I am not here to point fingers, but rather to tell those who are fostering the hate feelings against those unfortunate refugees in camps that they are attacking the wrong enemy. Their enemy is not the women and children seeking refuge from a bloodthirsty leader.

I should take this opportunity to salute Pope Francis for his call for mercy for the Syrian refugees in Europe.

Instead of dealing with this escalating crisis, this human tragedy, why are we not dealing with the source of the problem? We are looking at solutions to deal with its ramifications, rather than eliminating it at its root.

If Bashar Al Assad was dealt with in 2011, or when he used chemical weapons in 2013 against the Syrian people, then we would not be dealing with a world epidemic.

Did President Barack Obama not draw a red line to the Assad regime, and all the players on the ground, when sarin gas and other chemical weapons were being utilized?

I quote what President Obama said in 2013: "It's about humanity's red line. And it's a red line that anyone with a conscience ought to draw."

With all that is happening to Syrians so far, has this not yet crossed any "humanitarian red lines" for the US and the world? Two years later, and after continuous use of chemicals weapons in Syria, the world still fails to take any action and make good on its promise. Are five years not enough for the international community to intervene?

While world leaders are making plans to host refugees in their countries, all they offer is a temporary solution. But you must know that Syrians do not want to be refugees in Europe even more than Europe is reluctant to host them! What they need is to go back home to Syria.

A "safe zone" should be created within Syrian land, where Syrians can have a safe shelter from the butcher Assad while a solution is being found. A safe zone protected by NATO.

And the criminal Bashar Al Assad should be led to the International Criminal Court. Assad cannot be negotiated with. He should not be allowed an easy exit! He should be tried for all the crimes he committed against his own people. Assad must pay for the more than 350,000 innocent lives he has taken!

This is what the Syrian people need from you! If justice is not carried out against Assad, you will never be forgiven.

Let us not forget Syria is not the only troubled country in the Middle East. Iraq, Lebanon, Yemen are not any better. And the common denominator in all these problems is the Islamic Republic of Iran.

Iran's malicious fingerprints are left all over the region by supporting terrorist groups, such as Hezbollah in Lebanon, militant groups and destabilizing forces in Iraq, and most recently the Houthis in Yemen.

If Iran has managed to create all this turbulence and damage despite sanctions, what guarantees can ensure that it does not do more harm once sanctions are lifted?

Iran officially supports terrorism. It does not only back Shi'ite terrorist groups but Sunni ones, such as Al Qaeda itself. This is not an assumption, but a fact stated in official reports prepared by the US Department of State.

Most importantly, the Iranian regime regards the United States as the "Great Satan" and has – for decades – been involved in state-funded terrorism against America and its allies in the region. All that has happened despite the crippling economic sanctions over Iran. Imagine what will happen if the sanctions are lifted!

If an Arab country were perceived to be hostile to the US or the international community, it would be attacked without hesitation. On the other hand, this administration is treating its "favourite enemy" with a velvet glove instead of the iron fist it deserves.

Both the US and Iran have displayed exceptional commitment to the nuclear deal, and now a nuclear framework has been agreed. It is easy to understand Iran's willingness to compromise when sanctions have bit hard. But why the Obama administration has made supreme efforts to shake hands with America's long-time enemy is perplexing.

The P5+1 Iranian nuclear deal is set to enrich and empower Tehran once economic sanctions are lifted. President Obama says Iran's new wealth will be used to improve lives in Iran, rather than to fund Hezbollah, the Shi'ite Yemeni Houthis, or other troublemakers under the Iranian wing. One needs to be naive at best to believe that.

According to a *Daily Telegraph* report, Ali Khamenei – Iran's Supreme leader, controls "a financial empire" estimated to be worth $95bn. That alone should tell you that Iran has no intention of prioritizing the needs of its people over its regional troublemakers.

Iran's ayatollahs have been oppressing religious and ethnic minorities ever since they took power in 1979. Look at how they have treated Ahwazi Arabs in the occupied province of Arabistan, that they now call Khuzestan.

Although Arabistan provides Iran with 80 per cent of its oil requirements and half of its gas, Ahwazi Arabs are persecuted and oppressed on daily basis. They are not entitled to their basic human rights. Their identity is being destroyed. They are forced to study in Farsi if they are lucky enough to go to school; a meagre 50 per cent chance for boys, and 20 per cent for girls.

Over 30 per cent of Ahwazis under the age of 30 are unemployed. They have no access to drinking water. Their streets are open sewers, and they are deprived of electricity and gas. And more often than not, Arab farmers are stripped of their agricultural land.

There is no country on earth that oppresses its population underfoot, both politically and socially, while keeping over almost 11 million illiterate and 15 million struggling below the poverty line.

Meanwhile, Iran spends $15–30bn every year to support terrorists across the region, according to a recent report by the *Washington Times*.

Its proxy Hezbollah has hijacked Lebanon and turned it into a hub for terrorism in the Middle East. Whether it is the military or the political wing, there is no difference, Hezbollah is a terrorist organization created and nurtured by Iran to destabilize the Arab World.

It goes without saying that the United States is far better off on the side of its long-term and stability-seeking allies, the GCC countries. Contrary to Iran, our countries track down and punish terrorists and financers of such groups.

I would love to know why this entity that has been hostile to Western powers and their allies since its inception in 1979, is being rewarded for its terrorist associations and its regional will to power! Or is this hostility between Iran and the West just a farce to fool us?

Unfortunately, America no longer inspires the world. I say that with deep regret.

When President Obama signed up to the Iran nuclear deal, he placed the Middle East and the Gulf in danger from an enriched, empowered, and legitimized Tehran.

As the American people prepare to elect a new president, a man or a woman who will influence the future of the world, it is important that voters begin scrutinizing the presidential candidates through a new lens – one that is serious, positive and objective.

Americans should stop judging a man by his cover and dig deep to see who possesses the necessary tools as well as life experiences. Voters should not care about their candidates' personal lives, or what candidates do in their homes, behind closed doors. That is nobody's business. Instead voters should look for a shrewd businessman, with economic knowhow, a candidate who will create jobs for them.

Money is power, and money comes from smart and healthy economies.

Americans need employment. Americans need opportunities. They need investments in infrastructure. Most of all, they want to enjoy a healthy economy. They have tried the speakers who made empty promises or announced unrealistic policies – who have failed to return America to its former glory.

The US is a powerhouse of leaders, but this time instead of selecting a politician for president, it is best to vote for a successful businessman with a positive approach to run the country.

Some might say that the presidential election is an American matter, and as an Arab I should not interfere. Allow me to correct them! The choice of president, and his policies, will affect the whole world.

The world needs leadership. The American president needs to gain the admiration of your own people as well as ours. America's light of truth and justice should shine bright again!

To conclude, I invite you to please join me for a moment of silence to honour the UAE military men and women who sacrificed their lives in the line of duty in Yemen recently. May God bless their souls.

A large number of our finest UAE soldiers were killed while defending their Yemeni brothers and sisters from Iranian-sponsored Houthi rebels. We Emiratis are a population tied together by tribal roots and family connections. Every single Emirati life is precious to us, and we will not forget the sacrifice of our heroes. Our shared grief has joined us together as never before. We are very proud of the martyrs, they are defenders of the oppressed.

I am very proud of my country. The United Arab Emirates never skirts its duty and has proved its courage time and time again. My country is committed to the region's security and to fighting terrorism. Our hands are always open to help our friends and neighbours, be it with financial support or assistance in preserving their freedom.

We are determined to prevail over the threat of the Iranian thugs. Our resolve to fight on the side of right will never falter. We will never permit terrorist plotters to be victorious when the future of our nation is at stake.

We extend our hands to our allies, and it is my deepest hope that the United States of America, our long-time friend and ally, stands with us again in our common fight against terrorism to make our world safe again.

God bless America. And God bless our troubled Arab World. Thank you very much.

Rising Islamophobia in the West

17 December 2015

Al Arabiya Global Discussions Forum, Dubai, United Arab Emirates

I AM HAPPY TO BE speaking to you tonight. With everything happening around the world, your role as the media is more important than ever. We are living in extraordinary times when we do not know our friends from our enemies.

Over the past few years, the world has witnessed major change. We have seen an increase in terrorism by extremists who are falsely using Islam as a cover. They are not Muslims! Sadly, no place on earth is safe from their actions, and this has caused the biggest cross-cultural divide in living memory.

We have gone back to the Middle Ages. Why? We are in the 21st century where tolerance and respect of others' religions are a given. I do not know how we are going to get ourselves out of this dangerous situation. We are living in fear of our neighbours based on their religion and the colour of their skin. This is the sad truth!

Unfortunately, the media is not helping matters. It is fuelling the fire and widening the gap between the East and West, not to mention politicians who are supposed to look after their people. Instead they are causing hatred and encouraging cultural segregation.

Donald Trump's calls for banning Muslims from entering America are shocking. He wants to create a database to keep track of any Muslim in the United States, and has called for surveillance of mosques.

Why are Muslims considered criminals because of their beliefs? Cats and dogs can enter the US freely, but not Muslims.

And of course, the Western media is capitalizing on it. I was asked to give the Muslim view on Trump's statements as no one else was speaking out. Religion should not even come to it. Islam does not need defending. But someone had to counter Trump's disgraceful talk.

I wonder: is Trump simply ignorant or racist? I think he is both. And with people like Trump, the media has to act responsibly and write what is true. The media should be emphasizing the point that Islam is a peaceful religion. Maybe that is too boring for the audience who prefer headlines full of scandal and slander. But that is the truth!

The US media initially dismissed Trump as a one-minute wonder. But still gave him more air time while ignoring the real news.

The world's 1.7 billion Muslims are under attack by an individual aiming to be the so-called Leader of the Free World. I believe the American people are smarter than electing Donald Trump as their next leader, and I hope I am not proven wrong. I cannot imagine a world where Donald Trump is President of the United States of America.

But if he is, I am sure he would do everything within his power to ban Muslim visitors from entering his country.

When I heard what Donald Trump said, I believed he would be out of the presidential race. How wrong was I? There is a clear and present danger that he could actually make it to the White House.

Even after what he said, he is still ahead in the US polls, steaming away with 35 per cent of the Republican vote. It seems the more vulgar and offensive he is, the more the American voters love him. This shows that fear of Islam is dangerously on the rise.

This man – who could be democratically elected – is not only attacking Islam, he is attacking the Hispanics, the African Americans and others.

He is isolating everyone!

Through politics, and the media, Trump has successfully exploited people's fear of "The Other" with racism and bigotry being his tools of trade. Non-Muslims around the world are disgusted and they are speaking out. Various media commentators and news organizations have also done the right thing, calling Trump's provocative comments racist – and acknowledging that his policies are fuelled by racism.

But where is the defence from the Muslim world? I am shocked by the disturbing silence from the Muslim and Arab leaders and the business world. What is happening to us? We Muslims are the target. Our faith is under attack, but we are behaving like lambs to the slaughter.

Financial gain and politics aside, how can anyone of good conscience continue to do business with this person or his companies when Trump the man and Trump the brand are the same thing?

In any case, imagining that America can be kept safe by shutting out Muslims is wrong, and who can blame Muslims for thinking "if you do not want us, then you do not deserve our money".

Trump must remember that Muslim nations around the world are heavily invested in the United States. He promises to "Make America great again," but in fact he is gravely endangering his nation's economy with his vulgar and highly offensive talk. His policies are based on hot air, and he is attacking our great faith.

I would like to strongly urge anyone doing business with Donald Trump or any of his affiliated companies to stop. I urge the media to focus on what is important, and report facts. You have an incredible power in your hands. Do not fall prey to the game of politics.

Several years ago I launched a Foundation in my name, The Khalaf Ahmad Al Habtoor Foundation. Its mission is to promote East–West dialogue, and build respect and understanding between cultures. Sadly, this task is becoming more challenging by the day because of the stupidity of people like Donald Trump who do not make things any easier. He is spreading poison and hate.

It is people like Trump who are not allowing people to live in peace and harmony. I will continue to do everything in my power to break down the walls he is putting up.

In addition, I am planning a Round Table Event with people like me from around the world. It will focus on alleviating global poverty, one of the biggest threats to our planet. This is what we should be focusing on, not wasting valuable time on Donald Trump. We need to work on a realistic solution to help the poor. Our focus should be on saving humanity irrelevant of colour, race or religion.

It is not just Donald Trump who is abusing the media, creating fear and encouraging hatred of Muslims. There are others, which brings me to another article I wrote about Morten Storm who co-wrote a book about his life as a double agent for the CIA and Al Qaeda, and claims to have been a Muslim.

I was disappointed that Fox News recently invited him to comment in the aftermath of the Paris attacks. What an insult. A terrorist, claiming to be a Muslim, speaking on our behalf. He is a traitor, a liar and has blood on his hands.

Fox News should never have given him any air time. Storm has no moral standards and he is definitely not an authority on Islam. If Fox News wanted to learn about Islam, they should have invited a real Muslim, someone who knows and practices the faith.

The media has a responsibility to report the truth, and not show a fabricated version of a story to get mere ratings. Terrorists and racists should not be given a platform to air their views.

In our fragile world, media power should be used for good. To bring people together, to stamp out racism and hatred. A platform for peace and tolerance.

Thank you.

Glossary

Ahwazi Arab Refers to an Arab community in Iran centred mostly in the resource-rich **Khuzestan Province** (*cf.*) in the south of the country, bordering Iraq. The majority are Shi'ite, while a minority, concentrated in the coastal areas, are Sunni Muslims.

Air Force One Specific planes/aircraft equipped to carry the President of the United States of America.

Alawite Shabiha An armed militia in Syria, mostly Alawite, that supports the Ba'ath party and the Assad regime.

Al Mahdi Al Mountathar Also referred to as the Mahdi (Guided One) or the 12th Imam. Shi'ite Twelvers believe his return will bring justice to the world.

Al Qaeda Sunni Islamist militant organization founded in 1988 by Osama bin Laden, which gained prominence in the West in the aftermath of the September 11 terrorist attacks.

Al Shabaab Militant organization. The East African arm/wing of **Al Qaeda**. Al Shabaab means "the youth" in Arabic.

Amal Movement Also known as the Movement of the Dispossessed, or Hope Movement. A Lebanese political party co-founded by Musa al-Sadr and Hussein al-Husseini in 1974 and associated with Lebanon's Shi'ite community.

APEC Asia-Pacific Economic Cooperation. The APEC summit is a forum for the 21 countries in the Pacific Rim.

April 6 Youth Movement The political activist group in Egypt that played a leading role in the 25 January revolution that ousted Hosni Mubarak in January 2011.

AQAP Al Qaeda in the Arabian Peninsula, also known as Ansar al-Sharia in Yemen. Militant organization operating mainly in in Yemen and Saudi Arabia.

Arab League Also called the League of Arab States. A confederation established in 1945 for the purpose of securing Arab unity, currently comprising 22 member countries: Algeria, Bahrain, Comoros, Djibouti, Egypt, Iraq, Jordan, Kuwait, Lebanon, Libya, Mauritania, Morocco, Oman, Palestine, Qatar, Saudi Arabia, Somalia, Sudan, Syria, Tunisia, United Arab Emirates and Yemen.

Arab Spring Pro-democracy uprisings that originated in Tunisia in December 2010 and spread across parts of the Arab World in 2011.

Arab World Term to describe all the countries in the **Arab League** (*cf.*) and where Arabic is the principal language spoken.

Ayatollah A title of honour given to jurists in Shi'ite Islam, used predominantly in Iran where it is associated with political leadership.

caliphate A region controlled by a caliph, or religious leader, considered a leader of the Islamic nation, a successor to the Prophet (PBUH) and the Caliphs.

Camp David Accords Two framework agreements between Egypt and Israel signed on 17 September 1978 in the US under the presidency of Jimmy Carter, the second of which (A Framework for the Conclusion of a Peace Treaty between Egypt and Israel) led directly to the 1979 Egypt-Israel Peace Treaty.

Chilcot Report Also known as the Iraq Inquiry. A public inquiry, published by Sir John Chilcot on 6 July 2016, on Britain's role in the 2003 invasion of Iraq.

Coptic/Copts A Christian denomination in Egypt and North-east Africa.

Daesh Another term for **ISIL** or **ISIS** (*cf.*). An acronym for the Arabic phrase *al-Dawla al-Islamiya fi al-Iraq w-al-Sham* (Islamic State of Iraq and the Levant). A violent Islamic militia that purports to follow a fundamentalist doctrine and aims to establish a caliphate across Iraq and Syria.

DCIP Defense for Children International Palestine.

Doctors Without Borders Also Médecins Sans Frontières (MSF). An international humanitarian-aid non-governmental organization running projects in war-torn areas.

Druze Arabic-speaking monotheistic faith. The Druze community consider Jethro of Midian to be their ancestor and spiritual founder.

Fatah Palestinian nationalist movement founded by Yasser Arafat as the Palestinian National Liberation Movement in the 1950s to fight for an independent Palestinian state.

fatwa An Islamic legal ruling on a specific issue.

fedayeen Nationalist militant fighters from Palestine.

First Uprising *See* **Intifada**.

First World Generally refers to the countries of Western Europe, North America, Japan, Australia and New Zealand.

Free Patriotic Movement Lebanese political party also known as the FPM. Largely Christian, its Secretary General is Gebran Bassil, but is led by General Michel Aoun, the movement's central figure.

FSA Free Syrian Army. Group of fighters largely comprising defectors from the Syrian Armed Forces who wish to bring down the Assad regime.

Future Movement Party Lebanese Sunni political party led by Saad Hariri and established by his father, the former Prime Minister Rafic Hariri.

G8 Group of eight countries consisting of France, Germany, Italy, Japan, UK, US, Canada and Russia. Russia was temporarily suspended in 2014 after its annexation of the Crimea.

Gaza Strip A densely populated Palestinian area of the Mediterranean coast that was seized by Israel from Egypt in 1967 during the Six Day War.

GCC The Gulf Cooperation Council formed in 1981. A loose political and economic alliance made up of six Arab Gulf states: Saudi Arabia, Bahrain, Kuwait,

Oman, Qatar, and the United Arab Emirates.

Ghad Party Also known as Ghad al-Thawra Party. Egyptian political party led by Ayman Nour.

Goldstone Report An independent fact-finding mission to investigate alleged human rights in the Palestinian territories. Also known as the United Nations Fact Finding Mission on the Gaza Conflict. The report was headed by South African judge Richard Goldstone.

Hamas Palestinian Sunni organization fighting against Israeli occupation and aiming to establish a Muslim state in Israel, the West Bank and the Gaza Strip.

Haram Al Sharif The Arabic name for Islam's third holiest shrine, al-Aqsa Mosque in Jerusalem.

Hezbollah Lebanese Shi'ite Islamic militant group and political party, supported and funded by Iran and founded by followers of Ayatollah Ruhollah Khomeini.

hijab Veil that covers the head and chest. Worn by some Muslim women as a symbol of modesty.

IAEA International Atomic Energy Agency. Created in 1957 in response to fears about the future of nuclear energy, its work includes inspecting and verifying the whereabouts of nuclear material and checking safety standards.

ICC International Criminal Court based in The Hague in the Netherlands. It prosecutes individuals for international crimes, including genocide and war crimes.

IDF Israel Defense Forces, Israel's armed forces.

IEA International Energy Agency. Based in Paris, the IEA originally established to respond to disruptions in the supply of oil in the wake of the 1973 oil crisis. Nowadays, it has a broad role in providing advice and information as well as promoting alternative energy sources.

IMF International Monetary Fund. Created in 1945. An organization of 189 countries working to foster global monetary cooperation, secure finance stability, facilitate trade, promote high employment and sustainable economic growth, and reduce poverty around the world.

Intifada The Palestinian uprising against Israeli occupation of the West Bank and Gaza Strip. The First Intifada lasted from 1987 to 1993, and the Second Intifada (also known as Al-Aqsa Intifada) began in September 2000, when former Prime Minister of Israel Ariel Sharon made a highly provocative visit to **Haram Al Sharif** (*cf.*).

IRA Irish Republican Army. A militant/paramilitary organization dedicated to securing the independence of the whole of Ireland from the United Kingdom.

IRGC Islamic Revolutionary Guard Corps. Also known as the Army of the Guardians of the Islamic Revolution. A branch of Iran's armed forces, established with the particular mandate to protect the country's Islamic system.

ISIL or **ISIS** Acronyms for the Islamic State of Iraq and the Levant or the Islamic State of Iraq and Syria. *See* **Daesh**.

Islamic Da'wa Organization Also known as the Islamic Call Party. A Shi'ite political party in Iraq led by Nouri Al Maliki, Prime Minister of Iraq from 2006–2014.

Islamophobia Unwarranted fear of Muslims, dislike of or prejudice against Islam.

JCPOA Joint Comprehensive Plan of Action. Also known as "the Iran deal". An agreement reached on 14 July 2015 in Vienna between Iran and the **P5+1** (*cf.*) and the European Union. Iran agreed to reduce its stockpile of uranium and the quantity of its gas centrifuges along with granting access to the IAEA to inspect its nuclear facilities in return for a relaxation of sanctions against Iran.

jihad In Islam, the spiritual struggle within oneself against sin and the struggle to build a good Muslim society. A highly misunderstood term that is often misconstrued particularly in the West as meaning a holy war or a declaration of war against other religions.

jihadist or **jihadi** Term to describe violent Islamic militant movements that generally threaten the West. Not to be confused with **jihad** (*cf.*).

Khuzestan Province An oil-rich province in Iran where the **Ahwazi Arab** (*cf.*) community is centred.

madrassa(s) Islamic religious school(s).

majlis Literally means "a place of sitting" and is used to refer to a gathering place.

8 March Movement Named after the mass demonstration in Beirut in response to the Cedar Revolution. It is a coalition of pro-Syrian parties in Lebanon, which is opposed to the **14 March Movement** (*cf.*) and comprises mainly Hezbollah, Amal and the Free Patriotic Movement (FPM).

14 March Movement Named after the date of the Cedar Revolution, a mass anti-Syrian demonstration held in Beirut on 14 March 2005 following the assassination of former Prime Minister Rafic Hariri. It is a loose coalition of political parties and independents in Lebanon formed in 2005 that are united by their anti-Syrian regime stance and their opposition to the **8 March Movement** (*cf.*).

marjaaiya Refers to when a religious cleric becomes a reference for the people to rule among them, and offer them opinions and **fatwas** (*cf.*).

Maronite The largest Christian denomination in Lebanon.

Marshall Plan American aid plan designed to assist the rebuilding of Western European countries at the end of World War II. Named after Secretary of State George Marshall.

Mossad The national foreign intelligence agency of Israel.

Muslim Brotherhood The informal name for the Society of the Muslim Brothers founded by Hassan Al Banna in 1928. Considered by some Arab states to be a terrorist organization, it is a Sunni Islamist political party in Egypt that won the 2012 presidential elections, when Mohammed Morsi became President.

NAM Non-Aligned Movement. A group of states not formally aligned with or against any major power bloc.

NATO North Atlantic Treaty Organization. Also known as the North Atlantic Alliance. A group of countries allied under the North Atlantic Treaty signed in 1949, designed to safeguard the security of its members through peaceful resolution, or if not possible, through other political and military means. There are currently 28 members.

NGO A non-governmental organization.

NSA National Security Agency. An intelligence organization of the US government.

Occupied Territories Refers to the West Bank, Gaza Strip and the eastern part of Old Jerusalem, which were seized by Israel in 1967 from Jordan and Egypt during the **Six Day War** (*cf.*).

Organisation of Islamic Cooperation (OIC) Founded in 1969, it currently has 57 member states and aims to protect the interests of the Muslim world and promote international peace.

OPEC Organization of the Petroleum Exporting Countries.

Osirak Also known as Operation Opera and Operation Babylon. A codename for the Israeli Air Force strike of 7 June 1981 which destroyed an Iraqi nuclear reactor under construction 17km southeast of Baghdad.

Oslo Agreement Also known as the Oslo Accords. A peace deal agreed between Israel (led by Yitzhak Rabin) and the Palestine Liberation Organization (PLO, under Yasser Arafat) in Norway in 1993.

P5+1 Iran and five permanent members of the United Nations Security Council (US, France, Britain, China and the Russian Federation) plus Germany, who signed the Iran nuclear agreement in 2015.

PA *See* **PNA**.

PBUH Peace Be Upon Him. An expression used by Muslims when referring to a Prophet of God. Female reference is Peace Be Upon Her.

PBUT Peace Be Upon Them: the plural of the above.

Peshmerga Military forces of the autonomous region of Iraqi Kurdistan. Peshmerga means "one who confronts death".

PFLP Popular Front for the Liberation of Palestine. A secular Palestinian revolutionary organization, dubbed a terrorist group by some Western states.

PLO Palestine Liberation Organization. Founded in 1964 with the aim of achieving the independence of Palestine from Israeli occupation.

PNA Palestinian National Authority, also sometimes referred to as the Palestinian Authority (PA). Interim self-government authority established in 1994 to govern the Gaza Strip and certain parts of the West Bank, following the **Oslo Agreement** (*cf.*).

Qom A city in Iran, some 125km southwest of Tehran, which is the largest center for Shi'ite scholarship in the world, and is a significant destination of pilgrimage.

rabaa A four-finger salute that originated as a hand sign by pro-Mohammed Morsi protesters during demonstrations in Egypt's Rabia al-Adawiya Square.

Rafah Crossing The only crossing between the Gaza Strip and Egypt. Given the closures imposed by Israel on Gaza's land crossings, and the ban on air and sea travel to and from Gaza, Rafah Crossing is a vital route to the outside world for the residents of Gaza. Operating for only several days every month or two, the crossing remains completely closed the rest of the time.

Realpolitik A system of politics or principles based on practical rather than moral or ideological considerations.

SCAF Supreme Council of the Armed Forces. A council of senior military figures in Egypt, only to be convened in case of war and emergency. After the revolution in 2011, SCAF assumed power until June 2012.

Second Uprising *See* **Intifada**.

Shabiha *See* **Alawite Shabiha**.

Shia *See* **Shi'ite**.

Shi'ite Also known as **Shia**. A branch of Islam forged during a split in the 7th century. Shi'ite comes from the phrase "party of Ali" and Shi'ites consider the descendants of Ali, Mohammed's cousin and adopted son, to be the true inheritors of Mohammed (PBUH). Ali was the first Imam and all subsequent Imams are considered his descendants.

Shin Bet Israeli state security intelligence agency. The other two are **Mossad** (*cf.*) for foreign intelligence and Aman for military intelligence.

shock and awe Military term used to describe a period of enormous power and great displays of force to intimidate and demoralize the enemy.

Sinai Peninsula Desert region of Egypt, bordering Israel and Gaza.

Six Day War A series of pre-emptive strikes by Israel against Arab land in 1967. This included the seizure of Jerusalem and the West Bank from Jordan, the Golan Heights from Syria, and the Gaza Strip and Sinai Peninsula from Egypt.

Sunni A branch of Islam that holds that Islam's first caliph was Mohammed's (PBUH) father-in-law Abu Bakr. Sunnis constitute 85–90 per cent of the world's Muslim population.

Sykes-Picot Agreement Also known as the Asia Minor Agreement. A secret convention produced by British diplomat Mark Sykes and his French counterpart François George-Picot in 1916 during World War I, with the assent of Russia, for the dismemberment of the Ottoman Empire. The controlling powers were left free to determine state boundaries within their areas of influence, with Great Britain gaining command of Palestine that would eventually lead to the formation of an Israeli state in that territory.

Taif Agreement Also known as the National Reconciliation Accord or Document of National Accord. This agreement, which ended the civil war in Lebanon, was negotiated in Taif, Saudi Arabia, in September 1989. It was approved by the Lebanese parliament on 4 November 1989.

takfiri A Sunni Muslim who accuses another Muslim of abandoning their religious beliefs.

Taliban Islamic fundamentalist political movement in Afghanistan.

Trojan horse files Also referred to as "Operation Trojan Horse", this refers to attempts to introduce an Islamist or Salafist ethos into various schools in Birmingham, UK. The name is taken from a Greek legend, and is based on a leaked letter that was exposed in March 2014, which was alleged to be from Islamists in Birmingham discussing how to seize control of a school and replicate that strategy elsewhere.

UKIP UK Independence Party. A political party advocating Great Britain's departure from the European Union.

UNDP United Nations Development Programme. Provides advice and support to developing countries.

UNESCO United Nations Educational, Scientific and Cultural Organization. Promotes international collaboration through reforms in education, science and culture to improve human rights and freedoms.

UNHCR United Nations High Commissioner for Refugees. The UN entity centred on supporting refugees.

UNICEF United Nations Children's Emergency Fund. Provides assistance to children and mothers in developing countries.

UNRWA United Nations Relief and Works Agency for Palestine Refugees in the Near East. Provides assistance to refugees in the **Occupied Territories** (*cf.*).

UN Security Council United Nations Security Council. Established in 1946. It has the primary responsibility for the maintenance of international peace and security. The 15-member Security Council takes the lead in determining the existence of a threat to the peace or act of aggression.

WHO World Health Organization. A specialized agency of the United Nations that is concerned with international public health. It was established on 7 April 1948, and is headquartered in Geneva, Switzerland.

Wilayat al-Faqih Refers to a guardianship-based political system in contemporary Shi'ite political thought, which relies upon a just and capable jurist (*faqih*) to assume the leadership of the government in the absence of an infallible imam.

WMD Weapons of Mass Destruction.

World Assembly of Islamic Awakening An international body headed by Iran's Senior Advisor to Leaders of Islamic Revolution of Iran, Ali-Akbar Velayati. Iran regards the **Arab Spring** (*cf.*) as the Islamic Awakening and believes that the developments in the region are mainly inspired by the 1979 Iranian Revolution.

Xenophobia Hatred of strangers or foreigners, prejudice against people from other countries.

Yazidi(s) Kurdish religious group living primarily in the Nineveh province of Iraq, but also in Armenia, Georgia, Turkey, Iran and Syria.

zakat Third pillar of Islam (giving a proportion of one's wealth to the poor and needy).

Index

—